THE
AVENEL
DICTIONARY
OF SAINTS

Donald Attwater

THE
AVENEL
DICTIONARY
OF SAINTS

AVENEL BOOKS

NEW YORK

This book was formerly titled *The Penguin Dictionary of Saints.*

First published by Penguin Books Ltd. 1965.
Copyright © the Estate of Donald Attwater, MCMLXV
All rights reserved.

This edition is published by Avenel Books, distributed by Crown
Publishers, Inc., by arrangement with Penguin Books Ltd.
     c   d   e   f   g   h
AVENEL 1981 EDITION

Manufactured in the United States of America

Library of Congress Cataloging in Publication Data

Attwater, Donald, 1892–1977.
  The Avenel dictionary of saints.

  Reprint of the 1979 ed. published by Penguin Books,
New York, under title: The Penguin dictionary of saints,
which was issued as Penguin reference books; R30.
  Bibliography: p. 19.
  1. Christian saints—Biography.   I. Title.
[BX4655.8.A8 1981]   282′.092′ [B]   80-28073
ISBN: 0-517-33643-X

To my wife, Dorothy,
and my daughter, Sanchia

THE
AVENEL
DICTIONARY
OF SAINTS

INTRODUCTION

THE English word 'saint' is derived from the Latin epithet *sanctus*, which represents the Greek *hagios* and the Hebrew *qâdosh*. These words, *sanctus, hagios, qâdosh*, were applied to God himself, to people, and to things. When applied to people and things they meant hallowed, consecrated, set apart for a sacred purpose or office, made 'holy to God'; they did not of themselves necessarily connote that high moral quality which is now inseparable from such words as saint or holy when applied to a person. The original usage continues in some connexions: the pope of Rome is not the only Christian bishop who is referred to as 'his holiness' in virtue of his office; Jerusalem is the 'holy city'; Westminster Abbey, or any house of worship, is called a holy place.

Holiness as sacredness, as a state of dedication to God's service, is illustrated by the earliest Christian use of the noun 'saint'. St Paul, for instance, addresses himself to the saints in Achaia, at Ephesus, at Philippi, at Colossae: and by 'saints' he means all the members, the faithful, of the Christian communities in those places, God's holy people, the New Israel. The virtue, the doing of good and avoidance of evil, required of them (I Cor. vi, 9–11; Col. iii, 5–8) is a consequence of their state of sanctity, of their having been called to God's service: they have to live 'as becometh saints' (Eph. v, 3).

Paul and the other earliest writers refer to the saints only collectively, and the term came to be applied especially to particular categories among the faithful: to those who had died 'in the Lord', to the martyrs, and to the first monks. At the same time 'saint' in the singular began to be used as a term of individual appreciation or as a sort of official title, especially for a bishop. Finally 'saint' became the title of honour and respect used individually of persons distinguished among their fellow Christians for the degree of their devotedness to Christ and as commanding the public veneration of the faithful.

THE MARTYRS

The according of public veneration to a certain category of Christian men and women, and the giving to each of them of the appellation Saint, originated in the reverence given to martyrs. This was manifested first at the place where they had suffered and been buried; from there it often spread to other places and even to the whole church. Each year on the anniversary of the saint's martyrdom the faithful assembled at his grave; the Eucharist was celebrated there, and during this the martyr was named with honour: it was an occasion of rejoicing and triumph, a 'feast day', not a day of mourning. The first such annual commemoration of which there is record is that of ◊ *St Polycarp*, at Smyrna in the second half of the second century.

From early times Christians called on the dead, especially their close relatives, for their prayers; this custom was extended to, and was eventually superseded by, invocation of the martyrs.* Their bodily remains (at first carefully kept intact) and other relics were treasured and revered; their personal names were adopted or given at baptism; and in time churches were dedicated in their honour. Abuses and superstition became associated with these developments, and Tertullian (d. *c.* 220) was not the only early teacher who was moved to protest against such excesses.†

THE CONFESSORS

With Constantine's grant of toleration in 313 the classical age of acute but intermittent persecution of Christians by the Roman emperors came to an end. The faithful were then faced by new and more insidious forms of trial and temptation; and teachers such as St Basil and St John Chrysostom began to emphasize that ordinary Christian life, when lived consistently in a spirit of loving self-offering to God, can itself be a kind

---

* An example of each, from inscriptions in the Roman catacombs:
   'Januaria, be very happy and plead for us.'
   'Paul and Peter, pray for Victor.'
† The classical work on the veneration of saints in the early centuries is *Sanctus* (Brussels, 1954; in French), by Hippolyte Delehaye. Unfortunately it is not available in English.

of martyrdom. By the end of the fourth century the honours already given to the martyrs of old were being extended to the great ones among the ascetics in the wilderness; and to them were gradually added the names of outstanding bishops and teachers.

Those honoured as saints without having suffered martyrdom are known as 'confessors': a significant term, intimating that by confessing the Christian faith in their persevering lives they bear witness to Christ as effectively as a martyr does by his death. In time all the honours and reverence accorded to martyrs—anniversaries, commemorative services, invocation, dedications, and the rest—were accorded to confessors too. During the centuries that followed, down to our own day, the names of hundreds of new saints were added to church calendars. For the most part they were bishops and other clergy, monks and nuns, but there were also representatives of many other walks of Christian life. As can be seen from the pages of this book, that numerical disproportion has persisted (it is not found among the martyrs in any age). Among the reasons for it are such extrinsic considerations as that persons in a public position more easily attract notice, and that in later times religious orders have been able to press the claims of their members. The church can canonize only those whose repute is brought before her for examination and decision.

CANONIZATION

For legitimate public veneration of a person as a saint the sanction of at least the local church has always been necessary: he or she must be 'canonized',* and over the centuries this has been effected in various ways. The Virgin Mary, the apostles, and evangelists were recognized as saints by general consent; the early martyrs were spontaneously recognized as such by the faithful who had witnessed their sufferings; and so in a similar way were the early confessors. Later on, individual bishops canonized, by giving permission for a religious festival, or feast, to be kept in a dead person's honour. These local recognitions were frequently extended to other places, sometimes to the church at large. Many of the greatest saints were canonized

* This word originated from the insertion of a name in a 'canon' or list.

in this or a similar way, by a process of what may be called *informal* canonization, or by the prescription of long usage.

From the tenth century canonization in the West came more and more into the hands of the bishop of Rome; Pope Alexander III (d. 1181) in effect reserved future canonizations to the Roman see, and a process of *formal* canonization emerged.* But the present fixed process in the Roman Catholic church, involving a minute inquiry into the candidate's life, has been in full operation only since 1634. The Orthodox Eastern churches, notably the Greek and Russian, also now have systems of formal canonization, but less rigorous than the Roman and exercised, somewhat sporadically, on a less wide scale. The Anglican and Protestant churches, though some of them have retained certain elements of the public cultus (◊ p. 23) of saints, have not perpetuated the practice of canonization.

A man or woman is not 'made a saint' by canonization. Canonization, in which the voice of the people at large is often still a very powerful initiatory factor, is an authoritative declaration that such-and-such a person was a saint in his or her lifetime. Obviously these canonized saints are not the only saints, in the colloquial sense of the word. There must be countless uncanonized saints, known only to their neighbours or to God alone; but they also are honoured each year, on 1 November, the feast of All Saints, when all those who have left this world and are now in Heaven are also remembered.

It may be added that canonization does not imply a 'blanket' approval by the canonizing authority of all a saint's words and deeds, his opinions, policies, and politics. A saint is not faultless: he does not always think and behave well and wisely, one who has occasion to oppose him is not always wrong or foolish. Nor is he canonized because he 'had visions' or was reputed a wonder-worker. He, or she, is canonized because his personal daily life was lived, not merely well, but at an heroic level of Christian faithfulness and integrity (or, if a martyr, because of the circumstances of his violent death).

The key-word that distinguishes the saint is 'heroism'. The

* *Canonization and Authority in the Western Church* (Oxford, 1948), by E. W. Kemp, is a valuable book for students.

saint is the man or woman who gives himself, herself, to God *heroically*. And this giving, this loving self-offering to Him who is Holiness itself, is entirely independent of such circumstances as occupation in life, social or other status, education, temperament, natural abilities or lack of them. The lives of the saints present not only an extraordinary variety of human character and disposition. For all the great preponderance of clergy, monks, and nuns among the recorded saints, there are also found men and women of every human estate, from kings and queens to struggling peasants, from business-men and artisans to beggars in the street. What St Bernard of Clairvaux said eight hundred years ago of a holy man's relationship with his fellows is valid today, and it is an ideal which is open to all: he is 'seen to be good and charitable, living as a man among men, holding back nothing for himself but using his every gift for the common good; he looks on himself as every man's debtor, alike to friend and foe, to the wise and the foolish. Such a one, being wholly humble, benefits all, is dear to God and man.'

Sainthood – or any other degree of truly Christian life – is not achieved by anyone's own unaided efforts. It may be consciously taken as an ideal to be aimed at; it cannot be adopted and pursued as a 'career'. Men and women become saints by living 'in Christ', in whatever state of life to which they are called. They are enabled to do this by grace, the divine help – as Christians believe – which Christ freely offers to every man according to the circumstances, capacities, and needs of each one. The saints are those who accept and cooperate with grace more whole-heartedly and more selflessly than do others, to a superlative degree: they become Christ-like through the help Christ gives them. St Paul sums it up in a sentence: 'I live: yet not I, but Christ liveth in me.'

HISTORY OF THE SAINTS

There is no such thing as a 'canon of the saints', in the sense of a single authoritative register of all those holy men and women from the earliest times who have been publicly honoured in the church. Their names have ultimately to be sought in numerous ecclesiastical calendars, ancient and modern; in those compilations called variously in West and East martyrologies, menologies, and synaxaries; and in other sources. The number of names thus ascertainable is huge; the Roman Martyrology (◊ p. 25) contains some 4,500 names, and it is far from exhaustive.

Of many of the thousands of saints whose names are known, nothing more is known except, generally, their status (martyr, bishop, etc.), their place of death, their feast day, and the era at which they lived. Of the numerous written accounts of the early martyrs, a small proportion are authentic. Many of the rest were written after all memory of the true story had been lost, and are wholly fictitious; others are a combination of history and legend, and the respective elements cannot always be disentangled easily, or at all.

Other earlier writings about the saints are of very differing kinds and of very uneven historical value, ranging from biographies by contemporaries or near-contemporaries to later works full of errors, omissions, interpolations, and fictitious 'touchings-up'.* Ancillary sources of information are found in inscriptions (of which early epitaphs can have a special value), official secular records, memoirs (including autobiographies) and collections of letters, panegyrics preached on saints' feast days, and the works of historians and chroniclers.

Research into the lives of the earlier saints is beset with special difficulties. There are those which face other historians and biographers: fewness of records, their unreliability, uncertainties and contradictions, conflicting interpretations, and so on. But there is added to these, in particular, the 'selectiveness' of the material available and, not infrequently, what by later standards seems the unscrupulosity and absurd credulousness of many writers of the past. Most hagiographers were interested in nothing but the directly religious aspects of their subjects' lives: at the worst, a 'biography' became no more than a list of miracles, often puerile, or of voluntary physical austerities, or, in the case of a martyr, of repeated torments a single one of which no human body could survive. Or again, when material

---

* For the Celtic saints of Wales, Cornwall, and Brittany, wrote the Breton scholar Joseph Loth, 'it is not the saints' written Lives that tell us most about the existence of the saints and the national organization of religion, but the names of places'. These are a special case.

was lacking, the earlier hagiographer sometimes did not disdain to manufacture it himself or to borrow it: so that we may even come upon two saints whose written lives are almost word for word the same, with only names and places different. A high degree of authenticity and historical interest is a rather rare element in the huge whole of earlier hagioraphical literature; instead we find myth, folklore, legend, and romantic and 'edifying' fiction.*

Materials bearing on the lives of the saints have to be studied, analysed, and judged in the same objective way, with the same scientific spirit and method, as the materials relevant to any other sort of history and biography. The object of the study is to get at the truth, if that be possible (it often is not). But for centuries the object of writing saints' lives was solely to edify and gratify the reader (more often, the hearer), and to glorify the hero of the tale. Admirable objects: but unhappily they were too often attained at the expense of truth, reason, and common sense. This has constantly to be borne in mind. It accounts, for example, for the inordinate space and importance given to miracles or alleged miracles. During the middle ages miraculous happenings above all both edified and gratified the general public and redounded to the credit of the saint. We today can be almost as simple-minded, but in other ways.

These 'legendary Lives' became a recognizable literary form (*genre*), designed to honour the saints, to exalt their virtues and actions, and to kindle a more living spirit among lethargic or discouraged Christians. The narratives were meant to be taken seriously, but it may be questioned whether they were always meant to be believed as sober history. They have to be judged accordingly. We cannot but reject them as history and marvel that they could ever have been accepted as such; on the other hand, we may not withhold from the writers appreciation for their intentions and industry, and gratitude for not a few charming tales amidst the mass of 'common form'. That most critical of critical hagiographers, Father Hippolyte Delehaye, wrote of the *Golden Legend* (◊ p. 24): 'I confess that, when reading it, it is often difficult to refrain from smiling. But it is a sympathetic

---

* There is no general account of hagiography in English. In French, René Aigrain's *L'Hagiographie: ses sources, ses méthodes, son histoire* (Paris, 1953) is a valuable work.

13

and friendly smile, which does not at all disturb the religious response aroused by the picture of the goodness and heroic deeds of the saints.' Moreover, legendary narratives have this value: they are evidence for what people believed at the time the legends took shape. As Sir Arthur Quiller-Couch put it, writing in another context, 'a legend, however exaggerated upon fact, *is its own fact*, witnessing belief.'

It is only in more recent times that it has become generally recognized that the biography of a saint should simply provide a true record of an individual life, so far as it can be known; and that for this purpose use must be made of the methods and findings of scientific critical study. The fundamental requirements are, positively, the so-far-as-possible accurate recording of all that can with certainty or probability be found out about a saint, ancient or modern; negatively, the discarding of whatever is demonstrably untrue or unproved, and the acceptance of the fact that little or nothing is known about numerous saints, the names of some of whom are nevertheless famous. More than to anyone else, the emergence, development, and achievements of scientific hagiographical study are due to the labours of the Bollandists (◊ p. 22) since the middle of the seventeenth century.

Even in later writings about the saints for the general reader it has been a common fault, and sometimes still is, to present a saint as hardly a human being. Some writers make a distinction between 'the man' and 'the saint'. The distinction is unreal and false: a man or woman may turn to God and attain heroic virtue only late in life, or even in his last hours (as did some of the martyrs), but he was the same man all the way through. Or the writer glosses over or ignores the less attractive side of a saint's character, or may present the very virtues of his subject in such a way as to repel rather than attract the reader. It is such faults as these, together with the merciless emphasis on obvious moral or religious lessons, that have powerfully helped to restrict the reading of books about the saints: the very word has acquired an atmosphere of priggishness, fanaticism, miracle-mongering, sentimentality, and churchiness. But when proper attention is paid to historical truth, to science and criticism, when a saint's failings and mistakes are recorded as well as his achievements and heroism, it does not follow that the religious aspect, the element of 'edification', is overlooked or weakened. It is more and more being realized that religious profit is better served by letting saints' lives speak for themselves than by direct exhortation and moralizing about them.

This book is a work of quick reference to the lives and legends of the more important and interesting people among the saints, and the compiler has endeavoured to include as well most others whose names are likely to be met in the course of general reading or otherwise. In addition it contains entries about a number of lesser-known names which more extended reading or foreign travel might bring to the reader's notice.

Among the readers who consult the book there may perhaps be not a few for whom its subject has no antecedent attraction, who have no particular respect for the category of people called 'saints', who may indeed have a positive distaste for a subject which – understandably – they think of as specialized, monotonous, historically untrustworthy, and designed merely to arouse feelings of religious devotion in simple and credulous believers.

Such readers are invited to approach this compendium with an open mind, reading 'not to contradict and confute ... but to weigh and consider', as Francis Bacon wrote of studies in general. The lives of the saints are as worth while and rewarding a study as any other branch of biography, and more worth while and rewarding than some that are more popular. As has been said above, they cover a remarkable variety of human character and disposition, and a no less remarkable variety of human activity, social origin, and personal history. The saints range from obscure men and women who, but for the accident of their hidden lives becoming known, would never again have been heard of, to persons who made a mark on the history of their times, the influence of some of whom is powerful in human lives throughout the world today. Of no category of person is it more true than of the saint that he, 'being dead, yet speaketh'. Their lives, then, deserve the sympathetic and understanding attention of all, whether professing Christians or not, who are happy to call themselves humanists, saying, with the Roman playwright Terence, 'I am a man, and I am indifferent to nothing that is human.'

It is not within the scope of an introduction to a book of this kind to discuss such matters as miracles, either in themselves or in relation to narratives about the saints; or to examine the subject of religious visions or other phenomena so often recorded of them (and of other people too); or to seek to explain such anomalies as the disproportionate emphasis put by many writers on a saint's bodily austerities, real or supposed. The same applies to the various aspects of the public cultus of saints, their relics, their shrines and the pilgrimages thereto, dedication of churches in their honour, their choice as heavenly patrons, and the conventions of their representation in pictures and carvings. Each one of these is a subject 'on its own', requiring separate treatment; a few relevant books are included in the list that follows.

ABBREVIATIONS

B., b.   Born.

B.C.P.   Book of Common Prayer (calendar of).

c.   *circa*, about (with a date).

cd   canonized. The date of *formal* canonization (◊ p. 9) is given when known; unless otherwise stated, the canonization was by the Roman church since the tenth century. No doubt the records of some formal canonizations have been lost.

D., d.   Died. The day of the month (when known) is added to the year only when it is not the same, or nearly the same, as the feast day.

ed., edn   editor, edited, edition.

F.d., f.d.   feast day. The date on which a saint is or was commemorated.

ibid.   *ibidem*, in the same place or book.

id.   *idem*, by the same author.

Orth. ch.   Orthodox Eastern church.

R.C. ch.   Roman Catholic church.

tr., trans.   translator, translation, translated.

◊ ►   See.

◊► ►   See also.

Note The date of a saint's feast sometimes varies from place to place or in particular calendars. In the 1969 revision of the General Calendar of the Roman Church the number of days on which the commemoration of a saint is appointed or allowed has been drastically reduced. The dates of some of the saints' days retained have been adjusted: these include Philip and James, assigned to 3 May, Matthias to 14 May, Bede to 25 May, Augustine of Canterbury to 27 May, John Fisher and Thomas More together to 22 June, Thomas the Apostle to 3 July, Benedict to 11 July, Dominic to 7 August and Gregory the Great to 3 September. ◊ *Dies Natalis* on p. 23 herein.

SHORT GENERAL BIBLIOGRAPHY

K. S. LATOURETTE, *A History of Christianity* (1954).

PHILIP HUGHES, *A Popular History of the Catholic Church* (1958).

TIMOTHY WARE, *The Orthodox Church* (Penguin, 1963).

LOUIS LAVELLE, *The Meaning of Holiness* (1954).

CUTHBERT BUTLER, *Ways of Christian Life* (1932).

MARTIN THORNTON, *English Spirituality* (1963). The first half gives the background; the second covers thought and practice in England from St Anselm to William Law and the present day.

W. E. R. SANGSTER, *The Path to Perfection* (1943). An account and explanation of John Wesley's teaching on Christian perfection.

AN EASTERN MONK, *Orthodox Spirituality* (1945).

JACQUES DOUILLET, *What is a Saint?* (1958). A brief but very competent introduction to the subject of canonized saints, their history and veneration.

H. THURSTON and D. ATTWATER (editors), *Butler's Lives of the Saints* (4 vols., 1956). Accounts of some 2,500 saints, each followed by notes indicating sources, and suggestions for further reading.

E. C. E. OWEN, *Some Authentic Acts of the Early Martyrs* (1927). Translations of a dozen contemporary or very early narratives.

H. DELEHAYE, *The Legends of the Saints* (1962). The classical work on the origin and growth of legend, written in such a way as to be equally acceptable to the scholar and the general reader.

C. S. LEWIS, *Miracles: a Preliminary Study* (1963).

HERBERT THURSTON, *The Physical Phenomena of Mysticism* (1952). Deals with such matters as stigmatization, levitation, and 'second sight' as manifested in the lives of some saints and others.

FRANCIS BOND, *Dedications and Patron Saints of English Churches* (1914).

HELEN ROEDER, *Saints and their Attributes* (1955). The emblems and symbols of the saints in pictorial representations and statuary.

LOCAL COLLECTIONS

S. BARING-GOULD and J. FISHER, *The Lives of the British Saints* (4 vols., 1907-13). Since this work was published a great deal of fresh research has been done on the saints of the first centuries of Christianity in Celtic Britain; but these volumes still have value for reference, comparison and points of local in-information.

E. G. BOWEN, *The Settlements of the Celtic Saints in Wales* (1954).

G. H DOBLE, *The Saints of Cornwall*, Parts I (1960), II (1962), III (1964), IV (1965) and V (1970) published; others in preparation.

A. P. FORBES, *Kalendars of Scottish Saints* (1872).

D. D. C. POCHIN MOULD, *The Irish Saints* (1964).

ELEANOR DUCKETT, *The Wandering Saints* (1959). The Celtic 'pilgrim saints' in the British Isles and on the Continent, and the missionaries in Germany and the Lowlands, with some others.

H. VON CAMPENHAUSEN, *The Fathers of the Greek Church* (1963). *The Fathers of the Latin Church* (1964).

SIGRID UNDSET, *Saga of Saints* (1934). Historical sketches of the lives and times of six Norwegian saints.

LOUIS BOUYER, *The Cistercian Heritage* (1958).

C. DE GRUNWALD, *Saints of Russia* (1960).

V. YANICH and C. P. HANKEY, *Lives of the Serbian Saints* (1921).

D. M. LANG, *Lives and Legends of the Georgian Saints* (1956).

D. ATTWATER, *Saints of the East* (1963).

DE L. O'LEARY, *The Saints of Egypt* (1937). A documented compendium, mainly for students.

The bibliographical notes appended to some of the notices in this book are not exhaustive. They mostly refer to recent or fairly recent works, varying in level from 'popular' to learned.

GLOSSARY

ACTS (Latin *acta*; cf. the biblical Acts of the Apostles) A written account of the life and death of an early martyr or other saint, whether authentic, spurious, or mixed.

ALBIGENSES An heretical sect that flourished in the south of France during the twelfth and thirteenth centuries. The name is from the place Albi, but they called themselves Cathars, 'the pure ones', the name by which they were known elsewhere. The basis of their particular doctrines amounted to a revived form of ♢ MANI-CHAEISM.

APOCRYPHA (Greek, 'hidden things') Certain Jewish and Christian religious writings which the church has rejected from the canon of holy Scripture. Some few writings, the 'deuterocanonical books', excluded from the Hebrew Bible and by Anglicans and Protestants, are received as canonical by the Roman Catholic and Eastern churches (e.g. Tobit, Ecclesiasticus, the two books of Maccabees). Any work that is not authentic in authorship or content may be said to be apocryphal; but such writings are not necessarily wholly without historical or other value.

ARIANISM The very widely spread and damaging heresy, named from the Alexandrian priest Arius (d. *c.* 336), which denied the true Godhead of Jesus Christ. The Son, it claimed, was created by the Father, and therefore is not equal with the Father, not eternal, and not divine by nature. Arianism was condemned by the general council of Nicaea in 325, but it did not disappear for some time after; and among the Goths in Spain and North Africa and the Lombards in Italy it persisted for several centuries, not wholly for religious reasons.

ASCETIC (from Gk *askesis*, 'training') As a noun, 'ascetic' designates one who leads a life of systematic self-discipline, both inward and external, not as an end in itself, but as a means to uprightness of life and a more selfless love of God. The word is especially applied to the earliest monks, 'the desert fathers', and to their predecessors who followed a way of life in their homes more austere than that of the generality of Christians.

BEATUS (Lat., fem. *beata*) The existing Roman process of canonization is in two parts: the first, if successful, leads to beatification; the second normally to canonization proper. A beatified person is called *beatus*, 'blessed'; he or she may then be publicly venerated in varying ways, but this is usually limited to a particular country, diocese, or religious order. No names of *beati* are included in this book.

21

BEDE ◊ *St Bede the Venerable* is frequently quoted herein. His *History of the English Church and People*, finished in 731, is one of the world's great historical works, displaying an 'astonishing power of coordinating the fragments of information which came to him through tradition, the relation of friends, or documentary evidence' (Stenton). The most recent translation is by Leo Sherley-Price (Penguin Classics, 1955). Among Bede's other works is an historical ◊ MARTYROLOGY, probably the first of its kind, containing 114 historical notices of saints, together with some shorter entries.

BOLLANDISTS, THE The society of Jesuit scholars, named after their founder John Bolland, a Walloon (d. 1665), who devote themselves to the scientific study of the lives of the saints. The most famous of the Bollandist publications is the *Acta Sanctorum*, 'Acts of the Saints', containing principally critical texts of the relevant sources, copiously annotated. The first two volumes, covering the saints of January, were published in 1643; the work has now reached November 10 (sixty-seven folio volumes). The Bollandists were pioneers in the systematically critical approach to their subject and are still the most respected leaders in the field. Their headquarters is in Brussels.

BULL, PAPAL The most solemn and weighty form of papal communication, formerly authenticated by a leaden seal (Lat. *bulla*).

BYZANTINE Adjective from the noun Byzantium (Gk *Buzantion*), the original name of the city of Constantinople. It is used particularly of the later eastern Roman empire; and of the institutions, such as rites of worship, deriving from the church of Constantinople, and of those who use them.

CANONIZATION ◊ pp. 9–10.

CANONS REGULAR Priests bound by religious vows, living in community under a rule (*regula*). They are now differentiated from monks chiefly by being engaged in works of the active pastoral ministry. The principal orders of canons are the Augustinians (Black canons) and the Premonstratensians or Norbertines (White canons). *Canonesses* is the name given to certain orders of women, analogous to canons regular.

CATECHUMEN (from Gk, 'learner') The name given in the early church, and in modern foreign missions, to adults undergoing instruction and testing in the Christian faith preparatory to baptism.

CEMETERY The early Christian cemeteries of Rome and other places were underground, the constructions called 'catacombs'. The graves were niches in the walls, each closed by a stone slab or tiles. The fourth-century Roman list of martyrs notes the burial place of each one, with the day of the year on which the faithful would gather there to commemorate him or her in a celebration of the Eucharist.

CENOBITE (from Gk) A monk who lives in a community, in distinction from a hermit or anchorite, who lives alone or almost alone.

CHARTERHOUSE The English name for a monastery of Carthusian monks, derived from (La Grande) *Chartreuse,* their mother house near Grenoble in France.

CLERKS REGULAR Clergy bound by vows and life in common for the doing of particular ministerial or other work, but without other specifically monastic obligations. They first appeared in the sixteenth century. By far the greatest and most important of the orders of clerks regular is the Society of Jesus, or Jesuits.

CONFESSOR (*a*) One who bears witness to the Christian faith by word and deed. In the West, any male saint not a martyr is called a confessor. (*b*) A priest who hears confessions of sin and gives absolution to the penitent.

CULTUS, CULT (from Lat. *colere,* 'to honour') As regards the saints, cultus is the reverence evinced by individuals for a particular saint; but more especially it is the totality of the veneration, and its expression in public religious acts, given to a saint, constituting his 'public cultus', local or universal. Throughout this book the word is used in its Latin form, cultus, for the sake of definiteness. A common manifestation of cultus of a saint is prayer addressed to him or her; this is more exactly described as prayer to God through a saint, as when one Christian says to another, 'Please pray for me'.

DESERT FATHERS The first Christian solitaries and monks in the deserts and waste places of Egypt, Palestine, and Syria, from the third to the sixth centuries.

[DIES] NATALIS (Lat., 'anniversary' [literally, 'birthday']) The day of the year on which a saint's feast is celebrated. It is normally the day of his death or burial, but never the day of birth (except for ◊ *John the Baptist* and a secondary feast of the Virgin Mary).

DOCTOR OF THE CHURCH A theologian of special eminence, authority, and holiness of life, formally recognized as such by the church, who by his writings taught the church or some part of it (Lat. *doctor,* 'teacher').

EREMITICAL Adjective, pertaining to a hermit.

EUSEBIUS The Eusebius referred to several times herein was bishop of Caesarea in Palestine from *c.* 313–*c.* 338. Among his writings is a classical *Ecclesiastical History*; it is almost wholly concerned with the East and includes particulars of Palestinian martyrs in his time (Eng. trans 1927–8, and others).

FATHERS OF THE CHURCH Those writers and teachers from the second century onward whose works are traditionally considered of special weight and worthy of special respect as interpretations of the Gospel and as witnessing to 'the faith delivered to the saints' in the beginning. The age of the fathers is generally taken to end with ◊ *St John of Damascus* in the eighth century. Many of them figure in these pages, but not all the fathers are numbered among the saints.

FEAST DAY ◊ under DIES NATALIS

FRIARS (Lat. *fratres*, 'brothers') Members of orders of medieval origin who combine important elements of monastic life with an active ministry 'in the world'; they are quite distinct from monks. The principal orders of friars are the Franciscan Friars Minor (Grey friars), organized in three independent branches, Friars Minor, Conventuals, and Capuchins; the Order of Preachers or Dominicans (Black friars); the Carmelites (White friars); the Augustinian or Austin friars; and the Servites. Friars constitute what are known as the 'mendicant orders' because of their emphasis on corporate poverty.

GOLDEN LEGEND, THE The English title of the collection of saints' Lives written by James of Voragine (d. *c.* 1298), which after 1470 became the first printed best-seller in a number of languages. Its popularity was the means whereby legend after legend was perpetuated and spread far and wide. Caxton's charming version was printed at Westminster in 1483, and a new English translation, by G. Ryan and H. Ripperger, appeared in 1941.

HAGIOGRAPHY (from Gk *hagios*, 'holy', *graphein*, 'to write') The field of learning concerned with the writing and study of the Lives of the saints. Because of the excesses and credulity of many hagiographers the word is sometimes used in a depreciatory sense.

HERMIT ◊ under CENOBITE

ICONOCLASM (from Gk, 'image-breaking') A politico-religious policy of the Byzantine emperors during the periods 726–787 and 814–843. It attacked the lawfulness for Christians of the veneration of sacred images, *eikons*, which were destroyed in large numbers. The resulting dispute had far-reaching ramifications and was carried on with bitterness and violence on both sides; some of the victims of the iconoclasts were revered as martyrs for orthodoxy – the 'new martyrs'. In its theological aspect, Iconoclasm was a controversy about consequences flowing from the taking of a human body by God the Son.

ISLAM (Arabic, 'surrender' [to God]) The religion of the Moslems, followers of Mohammed.

JANSENISM A theological system deriving from the book *Augustinus* by Cornelius Jansen, bishop of Ypres (d. 1638). Jansenism impugned the reality of free will and denied that Christ died for all men without exception; its general tenor was harshly rigorist and pessimistic. Even after it had been condemned at Rome (1653,

1713) Jansenism continued to exercise an unhappy influence on Roman Catholics in various places for a considerable time.

JESUITS ◊ under CLERKS REGULAR

LAURA (Gk, 'alley') Originally, an Eastern monastic establishment whose members lived in rows of separate huts, under a single leader.

LEGEND (Lat. *legenda*, 'something to be read') A legend was originally an account of a martyr or other saint to be publicly read on his feast day; the contents might be true, false, or a mixture. In the course of time the word acquired in ordinary speech an almost wholly unfavourable meaning from the point of view of factual truth. It is in this sense that the word legend is used in this book, for a narrative or part of a narrative that is not historically true or is seriously untrustworthy.

MANICHAEISM (from Mani, a third-century Persian teacher) According to Manichaean doctrine there are two eternal and opposed first principles, Good and Evil ('light and darkness'); man is a mixture of the two, and his highest task is to purge out 'darkness' by the rejection of property, wine, flesh meat, sexual activity, and other matter, as intrinsically evil. Diluted forms of Manichaean ideas have from time to time appeared among Christians in later ages, e.g. among the ◊ ALBIGENSES, and the Paulicians and Bogomils in Asia Minor and the Balkans (7th to 15th cents.).

MARTYR (from Gk *martus*, 'witness') In Christian terminology a martyr is one who witnesses to Jesus Christ by willingly suffering death for him and his teaching or for any article of it, or for some Christian virtue, or for any act of virtue relating to God.

MARTYROLOGY A martyrology is a catalogue of martyrs and other saints, local or general, arranged in the order of their ◊ DIES NATALIS and giving the place of death; one that provides further particulars is an historical martyrology. The basic general martyrology is known as the *Hieronymianum*, first compiled before the seventh century. The Roman Martyrology, whose scope is world-wide, was officially approved in 1584 and has been added to since; it has long been in need of drastic historical revision and correction. An English translation of the current edition, edited by J. B. O'Connell, was published in 1962. In the East, menologies and synaxaries are somewhat similar works.

MONK (from Gk *monos*, 'alone') In the later development of Christian monasticism a monk is a man who lives in a community for life, under vows of poverty, celibacy, and obedience, and primarily engaged in communal worship of God and self-perfecting. What other work he undertakes varies with the customs of the house and individual aptitude. In the West all monks (except lay-brothers) are now normally ordained priest. The principal sorts of monk are the Benedictines (Black monks), the Cistercians (White monks), and the Carthusians. Eastern monks are not organized in different orders and, in accordance with original custom, a monk is not necessarily, or usually, a priest or deacon.

MONOPHYSISM (from Gk *monos*, 'one', *phusis*, 'nature') The doctrine that there is only one nature in the single person of Jesus Christ, his manhood being wholly absorbed in his divinity. This is as much as to say he was not really a man. Monophysism was condemned at the general council of Chalcedon in 451, but the decree was widely rejected in the Near East. The national churches of Egypt, Ethiopia and the Armenians, and of the Jacobite Syrians, are still reputedly monophysite.

MONOTHELISM (from Gk *monos*, 'one', *thelein*, 'to will') A somewhat artificial heresy produced by the efforts of the Byzantine emperor Heraclius to find a compromise formula to reconcile the monophysites with the orthodox (◊ previous entry). It affirmed that in Jesus Christ there is one, divine, 'energy' and one will; this is inconsistent with the reality of his human nature.

NESTORIANISM This heresy, taking its name from Nestorius, bishop of Constantinople, implies that Jesus Christ is not one divine-human person, but two persons joined together: God the Son and the man Jesus, who alone was born of Mary and died on the cross. This was condemned at the general council of Ephesus in 431. The once widespread Nestorian church, centred in Persia, is now reduced to a small body in Iraq and neighbouring lands.

NUNS AND SISTERS (from late Lat. *nonna*, fem. of *nonnus*, 'monk') Strictly speaking, nuns are members of a religious order of women having what are technically known as 'solemn vows'; all others, having 'simple vows', are called sisters. In ordinary speech, however, members of any female religious congregation are often referred to as nuns. Among the nuns proper are the Augustinian canonesses, the Benedictines, Poor Clares, Carmelites, and Ursulines; among sisters, the various congregations of Sisters of Charity, of Mercy, of the Sacred Heart, of Nazareth, of St Joseph, the Little Sisters of the Poor, and very many others.

OBSERVANTS A name formerly given to those Franciscan friars who observed a stricter form of the Rule of St Francis, in distinction from the followers of a mitigated form, the Conventuals.

ORDERS, RELIGIOUS What are commonly spoken of indiscriminately as religious orders are technically divided into orders properly so called, religious congregations, and societies, with various subdivisions.

PASSION (Lat. *passio*, 'suffering') (*a*) The sufferings and death of Jesus Christ. (*b*) The sufferings and death of any martyr; a martyrdom. (*c*) A written account of a martyr's death.

PATRIARCH (Gk, 'head of a family') A bishop of one of the five principal sees during the classical era of organization of the Christian church, each exercising a wide superior jurisdiction. They were the bishops of Rome, Constantinople, Alexandria, Antioch, and Jerusalem. Other patriarchates came into existence, through subdivision or through schism.

PELAGIANISM The teachings of a British or Irish monk, Pelagius, in the early fifth century: he denied that Adam's sin touched the rest of mankind ('original sin') and practically denied the need of God's grace for the attainment of salvation. Pelagius was condemned by several local church councils and by Popes Innocent I and Zosimus. Semi-Pelagianism was a modification of Pelagius's opinions.

SIMONY (from the name Simon Magus: ◊ Acts viii, 18–24) The buying and selling of sacred things, such as holy orders and other sacraments, ecclesiatical offices and preferment, and the like. At certain times and in certain places this abuse has been rife in the church.

SYNOD (Gk *sunodos*, 'meeting') 'Synod' is synonymous with 'church council', and is often used of lesser, local councils. It is also used for the permanent council of a patriarch or primate in the Eastern churches.

TERTIARY ◊ next entry

THIRD ORDER The medieval orders of friars gave rise to corresponding 'second orders' of nuns, and instituted 'third orders', of men and women living 'in the world' in close association, actual or moral, with the first order; these persons are called tertiaries. The chief third orders are those of the Franciscans, Dominicans, and Carmelites. There is also a number of 'regular tertiaries', living in community under religious vows.

TITULAR SAINT The saint in whose honour and under whose name a church or other building or institution is dedicated to God.

A

AARON and JULIUS, martyrs. Date uncertain; f.d. 3 July. Two Romano-Britons said to have been put to death at Caerleon in Monmouthshire, perhaps in the middle of the third century. Nothing else is recorded about them. The date c. 304, during the persecution under Diocletian, commonly given to these martyrs is only a conjecture (though a very old one); it is now believed that Diocletian's decree against Christians was not enforced in Britain.

Two other obscure martyrs, SS. *Socrates and Stephen* (f.d. 17 September), are noted in certain martyrologies as having suffered in Britain; in all probability, 'in Britannia' was written by mistake for 'in Bithynia', in north-western Asia Minor.

ABACHUM ◊ under Valentine

ABO, martyr. B. at Baghdad; d. at Tbilisi, 786; f.d. 8 January. He was a Moslem Arab who as a young man entered the service of a Georgian prince as a perfumer. At Tbilisi (Tiflis) he became convinced of the truth of Christianity, but was afraid to declare himself, for Georgia was then under Moslem rule. When, however, his master had to seek refuge among the Khazars north of the Caspian Sea, Abo accompanied him and was there baptized. In 782 they returned to Tbilisi, and some years later Abo was brought before the Moslem magistrate and charged as a renegade from Islam. He admitted that this was so, and after a short imprisonment he was beheaded. St Abo's feast is observed by the Christians of Georgia.

ABRAHAM OF KRATIA, monk. B. in Syria, c. 474; d. in Palestine, c. 558; f.d. 6 December. He became a monk at his native place, Emesa (Homs), but the community was soon after dispersed by nomad raiders. Abraham fled to Constantinople, and when only twenty-six was made abbot at Kratia in Bithynia. Ten years later he went away secretly to Palestine in search of a quieter life, but he was made to go back to his monastery, only to be made bishop of Kratia soon after. About 525 he again retired to Palestine, and lived in religious contemplation there for the rest of his life.

ABRAHAM OF SMOLENSK, abbot. D. at Smolensk, 1221; cd by Russian Orth. ch., c. 1549; f.d. 21 August. He became a monk at Smolensk, his birthplace, and devoted himself to biblical studies and preaching. He was a man of stern and militant character, who kept the day of judgement ever before himself and in the minds of others; but he had a great following among the lay people, whose sick and troubled were his care. Among the clergy, however, he incurred enmity and jealousy, and the time came when

29

serious charges, both moral and theological, were brought against him. The bishop of Smolensk took disciplinary measures, and for five years Abraham was under a cloud. Then the bishop re-examined his case, acquitted him of the charges, and made him abbot of a small monastery. Here St Abraham passed the rest of his days in peaceful ministry. He was a notable figure in pre-Mongol Russia, and a biography of him by his disciple Ephraem has survived.

ACHILLEUS ◊ *Nereus and Achilleus*

ADALBERT OF MAGDEBURG, bishop. D. at Merseburg, 981; f.d. 20 June. When, at the request of the Kievan princess St Olga, the Emperor Otto the Great decided to send Christian missionaries into Russia, he chose as leader of them a monk from Trier, Adalbert. They set out in 961, but had scarcely entered Russia when they encountered opposition from Olga's heathen son Svyatoslav. Some of the missionaries were killed; but Adalbert got back to Germany, where he became abbot of a monastery at Weissenburg and did much to encourage learning among his monks. In 968 he was made first archbishop of Magdeburg, and for thirteen years ruled that see, doing missionary work among the Wends and founding three new dioceses.

ADALBERT OF PRAGUE, bishop and martyr. B. in Bohemia, *c.* 956; d. in Pomerania, 997; f.d. 23 April. He was christened Voytech, but took the name of his preceptor at Magdeburg, ◊ *St Adalbert.* While still under thirty he became bishop of Prague, but the pastoral and political difficulties were such that in 990 he withdrew in desperation to Rome. Pope John XV sent him back to his diocese, where he founded the great abbey of Brevnov; but again he met with opposition to his ministry from the nobility, and again he retired to Rome. At length it became apparent that there was no hope of his working unmolested in Prague, and he was allowed to turn his attention to the heathen Prussians of Pomerania. But here he had no more success. He and his fellow missionaries nevertheless persevered in their mission, and were eventually murdered, perhaps near Königsberg. Despite the disappointments of his career, St Adalbert of Prague seems to have had considerable influence. He was a friend of the Emperor Otto III, encouraged the evangelization of the Magyars, and inspired ◊ *St Boniface of Querfurt;* his cultus was widespread in central Europe. He in his turn was influenced by the ideals of the great monastery of Cluny.

ADAMNAN, abbot. B. in Iieland, *c.* 628; d. on Iona, 704; f.d. 23 September. Adamnan (or Adomnan, Eunan) was descended from a grandfather of ◊ *St Columba,* and in 679 he became the ninth abbot of Iona. After a mission to Northumbria on behalf of Irish captives there, and a later visit to the monasteries of Wearmouth and Jarrow, he rejected the Celtic customs relative to the date of Easter and other matters; this displeased the Iona monks, and from c. 692 Adamnan seems to have been there only from time to time. Instead he popularized the Roman Easter in Ireland itself, and may have founded the monastery of Raphoe. At Birr in Offaly in 697 he was instrumental in the enacting of 'Adamnan's Law' for the protection of women, children and clergy, especially during warfare. He was a peace-loving man, and Ceolfrid of Wearmouth, who knew him personally, praised his moderation and humbleness. St Adamnan wrote a book *On the Holy Places*, from notes taken down from a Frankish bishop, Arculf, who had been in Palestine. The text of this still exists; but Adamnan's most famous work is the *Life of St Columba*, which was written on Iona after 688, and has several times been translated into English.

ADAUCTUS ◊ *Felix and Adauctus*

ADDAI and MARI, bishops. Second century (?); f.d. various dates. The traditional envangelizers of Mesopotamia. According to the story, Addai was one of Christ's disciples and was sent by the apostle ◊ *St Thomas* to Edessa (Urfa in Iraq), where he founded the church. This legend is associated with that of Christ's letter to King Abgar at Edessa. It is possible that Addai was a missionary in Mesopotamia during the second century. Nothing at all is known of Mari; tradition connects him with Nisibis and Nineveh. The Nestorian Christians ('Assyrians') and the Catholic Chaldeans still reverence the memory of 'the Holy Apostles Addai and Mari'.

ADELAIDE, empress. B. in Burgundy, c. 931; d. near Strasbourg, 999; cd c. 1097; f.d 16 December. After the death of her first husband, King Lothair of Italy, in 950, Adelaide became the second wife of Otto the Great, whose first had been Edith, sister of Athelstan of England. In 962 they were crowned emperor and empress by Pope John XII. Otto died in 973, and for twenty years his widow's life was a turmoil of family and political troubles. Her son, Otto II, was turned against her by his Greek wife Theophano, and Adelaide had to leave the court for a time to live with her brother in Burgundy. The same thing happened under her grandson, Otto III; but from 995 she was able to live more peacefully. She was a conscientious and generous-hearted woman, who profited from the friendship and advice of such men as ◊ *St Adalbert of Magdeberg, St Willigis of Mainz*, and the Cluniac abbots ◊ *SS. Mayeul and Odilo*. The last named wrote a memoir of her, calling her 'a marvel of beauty and goodness'. St Adelaide died in the convent she had founded at Seltz in Alsace.

ADRIAN and NATALIA, martyrs. D. at Nicomedia, c. 304 (?); f.d.
8 September, 1 December. The story told of these two is that
Adrian, an imperial officer at Nicomedia, was so impressed by the
patient suffering of some persecuted Christians that he openly
declared he was a Christian himself, though he had not been
baptized. He was at once thrown into jail, where his young
Christian wife, Natalia, visited him and arranged for his instruction in the faith there. After he had been sentenced to death
visitors were forbidden him, but Natalia disguised herself as a
boy and bribed her way in to ask his prayers for her in Heaven.
She was present at his execution, when he was broken limb by
limb, and had to be restrained from casting herself into the fire
when Adrian's body was burned with those of other martyrs.
A rain storm put out the fire, and Christians gathered the remains
and buried them at Argyropolis, on the Bosporus. There Natalia
went to live, taking with her a hand of her husband which she
had recovered; and when she died she was buried among the
martyrs. It is not known what, if any, truth lies behind this romantic tale. There were apparently two Adrians martyred at Nicomedia, one under Diocletian, the other under Licinius.

ADRIAN OF CANTERBURY, abbot. B. in Africa; d. at Canterbury,
710; f.d. 9 January. While abbot of a monastery near Monte
Cassino, this Adrian was twice offered the vacant archbishopric of
Canterbury by Pope St Vitalian. Twice he declined, but on the
second occasion suggested the Greek monk Theodore (◊ *Theodore of Canterbury*) as a suitable candidate. The pope agreed,
but stipulated that Adrian should accompany the new archbishop
to England. They set out in 668, and reached Canterbury separ-
ately after long delays on the road. There Adrian was soon installed at the abbey of SS. Peter and Paul (later St Augustine's).
He was a man learned in the Scriptures, an experienced administrator, and a good Greek and Latin scholar, and under his direction the Canterbury monastic school had far-reaching influence.
As well as sacred learning, poetry, astronomy and calendar cal-
culation were taught, and Bede even alleges that some of its students knew Latin and Greek as well as they did English. The
abbot helped his archbishop in pastoral undertakings, and there
can be no doubt that the flourishing state of the English church
in St Theodore's time owed much to St Adrian. He was buried
in the church of his monastery.

AEDAN ◊ *Aidan*

AEGIDIUS ◊ *Giles*

ÆLFHEAH ◊ *Alphege*

ÆLRED or AILRED, abbot. B. at Hexham, 1109; d. at Rievaulx,
12 January 1167; f.d. 3 March. Ælred, an Englishman, son and

grandson of parish priests of Hexham, was at an early age taken into the service of King David of Scotland. When he was twenty-four, after a sharp inward struggle, he entered the monastery of Rievaulx in Yorkshire, founded in the previous year as the first Cistercian house in England. Ten years later he was made abbot of a new house of his order at Revesby in Lincolnshire, and in 1147 returned to Rievaulx as its abbot. Throughout his busy life Ælred was distinguished for his energy and his sympathetic gentleness. His biographer, Walter Daniel, records: 'I lived under his rule for seventeen years, and in that time he did not dismiss anyone from the monastery.' Ælred's name, indeed, is particularly associated with friendship, human and divine, and one of the two best known of his writings is a little work *On Spiritual Friendship*; the other is the *Mirror of Charity*, a treatise on Christian perfection (both have been translated into English). His writings and sermons are characterized by a constant appeal to the Bible and to a love of Christ as friend and saviour that was the mainspring of his life. During his abbacy the number of monks at Rievaulx rose to over six hundred, and in addition to looking after these he had every year to visit other Cistercian houses in England and Scotland, and even to go as far afield as the Cistercian centres of Cîteaux and Clairvaux. These journeys must have been a great trial, for during his later years Ælred suffered from a very painful disease; but such travellings, together with his writings, did much to extend the influence of this man who has been called 'the St Bernard of the north'. After being for a time virtually in a state of physical collapse, St Ælred died at his monastery, in a shed adjoining the infirmary which he had made his quarters. The historian of monasticism in England, Professor David Knowles, writes of him that he is 'a singularly attractive figure. ... No other English monk of the twelfth century so lingers in the memory'.

F. M. Powicke (tr.), *The Life of Ailred of Rievaulx by Walter Daniel* (1950); A. Squire, *Aelred of Rievaulx: A Study* (1969).

ÆTHELBURH, ÆTHELTHRYTH ✧ *Ethelburga, Etheldreda*

AFRA, martyr. D. at Augsburg, *c.* 304(?); f.d. 5 August. The existence at Augsburg of an early martyr named Afra seems established, but there is no historical value in the particulars given in her legend. This relates that she was a prostitute who was arrested as a Christian during the persecution under Diocletian. When brought to trial and ordered to sacrifice to the gods she replied, 'My body has sinned, let it suffer. But I will not corrupt my soul by idolatry.' So she was burned to death on an islet in the river Lech. Her mother and three servants carried away the body and gave it honourable burial, for which they too were put to death.

This story seems to be an embroidery on some historical record or reference.

AGAPE, CHIONIA, and IRENE, martyrs. D. at Salonika, 304; f.d. 3 April. The martyrdom of these three maidens, sisters, is related in a document that is a somewhat amplified version of genuine records. They were brought before the governor of Macedonia, Dulcitius, on a charge of refusing to eat food that had been offered in sacrifice to the gods. When asked from whom they had learned such strange ideas, Chionia replied, 'From our Lord Jesus Christ', and she and Agape again refused to eat the impious food. Whereupon they were burned alive.

Meanwhile Dulcitius had learned that Irene had kept Christian books in her possession, instead of giving them up as the law required. He examined her again, and she said that when the emperor's decree against Christians was published, she and others fled to the mountains. She avoided implicating those who had helped them, and declared that nobody but themselves knew they had the books: 'We feared our own people as much as anybody.' After they returned home they hid the books, and were very unhappy at not being able to read them at all hours as was their wont. The governor ordered Irene to be stripped and exposed in a brothel; but she was unmolested there, so, after being given a last chance to conform, she was sentenced to death. The books also, the sacred Scriptures, were publicly burnt. Three other women and a man were tried with these martyrs, of whom one woman was remanded because she was pregnant. It is not recorded what happened to them.

AGATHA, martyr. Third century (?); f.d. 5 February. There was certainly a virgin martyr named Agatha at Catania in Sicily, who was venerated from early times; but nothing more is known about her. Her worthless legend, of which there are many versions, tells us that she was a girl of noble family who was pursued by a man of consular rank, named Quintian. When she rejected him resolutely, he proceeded against her as a Christian. Having been handed over to a woman who tried in vain to corrupt her, Agatha was tortured in various ways, and we are told that at one point ◊ St Peter appeared in a vision and healed her hurts. But eventually she died from her sufferings. Among the barbarities to which St Agatha was said to have been subjected was the cutting off of her breasts, and she is often represented in art carrying them on a dish, with curious consequences. For the resemblance in shape of breasts to bells led to the adoption of Agatha as patron saint of bell-founders; and their resemblance to round loaves apparently accounts for the custom observed in some places of blessing bread in church on her feast day.

AGAUNUM, MARTYRS OF. Third century (?); f.d. 22 September. A tradition, first recorded *c.* 445 by ◊ *St Eucherius of Lyons*, relates that a Roman legion of Christian soldiers from Egypt, the 'Theban Legion', was serving in Gaul, when it mutinied at Agaunum (Saint-Maurice en Valais in Switzerland). The mutiny was caused by their being ordered to take part in heathen sacrifices or, according to another interpretation, by their prospective use to punish Christians. For this insubordination they were twice decimated; encouraged by their commanding officer Maurice and two others, they still refused to obey, and the rest of the legion was butchered to a man.

What truth, if any, lies behind the story of this unexampled happening has been much debated. It would seem that a group or small unit of soldiers was put to death at Agaunum near the end of the third century, and that this was subsequently exaggerated into a legion. Later on hagiographers identified a number of obscure martyrs, from Cologne to Piacenza, as stragglers from the Theban Legion (cf. ◊ *St Gereon*). The sixth-century monastery established at the place of martyrdom still exists at Saint-Maurice en Valais as an abbey of canons regular.

AGNES, martyr. D. *c.* 304 (?); f.d. 21 January. St Agnes is unquestionably one of the most famous of Roman martyrs: it is therefore the more disappointing that so little is known about her for certain. There is no doubt whatever that she was martyred in Rome and was buried in the cemetery on the Via Nomentana, where a church was built in her honour *c.* 350, and her name and the date of her feast occurs in the calendar of martyrs drawn up in 354. From then on much was written about her, including a celebrated epitaph by Pope ◊ *St Damasus*; unfortunately, it is clear from the contradictions in these earliest accounts that memory of the real story of St Agnes was already confused. One learned attempt to reconstruct her story from the unsatisfactory evidence now available may be summarized thus: Agnes was little more than a child; she refused to consider marriage, and consecrated her maidenhood to God; when persecution broke out she left home and offered herself for martyrdom; she resisted all threats, and was executed by being stabbed in the throat (a common Roman form of execution). Some such relatively simple sequence as this is probably what happened, contrasting with the exaggerations and fancies of later accounts. There is general agreement that St Agnes was very young, twelve or thirteen; and if her relics preserved in Rome are genuine, which some competent archaeologists maintain is probable, they bear out this point. Her emblem in art is a lamb.

AGNES OF MONTEPULCIANO, nun. B. in Tuscany, *c.* 1268; d. at

Montepulciano, 1317; cd 1726; f.d. 20 April. She was confided to the care of nuns as a child, and at a very early age was made superioress of a convent. About 1298 she was invited to establish a nunnery at Montepulciano, which she did, putting it under the direction of the Dominican Order. St Agnes led an extremely mortified life, and a number of visions, miracles, and other remarkable occurrences are related of her. ◊ *St Katherine of Siena* held her memory in special veneration.

AIDAN, missionary. B. in Ireland; d. at Bamburgh, 651; f.d. 31 August. This Irishman, who played a decisive part in the evangelization of northern England, is first heard of *c.* 635, when he was a monk in the monastery of Iona: he was chosen to replace one of his fellows who failed as a missionary in Northumbria because of the roughness of his methods. Aidan was consecrated bishop, and made his headquarters on the island of Lindisfarne. From there he made journeys on foot far and wide, visiting his flock and establishing missionary centres, work which had the wholehearted support of the king, ◊ *St Oswald*. He organized a monastery on Lindisfarne, where English boys were educated and trained to be missionaries among their countrymen. No wealth was allowed to accumulate; surpluses were applied to the needs of the poor and to the manumission of slaves: Aidan made his teaching acceptable by its practice. The death of King Oswald, friend as well as patron, was a great blow to Aidan, but his successor Oswin was no less dear to him. When Oswin was murdered at Gilling in 651 (he was afterwards venerated as a martyr), Aidan himself died within the fortnight, seemingly of grief. He was buried on Lindisfarne. St Aidan 'was a man of remarkable gentleness, goodness, and moderation, zealous for God; but not', adds Bede, 'fully according to knowledge . . .': that is, he followed and taught the liturgical and disciplinary customs of the Celtic Christians, which in certain respects differed from those usual in the Western church. In art, St Aidan's emblem is a stag.

AIDAN, or MAEDOC, of FERNS, bishop. D. 626; f.d. 31 January. Among a number of saints in Ireland named Aidan (Aedan), this one seems to have been the most important. Apparently he was a native of Connacht, and as a youth, 'desirous of becoming learned in holy Scripture', he studied under ◊ *St David* in Wales. Returning to Ireland, he established a monastic community at Ferns in Co. Wexford, and became the first bishop there. The written Lives of St Aidan are mostly composed of miracles attributed to him, showing his generosity and kindness. A bronze reliquary in which this saint's relics were kept in the eleventh century is preserved in Dublin.

AILRED ◊ *Ælred*

ALBAN, martyr. D. at Verulamium, *c.* 209 (?); f.d. 22 June (B.C.P. 17 June). St Alban is venerated as the first martyr in the Island of Britain. The first known reference to him is in the fifth century Life of ◊ *St Germanus of Auxerre,* and Gildas, writing *c.* 540, gives the core of the tradition: Alban was a Romano-Briton living at Verulamium (now the city of St Albans); during Diocletian's persecution he gave shelter to a fleeing Christian; he was himself arrested and put to death amidst supernatural happenings. Bede gives an amplified account, which includes a lively description of the execution by beheading and more details of the signs from Heaven. The traditional scene of the martyrdom was Holmhurst Hill, where it was commemorated by a church and shrine in Bede's day; the great abbey of St Alban afterwards rose on the same site. Some elements in the narratives are clearly quite untrustworthy, and the question of Alban's date has been very much discussed. The latest study uses the Turin manuscript of a *Passio Albani* to show that he was martyred in 209.

J. Morris, in *Hertfordshire Archaeology,* vol. 1 (1968).

ALBERIC or AUBREY, abbot. D. at Cîteaux, 1108; f.d. 26 January. He was co-founder with ◊ *St Stephen Harding* and *St Robert of Molesme* of the mother house of that branch of Benedictine monastic life called 'Cistercian', from the Latin name of its cradle, Cistertium (Cîteaux in Burgundy). After several abortive attempts to find a form of monastic life whose austerity and simplicity would satisfy them, these three monks, with others, settled in 1098 at Cîteaux, which was then a wilderness. Robert was their leader, but in the following year he returned to his former monastery at Molesme, and Alberic became abbot of Cîteaux in his place. During the few years of his abbacy the foundations were laid of what was quickly to grow from a single obscure house into a ramifying and influential religious order, which still exists. Alberic set the example of humble poverty and hard work in God's service; when he died, his successor Stephen told the community, 'You have lost a revered father and spiritual guide; I have lost, not only a father and guide, but a friend and fellow soldier of the Lord.'

ALBERT THE GREAT, theologian. B. in Swabia, 1206; d. at Cologne, 1280; cd 1931; f.d. 15 November. He studied at the University of Padua, and then, against the wishes of his noble family, joined the newly founded Order of Preachers; he was a lecturer in several German friaries, gaining his master's degree in theology at Paris in 1244. From 1248 his headquarters was at Cologne where, as director of studies, he had ◊ *St Thomas Aquinas* among his pupils for four years. After being professor of holy Scripture in Rome for a time, he took part in the organization of the studies of the whole Dominican Order. In 1260 Albert was appointed bishop of Regensburg, but resigned two years later, believing that he could be more useful as a teacher in the schools. For the last dozen years of his life he taught theology in Cologne, with a break in 1274 when he took an active part in the general council at Lyons.

Not for nothing is St Albert called 'the Universal Teacher': his written works are voluminous in bulk and encyclopaedic in scope: they include, as well as biblical and theological works and sermons, treatises on logic, metaphysics, ethics, and the physical sciences. His interests extended to physics, astronomy, chemistry, and biology, to human and animal physiology, to geography, geology, and botany. But he stands out in particular for his recognition of the autonomy of human reason in its own sphere, of the validity of knowledge gained from sense-experience, and of the value of Aristotle's philosophy in systematizing theology. Aquinas perfected the synthesis. St Albert was canonized by being enrolled among the doctors of the church by Pope Pius XI in 1931. He was also named patron saint of students of the natural sciences, for he had, said the pope, 'that rare and divine gift, scientific instinct, in the highest degree ...; he is exactly the saint whose example ought to inspire the present age'.

H. Wilms, *Albert the Great* (1933).

ALDHELM, bishop. B. in Wessex, *c.* 640; d. at Doulting in Somerset, 709; f.d. 25 May. St Aldhelm was the first English scholar of distinction. In earlier life he studied under an Irish teacher, Maeldubh, who was head of a religious community at Malmesbury, and later for a short time under ◊ *St Adrian* and *St Theodore* at Canterbury. About 675 he became abbot of Malmesbury; he visited Rome at the request of Pope Sergius I, and in 705 King Ine appointed him first bishop of Sherborne. His brief episcopate was marked by energy and enterprise: we are told he would go into public places and sing hymns and passages from the gospels, mixed with bits of clowning, hoping thus to 'win men's ears, and then their souls'.

His English writings, hymns and songs, with their music, have all perished; of his Latin works, the longest are a poem in praise of holy maidens and a treatise on virginity written for the nuns of Barking in Essex. He addressed a famous letter to Gerent, king of Dumnonia (Devon and Cornwall), explaining the date on which Easter ought to be kept by the Celtic clergy there. In his lighter moments he composed Latin verse and metrical riddles. As a scholar, St Aldhelm has been described as 'ingenious', and it has been well said that the Latin language went to his head. He liked to play with words, and his writing was so involved and obscure as often to be unintelligible; but his reading was extensive, and in his own day he had a wide influence in southern England. He was buried at Malmesbury abbey. The cape in Dorset usually called St Alban's Head is properly St Aldhelm's Head.

E. S. Duckett, *Anglo-Saxon Saints and Scholars* (1947).

ALEXANDER, martyr. Date unknown; f.d. 10 July. He is among the martyrs named in the canon of the Roman Mass, added thereto by Pope St Symmachus early in the sixth century, but his history is no longer known. He was buried in the cemetery of the Jordani on the Salarian Way, one of the seven martyrs commemorated on 10 July who later on were alleged to be sons of the Roman ◊ *St Felicity.* – There are many other saints named Alexander, about most of whom little is known.

ALEXANDER NEVSKY, prince. B. at Pereaslavl, 1219; d. at Vladimir, 1263; cd by the Russian Orth. ch., 1547; f.d. 23 November. Grand-prince of Novgorod, Vladimir and Kiev, who saved Russia by his policy of conciliation towards the invading Tartars and firm resistance to enemies on the west. His name of Nevsky came from his victory in 1240 over the Swedes on the river Neva; he defeated the Teutonic Knights at Lake Peipus in 1242, and drove out the Lithuanians soon after. But he was no mere ambitious conqueror: 'God is not on the side of force', he said, 'but of truth and justice.' He had several times to make long journeys to the Tartar overlords to intercede for his people, and earned much obloquy thereby from those who disapproved his policy. He bore the unjust accusations patiently, and the religious integrity of his life, together with his great services to his people, caused him to be venerated as a saint: 'God glorified his righteous servant', it was said, 'because he laboured greatly for the land of Russia and for the true Christian religion.' In 1938 Alexander Nevsky was made the subject of a film by Eisenstein, with music by Prokofiev.

ALEXANDER SAULI ◊ under *Charles Borromeo*

ALEXIS, called 'the Man of God'. Fifth century; f.d. 17 July. According to an almost contemporary account there died in a hospital at Edessa in Mesopotamia *c.* 430 a nameless man who had lived by begging, and shared the alms he received with other poor people; after his death, it was learned that he was the son of a Roman patrician, who had left a wealthy bride on his wedding day and gone to live in poverty in Syria. An account of this man, which called him Alexis, was written in Greek, and a further narrative was produced in Latin; this made the extravagant claim that Alexis returned to Rome and spent his last seventeen years there, unrecognized, as a servant in his father's house, sleeping in a corner under the stairs. The legend of St Alexis had a widespread popularity in the later middle ages; in the eleventh century he was made the subject of a long epic poem, and c. 1350 he was chosen as patron saint of the nursing society called Alexian Brothers.

ALEXIS FALCONIERI ◊ under *Seven Founders*

ALMACHIUS or TELEMACHUS, martyr. D. in Rome, c. 400; f.d. 1 January. He was a monk from the East who, while in Rome, sought to put an end to gladiatorial contests. One day he ran into the arena to separate the combatants, and was killed, either by the infuriated spectators or by gladiators at the order of the city prefect. It is said that in consequence the emperor Honorius abolished such shows; certainly Almachius was revered as a martyr.

ALOYSIUS, Jesuit student. B. in Lombardy, 1568; d. in Rome, 1591; cd 1726; f.d. 21 June. Aloysius (Luigi) Gonzaga, eldest son of the Marquis of Castiglione, was intended by his father to be a soldier. But the youth was revolted by the violence and licentiousness of noble society as he experienced it in Italy and Spain; he was fired with the idea of being a missionary, and at the age of sixteen he determined to join the Society of Jesus. His father was furious, but eventually in 1585 Aloysius was allowed to enter the Jesuit novitiate in Rome. He was a model novice, and all was going smoothly when an epidemic of plague broke out. The Jesuits opened a hospital for the stricken, and Aloysius was working very hard in it when he was taken with a lingering fever, from which he never recovered. During his sickness he was ministered to by ◊ *St Robert Bellarmine*, who afterwards testified to his holiness. The biographies of St Aloysius and his own letters and religious writings show a type of character but little attractive to many people of a different time and society, with perhaps a different religious background; but he was strong enough to pass unscathed through the dangers of his youth, and when there was a serious quarrel between his brother and the Duke of Mantua to be composed, it was Aloysius who was sent for.

Mention may be made here of two other young Jesuit saints who resembled St Aloysius in personality and history: *St Stanislas Kostka*, a Pole (1550–68); f.d. 13 November, and *St John Berchmans*, a Brabanter (1599–1621; f.d. 26 November).

C. C. Martindale, *The Vocation of Aloysius Gonzaga* (1927); *Lives of St John Berchmans* by H. Delehaye (1921) and R. Brenan (1964).

ALPHEGE, bishop and martyr. B. 954; d. at Greenwich 1012; f.d. 19 April. Alphege (Ælfheah) was a monk first at Deerhurst in Gloucestershire and then at Bath, and in 984 was made bishop of

Winchester, where he presided for over twenty years. He was then raised to the archbishopric of Canterbury, at a time when England was being ravaged by the Danes. Canterbury was betrayed to the marauders, and the archbishop was captured and carried away to Greenwich. A ransom was demanded for him, which he would not allow to be paid. In a drunken fury the Danes set on him, pelting him with bones, and although one of them, Thorkell the Tall, tried to save him, he was killed by a blow on the head with an axe. It cannot be said that St Alphege died for the Christian faith; but ◊ *St Anselm* vindicated his public veneration as a martyr, and his feast is still observed.

ALPHONSUS LIGUORI, founder and theologian. B. near Naples, 1696; d. 1787; cd 1839; f.d. 2 August. He was a rising young barrister until, having lost an important case, he forsook the law in 1723 and in due course was ordained priest. He did mission work in and around Naples, making his mark as a preacher, and in 1732 he organized at Scala a group of missioners intended specially for work in rural districts. This was the beginning of the congregation of priests known as Redemptorists, but it was handicapped in its early days by grave internal dissensions. In 1748 Liguori published the first version of his work on moral theology, so famous that it has a little overshadowed his other achievements, and he continued with this and many other writings.

In 1762 he was made bishop of Sant' Agata dei Goti, a small diocese but a difficult one. In pastoral work he insisted continually on simple preaching, dignified and unhurried celebration of the Eucharist, and the firm handling of obstinate wrongdoers. For the last twenty years of his long life he had to contend with chronic ill-health, resulting in a permanent deformity, with attacks on his teaching, and with the troubles of the Redemptorist congregation. In 1775 he was allowed to resign his bishopric, only to be faced by another and worse crisis in Redemptorist affairs. Alphonsus was tricked into signing a document of which the result was the splitting of the congregation into two separate factions. He found himself excluded from the society he had founded, and did not live to see its reunification. For eighteen months he was afflicted with acute spiritual trials and temptations; but he was enabled to overcome them, and he died peacefully in retirement at Nocera dei Pagani.

St Alphonsus once claimed never to have preached a sermon which the simplest old woman in the congregation could not understand; on the other hand, his system of moral theology was marked by great subtlety, and he incurred charges of laxity in moral teaching. But he was in fact opposing the rigours of Jansenism, and sought to win back sinners by patience and moderation rather than to repel them by severity and fear. His numerous devotional writings, very 'flowery' in expression, had a wide influence; *The Glories of Mary* is perhaps the best remembered of them.

A. C. Berthe, *Life of St Alphonsus de' Liguori* (2 vols., 1905).

ALPHONSUS RODRIGUEZ, Jesuit laybrother. B. at Segovia, 1531; d. in Majorca, 1617; cd 1888; f.d. 30 October. This Alphonsus was the son of a successful wool-merchant, whose business he inherited when he was twenty-three. But the business declined, and his wife and two children died young: he had always taken religion seriously, so at the age of forty he applied for admittance as a lay helper to the Jesuits at Valencia. After some hesitation he was accepted, and sent to the college at Montesión in Majorca. He lived there for the rest of his life, employed as hall-porter. Many of the varied people who were thus brought into contact with Brother Rodriguez learned to respect him and value his advice; in particular, ◊ *St Peter Claver* as a student used to consult him frequently and received from him impetus for his future work among the slaves of South America. Alphonsus bears considerable resemblance to the Carmelite Brother Lawrence, of the next generation. He was a man of practically no education, but he had deep religious sensibility of a mystical kind, and he wrote down some of his thoughts and experiences at the request of his superiors. This Alphonsus Rodriguez must not be confused with two Jesuit contemporaries of the same names, one a writer of well-known religious books, the other a martyr in Paraguay. Neither of these has been canonized, though the second is venerated as a *beatus*. There is a sonnet on St Alphonsus Rodriguez among Gerard Manley Hopkins' *Poems* (2nd edn, 1930).

Autobiography, tr. W. Yeomans (1964).

AMADOUR, hermit. Date unknown; f.d. 20 August. St Amadour is the legendary founder of the shrine of our Lady at Rocamadour in France. After the finding there in 1162 of an ancient tomb containing an unidentified body, the legend underwent surprising developments. Amadour was represented as a servant of the ◊ *Virgin Mary*, who married ◊ *St Veronica* and came as a missionary to Gaul; later on he was identified as Zacchaeus (Luke xix, 2–9). It is very probable that Amadour is a wholly imaginary person: the idea that he was really a certain *St Amator*, bishop of Auxerre (d. 418), is baseless.

AMALBURGA ◊ under *Gudula*

AMAND OF MAASTRICHT, missionary bishop. B. in Poitou, *c.* 584; d. at Elnone, 679; f.d. 6 February. He lived at Bourges as a hermit for fifteen years, before embarking on a long and fruitful missionary career at the age of forty-five. Having been made a bishop without a fixed see, he preached the gospel in Flanders, among the Danubian Slavs, possibly in Gascony, and around Antwerp, where he was not very successful. Then for a short time he was resident bishop at Maastricht; but the difficulties there were too great for him and, although Pope ◊ *St Martin I* had encouraged him to persevere, he returned to his itinerant life of evangelization. St Amand had the support of the Frankish kings, but often met strong opposition from the peoples he tried to convert; he sharply reproved King Dagobert I for encouraging the use of force for this purpose, and for other crimes as well. To solidify his missionary work Amand founded several religious houses, notably Mont-Blandin (and perhaps Saint-Bavon) at Ghent and the abbey of Elnone. To this last he retired when he was nearly ninety, and there died, after dictating his testament, whose text has survived. – There are several other saints named Amand venerated in France.

E. S. Duckett, *The Wandering Saints* (1959).

AMATOR ◊ under *Amador*

AMBROSE, bishop and doctor. B. at Trier, *c.* 334 or 340; d. at Milan, 4 April 397; f.d. 7 December (B.C.P., 4 April). He was son of a praetorian prefect of Gaul. While practising law in the Roman courts he was appointed, *c.* 370 , governor of the province of Aemilia and Liguria, whose capital was Milan. When that see became vacant in 374 Ambrose was chosen to be its bishop by the acclamations of the people: he accepted unwillingly, for at the time he was but a catechumen, not yet baptized. The bishopric was one of the highest responsibility. Milan was then the administrative centre of the western part of the Roman empire; its bishop was inevitably involved in politics; there was a flood of new converts to be instructed in Christianity, but paganism was still widespread; and many of the Christians themselves were adherents of Arianism, which was given support in high quarters. These were the problems facing the new bishop. A group of senators tried to get the statue of the goddess of victory restored to the senate-house in Rome; Ambrose intervened, and persuaded the young emperor, Valentinian II, not to give permission. The empress-regent, Justina, ordered him to hand over a building to the Arians for a church: Ambrose refused. At Salonika, in 390, rioters killed the Roman governor, and the Emperor Theodosius I in punishment ordered a massacre of monstrous savagery: Ambrose wrote and told him that such a crime needed to be expiated by public penance. The emperor submitted to it. Ambrose always acted on the principle that he himself enunciated: 'The emperor is within the church: he is not above it.' More far-reaching in a different way was a happening in the autumn of 386: ◊ *Augustine*, later of Hippo, came from Africa to Milan, and six months later was baptized by St Ambrose.

Ambrose is numbered among the four great Latin doctors of the church, with ◊ *Augustine, Jerome*, and *Gregory the Great*. His teaching, as befitted a bishop, was more by his sermons than his writings; his primary business was not with emperors or theologians but with the people, and his discourses were very practical. His writings on doctrinal subjects include 'catechism lessons' (*De mysteriis*; Eng. trans., 1950) to the newly baptized on baptism, confirmation, and the eucharist, and his few letters are valuable for the history of his time. He was the first teacher in the West successfully to make extensive use of hymns as a popular means of divine praise and of fostering right belief. A few have survived and are still in use, e.g. *Aeterne rerum conditor*, and his influence is found in many others. On the other hand, the *Te Deum* is not his work, though the so-called Athanasian Creed possibly is.

F. H. Dudden, *Life and Times of St Ambrose* (2 vols., 1935); A. Paredi, *St Ambrose, his Life and Times* (1964).

ANACLETUS ◊ under *Clement the First*

ANASTASIA, martyr. D. at Sirmium, 304 (?); f.d. 22 December. This saint now has a commemoration only in Byzantine churches. Nothing is known about her except that she was martyred at the place now called Sremska Mitrovica in Yugoslavia. Later legend makes her a Roman matron, associating her with ◊ *St Chrysogonus* at Aquileia and attributing incredible adventures to her.

ANASTASIUS THE PERSIAN, martyr. D. at Bethsaloe, 628; f.d. 22 January. According to his Greek biographer, this young soldier, whose name was Magundat, was serving in the army of King Chosroes II of Persia when it captured Jerusalem in 614. There he became a Christian, was christened Anastasius, and entered a monastery. Some years later he was allowed to go to Caesarea to preach the gospel to the Persian garrison. He was there arrested, flogged, and put to hard labour. Having repeatedly refused to renounce his faith, he was taken in chains eastward to the Euphrates, where an officer of Chosroes also failed to make him apostatize, even with the help of torture. At length, with many other Christians, Anastasius was strangled, at Bethsaloe on the Euphrates. He was buried first at Resapha, near by, but his relics are said now to be in the church of St Vincent and St Anastasius at Rome.

ANDREW, apostle. First century; f.d. 30 November. He was a Galilean fisherman of Bethsaida and the first-called of the followers of Christ, to whom he brought his brother Simon, afterwards ◊ *St Peter* (Mark i, 16–18; John i, 40–42). Andrew is mentioned several times in the gospels, but later accounts of his life are very unreliable. They associate him with Scythia and Epirus, and say he was martyred by crucifixion at Patras in Achaia. The idea that he suffered on an X-shaped cross seems to have been unknown before the late middle ages. The claim that he was the first bishop at Byzantium (Constantinople) is without historical foundation. St Andrew is the patron saint of Scotland, and his emblem is a cross saltire, X.

ANDREW OF CRETE, preacher and poet. B. at Damascus, *c.* 660; d. in Crete, 740; f.d. 4 July. He is sometimes called 'of Jerusalem', as he was a monk there for ten years. He was then in charge of an orphanage and old men's home in Constantinople, and *c.* 700 was made archbishop of Gortyna in Crete. Andrew was an exceptionally eloquent preacher, but he is known best of all for his Greek liturgical poetry. He wrote many short hymns, each with its own melody, called *idiomela,* and is said to have been the first writer of the compositions called *kanons.* This is a form that tends to length and verbosity: St Andrew's 'Great Kanon', a penitential hymn for Lent, runs to 250 strophes; it is still sung in the Byzantine liturgy.

There is another *St Andrew of Crete,* who was killed by an iconoclast at Constantinople in 766 (f.d. 20 October).

ANDREW OF FIESOLE ◊ under *Donatus of Fiesole*

ANDREW AVELLINO, priest. B. near Naples, 1521; d. at Naples, 1608; cd 1712; f.d. 10 November. He was christened Lancelot, and in his youth determined to become a priest. After ordination he was employed in the ecclesiastical courts, and in 1556 was entrusted with the reform of a rather disorderly convent of nuns; he made earnest efforts to achieve this, but failed. In the same year he joined the newly founded congregation of Theatine clerks regular in Naples, and it was then that he changed his name to Andrew. He proved an effective preacher and zealous missioner, and was invited by ◊ *St Charles Borromeo* to establish a Theatine house in Milan. St Andrew was much in request as a confessor, keeping up an extensive religious correspondence, and among his disciples was Lorenzo Scupoli, author of *The Spiritual Combat.*

ANDREW BOBOLA ◊ under *Josaphat of Polotsk*

ANDREW CORSINI, bishop. B. in Florence, 1301; d. at Fiesole, 6 January 1373; cd 1629; f.d. 4 February. He was a bad-tempered and troublesome youth, but underwent a sudden change of heart and joined the Carmelites at Florence in 1316. He proved an exemplary friar, and in 1349 was chosen to be bishop of Fiesole. To avoid this office he ran away, and had to be brought back from the charterhouse at Enna to be consecrated. As bishop he showed a special talent for composing quarrels; for this reason he was sent as papal legate to deal with civil disorders in Bologna. In 1737 a chapel was built in his honour in St John Lateran at Rome by Pope Clement XII, who was a member of the Corsini family.

ANDREW FOURNET, priest. B. near Poitiers, 1752; d. at La Puye, 1834; cd 1933; f.d. 13 May. As a young man he was bored by religion, and apparently by life in general; but under the influence of an uncle, who was a country clergyman, he himself became a priest, and eventually *curé* of his birthplace, Maillé. At the French Revolution he refused the oath of the civil constitution of the clergy; he continued his ministry in secret, and on Good Friday 1792 was arrested: he declined to go to jail in a carriage, for 'From the day that Jesus Christ carried his cross it has behoved his followers to travel on foot'. On another occasion he escaped the police by taking the place of a dead body on a bier. Fournet had made the acquaintance of ◊ *St Elizabeth Bichier*, and after 1801 he collaborated with her in the establishment of her congregation of Daughters of the Cross, whose rule he drew up. He is said more than once to have miraculously multiplied food for the sisters and their young charges. St Andrew retired from his parish in 1820, but continued to direct the sisters till his death.

ANGELA OF BRESCIA, foundress. B. at Desenzano, 1474; d. at Brescia, 27 January 1540; cd 1807; f.d. 1 June. Angela Merici was born on the shore of Lake Garda and was early left an orphan. She joined the Franciscan tertiaries, and began giving catechism lessons to the children of her village, with such success that in 1516 she was invited to do similar work in Brescia. After a pilgrimage to the Holy Land and to Rome, she continued to teach in Brescia and, when war drove her out, at Cremona. In 1535, Angela and a number of younger companions, in the church of St Afra at Brescia, bound themselves before God to devote the rest of their lives to his service, especially by the education of girls. This was the beginning of the Company of St Ursula (Ursuline nuns), the first teaching order of women to be established. But in the beginning there was no community life, no vows, no religious habit: these things were not to come till a quarter of a century after Angela's death. At the start much of the teaching was done in the children's own homes: but in her conception of an uncloistered, flexible society of women St Angela was before her time. She survived to direct her foundation for only four years.

P. Caraman, *St Angela* (1963).

ANN ◊ *Joachim and Ann*

ANSELM, bishop and theologian. B. at Aosta, *c.* 1033; d. at Canterbury, 1109; cd 1720; f.d. 21 April. Anselm, the son of a Lombard nobleman, was one of the outstanding figures of the church in England. After a restless youth, in 1059 he entered the monastery of Bec in Normandy, whose prior was then Lanfranc, who was to precede him in the see of Canterbury. During the next thirty years Anselm wrote several of the philosophical and theological works that have been so influential, works that are characterized by a use of rational argument that made him 'the father of Scholasticism'; but his intellectual rigour was softened by the sensitiveness of his mind and the generosity of his heart. 'I want', he wrote, 'to understand something of the truth which my heart believes and loves. I do not seek thus to understand in order to believe, but I believe in order that I may understand.' He was elected abbot of Bec in 1078, and in 1093 King William II consented to nominate him to the archbishopric of Canterbury.

Henceforward, Anselm's public life was almost wholly conditioned by dissensions with William II and Henry I over relations between the church, and the state as represented by the king. Among the principles at stake was the election of bishops without interference from the crown. William II soon made determined efforts to get rid of the archbishop, and in 1097 Anselm went to Rome, where he remained for three years. During that time he wrote *Cur Deus Homo?*, one of the best known of all works on the Atonement, and the only one of Anselm's books to be published in English in a cheap edition. He also attended the Council of Bari, and was instrumental in resolving the doubts of the Greek bishops in southern Italy about the Holy Spirit proceeding from the Son (*Filioque*). He returned to England when Henry I came to the throne, but Henry soon claimed rights in respect of bishops and abbots that a council in Rome had been unable to recognize: Anselm was again in exile abroad from 1103 to 1107. As a pastor he encouraged the ordination of native Englishmen among his clergy, for whom he enforced celibacy; he emulated ◊ *St Wulfstan* in his opposition to slavery; and he restored to the calendar the names of some of the English saints that his predecessor Lanfranc had removed. As a statesman he was deficient: the monastery, not the court, was where he was at home. Many incidents recorded of his life testify no less than his writings to the attractiveness of his personal character. In the *Paradiso* (canto xii) Dante mentions him among the spirits of light and power in the Sphere of the Sun. Anselm was canonized by being included among the doctors of the church by Pope Clement XI in 1720. In art, St Anselm's emblem is a ship.

R. W. Southern (tr.), *The Life of St Anselm by Eadmer* (1962); id., *St Anselm and his Biographer* (1963); R. W. Church, *St Anselm* (1892).

ANSKAR, missionary. B. near Amiens, 801; d. at Bremen, 865; f.d. 3 February. St Anskar was the first missionary to north-western Europe. He was a monk, first of Corbie in Picardy, then of New Corbie (Corvey) in Westphalia. In 826 he went to preach the gospel in Denmark, but was soon driven out, whereupon he turned his attention to Sweden, with some success. In 831 he was consecrated archbishop of Hamburg, and Pope Gregory IV confided the Scandinavian peoples to his care. The Danes destroyed Hamburg in 845, and Anskar was given the see of Bremen, but he was unable to establish himself there for a long time. Meanwhile, he returned to Sweden for a time, and to Denmark, where he laboured under more encouraging conditions. But after his death the work he had begun came to a stop; Christianity did not begin to make headway in Scandinavia until two centuries later. In answer to one who 'cracked up' the miracles with which the bishop was credited, St Anskar spoke words which represent the attitude of all the saints in this matter: 'Were God to choose me to do such things, I would ask him for one miracle only – that by his power he would make me a good man.' A Life of him was written by his fellow missionary in Scandinavia, St Rembert (d. 888).

C. H. Robinson, *Anskar, Apostle of the North* (1921; includes trans. of Rembert's Life).

ANTHELM, bishop. B. near Chambéry, 1107; d. at Belley, 1178; f.d. 26 June. When he was thirty years old, Anthelm resigned his ecclesiastical benefice at Belley, in south-eastern France, and became a Carthusian monk at Portes. Only two years later, in 1139, he was made prior of the mother house of his order, the Grande Chartreuse, which flourished under his direction: the community grew in number and fervour, its buildings were improved, and the other monasteries brought into closer relation with the mother house. Among his monks was ◊ *St Hugh*, afterwards of Lincoln, who had a great affection for him. With one short interval Anthelm continued in office for twenty-four years; he then had to leave his solitude in the Alps of Dauphiné to be bishop of Belley. It was said that the diocese had never had so fearless and uncompromising a bishop. There was an instance in 1175, when he excommunicated Count Humbert of Maurienne for his misdeeds. The count appealed to the pope, Alexander III, who raised the excommunication; whereupon Anthelm withdrew from his see for a time in protest, on the ground that Humbert was impenitent. Shortly afterwards the pope commissioned Anthelm to go to England to try to reconcile King Henry II with ✞ *St Thomas of Canterbury*; but the mission never took place.

ANTHONY ✞ *Antony*

ANTONINO, bishop. B. in Florence 1389; d. there, 1459; cd 1523; f.d. 10 May. Antonino Pierozzi joined the Order of Preachers in 1405, and for forty years lived at various Dominican houses in Italy, for much of the time as local superior and twice as superior of a province. At Florence in 1436 he founded the famous friary of San Marco, with the financial help of Cosimo dei Medici; Fra Angelico decorated its walls, and it became a centre of Renaissance humanism. In 1446 Antonino was appointed archbishop of Florence, and he discharged his office with inflexible justice and overflowing charity. Because of his reputation for wisdom and ability he was often called to help in public affairs, civil and ecclesiastical; but his first concern was always for the people of his diocese, to whom he set an example of simple living and inflexible integrity. He preached regularly, made a yearly visitation of parishes and no one appealed for his help, material or spiritual, in vain. St Antonino's writings as a practical moralist are of particular interest today. He was conscious of the new problems presented by social and economic development, and taught that the state had a duty to intervene in mercantile affairs for the common good, and to give help to the unfortunate and needy. It is significant that the canonization of St Antonino was decreed by the short-lived Pope Adrian VI, whose ideas for church reform were radical and drastic.

B. Jarrett, *St Antonino and Medieval Economics* (1914).

ANTONY, hermit. B. near Memphis, *c.* 251; d. on Mount Kolzim, 356; f.d. 17 January. St Antony is looked on as the founder of monasticism, in the later sense of the word, because he gathered hermits into loosely-knit communities and exercised a certain authority over them; but he himself passed most of his long life more or less in solitude. When he was about twenty he went to live alone in various spots in the neighbourhood of his home in Lower Egypt, spending his time in prayer, study, and the manual work necessary to earn his living. He underwent violent temptations, spiritual and physical, but he overcame them; and in time a number of disciples gathered round him. In *c.* 312 he went further away and took up his abode in a cave on Mount Kolzim, near the north-west corner of the Red Sea; this remained his home for the rest of his life.

People of all kinds sought out St Antony, to get his advice or simply from curiosity, and from time to time he visited his followers in their hermitages; towards the end of his life he went to Alexandria to encourage the opposition to Arianism. If the traditional date is right, he was over a hundred when he died, in perfect health. A good deal is known about St Antony because a biography has survived, written by ◊ St Athanasius, who knew him personally. The desert monks were not seldom characterized by extravagance and fanaticism: not so Antony. He was notably moderate for his time, a man of spiritual wisdom, whose great austerity of life was always consciously directed to the better service of God. Both during his life and after his death his influence was very great, and veneration for him, sometimes for extrinsic reasons, was strong all over Christendom right on into the middle ages.

The 'desert fathers' of whom St Antony is the classic representative lived in more or less remote places in huts, caves or abandoned buildings, seeking God through intellectual and physical self-discipline in a life of prayer and meditation, austerity and manual work. The last was provided by the need to supply a minimum of food, clothing and shelter, and by such occupations as the making of palm-leaf baskets and mats. Many writers (and painters) have tended to dwell on the abuses of this life – unbridled self-mortification for its own sake, competitive fasting, an 'orgy of the "supernatural"'. At its best it was able to, and did, produce characters of impressive integrity and wisdom, one of whose traits was a keen understanding of human psychology and an ability to express it in telling words. St Antony's emblems in art are a pig and a bell.

R. T. Meyer (tr.), *The Life of St Antony, by St Athanasius* (1950).

ANTONY OF THE CAVES, abbot. B. near Chernigov, 983; d. at Kiev, 1073; f.d. 10 July. About the year 1028 he went to live as a hermit in the Balkans or on Mount Athos; then, returning to Russia, he settled at Kiev, in a cave by the river Dnieper, where others joined him. This was the beginning of the first purely Russian monastery, of the Caves of Kiev (Kievo-Pecherskaya Lavra), which was more firmly established by his contemporary ◊ St Theodosius of the Caves. Antony was an austere and uncompromising follower of the example of his namesake of Egypt, and he early left his community to seek greater solitude elsewhere; but he came back to Kiev to die, at the age of ninety.

ANTONY OF PADUA, preacher. B. at Lisbon, 1195; d. near Padua, 1231; cd 1232; f.d. 13 June. Until the age of twenty-five he was a canon regular in his native Portugal, pursuing religious studies at Coimbra. Fired with the desire to be a missionary, and perhaps a martyr, he then joined the Franciscan friars, and was sent to work among the Moslems in Morocco. But his health betrayed him, and he had to return to Europe, where he was for a time at a hermitage near Forlì in Italy. It was soon realized that he had a most unusual gift for preaching, and he exercised it to the full for nine years, as well as filling several teaching and other posts of his order in Italy and France. He had a remarkable knowledge of the Bible, and his sermons impressed the learned no less than the simple, whether he was speaking on behalf of right living or against false doctrine. He was buried at Padua, where his shrine is a place of pilgrimage, and many miracles have been attributed to his intercession. The statues of St Antony that are so often seen, showing him as a rather 'soft' looking young man, carrying the child Jesus and a lily, do not do him justice. He was strong and fearless, merciless towards oppressors of the defenceless and towards ill-living clergy, and was called in his lifetime a 'hammer of heretics'. The text of many of his sermons has survived, and because of these and his reputation as a biblical scholar the Roman Catholic church reckons him among the doctors.

E. Gilliat-Smith, *St Antony of Padua according to his Contemporaries* (1926).

ANTONY CLARET, bishop and founder. B. in Spain, 1807; d. near Narbonne, 1870; cd 1950; f.d. 23 October. He was the son of a weaver, and was ordained priest in 1835. Five years later he began giving parochial missions and retreats all over Catalonia, and in 1849 founded a congregation, now commonly called the Claretian Fathers, to carry on the work on a wider scale. In the same year, at the request of Queen Isabella II, he was made archbishop of Santiago in Cuba. The people of this diocese were in a shocking state, and Claret's vigorous reform measures provoked several attempts on his life. In 1857 the queen recalled him to be her chaplain, a position that gave him time to carry on his mission work by preaching and publishing; he also established a science laboratory in the Escorial, a natural history museum, schools of music and languages, and a religious library at Barcelona. During the revolution of 1868 he accompanied Queen Isabella into exile, and was never able to go back to Spain.

ANTONY DANIEL, martyr. B. at Dieppe, 1601; d. at Teanaustaye 4 July 1648; cd 1930; f.d. 26 September. He joined the Society of Jesus, and was sent as a missionary to the Red Indians of Canada, where for a time he taught in an Indian school. In 1637 he was posted to Georgian Bay, and ministered there for ten years. When the Huron village of Teanaustaye, near Hillsdale in Ontario, was raided by Iroquois, Daniel refused to fly with the rest; after doing all he could to safeguard his flock, he submitted to death: the Iroquois shot him down and flung his body into his burning church.

ANTONY ZACCARIA ⟡ under *Cajetan*

APLONAY ◊ under *Apollinaris*

APOLLINARIS OF RAVENNA, bishop and martyr. Date unknown. The name of this saint is well known from the famous church of Sant' Apollinare 'in Classe' at Ravenna. By tradition he was the first bishop of Ravenna and the first and only known martyr there, but no reliable information about him has survived; even his martyrdom is doubtful.

Under the colloquial name of Aplonay, *St Apollinaris of Valence* (d. *c.* 520) is honoured as the patron of the diocese of Valence in France, of which he was bishop.

APOLLINARIS ◊ *Sidonius Apollinaris*

APOLLONIA, martyr. D. at Alexandria, 249; f.d. 9 February. During a riot against Christians the Alexandrian mob put several of them to death, including this aged deaconess. She was repeatedly struck in the face, her teeth being knocked out; then a bonfire was made and her tormentors threatened to burn her alive if she did not renounce her faith. She uttered a short prayer, walked into the flames, and was consumed. These particulars were related in a letter by ◊ *St Dionysius*, who was bishop of Alexandria at the time. From the nature of her torments St Apollonia was invoked against toothache, and her emblem is a forceps gripping a tooth.

ARAGHT ◊ *Attracta*

ARNULF OF METZ, bishop. B. near Nancy, 582; d. near Remiremont, 18 July 641; f.d. 19 August. This Arnulf (Arnoul) passed his earlier life at the court of Theodebert II, king of Austrasia; through the marriage of his elder son with a daughter of Pepin of Landen, St Begga, he became an ancestor of the Carolingian dynasty. At the age of thirty he wanted to retire from public life, but instead in 614 he was chosen bishop of Metz, though still a layman. He continued to act as adviser to King Chlotar II, whom he had helped to the Frankish throne, and was tutor to his son Dagobert. Arnulf made further attempts to resign his offices, but it was not till 629 that he was able to retire to the Vosges mountains. Here his friend St Romaric had preceded him and begun the monastic community at Habend that was later called Remiremont. St Arnulf settled near by, and lived there till his death twelve years later.

ARSENIUS, monk. B. *c.* 354; d. near Memphis, *c.* 412 (?); f.d. 19 July. He appears to have been born in Rome, and is said first to have been a deacon there and afterwards tutor to the sons of Emperor Theodosius I at Constantinople, but both these things are doubtful. Somewhere about the year 400 he joined the desert monks in Egypt, first in the Wadi Natrun (Scetis) and then at Canopus and Troë. The sayings and doings recorded of him are characteristic of the desert fathers, marked by strict self-discipline and shrewdness about human nature: he had learned in a hard school, and expected others to do the same, and he seems to have been more than usually averse to the company of his fellow men. But he was not wanting in compassion, and sometimes modified his brusqueness. A saying of his that has constantly been repeated since is: 'I have often been sorry for having spoken, but never for having held my tongue.' Ancient writers emphasize that Arsenius had the 'gift of tears' in a surprising degree – his hand-kerchief (*sudarium*) was always handy – and his self-depreciation sometimes seems excessive. He died at Troë, and his life was written by ◊ *St Theodore the Studite*, but this was too long after to be very reliable. Forty-four written maxims and moral anec-dotes are attributed to St Arsenius.

ASAPH, bishop. Sixth century; f.d. 11 May. He was no doubt the founder of the church of Llanasa in Flintshire, and it was prob-ably he (and not ◊ *St Kentigern*) who established the monastery at Llanelwy near by; when this place was organized as an episcopal see by the Normans it was renamed Saint Asaph. A late medieval writing speaks of Asaph's 'charm of manners, grace of body, holiness of heart, and witness of miracles'. He is a very shadowy figure.

ATHANASIUS, bishop and doctor. B. at Alexandria, *c.* 296; d. there, 373; f.d. 2 May. When a deacon, Athanasius accompanied his bishop to the first Council of Nicaea in 325, at which the Arian heresy was condemned, and three years later he was him-self elected to the see of Alexandria. He presided over this church for forty-six years, of which over seventeen were passed in exile on account of his vigorous opposition to the spread of Arianism, which had the support of certain of the emperors. He was first banished, to Trier, in 335, but was allowed to return in 337, only to be banished again two years later. This time he went to Rome and was away for seven years. From 346 to 356 was relatively his most peaceful period and some of his most important writings date from this time. But the emperor, Constantius, was bent on getting him deposed, and soldiers were sent to arrest him. Athanasius went into hiding in the desert, and guided his flock from there till Constantius died in 361. There were two more short periods of exile, and then from 366 he was able to rule his church in peace until his death. He devoted himself to repairing the harm done by all the years of dissension and violence, and was able to return to his writing and preaching undisturbed.

St Athanasius was a man small in physical stature but of tower-ing spirit. John Henry Newman declared that, in the troubles that followed the Council of Nicaea, the laity were firm champions of

Christian orthodoxy and the bishops were not. There were, of course, exceptions to both sides of this generalization, and among these Athanasius was outstanding: it was Newman again who wrote of him as 'that extraordinary man ... a principal instrument after the Apostles by which the sacred truths of Christianity have been conveyed and secured to the world'. As well as his expository treatises and controversial writings against the Arians, Athanasius wrote several works of historical value, including the *Life of St Antony*, and commentaries on Scripture, notably the Psalms, and some of his letters are extant; but he was not the author of the so-called creed that bears his name. An eighth-century monk wrote, 'If you find a book by Athanasius and have no paper on which to copy it, write it on your shirts.' St Athanasius is one of the four great Greek doctors of the church, together with ◊ *Basil the Great, John Chrysostom,* and *Gregory of Nazianzus.*

ATHANASIUS THE ATHONITE, abbot. B. at Trebizond, *c.* 920; d. on Mount Athos, *c.* 1003; f.d. 5 July. From an early date Mount Athos in Greece was peopled by hermits, but it was not till the tenth century that communal monasticism was introduced there, by this Athanasius. After being a teacher in Constantinople he joined the monks at Mount Kyminas in Bithynia, under St Michael Maleinos, and then in 958 migrated to Athos. With money from the Emperor Nicephorus II he built the first monastery there, dedicated in 963: it is still in being and is commonly known simply as *Lavra*, 'The Monastery'. Other foundations followed, three of which survive as leading monasteries of the Holy Mountain. The founder met much opposition from the hermits already in possession. They resented the intrusion of a stranger, who sought to bring order and discipline into their old-established life and ways. It took the intervention of another emperor, John Tzimisces, finally to establish the authority of Athanasius, who had gained the trust and reverence of his own followers. He met his death in an accident, killed by falling masonry when the cupola of his church fell in.

ATTRACTA, nun. Fifth or sixth century (?); f.d. 11 August. There is no reliable information about the Irishwoman St Attracta (Araght). According to her legend she fled from home and was given the veil of a nun by ◊ *St Patrick* at Coolavin; she then settled by Lough Gara, and founded a shelter for travellers at the place now called Killaraght. Other references would suggest that she lived in the sixth rather than the fifth century. Several very surprising miracles were attributed to her.

AUBERT OF AVRANCHES, bishop. D. *c.* 725; f.d. 10 September. Nothing is known about the life of this bishop of Avranches ex-

cept that he was the originator of the great pilgrims' shrine of
Mont-Saint-Michel. It is said that three times between the years
706 and 708 he fell asleep on the Rocher de la Tombe and
dreamed that ◊ *Michael the Archangel* told him to build a church
in that place. The church was certainly built, and dedicated on
16 October 709; St Aubert was buried in it. A Benedictine monastery was subsequently established on the Mount. ◊ under
Michael the Archangel.

AUBIERGE ◊ under *Ethelburga*

AUBREY ◊ *Alberic*

AUDOENUS ◊ *Ouen*

AUDOMARUS ◊ *Omer*

AUDREY ◊ *Etheldreda*

AUDIFAX and ABACHUM ◊ under *Valentine*

AUGUSTINE, bishop and doctor. B. in Numidia, 354; d. at Hippo,
430; f.d. 28 August. This great Latin doctor of the church was a
native of Thagaste in what is now Algeria. He was the son of a
pagan father, but his mother, ◊ *St Monica*, was a Christian, and
as such he was brought up, though baptism was yet to come. At
sixteen he was sent to Carthage to finish his education, and here
he was soon living with a young woman, to whom he was devoted
for fourteen years; they had a son, Adeodatus, whom his father
always cherished. His studies ended, Augustine found it difficult
to settle down to teaching; he was seeking a philosophy of life,
and for long was attracted by the teachings of Manichaeism. In
383 he went to lecture in Rome, and then received an appointment
at Milan, where he came under the influence both of Neoplaton-
ism and the preaching of ◊ *St Ambrose*. He underwent agonizing
inward conflicts, between honours, wealth, marriage, on the one
hand, and the call to a life dedicated wholly and directly to God
on the other. His decision was made, in a garden, when he took
up the book of St Paul's epistles and his eye fell on Romans xiii,
12–14. With his friend Alipius and his son Adeodatus, Augustine
was baptized on Easter eve in 387. He went back to Africa and
formed a kind of monastic community; but in 391 he was ordained priest, against his wishes, and five years later was chosen
bishop of Hippo.

For thirty-four years St Augustine was one of the greatest
bishops in the history of the Christian church in a diocese of
North Africa, exercising pastoral authority as a ministry of
equity, disinterestedness, sympathy, and care for people's welfare.
He lived in community with his cathedral clergy, under strict
rule, presiding at public worship daily, preaching every Sunday
and feast day, preparing catechumens for baptism, looking after
the material needs of the church and of the poor, even adminis-

tering justice in civil affairs. And always writing whenever he he could, writing not only for his friends or to meet local needs, as against the Donatists, but for a wider audience, as against the Manichees and Pelagianism; and producing also the great treatise on the Holy Trinity and writings on grace. His written output was vast; there still survive 113 books and treatises, over 200 letters, more than 500 sermons. Two of his longest works, his *Confessions*, an autobiography down to his conversion, and *The City of God* (both available in English), have found numberless readers beyond the ranks of students and theologians. The second of these was prompted by the capture of Rome by Alaric the Goth in 410; when Roman civilization was collapsing in the West, St Augustine sat down and wrote a book; still later, as he lay on his deathbed in 430, the invading Vandals were at the gates of Hippo, but that book and its author's spirit have survived other empires as well. But his mighty influence on Western Christian thought has not always been wholly beneficial; some aspects of his teaching have been so interpreted as to precipitate grievous contention, as in the case of the Jansenists. His monastic rule has been adopted and adapted by numerous orders of men and women, notably by the canons regular and the friars who bear his name.

The *Confessions of St Augustine* (Penguin); C. Dawson and others, *A Monument to St Augustine* (1934); H. Marrou, *St Augustine and his Influence* (1957); G. Bonner, *St Augustine of Hippo* (1963).

AUGUSTINE, or AUSTIN, OF CANTERBURY, missionary bishop. D. at Canterbury, c. 605; f.d. 26 May. In the year 596 Pope ◊ *St Gregory the Great* sent a band of forty monks, led by this Augustine, to preach the gospel to the heathen English. They arrived in Kent in 597, and were well received by the local king, ◊ *Ethelbert*, who himself soon became a Christian, with many of his subjects. Augustine went to Arles to be consecrated archbishop of the English, and established his see at Canterbury, where he also founded the monastery of SS. Peter and Paul (afterwards called St Augustine's). The mission continued to prosper, and shortly before his death Augustine founded two more episcopal sees, in London for the East Saxons and at Rochester. But he was not successful in his attempt to extend his authority to the existing Christians in Wales and south-west England (Dumnonia). These Britons were suspicious and wary, Augustine was perhaps insufficiently conciliatory, and the British bishops refused to recognize him as their archbishop. From early times St Augustine has been venerated as the evangelizer of England (as distinct from Roman Britain), though his comparatively short mission was perforce confined to a limited area. That he was a very conscientious missionary is clear from the pages of Bede, who gives what purports to be the text of Pope Gregory's answers to Augustine's requests for direction on various matters arising out of his mission.

M. Deanesly, *Augustine of Canterbury* (1964).

AURELIUS and NATALIA, martyrs. D. 852; f.d. 27 July. They were two of a group of five martyrs at Córdova who suffered in the persecution by Emir Abd ar-Rahman II during the Moslem domination of Spain. Aurelius, son of a Moor and a Spanish woman, was a secret Christian, as was his half-Moorish wife Natalia. Aurelius had a relative, Felix, who accepted Islam for a time, but returned to Christianity and married a Christian wife, Liliosa. All four at length openly professed their Christianity, the two women going about with faces unveiled. They were arrested as apostates from Islam, and beheaded. With them was executed the monk George, who had spoken openly against the prophet Mohammed.

AUSTIN ◊ *Augustine*
AUSTOL ◊ under *Méen*

B

BACCHUS ◊ *Sergius and Bacchus*
BALDHILD ◊ under *Bathild*
BARBARA, martyr. No date; f.d. 4 December. The kernel of the story of St Barbara, as told, for instance, in the *Golden Legend*, is that she was a maiden of great beauty whose father, Dioscurus, shut her up in a tower to discourage the attentions of numerous suitors. On discovering that she had become a Christian, Dioscurus made to kill her, but she was miraculously transported out of his reach. He then denounced her to the authorities, who subjected her to torture. She refused to renounce her faith, whereupon her father was ordered himself to put her to death. This he did, and straightway was struck by lightning and reduced to ashes. The various versions differ as to when and where: from 235 to 313, in Egypt, Rome, Tuscany, or elsewhere. This spurious legend first appears only in the seventh century and appears to have been written as a pious romance, for there is no evidence that a martyred St Barbara ever existed. Nevertheless from the ninth century her cultus became very widely spread; because of her father's fate she was invoked against danger from lightning, and by an extension of this idea she later became the patron saint of gunners and miners. Her special emblem is a tower.

BARBA'SHMIN ◊ under *Simeon Barsabba'e*

BARLAAM and JOSAPHAT. No date; f.d. 27 November. These 'saints' never existed: they are the principal characters in a fictional narrative adapted from the Indian story of Siddhartha Buddha. It relates that Josaphat (Joasaph) was the son of an Indian king, who kept the young man in close confinement to prevent his becoming a Christian. He was nevertheless converted by an ascetic named Barlaam, and eventually resigned his throne and became a hermit with Barlaam. ◊ *St John of Damascus* is traditionally the author of the Greek text of this legend, but this has been questioned; further translations carried it all over Christendom; its original version was probably in Arabic.

There is a genuine *St Barlaam of Antioch* (f.d. 19 November), who was martyred *c.* 304.

BARNABAS, apostle. First century; f.d. 11 June. Barnabas, 'a good man, full of the Holy Ghost and of faith' (Acts xi, 24), is styled 'apostle', though he was not one of the Twelve. He was a Cypriot Jew, and is remembered for his close association with the work of ◊ *St Paul*, from the time that he vouched for Paul to the nervous Christians of Jerusalem until the disagreement over John Mark (◊ *St Mark*). It was Barnabas who was sent to the growing Christian centre at Antioch, and he fetched Paul from Tarsus to help him; later the teachers there, prompted by the Holy Spirit (Acts xiii, 2), sent Barnabas and Paul on the first missionary journey, beginning with Cyprus, of which church St Barnabas is esteemed the founder. He was still at work when St Paul wrote his first letter to the Christians at Corinth, but probably died not long after. He is said to have been martyred at Salamis, the Cypriot port, but the New Testament says nothing of this. The ancient work called the *Epistle of Barnabas* was not written by him.

BARR ◊ *Finbarr*

BARTHOLOMEA CAPITANIO and VINCENTIA GEROSA, foundresses. B. 1807, 1784; d. 1833, 1847; both cd 1950; f.d. 26 July, 28 June. They founded together the Sisters of Charity of Lovere, the town in Lombardy of which they were both natives. They were moved by the state of ignorance and neglect in which so many people lived, and their congregation was designed to teach the young and nurse the sick; it is based on the principles of ◊ *St Vincent de Paul*. Vincentia was already forty when she got to know Bartholomea, and the latter was only twenty-six when she died; it was a partnership of persons of remarkable determination and selflessness, and their foundation has spread widely.

BARTHOLOMEW, apostle. First century; f.d. 24 August. Except that he was called to be one of the twelve apostles, nothing certain is known about him; but it is possible that he is the same man as Nathanael, 'an Israelite indeed, in whom is no guile', of whose meeting with Christ there is a remarkable account in St John's gospel (i, 45–51; see also xxi, 2). Later writers associate St Bartholomew with the spreading of the gospel in Lycaonia, India and, more particularly, Armenia, where he is said to have been martyred by being flayed alive; but there is no certainty about any of this. His emblem in art is a butcher's knife.

BARTHOLOMEW OF GROTTAFERRATA ◊ under *Nilus of Rossano*
BASIL THE BLESSED ◊ under *Simeon Salus*
BASIL THE GREAT, bishop and doctor. B. at Caesarea in Cappadocia, *c.* 330: d. there, 1 January 379; f.d. 14 June. Basil was born into an old Christian family of wealth and distinction, with a remarkable religious history: his grandmother, Macrina the Elder, his father, Basil the Elder, his mother, Emmelia, his elder sister ◊ *Macrina*, and two younger brothers ◊ *Gregory of Nyssa* and Peter of Sebastea, are all numbered among the saints. He was educated in the schools of Caesarea, Constantinople, and Athens, where he formed a deep friendship with ◊ *St Gregory of Nazianzus*. About 357 he visited the chief monastic centres of the East, and then settled as a monk at Annesi, on the river Iris in Pontus. Basil lived with his community for only about five years, but he is justly accounted the father of Eastern communal monasticism; he was not a legislator as ◊ *St Benedict* was in the West, but his influence was vast and the monastic life of the Orthodox church is still based on the principles he laid down.

Having been ordained priest, St Basil was from 365 practically responsible for the diocese of Caesarea, and in 370 was made bishop there. As such, he had to stand up against the persecution of orthodox Christians by the Arian emperor Valens, and was called before the local prefect to justify himself. So stiff was Basil's attitude that the prefect expressed astonishment at his temerity: 'Perhaps you have never before had to deal with a proper bishop,' retorted Basil. This and other controversies disturbed the whole of his episcopate, and he was involved in difficult relations with Pope ◊ *St Damasus* and the Western church. Valens feared him, and sought to diminish his authority by administrative measures; a by-product of this was an unhappy breach between Basil and his friend Gregory of Nazianzus (and Basil set a very high value on friendship). The weeping crowds at his funeral testified to Basil's popularity with his flock. One of his greatest works had been the provision at Caesarea of an estate which included dwelling-houses, a church, a hospital for the sick, a hospice for travellers, a staff of doctors, nurses, and artisans, the whole on such a scale as to be called a new town.

A good deal of what is known of St Basil's life is derived from his own letters and sermons, which give a vivid picture of his many-sided character and activities. He had a strong practical sympathy with the poor and downtrodden and was merciless towards the enormities of the wealthy. But he was inclined to be headstrong and tactless, which contributed to some of his disappointments: 'For my sins, I seem to fail in everything,' he once wrote dispiritedly. Among his writings is a treatise in which he advises his nephews to make prudent but full use of classical pagan literature in preparing themselves for a deeper understanding of Christianity, a point of view not very common in his day. The influence of St Basil did not a little to help bring about the ending of the controversy about Arianism two years after his death, and he is included among the four great Greek doctors of the church.

M. M. Fox, *Life and Times of St Basil* (1939).

BATHILD, queen. B. in England; d. near Paris, 680; f.d. 30 January. Bathild (Baldhild) was an English girl who in 641 was carried off by pirates and sold into the household of Erchinoald, mayor of the palace to Clovis II, king of the Western Franks. Some years later the king made her his wife, and on the death of this profligate young man in 657 Bathild became regent for their eldest son, Chlotar III. In this office she opposed the slave-trade, of which she had been both a victim and a beneficiary, and encouraged monasticism by numerous benefactions. An English writer living at the time, Eddi (the biographer of ◊ *St Wilfrid*), asserts that Queen Bathild was responsible for the political assassination of Bishop Annemund (Dalfinus) of Lyons and others; what actually happened is obscure, and it is unlikely that Bathild was guilty of the crime. About 665 her regency came to an end and ambitious nobles unceremoniously removed her from court to the nunnery she had founded at Chelles. Here St Bathild passed the rest of her days in religious retirement, at the service of the nuns and obeying the abbess like the least of them.

BAVO, penitent. B. in Brabant; d. *c.* 653; f.d. 1 October. Bavo (christened Allowin) was a wealthy landowner, who made a good marriage and was father of a daughter; but he led a very disorderly life. Shortly after the death of his wife he determined to mend his ways: he gave away his possessions to the poor, and put himself under the direction of ◊ *St Amand*, whom he accompanied for a time on his missionary journeys in France and Flanders. On one occasion Bavo met a man whom he had years before sold into serfdom; in reparation, he made the man lead him by a chain to the town lock-up. He was eventually given permission to live as a hermit in a wood near Abbot Florbert's monastery at Ghent, and so passed the last years of his life. Bavo was buried at the neighbouring monastery, afterwards called by his name, Saint-Bavon.

BEDE, THE VENERABLE, monk. B. in Northumbria, 673; d. at Jarrow, 735; f.d. 27 May. He was sent to school at the newly-founded monastery of Wearmouth, and soon after to the twin house of Jarrow; there he became a monk and a priest, and there he passed his whole life, probably never going further afield than Lindisfarne and York. In his own words, 'I have devoted my energies to the study of the Scriptures, observing monastic discipline, and singing the daily services in church; study, teaching, and writing have always been my delight'. Bede's biblical writings were extensive and important in their time, but it is as an historian that he is famous. His most valuable work, the *History of the English Church and People*, is referred to on p. 22 herein; to it he added Lives of five early abbots of Wearmouth and Jarrow. He also wrote grammatical and chronological works, hymns and other verse, letters and homilies, and compiled the first martyrology with historical notes. These are in Latin, but Bede was also the first known writer of English prose; unhappily his vernacular prose writings and translations have been lost. During his last illness he was translating St John's gospel and extracts from the writings of ◊ *St Isidore of Seville*; he dictated the last sentence just before he died, sitting on the floor of his cell, surrounded by the brethren among whom he had lived. Of all the writers in western Europe from the time of ◊ *St Gregory the Great* until ◊ *St Anselm*, St Bede was perhaps the best known and most influential, especially in his native land; already in 836 a church council at Aachen referred to him as 'the venerable', i.e. worthy of honour, but it was not till 1899 that Pope Leo XIII gave him formal recognition as a doctor of the church. ◊ *St Boniface* called Bede 'a light of the church, lit by the Holy Spirit'; to Alcuin, himself 'the schoolmaster of his age', he was 'blessed Bede, our master'; and he is the only Englishman whom Dante names in the *Paradiso*. The Latin of the hymns 'The hymn for conquering martyrs raise' and 'Sing we triumphant hymns of praise' was written by him.

A. Hamilton Thompson (ed.), *Bede: his Life, Times and Writings* (1936); E. S. Duckett, *Anglo-Saxon Saints and Scholars* (1947).

BEE, nun. Seventh century; f.d. 31 October. The origin of the name of a village and headland on the coast of Cumberland, Saint Bees, is a matter of uncertainty. It seems more likely that they are named after a Bega, legendarily said to have been a refugee from Ireland, veiled a nun by ◊ *St Aidan*, than after either of the two seventh-century Northumbrian nuns, Begu and Heiu, mentioned by Bede.

61

BEGGA ◊ under *Gertrude of Nivelles*

BENEDICT, patriarch of Western monks. B. at Norcia in Umbria, *c.* 480; d. at Monte Cassino, *c.* 547; f.d. 21 March. Few particulars are known of the life of this man whose monastic rule and the monks who followed it have been so influential in the western world; what little information there is comes from the *Dialogues* of ◊ *St Gregory the Great*, who gives an excessive proportion of his space to Benedict as a wonderworker. He was sent to Rome for his studies, but the disturbed and profligate life of the city drove him into the wilds, and when he was about twenty he became a solitary at Subiaco. He left there at the request of a community of monks to be their abbot, but some of them were dissatisfied by his high standards and we are told they attempted to poison him. Returning to Subiaco, he gradually organized twelve small communities in various places, and *c.* 529 established the monastery of Monte Cassino under his own direction. There is no evidence that he was ever a priest, as indeed very few monks were until much later times. It was now that he drew up his monastic rule, in which he made use of previous 'rules', especially those of ◊ *St John Cassian* and *St Basil*. Benedict's reputation spread rapidly, and towards the end of his life he was even visited by the Gothic king Totila. He had a visitation of another kind when, standing one night praying by his window, 'the whole world seemed to be gathered into one sunbeam and brought thus before his eyes'.

When death was at hand, St Benedict was carried into the chapel, where he received communion and died, standing erect supported by his disciples; he was buried in the same grave as his sister, ◊ *St Scholastica*. A clear idea of what sort of man he was can be gained from the text of his Holy Rule (available in English): single-minded, composed and upright, a man of peace and moderation, a loving father who combined insistence on good discipline with respect for human personality and individual capabilities, thoroughly practical. He called his rule one for beginners, a 'school of the Lord's service, in which we hope to order nothing harsh or rigorous'. That simple and profound document was destined to play a considerable part in the history of Europe; and in numerous monasteries of men and women throughout the world today St Benedict, 'being dead, yet speaketh'. His emblems are a broken cup and a raven.

J. McCann, *St Benedict* (1938); T. F. Lindsay, *St Benedict, his Life and Work* (1949).

BENEDICT THE BLACK, laybrother. B. in Sicily, 1526; d. at Palermo, 1589; cd 1807; f.d. 4 April. He was the son of African parents, who were slaves on an estate near Messina, but was freed by his master at an early age. He was about twenty-one when he was publicly insulted on account of his colour, and his patient and dignified bearing on that occasion was observed by the leader of a group of Franciscan hermits. Benedict was invited to join the group; he did so, and himself in time became their leader. About 1564 the group was dispersed, and Benedict was accepted as a laybrother by the Franciscan friary at Palermo; he worked in the kitchen. In 1578 the friars required a new guardian (i.e. superior), and Benedict was chosen, for all he was simply a laybrother, and illiterate at that. With understandable reluctance he accepted the office, and successfully carried through the adoption of a stricter interpretation of the Franciscan rule. He later filled other offices, including that of novice-master. His sympathy and understanding as a religious counsellor, helped by a reputation as a healer of bodies, brought him many visitors of all sorts, and this continued when he returned to the kitchen in his later years. It seems that St Benedict the Black was not a Negro but a Nubian.

BENEDICT OF ANIANE, abbot. B. *c.* 750; d. 821; f.d. 11 February. When a young man he left the court of Charlemagne to become a monk, and *c.* 780 formed a community on very austere lines by the river Aniane (Corbière) in Languedoc. The results being disappointing, he adopted the Rule of St Benedict (◊ *Benedict*) and established a large monastery in the same place. From here the founder's influence spread; he reformed and inaugurated other houses, and became at length virtually supreme abbot over all the monasteries of Charlemagne's empire. Under his presidency, a council of abbots, held at Aachen in 817, issued a code of regulations binding on all their houses. This systematizing and centralizing innovation fell into desuetude after the death of Benedict of Aniane and his patron, Emperor Louis I, but it had lasting effects on Western monasticism. He died at Cornelimünster, the monastery built for him by Louis near Aachen from which to direct his supervisory work. St Benedict of Aniane was a religious reformer in every direction and throughout his life he maintained the rigorous austerity of his earlier years.

BENEDICT, or BENET, BISCOP, abbot. B. in Northumbria, *c.* 628; d. at Wearmouth, *c.* 690; f.d. 12 January. Biscop Baducing when about twenty-five left the service of King Oswy and travelled to Rome with ◊ *St Wilfrid*; after a second visit there he became a monk at Lérins, off Cannes, taking the name of Benedict, and in 669 returned to England with ◊ *St Theodore of Canterbury*. After being abbot of SS. Peter and Paul's for two years he went back to Northumbria, and in 674 founded a monastery at Wearmouth, and eight years later its sister house at

Jarrow. Abbot Benedict made other visits to Rome, from whence and from Gaul he brought back sacred images and relics, stonemasons, glaziers, and even the precentor of St Peter's to teach his monks to sing in the Roman fashion. He never missed an opportunity of obtaining books, and the libraries he formed in the two monasteries made possible the work of ◊ *St Bede*, who was one of his pupils. Doubtless, too, he organized the *scriptorium* in which was written the manuscript of the Bible which his successor, St Ceolfrid, took with him in 716 as a present to Pope St Gregory II: the very book was identified in the Bibliotheca Laurentiana at Florence in 1887, the famous Codex Amiatinus. Altogether St Benedict Biscop had an important part in the development of the church in northern England, which was early recognized in the veneration paid to his memory. During his last three years he was bedridden, an affliction borne with exemplary patience and faith.

BENEDICT LABRE, mendicant. B. near Boulogne, 1748; d. in Rome, 1783; cd 1881; f.d. 16 April. Benedict Joseph Labre was the eldest of fifteen children of a prosperous shopkeeper. Between 1766 and 1770 he made several attempts to join one or other religious order, but was rejected as too young, too delicate, or of insufficiently stable disposition. He then went on pilgrimage to Rome, on foot and begging his way. For the next three or four years he wandered about western Europe, going from shrine to shrine: to Loreto, Assisi and Bari in Italy, to Einsiedeln in Switzerland, to Aix-en-Provence and Paray-le-Monial in France, to Compostela in Spain. He always travelled on foot, slept in the open or in some corner, his clothing in rags, his body filthy, picking up food where he could, and sharing any money given him. He talked little, prayed much, and accepted abuse unmurmuringly. From 1774 he stayed in Rome, spending his days in the churches and his nights in the Colosseum ruins, till failing health forced him to seek the shelter of a home for the destitute. At length he collapsed in church, and died in the back room of a butcher's shop to which he had been carried. The people of Rome had never had any doubt about the holiness of this 'new St Francis', and he was eventually canonized. St Benedict Labre is a late Western example of an ascetical vocation better known in the East, that of the pilgrim or wandering holy man; he has also points of resemblance with the Greek *saloi* and Russian *yurodivy*, 'fools for Christ's sake'.

A. de La Gorce, *St Benedict Joseph Labre* (1952).

BENIGNUS, martyr. Second century (?); f.d. 1 November. The cultus of this martyr began in the early sixth century with the discovery of an ancient tomb at Dijon. Subsequently a Passion of St Benignus made its appearance; it was said to have had its origin in Italy, but the story it tells is manifestly spurious in all its versions. There is a remote possibility that Benignus was a missionary priest from Lyons, martyred at Épagny, near Dijon, in the late second century.

BERARD and his companions, martyrs. D. in Morocco, 1220; cd 1481; f.d. 16 January. In 1219 St Francis of Assisi sent Berard and four others of his friars, Otho, Peter, Accursio, and Aiuto, to preach the gospel to the western Moslems. They began their mission with the Moors in Seville; they were at once imprisoned and then driven out. They then made their way to Marrakesh in Morocco, where they preached in the streets, though Berard was the only one who knew any Arabic. At first the Moors were forbearing, thinking they were mad; but when they would not go away, and continued openly to denounce the teachings of Mohammed, they were beaten and put to death, it is said by the hand of the sultan himself. These were the first martyrs of the Franciscan order. Seven years later *St Daniel* and six more Italian friars perished at Ceuta in Morocco, after they had refused to apostatize to Islam (f.d. 10 October).

BERNADETTE, visionary. B. at Lourdes, 1844; d. at Nevers, 1879; cd 1933; f.d. 16 April. Marie Bernarde ('Bernadette') Soubirous was the eldest child of an impoverished miller. At the age of fourteen she was ailing and undersized, sensitive and of pleasant disposition but accounted backward and slow. Between 11 February and 16 July 1858, in a shallow cave on the bank of the river Gave, she had a series of remarkable experiences. On eighteen occasions she saw a very young and beautiful lady, who made various requests and communications to her, pointing out a forgotten spring of water and enjoining prayer and penitence. The lady eventually identified herself as the Virgin Mary, under the title of 'the Immaculate Conception'. Some of these happenings took place in the presence of many people, but no one besides Bernadette claimed to see or hear 'the Lady', and there was no disorder or emotional extravagance. After the appearances ceased, however, there was an epidemic of false visionaries and morbid religiosity in the district, which increased the reserved attitude of the church authorities towards Bernadette's experiences.

For some years she suffered greatly from the suspicious disbelief of some and the tactless enthusiasm and insensitive attentions of others; these trials she bore with impressive patience and dignity. In 1866 she was admitted to the convent of the Sisters of Charity at Nevers. Here she was more sheltered from trying publicity, but not from the 'stuffiness' of the convent superiors nor from the tightening grip of asthma. 'I am getting on with my job,' she would say. 'What is that?' someone asked. 'Being ill,' was the reply. Thus she lived out her self-effacing life, dying at the age of thirty-five. The events of 1858 resulted in Lourdes becoming one of the greatest pilgrim shrines in the history of Christendom. But St Bernadette took no part in these developments; nor was it for her visions that she was canonized, but for the humble simplicity and religious trustingness that characterized her whole life.

F. Trochu, *St Bernadette Soubirous* (1957); B. G. Sandhurst, *We saw Her* (1953).

BERNARD, abbot and theologian. B. at Fontaines, near Dijon, 1090; d. at Clairvaux, 1153; cd 1174; f.d. 20 August. St Bernard of Clairvaux was not among the three founders of the abbey of Cîteaux, but he must be accounted a founder of the Cistercian Order that emerged from it. He was one of the six brilliant sons of a Burgundian nobleman, and after wavering for a time he decided in 1113 to join the new monastery at Cîteaux; he won over four of his brothers and twenty-seven other friends to come with him. Two years later he was sent to establish a new house at Clairvaux in Champagne. It prospered and grew and planted out no less than sixty-eight daughter houses, including Rievaulx and, in a way, Fountains in England and Mellifont in Ireland; knowledge of the Cistercian reform was thus carried far and wide. Bernard's personal fame spread quickly and, in spite of his diffidence and serious ill-health, he was soon drawn into public affairs: a conflict between the Cistercian and the Cluniac monks, the disputed papal election of 1130, the contest with Peter Abelard, whose teaching Bernard opposed with relentless vigour. With all his charity and attractiveness he was a hard hitter, as when he attacked luxury among the clergy, or persecution of the Jews, or what he considered the invalid election of ◊ *St William of York* to that see.

In 1145 a former Clairvaux monk, Eugenius III, was elected pope. Bernard wrote for him a remarkable treatise on the duties of the papal office, in which he castigates the abuses of the Roman *curia* and expounds the religious mysteries which the pope should always keep before his eyes (this work, *De consideratione*, is available in English). Eugenius had great confidence in Bernard, who was sent into Languedoc to preach against Albigensianism (with no lasting effect), and was commissioned to stir up enthusiasm for the Second Crusade in France and Germany; when that military expedition proved a disastrous failure, abuse was heaped on the man who had recommended it so zealously. With all these activities, and in spite of distressing ill-health, St Bernard was yet a prolific writer. His letters, his *Life of St*

Malachy of Armagh, and the treatise *On the Love of God* have been published in English, as well as the sermons to his monks *On the Song of Songs*, perhaps his most famous work. He made very extensive use of the Bible in his writing and preaching, 'not so much', as he said, 'in order to expound the words as to reach people's hearts'. This affective quality to St Bernard's writing and devotion makes an instant appeal to many today. He has been praised by men of very diverse beliefs and temperaments, and was early accorded the title of *Doctor mellifluus*, 'the Honey-sweet Teacher'; Pope Pius VIII included him among the doctors of the church in 1830. As a theologian he belongs to the pre-scholastic era, and he is sometimes spoken of as 'the last of the Fathers'. His emblem is a beehive.

St Bernard of Clairvaux, the first Life, tr. G. Webb and A. Walker (1960); W. Williams, St Bernard, the Man and his Message (1952); B. Scott James, St Bernard of Clairvaux (1957).

BERNARD OF MONTJOUX, priest. B. 996 (?); d. at Novara, 1081 (?); f.d. 28 May. There is little certainty about the early life of Bernard of Montjoux (often called 'of Menthon'), but later he was said to have been a canon serving the cathedral of Aosta, and to have been made archdeacon. As such he had oversight of the local Alpine passes, which he cleared of highway robbers, and he ministered to the welfare of the scattered inhabitants for over forty years. His memorable achievement was the building of permanent rest-houses for travellers at the top of the two passes now known after him as the Great and the Little St Bernard. He collected endowments for them and staffed them with Augustinian canons regular, the order still responsible for the hospice (the dogs did not come till very much later). This benefactor of travellers died while on a journey, at Novara in Lombardy; the year of his death has been much debated. In 1932 Pope Pius XI, himself formerly an Alpinist, named St Bernard of Montjoux patron saint of Alpinists and other mountaineers; he also severely criticized the fictions which have been incorporated in the written Lives of the saint.

BERNARDINE OF SIENA, preacher. B. at Massa di Carrera, 1380; d. at Aquila, 1444; cd 1450; f.d. 20 May. As a young man he took charge of La Scala hospital at Siena when most of the staff had been carried off by an epidemic, and afterwards looked after a bed-ridden aunt until her death. Then, in 1402, he became a Franciscan friar, and soon began to make a name as a preacher. For many years he journeyed on foot, preaching up and down Italy, in churches and in the open, to crowded assemblies and often at great length, and the effect of his sermons was commensurate with his efforts. He made much use of the name of Jesus as a symbol of the Lord himself, using as a badge the monogram of the letters IHS (from the Greek form of the sacred name). Some of his teaching was criticized by the University of Bologna, but this controversy, which troubled him for eight years, ended in his favour. He attacked usury relentlessly, and denounced the party strife of the Italian cities as a fundamental evil of the age and place; on the other hand he did not rise above such contemporary characteristics as hostility to Jews and belief in widespread witch-craft.

It has been said of St Bernardine, 'the people's preacher', that he inaugurated in Italy 'one of those rare periods in history when the rule of Jesus made visible progress in society'. He was a leader in the movement in the Franciscan order to restore a stricter observance of its rule, and these 'Observants' greatly in-creased in number during his time. He assisted at the Council of Florence, and in 1444 set out on his last preaching journey, be-ginning at his birthplace and intending to go on to Naples. But at Aquila in Abruzzi his strength failed, and he died and was buried there.

I. Origo, *The World of San Bernardino* (1963).

BERNARDINE REALINO ◊ under *Januarius*

BERNWARD, bishop. B. *c.* 960; d. at Hildesheim 1022; cd 1193; f.d. 20 November. He was ordained priest by ◊ *St Willigis* at Mainz, and after serving as chaplain to Emperor Otto III was made bishop of Hildesheim in 993. His episcopate was disturbed by political and ecclesiastical troubles, including a dispute with St Willigis about the nunnery at Gandersheim, which went on for seven years. It is as an encourager of the arts that St Bernward is remembered. He was himself a painter and metal-worker, and Hildesheim became famous for its 'school' of sacred art: the Bernward bronze doors, cross, column, and candlesticks are still there to testify to its achievements. He was also responsible for the building of St Michael's abbey church at Hildesheim, which has been said to 'represent religious architecture in the absolute'. In the crypt of this church St Bernward lies buried.

BERTHOLD and BROCARD, hermits D. on Mount Carmel, 1198, 1231 (?); f.d. 29 March, 2 September. In the second half of the twelfth century there was a group of Frankish hermits living on Mount Carmel in Palestine, under the direction of St Berthold of Solignac. On his death he was succeeded by another Frenchman, St Brocard, who *c.* 1207 had the customs of the hermits incor-porated in a formal rule by the Latin patriarch of Jerusalem, St Albert of Vercelli. This is now generally understood to represent the origin of the order of Carmelite friars, but of the lives of the first two superiors very little is known.

BERTILLA BOSCARDIN, nursing sister. B. near Vicenza, 1888; d. at Treviso, 1922; cd 1961; f.d. 20 October. Anna Francesca Boscardin was a peasant girl, none too 'bright', who in 1904 was accepted by the Sisters of St Dorothy at Vicenza. After working for three years as a kitchen maid, she was promoted to help in a children's ward at Treviso. During air-raids here in 1917 Sister Bertilla was imperturbably careful of her patients and attracted the admiring notice of the authorities of a military hospital near Como. But the local superioress did not appreciate her and sent her to work in the laundry, whence she was rescued by a more perceptive higher superior. In 1919 she was put in charge of the children's isolation ward at Treviso, but soon her health, never good, gave way altogether. A serious operation became necessary, and she did not survive it. St Bertilla's life was a simple record of devoted hard work; she had made a deep impression, and miracles of healing were attributed to her intercession: in 1961 she was canonized, in the presence of crowds which included members of her family and patients whom she had nursed.

BERTIN, missionary. B. near Coutances; d. at Sithiu, c. 700; f.d. 5 September. Bertin and his companions were missionary monks among the Morini in the low-lying marshy country of the Pas-de-Calais, persevering there in face of great difficulties and physical hardship. Their first centre was at Saint-Mommolin, as it is now called after the first abbot; then a monastery (Saint-Bertin) was established at Sithiu, and from here for many years Bertin continued his work of evangelization and civilization. The town of Saint-Omer grew up round the monastery. These monks were followers of the Rule of ◊ St Columban, and worked in association with Omer. When it was desired to establish another monastery among the Morini, St Bertin selected St Winnoc (d. 715? 6 November), who with three companions settled at Wormhoudt, near Dunkirk. These monks were either Bretons or Britons from Wales, and Winnoc's name figures in many medieval English calendars; he is apparently the titular saint of Saint Winnow near Lostwithiel. St Bertin's emblem in art is a ship.

BEUNO ◊ under Winifred

BIBIANA ◊ Viviana

BIRINUS, missionary. D. at Dorchester, c. 650; f.d. 5 December. This bishop came from Rome intending to preach the word of God in the 'inner parts' of England, but finding the people of Wessex still heathen he decided he had to work among them instead. He baptized their king, Cynegils, in 635 and was allowed to set up his see at Dorchester on the Thames. Bede tells us that he built churches and 'called many to the Lord by his holy labours'. St Birinus may have been a man of Germanic descent, as his name, Birin, suggests. After the diocese of Dorchester had been divided, the first separate bishop of the Winchester part was *St Hedda* (d. 705; f.d. 7 July); Bede says of him that he was 'a good and just man, who in carrying out his duties was guided rather by an inborn love of virtue than by what he had read in books'.

BLAAN, or BLANE, bishop. Late sixth century; f.d. 11 August. He was born on the island of Bute and is said to have been trained in Ireland by ◊ *St Comgall* and *St Canice*, returning to Scotland to finish his education under his uncle St Cathan. He founded a church or monastery at Dunblane, where the former cathedral now stands, and worked among the Picts. There are several dedications in St Blaan's honour in Bute and other parts of Scotland, but the particulars of his life are few and legendary.

BLAISE, bishop and martyr. Date unknown; f.d. 3 February. There is said to have been a bishop of Sebastea in Armenia named Blaise, who was martyred, perhaps under Licinius; but the traditional account of him is very late and mostly given over to marvels and tortures, and all historical particulars are lacking. From the eighth century his cultus spread rapidly in East and West; he was invoked especially on behalf of diseased creatures, human and animal, on account of the nature of some of the miracles attributed to him. From this derives the still existing observance called the Blessing of St Blaise, asking God's protection against affections of the throat. His emblems are a comb or two crossed candles. The name appears in some English dedications as Blazey, and also in other forms.

BLANDINA, martyr. D. at Lyons, 177; f.d. 2 June. One of the martyrs who suffered at Lyons with their bishop, ◊ *St Pothinus*. Blandina was a slave girl (her mistress was one of the victims) in whom 'Christ showed that those who appear weak and worthless to men may be glorious in God's sight because they love him in deed rather than in outward show'. She was tortured relentlessly, but would only say 'I am a Christian, and we do nothing vile' (the Christians had been accused of incest and cannibalism). Her tormentors themselves declared that 'they had never known a woman show such endurance'. At length she was tied in a net and thrown to a bull, which gored her to death. With Blandina there died a fifteen-year-old boy, Ponticus, whom she encouraged to endure bravely.

BONAVENTURE, bishop and theologian. B. at Bagnorea, 1221; d. at Lyons, 1274; cd 1482; f.d. 14 July. He left Italy to study at the University of Paris, where one of his teachers was the Englishman Alexander of Hales, whom he followed into the Franciscan Order. Bonaventure himself taught and preached in Paris for

70

many years, concentrating on the elucidation of some of the problems that especially exercised men's minds in his day. With ◊ *St Thomas Aquinas* he defended the mendicant friars against their opponents, and in 1257 was chosen minister general (head) of the Franciscans. He discharged this office with such effect that he is regarded as the greatest friar minor after ◊ *St Francis of Assisi* himself and, as it were, a second founder of the order. In 1265 he declined the archbishopric of York, but eight years later was made cardinal bishop of Albano, in time to take a prominent part at the second Council of Lyons, when the Greeks were briefly reconciled with the Latins. He died during the council and was buried at Lyons.

St Bonaventure was a man of the highest intellectual attainments, but he would emphasize that a fool's love and knowledge of God may be greater than that of a humanly wise man. His personal simplicity is illustrated by the story that when his cardinal's hat was brought to him he told the legates to hang it on a near-by tree, as he was washing the dishes and his hands were wet and greasy. He left many important works of philosophy, theology and mysticism, which have been extremely influential; several of them have been published in English, including his biography of St Francis of Assisi and the *Journey of the Soul to God*. The hymn 'In the Lord's atoning grief' is a translation from St Bonaventure. He was known as the Seraphic Teacher, and in 1588 Pope Sixtus V declared him to be a doctor of the church. His emblem is a cardinal's hat.

L. Costelloe, *St Bonaventure* (1911); E. Gilson, *The Philosophy of St Bonaventure* (1938).

BONIFACE OF CREDITON, missionary and martyr. B. probably at or near Crediton, *c.* 675; d. in Friesland, 754 or 755; f.d. 5 June. He was christened Wynfrith, but is always known as Boniface, the name he used later on. Until he was about forty he was a monk, first at Exeter and then at Nursling, near Southampton; his chief concern in those days was study and the handing on of the fruits of his study by teaching and preaching: he expounded the Bible, and compiled the first Latin grammar written in England. In the year 718 Boniface left his homeland, never to return, to take the gospel to the heathen tribes of Germany. He made an immediate impression as one who moved with power, and the results of his mission were lasting. St Boniface's activities ranged over Hesse, Bavaria, Westphalia, the Thuringenland, and Württemberg. Three times he journeyed to Rome to report progress to the pope, and on the second visit he was made a bishop, eventually establishing his see at Mainz. To help in his work he enlisted other English missionaries from Wessex, women as well as men, ◊ *Lull, Willibald, Walburga,* and *Lioba* among them.

The text of many letters written by and about Boniface still exists; they are valuable historical documents and give a picture of a great and lovable man. Probably in the year 732, Pope Gregory III made him archbishop, and his later years were busy with organizing the West German and reforming the Frankish church, in concert with King Pepin the Short. When he was over seventy he still had no thought of rest, and turned his attention to Holland. There he ended his life in martyrdom. At a place called Dokkum, he and his companions were set upon by heathen Frieslanders and put to the sword; when they broke in on him he was sitting quietly in a tent, reading. Shortly after, Archbishop Cuthbert of Canterbury wrote to St Lull that 'we in England lovingly reckon Boniface among the best and greatest teachers of the faith' and among our special patrons. St Boniface is an important figure in the history of western Europe, but today he is much better remembered in Germany than among his fellow countrymen: his tomb at Fulda (where he founded a monastery) is revered as a sacred spot.

The Life of St Boniface by Willibald, with selected correspondence, in C. H. Talbot, *The Anglo-Saxon Missionaries in Germany* (1954); G. F. Browne, *Boniface of Crediton* (1910); G. W. Greenaway, *St Boniface* (1955).

BONIFACE OF QUERFURT, bishop and martyr. B. at Querfurt, *c.* 974; d. at Braunsberg, 14 March 1009; f.d. 19 June. This Boniface (baptized Bruno) was educated at the Magdeburg cathedral school, and became one of ◊ *St Romuald's* monks near Ravenna. While there he heard a call to take up the work of ◊ *St Adalbert of Prague* and be a missionary among the Prussians. He was authorized to do so by Pope Silvester II and was consecrated bishop *c.* 1004; but at first, because of political difficulties, he worked among the Magyars and among the Pechenegs in southwest Russia. At length, with the help of Boleslav I of Poland, he was able to reach the borderland heathen of eastern Masovia. He encountered fierce opposition, and was soon put to death, with eighteen companions.

BORIS and GLEB, sufferers. D. 1015; f.d. 24 July. When the first Christian prince in Russia, ◊ *St Vladimir,* died in 1015, his eldest son, Svyatopolk, sought to consolidate his position by getting rid of two half-brothers, Boris and Gleb. Within a short time of one another these young men were murdered, each of them refusing to allow his men to defend him. From the first the highest motives were attributed to their attitude of resignation – unwillingness to repel injustice to themselves by force and violently to oppose an elder brother. They were reverenced as 'passion-bearers', voluntary sufferers for Christ's sake, and enrolled among the saints; their feast day is still observed in Russian and Ukrainian churches. SS. Boris and Gleb are sometimes referred to by their christening names, Romanus and David.

G. P. Fedotov, *The Russian Religious Mind* (1946).

BOTOLPH, abbot. D. *c.* 680; f.d. 17 June. Botolph (Botulf) was a very popular saint in medieval England, but little is known about him. With his brother St Adulf he became a monk abroad, and in 654 established a monastery at Icanhoh, usually identified with Boston ('Botulf's stone') in Lincolnshire. St Ceolfrid is said to have journeyed all the way from Wearmouth to converse with this man 'of remarkable life and learning'.

BRAULIO, bishop. B. *c.* 590; d. at Saragossa, 651; f.d. 26 March. He was the son of a Spanish bishop and in 631 succeeded his own brother in the see of Saragossa. He played an important part as a reformer in the ecclesiastical life of his time, and followed his master and friend ◊ *St Isidore of Seville* as the most influential and respected bishop in Spain. Like Isidore, too, he was devoted to learning; a number of his letters are in existence, which show his familiarity with classical authors of Roman antiquity as well as his desire to extend his knowledge of Christian writers. It was St Braulio who induced St Isidore to undertake his encyclopedic work called *Etymologies*, and after Isidore's death he gave the book its final form.

C. H. Lynch, *St Braulio* (1938).

BRENDAN THE VOYAGER, abbot. B. in Kerry, *c.* 486; d. at Annaghdown, 578; f.d. 16 May. As a child he was in the care of ◊ *St Ita* at Killeedy and in due course became a monk and a priest. Little reliance can be put on the accounts of his life; but it is clear that he founded the monastery of Clonfert in Galway *c.* 560, which continued to exist until the sixteenth century. The fame of St Brendan was spread far and wide by the translation into various languages of a tenth-century tale, *Brendan's Voyage*, which relates his astonishing adventures when, with a company of monks, he sailed to a beautiful Land of Promise in the Atlantic; this was afterwards identified with the Canary Islands and other places. In fact, Brendan visited Iona and western Scotland, and perhaps the west of Britain and Brittany, as other Irishmen did in his time. There is another St Brendan, 'of Birr', who was a contemporary of the above.

G. A. Little, *St Brendan the Navigator* (1945); J. F. Webb, *Lives of the Saints* (Penguin).

BRICE, bishop. B. in Touraine; d. at Tours, 444; f.d. 13 November. Brice (Brictio) was one of ◊ *St Martin of Tours*'s clergy, and succeeded him as bishop of Tours in 397. After allowing for exaggeration and malice, Brice still seems to have been of insubordinate and troublesome character; and, whatever the true circumstances, he had to leave his see *c.* 430 and was in exile for seven years. On his return he mended his ways, and the formation of a number of new Christian centres is credited to him. Perhaps his early association with St Martin partly accounts for the reverence afterwards paid to Brice's memory: his name appears in many early English church calendars, and it still figures in the calendar of the Book of Common Prayer, in a Latin form, Britius.

BRIDE ◊ *Brigid*

BRIDGET, foundress. B. in Sweden, *c.* 1303; d. in Rome, 23 July 1373; cd 1391; f.d. 8 October. This Bridget (Birgitta) is often called 'of Sweden', though she was never a queen or royal princess. About 1317 she married a nobleman, Ulf Godmarsson, and they had eight children, including St Katherine of Vadstena, and a son Charles, who caused his mother great distress in later years. About 1335 Bridget was appointed principal lady-in-waiting at court, where she zealously endeavoured to get Queen Blanche, and her husband, King Magnus II, to take life more seriously. Her own husband died in 1344, and Bridget later applied herself to the founding of the Order of the Holy Saviour ('Bridgettines'), primarily for women; its mother house was at Vadstena, which became an important Swedish religious centre. She spent much time in Rome, living very austerely, looking after the poor and sick, and proffering very outspoken advice to the popes about the serious ecclesiastical and political problems of the time. She died in Rome on returning from a pilgrimage to the Holy Land.

St Bridget appears as an intense personality, and throughout her life she claimed to have visions and religious inspirations, on the strength of which she sometimes acted, as in her mission to the popes. Her dictated book of 'Revelations', chiefly about Christ's sufferings and about future events, exercised wide influence and provoked strong controversy, especially at the time of her canonization and at the Councils of Constance and Basle (1414, 1431). Some theologians averred that she was deceived and not always orthodox; others maintained that her experiences were authentic and in accord with sound doctrine.

St Bridget's daughter *Katherine of Vadstena* is also venerated as a saint, though never formally canonized (d. 1381; f.d. 24 March). She finished her mother's work by obtaining official approval for the Bridgettine Order at Rome, and died in retirement at Vadstena. ◊ *Brigid*

J. Jörgensen, *St Bridget of Sweden* (2 vols., 1954); H. Redpath, *God's Ambassadress* (1947).

BRIEUC, abbot. Sixth century; f.d. 1 May. He was the founder of the monastery near Tréguier in Brittany which grew into the town and see called Saint-Brieuc. He was probably born in Ceredigion (Cardiganshire), and seems to have worked in southwestern Britain before going to Brittany; there is a place called Saint Breock or Breoke in Cornwall, and Saint Briavels in the Forest of Dean is at root the same name. St Brieuc's medieval biography contains a number of particulars and marvellous tales, but its historical value is very slight; it says, for instance, that he was trained in Gaul by an unidentified St Germanus.

BRIGID, abbess. B. at Faughart (?), c. 450; d. at Kildare, c. 523; f.d. 1 February. In Ireland St Brigid, 'the Mary of the Gael', is revered only less than ◊ St Patrick himself, but ascertainable facts about her life are few. The numerous accounts written during the centuries immediately following her death consist principally of miracles and anecdotes, sometimes very far-fetched and not unmixed with folklore. But they have a background of beauty, and give an impression of a strong, gay, compassionate character, imbued with a shining charity: so many of the wonders related of her were to meet the spiritual and physical needs of her neighbours. The great fact of her life is the foundation of a community of dedicated women at Kildare, though even about this not much is known. But Brigid has always been looked on as the initiator and abbess of the first women's religious community among the Irish, and she seems to have had a unique position in the Irish church even in her lifetime. She died and was buried at Kildare, but during the Danish invasions her remains were removed to Downpatrick, to be reburied, it is said, with those of St Patrick. The cultus of St Brigid spread far beyond her native land; in England and Scotland churches were dedicated in her honour as St Bride, and in Wales as Ffraid Santes.

F. O'Briain, *St Brigid, her Legend, History and Cult* (1938); A. Curtayne, *St Brigid of Ireland* (1954).

BROCARD ◊ under *Berthold*

BRUNO, founder. B. at Cologne, c. 1033; d. in Calabria, 1101; f.d. 6 October. The founder of the order of Carthusian monks was a man of noble birth. He studied in the cathedral school at Rheims, was ordained priest, and c. 1056 was called to teach theology at Rheims, which he did successfully for twenty years. Then he fell foul of his archbishop, a man who had obtained the see of Rheims by simony; Bruno denounced him, and was discharged from his office at the school. In 1084, with six companions, he withdrew to the Grande Chartreuse, a wild and lonely spot in the mountains near Grenoble. They built a small church, with scattered huts for their accommodation, and entered on that combination of solitary and communal living that characterizes Carthusian monks to this day (the Chartreuse gives its name to all their monasteries – in English, 'charterhouse'). Their life of worship, work, and penitence was (and is) an extremely hard one, but it attracted recruits and all was going well when, after six years, their leader was called away.

Pope Urban II, a former pupil of Bruno's, summoned him to Italy to be his adviser. Bruno was unhappy at being thus called back 'into the world', and before long the pope allowed him to make another foundation like the Grande Chartreuse, but not so far from Rome, at La Torre, near Squillace in Calabria. He never saw his brethren in France again, but he kept in touch with them, and a letter of encouragement he wrote has survived. There is also a long letter to an old friend, in the course of which he speaks of the rest and refreshment brought to the spirit by the sight of natural beauty: 'Only those who have experienced it can know the benefit and delight to be had from the quietness and solitude of a hermitage.' As well as at La Torre, a charterhouse had been started at San Stefano-in-Bosco, and it was while on a visit there that St Bruno died.

Another *St Bruno*, also of Cologne, was archbishop of Cologne from 953 to 961 (f.d. 11 October).

E. I. Watkin, in *Neglected Saints* (1963).

BRUNO OF QUERFURT ⟡ *Boniface of Querfurt*

BUDOC, bishop. Sixth century; f.d. 8 December. A saint of this name (Beuzec in Breton) was honoured in Pembrokeshire, Cornwall, and Devon (Saint Budeaux, near Plymouth). His Life, written in Brittany, is a fantastic composition. It relates that his mother, Azenor, was thrown into the sea off Brest, in a cask wherein she gave birth to Budoc; five months later they were cast up, alive and well, on the coast of Ireland. Budoc, we are told, grew up to be bishop of Dol in Brittany. His name is found associated with that of *St Mawes* (Maudez in Breton; f.d. 18 November) in both Cornwall and Brittany; no doubt they were missionary monks, probably of Welsh origin.

BURGUNDOFARA ⟡ under *Faro*

C

CADOC, abbot. Sixth century; f.d. 25 September. Cadoc (Cadog) was one of the outstanding Welsh saints, and he must have been an important missioner. He was the traditional founder of the monastery of Nant Carfan (later Llancarfan), west of Cardiff, he was widely venerated in South Wales and Brittany, there is some evidence that he visited Cornwall and Scotland, and his influence extended to Ireland. He seems to have been a contemporary of ◊ *St Samson* and *St Gildas*, but the written evidence about him is of a date and character that deprives it of almost all historical value. Its wildest flight concerns the end of his life: we are told that he was transported in a cloud from Llancarfan to Benevento in Italy, where he was made bishop and met a martyr's death while celebrating Mass. St Cadoc's parents, Gwynllyw and Gwladus, are said to have lived on Snow Hill at Newport (Monmouthshire), where the church of St 'Woolos' is dedicated under his father's name.

CAESARIUS OF ARLES, bishop. B. at Chalon-sur-Saône, 470; d. at Arles, 543; f.d. 27 August. He came of a good Gallo-Roman family, and after being a monk at Lérins, he was chosen bishop of Arles in 503. His episcopate was politically and religiously disturbed by the Arian Visigoths and Ostrogoths and then by the Franks; but his authority was made secure when he went to Rome in 513 and obtained recognition of the primatial status of his see from Pope Symmachus. Caesarius was an energetic bishop and an effective preacher; not too lengthy, he expressed himself in simple language, as his many surviving discourses show. He presided at several councils, notably that of Orange in 529, at which Semi-Pelagianism was condemned. In his will St Caesarius left most of his property to the nunnery he had founded at Arles, of which his sister St Caesaria was abbess: this was the first known convent of women in Gaul. He drew up the rules of the house, among its provisions being that every nun should learn to read and write and that they should have the sole right to choose their abbess.

CAGNOALD ◊ under *Faro*

CAJETAN, founder. B. at Vicenza, c. 1480; d. at Naples, 1547; cd 1671; f.d. 7 August. St Cajetan (Gaetano) was prominent among the Roman Catholic reformers before the Council of Trent. He studied at the University of Padua and was given an ecclesiastical office in Rome, but was not ordained till he was thirty-six. There and in several cities of northen Italy he was active in religious and charitable work among the people, and became acutely conscious of widespread disorder in the church. In 1524, with the object of providing better clergy, he joined with Bishop John Peter Caraffa (afterwards Pope Paul IV) in founding the first congregation of clerks regular: they were called 'Theatines', from the Latin name of Caraffa's see of Chieti. These priests were given special training, among its emphases being study of the Bible. When Rome was sacked by imperial troops in 1527 the Theatine headquarters was removed to Naples, where St Cajetan spent most of the rest of his life. They were hard years; success came but slowly to the Theatine congregation, and Naples was in a shocking state. Among Cajetan's good works for the people there was the establishment of pawnshops, run not for profit but to help those in temporary difficulties.

St Cajetan must not be confused with his contemporary *Cardinal Cajetan* (Thomas de Vio), another eminent Catholic reformer, who has not been canonized.

Other founders of clerks regular were ◊ *St Ignatius of Loyola*; ◊ *St Joseph Calasanz*; ◊ *St Camillus de Lellis*; *St Antony Zaccaria* (d. 1539; cd 1897; f.d. 5 July), who founded the Congregation of St Paul ('Barnabites'); *St Jerome Emiliani* (d. 1537; cd 1767; f.d. 20 July), founder of the Somaschi; *St John Leonardi* (d. 1609; cd 1938; f.d. 9 October), who founded the Order of the Mother of God and *St Francis Caracciolo* (d. 1608; cd 1807; f.d. 4 June), who founded the Lesser Clerks Regular. With the exception of Loyola and Calasanz all these were Italians.

CALLISTUS THE FIRST, pope and martyr. D. *c.* 222; f.d. 14 October. The earlier years of Callistus were unpromising. He was a slave of a Christian master in Rome, and was involved in some financial operations and disturbances which led to his being sentenced to hard labour in the Sardinian quarries. After his release he was emancipated from slavery and made a deacon, and Pope Zephyrinus put him in charge of the Christian cemetery on the Appian Way which still bears his name. He was an able man, and on the death of Zephyrinus in 217 was chosen to be bishop of Rome in his place. The choice was strongly opposed by a rigorist party, including ◊ *St Hippolytus* (from whom most of what is told about Callistus is derived). This party objected to him on both doctrinal and disciplinary grounds: for instance, his gentle treatment of sinners; but within a few years Callistus was dead. From the fourth century he was venerated as a martyr; there was no official persecution at the time and he was probably killed by a rioting mob. Curiously enough, St Callistus was not buried in the catacomb of San Callisto but on the Aurelian Way.

CAMILLUS, founder. B. in Abruzzi, 1550; d. in Rome, 1614; cd 1746; f.d. 14 July. From his seventeenth to his twenty-fifth year Camillus de Lellis was a soldier of fortune. He was physically a very big man, hasty of temper, and so addicted to gambling that eventually he lost everything and had to take a job as a builder's labourer. A sermon having wrought a great change in him in 1575, he twice tried to join the Franciscan Order, but had to leave because of a disease of the leg that afflicted him all his days. His own sufferings drew his attention to those of others, and he offered himself to the hospital of San Giacomo in Rome, of which in time he became bursar. This experience opened his eyes to the shocking state of the hospitals and the gross inadequacies, and often brutalities, of the nursing staffs. On the advice of ◊ St Philip Neri he was ordained priest in 1584 (by an English bishop exiled in Rome, Thomas Goldwell), having already begun to organize a congregation of priests and lay brothers, the Servants of the Sick; they were to look after the sick both in hospitals and in their own homes.

Before the end of the century St Camillus had opened other houses and hospitals in Naples and elsewhere, and sent out the first recorded nursing unit to troops in the field. He insisted on such innovations as open windows, suitable diets, and isolation of contagious cases; his priests were always at hand to minister to the dying, and experience had taught him the necessity of special precautions lest patients be buried while still alive. His own health became worse and worse, with a complication of disabilities, and in 1607 he resigned the headship of his order; but he continued personally to visit his hospitals and wait on the patients almost till the day of his death. St Camillus de Lellis is a patron saint of nurses and the sick.

C. C. Martindale, *St Camillus* (1946).

CANICE, abbot. D. at Aghaboe, *c.* 600; f.d. 11 October. Canice (Cainnech; in Scotland, Kenneth) came from modern Derry, and is said to have been a pupil of ◊ St Finnian at Clonard. For a time he worked in the Western Isles and on the mainland of Scotland, where a number of place-names and old dedications confirm his presence, notably the islet called Inch Kenneth in Mull. He may have gone with ◊ St Columba on his mission to the Picts. When he returned to Ireland he founded the monastery of Aghaboe in Ossory, *c.* 577. St Canice is said also to have had a foundation at Kilkenny.

CANUTE THE FOURTH, king of Denmark. D. at Odense, 10 July 1086; f.d. 19 January. This Canute (Cnut) is remembered in English history for a raid on Yorkshire in 1075 and a more serious projected invasion in 1085. In the following year he was assassinated by a band of rebellious subjects, in St Alban's church at Odense. His supporters looked on this as martyrdom, miracles were duly reported at his grave, and in 1100 King Eric III's legates persuaded Pope Paschal II to permit the cultus.

St Canute Lavard (f.d. 7 January) provides a very similar case, though he seems to have been a more worthy person than Canute IV. While duke of Schleswig he was recognized by Emperor Lothair III as sovereign over the western Wends. This alarmed his uncle, King Niels of Denmark, and Canute was murdered in an ambush near Ringsted in Zealand in 1131. He was formally canonized as a martyr by Pope Alexander III in 1169, at the request of his son, King Valdemar I. Canute Lavard gave his support to the earlier missions of *St Vicelin* (d. 1154; f.d. 12 December), evangelizer of the Wends, who was afterwards bishop of Staargard, now Oldenburg.

CARPUS and PAPYLUS, martyrs. D. at Pergamum, *c.* 170 or 250; f.d. 13 April. Carpus was bishop of Gordus in Asia Minor and Papylus was a deacon of Thyatira. They were brought before the Roman governor at Pergamum and required to sacrifice to the gods. They refused, and no arguments or ill treatment could overcome their resistance. They were therefore burnt alive. At the same time there suffered St Agathonice, a married woman : urged not to make her children motherless by her obstinacy, she replied, 'God will look after them', and went to the stake.

CARTHAGE, abbot-bishop. D. at Lismore, 637; f.d. 14 May. Carthage (Carthach, Mochuda) was a native of Kerry. After being a hermit for a time he lived in several monasteries, and then, *c.* 595, settled at Rathan in Offaly to form his own community. The rule he drew up for these monks, written in verse, is still extant, though not in its original form. The foundation in time provoked the jealousy of monasteries that had adjacent lands, and in 635 Carthage and his monks were turned out by the local chieftain. He re-established them at Lismore, where he survived long enough for him to give a firm foundation to what was to become one of the most famous of all Irish monastic schools. St Carthage was exceptionally strict about the holding of property : at Rathan he would not allow the community to have horses or oxen for help in the tillage.

Fr Carthage, *The Story of St Carthage* (1937).

CASIMIR, prince. B. at Cracow, 1458; d. at Grodno, 1484; cd 1521; f.d. 4 March. He was the second son of King Casimir IV of Poland and had as his tutor John Dlugosz, the historian of his country, from whom he learned to be virtuous and devout. In 1471 an attempt was made to put the boy on the throne of Hungary; the attempt failed, to young Casimir's satisfaction, and his angry father banished him for a time to a castle near Cracow. Later he was viceroy in Poland during the king's absence in Lithuania, but his real interests were in religious retirement and the arts of peace. In 1483 he rejected a proposed marriage with a daughter of Emperor Frederick III, having bound himself to a life of celibacy, and in the following year he died of phthisis. He was buried at Vilna, and miracles were reported at his tomb. St Casimir was named patron saint of Poland in 1602. The attribution to him of the Latin original of the hymn 'Daily, daily sing to Mary' is erroneous.

CASPAR DEL BUFALO, founder. B. in Rome, 1786; d. there 1836; cd 1954; f.d. 2 January. He was the son of a cook. Having been ordained priest, he was banished with the other clergy who refused the oath of allegiance to Napoleon Bonaparte after the deportation of Pope Pius VIII. On his return he became a general missioner, and founded, in face of considerable difficulties, a society of priests to carry on the work, the Missionaries of the Precious Blood. St Caspar's missionary methods were dramatic in a high degree: the contemporary St Vincent Strambi said of his preaching that it was 'like a spiritual earthquake'. He died in the cholera epidemic of 1836, during which he had given his last mission in Rome.

St Vincent Strambi, just mentioned, was also a missioner, of the Passionist congregation, and bishop of Macerata in Italy; he was cd in 1950 (f.d. 25 September).

CASSIAN ◊ *John Cassian*

CASSIAN OF IMOLA, martyr. Date unknown; f.d. 13 August. That there was an early martyr named Cassian at Imola admits of little doubt, but his traditional story seems certainly fictitious. This tells that he was a Christian schoolmaster who would not sacrifice to the gods. So he was handed over to his pupils, who disliked him; they fell upon him and stabbed him to death with their iron pens. This form of death occurs in the legends of three other martyrs, of whom the best known is the fourth-century *St Mark of Arethusa* in Syria (f.d. 29 March).

CASSIAN OF TANGIER ◊ under *Marcellus the Centurion*

CATHERINE ◊ *Katherine*

CEADDA ◊ *Chad*

CECILY, or CECILIA, martyr. Date unknown; f.d. 22 November. At some uncertain date a lady named Cecily founded a church in the Trastevere quarter of Rome; at her death her body was buried in a specially honourable place in the cemetery of St Callistus. No more is known of her. But by the year 545 she was called *Saint* Cecily and honoured as a martyr, and a Passion of St Cecily had been written (there was possibly confusion with some other Cecily, who had been martyred). According to this document, she was a Christian girl of patrician rank who was betrothed to a young pagan, Valerian. On her wedding day she informed him that she had consecrated her virginity to God, and won him over to respect her vow and to be baptized. His brother Tiburtius likewise became a Christian. Eventually the two brothers were arrested and put to death as obstinate Christians, together with a man called Maximus. Then Cecily was brought before the prefect, and upon her refusing an act of idolatry she was sentenced to be stifled to death in the bathroom of her own house. The steam and heat failed to suffocate her, so a soldier was sent to behead her; he struck three ineffective blows, and she was left to linger three days before she died. Afterwards her house was turned into a church.

Valerian, Tiburtius, and Maximus are historical characters; they were Roman martyrs, buried in the cemetery of Praetextatus, but, though nothing else is known about them, there is no reason to suppose that they had anything to do with the lady Cecily. Her story as outlined above can only be regarded as a fabrication; but it was not till recent times that scholars were able to elucidate it, and from the sixth century onwards St Cecily, virgin and martyr, was held in high honour by Christians in the West. Since the sixteenth century she has been regarded as the patroness of musicians; the *passio* speaks of her singing to God 'in her heart' while instruments were making music at her wedding, and so the idea may have arisen: an organ is often shown as her emblem. The history of the reputed relics of St Cecily is as full of mysteries and contradictions as the rest of her story.

CEDD ◊ under *Chad*

CELESTINE THE FIRST, pope. B. in Campania; d. in Rome, 432; f.d. 27 July. He was elected bishop of Rome in 422 and is chiefly remembered for his energetic measures against the heresies of Pelagius and Nestorius. ◊ *St Prosper of Aquitaine* says that it was St Celestine who, on the suggestion of St Palladius, commissioned ◊ *St Germanus of Auxerre* in 429 to deal with Pelagianism in Britain; and that in 431 he sent Palladius himself to Ireland as the first bishop of the Christians there; but this mission was very short-lived. Of St Celestine personally, nothing is known.

CELESTINE THE FIFTH, pope. B. in Abruzzi, *c.* 1214; d. near Anagni, 1296; cd 1313; f.d. 19 May. After the death of Pope Nicholas IV over two years passed without any agreement on a successor, till in 1294 the cardinals despairingly sought to end the deadlock by electing a 'stop-gap': their choice fell on an eighty-year-old hermit, Peter of Morrone. He came of a peasant family and had been professed a Benedictine monk, but for many years he had lived as head of a group of solitaries on Monte Morrone in the Abruzzi hills. Peter was shocked by the cardinals' choice, but he submitted, taking the name of Celestine, and was consecrated bishop of Rome at Aquila. The results were disastrous, for Celestine was unfitted for the papal office in every respect except his holiness.

In his simplicity and ignorance he made the most elementary blunders; he became the innocent tool of the politics of King Charles II of Naples, and, conscious of his failure, miserable in his new surroundings, he abdicated his office before a consistory of cardinals at Naples. He had been pope for five months. A few days later the stern and rigid Boniface VIII was elected in his place, and Boniface feared lest his adversaries should make use of Celestine for their own ends. The old man tried to slip away to the mountains or across the sea, but he was found and at Boniface's orders shut up in narrow quarters at the castle of Fumone, near Anagni. 'I wanted nothing in the world but a cell', said St Celestine, 'and a cell they have given me.' Ten months later he died, and was buried at Aquila, the most pathetic figure in the history of the papacy.

J. Ayscough, *San Celestino* (c. 1920).

CELSUS ◊ under *Gervase and Protase*

CHAD, bishop. B. in Northumbria; d. at Lichfield, 672; f.d. 2 March. Chad (Ceadda) was a pupil of ◊ *St Aidan* at Lindisfarne, and succeeded his brother Cedd as abbot of Lastingham in Yorkshire. From there he was called to be bishop in York, but in 669 ◊ *St Theodore of Canterbury* judged him to have been irregularly consecrated. Chad accepted the decision humbly and went back to Lastingham. Impressed by Chad's character, Theodore soon made him bishop of the Mercians, with his see at Lichfield, the defect in his consecration having been made good. He lived less than three years longer; during that time, says Bede, 'he administered his diocese in great holiness of life, following the example of the ancient fathers.' He always travelled on foot until Archbishop Theodore insisted on his riding a horse, and he founded a monastery in Lincolnshire, probably at Barrow upon Humber.

St Chad's brother, *St Cedd*, was founder of Lastingham abbey; he became bishop of the East Saxons and founded many churches, including monasteries at Bradwell-on-Sea and Tilbury (d. 664).

CHARITY ◊ under *Faith*

CHARLES OF SEZZE ◊ under *Diego*

CHARLES BORROMEO, bishop and cardinal. B. near Lake Maggiore, 1538; d. at Milan, 1584; cd 1610; f.d. 4 November. At the age of twenty-two, while not yet a priest, he was made a cardinal by his uncle, Pope Pius IV, and appointed administrator of the vacant see of Milan. The young man was acutely conscious of the needs of the church at that time, and took an important part in the final sessions of the reforming Council of Trent. In 1563 he was made priest and bishop, and archbishop of Milan in the following year. He now modified his aristocratic way of living, and set himself to apply the principles of the Council of Trent in the reformation of a large diocese that badly needed it. To help remedy the people's religious ignorance he established 'Sunday schools'; seminaries were opened for the training of clergy (he was a benefactor of the English College at Douay); the dignity of public worship was insisted on. Borromeo set his clergy an example of virtuous and selfless living, of caring for the needy and sick, of making Christ a reality to society, and his influence was felt outside his own diocese. During the plague of 1576, in particular, he worked unceasingly for his flock and used up much of his means in relieving sufferers.

St Charles's uncompromising reforms were not carried on without opposition, not least from highly-placed lay people whose disorderly lives he used stringent measures to curb: efforts were made to get him removed from office, and an attempt was even made to assassinate him, by a member of a religious order, the Humiliati, which the archbishop had sought to control. In his earlier years St Charles suffered from a speech impediment, which he at length overcame, but he was unable to preach with ease; nevertheless he always spoke convincingly, and constantly preached and catechized on his visitations. He was only forty-six when he died, in the arms of his confessor, a priest from Wales, Dr Gruffydd Roberts. St Charles Borromeo was an outstanding figure among Roman Catholic reformers after the Council of Trent, and has been called 'another ◊ *St Ambrose*'; his rigorism in some directions and his imperiousness have not escaped criticism, but such work of his as the religious education of children has been very widely appreciated. Among Walter Savage Landor's poems is one addressed to St Charles, invoking his pity on Milan at the time of the troubles in 1848.

Another confessor of Borromeo was himself canonized, in 1904. This was *St Alexander Sauli* (d. 1592; f.d. 11 October), a Barnabite clerk regular, who afterwards spent twenty years as a bishop carrying out religious reforms in Corsica – reforms that were as unwelcomed as they were necessary and overdue. Just before his death Bishop Sauli was advanced to the Italian see of Pavia.

G. Orsenigo, *St Charles Borromeo* (1943); M. Yeo, *A Prince of Pastors* (1938).

CHARLES GARNIER, martyr. B. in Paris, 1606; d. in Canada 7 December 1649; cd 1930; f.d. 26 September. He became a Jesuit priest and in 1636 sailed for Quebec to work among the Indians. In 1649 the Huron village where he was stationed, Saint-Jean, was attacked by Iroquois. While ministering to his flock and helping them to escape, Garnier was shot down; he struggled to his feet and tried to reach a dying Huron to give him absolution; but as he staggered forward an Iroquois clove his head with a tomahawk and he fell dead. Father Garnier's superior wrote of him that 'his very laugh spoke of goodness'.

CHIONIA ◊ *Agape, Chionia, and Irene*

CHRISTINE, martyr. Date unknown; f.d. 24 July. The legend of the St Christine venerated at Lake Bolsena in Latium is simply that of St Christine of Tyre, imported from the East and adapted to local conditions. Both legends are narratives of ordeals endured and of miraculous happenings, without historical value. There are remains of an early Christian cemetery at Bolsena, but the evidence for its being the burial place of a martyred Christine is not satisfactory.

CHRISTOPHER, martyr. Date unknown; f.d. 25 July. The core of the legend of St Christopher as told in the West (the Greek story is different) is that he was a man of gigantic stature who wished to serve the mightiest of masters. A king and Satan having both disappointed him, he sought Christ, living alone by a ford where many travellers passed. One night he was carrying a child across the river when the child became so heavy that Christopher could hardly get across. 'No wonder!' said the child. 'You have been carrying the whole world. I am Jesus Christ, the king you seek.' In due course Christopher was put to death for his faith.

This story, which has delighted so many generations and took its final form only gradually, doubtless owes much to its hero's name: *Christophoros* in Greek means 'one who carries Christ', and its original connotation was spiritual, not physical. A church was built in St Christopher's honour at Chalcedon as early as 450, but the most that can be surmised about him is that he was a martyr in Asia Minor, perhaps in the third century. It was a common medieval belief that he who looked on an image of St Christopher would suffer no harm that day, which led to the painting of large pictures of him on church walls; he is the patron saint of wayfarers, and now of motorists.

CHRODEGANG, bishop. B. near Liège, c. 715; d. at Gorze, 766; f.d. 6 March. This bishop is of importance because of his continuation of the work of ◊ *St Boniface of Crediton* in reforming the Frankish church. In particular, he sought to raise the standard of the clergy by suitable education and by encouraging them when possible to live a common life together. For such communities he drew up a rule, based in part on that of ◊ *St Benedict*; this movement spread and was widely influential. St Chrodegang was appointed to the see of Metz in 742, and as well as thus organizing his cathedral clergy he introduced Roman chant and liturgical usages into his diocese. Pope Stephen II having conferred archiepiscopal rank on him, and having the full support of King Pepin the Short, he was able to get his reforms taken up in neighbouring dioceses. In 748 he founded the abbey of Gorze which, like the Metz school of church music, became famous. St Chrodegang, we are told, was a man of handsome appearance and generous disposition, a ready writer in Latin and his own tongue, a man whose character and abilities eminently fitted him to carry on the work St Boniface had begun.

CHRYSANTHUS and DARIA, martyrs. Date unknown; f.d. 25 October. These two were certainly early martyrs, buried on the New Salarian Way outside Rome, but their popular and much-discussed legend is no more than a romance. According to it, Chrysanthus was a young Alexandrian at Rome, whose father tried to wean him from Christianity by means of the blandishments of a priestess of Minerva, Daria; instead, he converted her and they entered into a virginal marriage. They in turn brought about many conversions, including a company of soldiers who were all beheaded, and they were themselves martyred by being buried alive in a sand-pit on the Salarian Way. While Christians were praying at their tomb, the emperor ordered its entrance to be blocked up and the worshippers were left there to perish.

CHRYSOGONUS, martyr. D. 304 (?); f.d. 24 November. This martyr is among those named in the canon of the Roman Mass, but nothing is now known about him, except that he probably suffered at Aquileia in northern Italy. He figures in the worthless Passion of ◊ *St Anastasia* and has been venerated in Rome since at least the end of the fifth century.

CHRYSOSTOM ◊ *John Chrysostom*

CIARAN, or KIERAN, OF CLONMACNOIS, abbot. B. in Connacht, *c.* 516; d. at Clonmacnois, *c.* 549; f.d. 9 September. He was born of a Meath family of pre-Celtic descent, and as a boy he left home, driving a dun cow before him for his keep, to be trained in ◊ *St Finnian*'s monastery at Clonard. Then he migrated to the Arans to learn from ◊ *St Enda*, and left there at the prompting of a vision which Enda interpreted for him. Ciaran travelled slowly eastwards, settling at length at Clonmacnois, on the Shannon south of Athlone. Here he began the establishment of what was to become one of the greatest of Ireland's monasteries, whose school attracted learners from all over the land. But he seems not to have survived long to direct it, apparently dying in early middle life; a moving and probably authentic account of his last moments has survived, to which has been appended a fabulous resuscitation for twenty-four hours. Other fabulous tales are told of St Ciaran, and yet others illustrating his religious spirit more convincingly. One community of monks found his generous charities too great a strain on their resources: 'Go away', they said, 'for we cannot suffer you here with us.'

R. A. S. Macalister (tr.), *The Latin and Irish Lives of St Ciaran* (1921).

CIARAN OF SAIGHIR, bishop. Fifth or sixth century; f.d. 5 March. There is a conflict of evidence about the era in which this Ciaran lived, but he may have been one of several missionaries in Ireland before ◊ *St Patrick*. In any case, most of what is related about him, however entertaining or edifying, has no value as sober history. Round his monastery there grew up the town called Sier-Ciaran (Saighir), and he is said to have founded a convent which he put in the charge of his mother. He is honoured as the first bishop in his native Ossory, and is sometimes called 'of Ossory'. The identification of this St Ciaran with the Cornish ◊ *St Piran* is now rejected by scholars.

CLARE OF ASSISI, foundress. B. at Assisi *c.* 1194; d. there, 1253; cd 1255; f.d. 12 August. She came of a noble family. In her youth she refused two proffered marriages, but did not finally make up her mind to 'leave the world' until she came under the influence of ◊ *St Francis* in her native town. Then, when she was eighteen, she left home secretly and Francis put her in the care of Benedictine nuns at Bastia. Her family tried to induce her to return home, but in vain, and she was joined by her sister, St Agnes (and, later on, by her widowed mother). St Francis installed them as the nucleus of a community in a house by the church of San Damiano at Assissi, drawing up a 'way of life' for them, and this was the beginning of the order of Poor Ladies, formerly called Minoresses in England and now Poor Clares.

From Pope Innocent III St Clare obtained, *c.* 1215, the 'privilege of poverty', that is, permission for her nuns to live wholly on alms, without possessing any property whatever, either personal or communal. From time to time throughout her life St Clare had to fight for the maintenance of this privilege, and for the nuns' rule of life as designed by St Francis, against the modifications desired by popes and other prudent church authorities. The Poor Clares' mode of life was harder than that of any other nuns at that time. Clare herself was in the front rank of medieval contemplatives, and she has been called 'the most authentic expression of evangelical perfection as understood by St Francis of Assisi'. She guided her community with discretion for forty years, during many of which she was suffering from serious ill-health. We are given glimpses of her walking among her nuns at night and tucking in their bedclothes, and she wrote to a nun who had started a Poor Clare convent in Prague, telling her not to overdo her austerities, 'for our bodies are not made of brass'. St Clare outlived St Francis by twenty-seven years. She is shown in art carrying a monstrance.

P. Robinson (tr.), *The Life of St Clare* ascribed to Thomas of Celano (1910); E. Gilliat-Smith, *St Clare of Assisi* (1914).

CLEMENT THE FIRST, pope. D. at the end of the first century; f.d. 23 November. ◊ *St Peter*'s first successor in the see of Rome was *St Linus* (f.d. 23 September), probably followed by *St Cletus* (f.d. 26 April), who is the same as St Anacletus; nothing is now known about either of them, but they are both venerated as martyrs. Linus may be the man of that name mentioned in II Tim. iv, 21. Clement I is generally reckoned to be Peter's third successor. Little is known of his life either: ◊ *St Irenaeus* says that 'he had seen and consorted with the blessed apostles', and he was identified by some with the Clement mentioned by ◊ *St Paul* in his epistle to the Philippians (iv, 3). But he is famous for the letter sent by him from the church of Rome to the church of Corinth, the occasion of which was the revolt of some Corinthian Christians against the leaders of their church. It is the first known example of a bishop of Rome intervening in the affairs of another church, and is a model of pastoral solicitude and firm paternal admonition; it also contains valuable historical and other references. The letter was well received by the Corinthians, who for many years used to have it read out in their religious assemblies. Another letter (really a sermon) and other writings bore Clement's name, but it is now known that they are not his.

On the strength of the authentic letter St Clement is accounted the first of the Apostolic Fathers. He is venerated as a martyr, but there is no good evidence that he was one. The tale that he was sentenced to hard labour in the Crimea and was there lashed to an anchor and thrown into the sea is legendary; but it became popular, and it accounts for such marine dedications as St Clement's Isle in Mount's Bay and the Gild of the Holy Trinity and St Clement (now called 'Trinity House') in London. An anchor is St Clement's emblem.

CLEMENT HOFBAUER, priest. B. in Moravia, 1751; d. in Vienna, 1820; cd 1909; f.d. 15 March. He was a Czech by birth (his original name was Jan Dvořák) and at first a baker by trade. But he aspired to be a solitary and for some years led a rather wandering life between Rome and Vienna, till at the age of thirty-four he was ordained priest in the Redemptorist congregation of ◊ *St Alphonsus Liguori*. For twenty years he laboured in Poland, being the first to establish the Redemptorists north of the Alps; but his remarkably fruitful religious and social work came to an end in 1808 when Napoleon Bonaparte dispersed the religious communities in Poland. Hofbauer spent the rest of his life in Vienna, where he battled unceasingly against state control of the church and religious affairs. He had had no advantages of birth or general education, but he earned a great reputation for wisdom in religious and social matters, and succeeded in establishing a new college in the city; he even had a certain influence in ecclesiastical concerns behind the scenes at the Congress of Vienna in 1814–15. He was distinguished by a deep and sensitive understanding of the causes of the Protestant Reformation and of its religious motives among the German peoples.

J. Hofer, *St Clement Mary Hofbauer* (1926).

CLEMENT SLOVENSKY, missionary. D. at Okhrida, 916; f.d. 27 July. He was probably a Macedonian Slav; he was a missionary with St Methodius (◊ below) in Moravia, on whose death in 885 he was driven out by the German element there. With four others who had been expelled he went to the Bulgars to carry on the work of evangelism among them. They were well received, Clement was consecrated bishop, and he probably established his see somewhere near Okhrida. The text of a number of sermons attributed to St Clement still exists; they are clearly intended for new converts, but it is doubtful how many of the discourses are his. Clement and his companions, SS. Gorazd, Naum, Sava and Angelar, together with ◊ *SS. Cyril and Methodius*, are honoured in Bulgaria as the evangelizers of the country.

CLETUS ◊ under *Clement I*

CLOTILDA ◊ below, under *Cloud*

CLOUD, prince. B. *c.* 520; d. *c.* 560; f.d. 7 September. When his father died in battle in 524 Cloud (Clodoaldus) and his two brothers were taken into the care of their grandmother Clotilda, widow of the Frankish king Clovis. Their ambitious uncle Childebert compassed the murder of the two elder children, but Cloud was rescued from this fate and taken to a place of safety. When he grew up he resigned all claim to the Frankish throne by being tonsured a monk; he was then ordained priest, and lived out his days in quietness and good works. The place where he died, now a *commune* of Versailles, was named Saint-Cloud after him. His grandmother *Clotilda*, after a long widowhood made miserable by the atrocious behaviour of her sons, died in 545, and she too is revered as a saint in France (f.d. 3 June).

G. Kurth, *St Clotilda* (1896).

COEMGEN ◊ *Kevin*

COLETTE, nun. B. at Corbie, 1381; d. at Ghent, 1447; cd 1807; f.d. 6 March. Nicolette Boylet was the daughter of a carpenter in Picardy. She joined the Franciscan third order, and at the age of twenty-one began to live alone in a hermitage lent by the abbot of Corbie. Here she had a vision of ◊ *St Francis of Assisi*, who charged her to bring his Poor Clare nuns back to their original strict rule of life. On the advice of Friar Henry de Baume, Colette in 1406 went to Nice to interview the papal claimant, Peter de Luna. He was so impressed that he admitted her to the Poor Clare order and authorized her to reform existing convents and establish new ones. She was strongly opposed by the nuns of

Picardy and Savoy, but from 1410, with the support of Henry de Baume, she had more and increasing success. She founded seventeen convents of strict observance in France and Flanders, and reformed a number of others, including one at Le Puy-en-Velay which survived the French Revolution. St Colette was untrained and unprepared for any such work; she achieved it by the power of faith and holiness, and a determination that no opposition could discourage. After her death her work spread beyond its original territory, and Poor Clares of the Colettine reform are found in many parts of the world today.

S. M. Perrin, *St Colette* (1923).

COLMAN OF LANN ELO, abbot. B. in Tyrone, 555; d. at Lynally, 611: f.d. 26 September. There is a story in the Life of ◊ *St Carthage* that once when a party of his monks was working by a stream the one in charge called out, 'Colman, get into the water!'; whereupon twelve Colmans at once jumped in. Colmans can in fact be found literally by scores in lists of early Irish saints, and about most of them nothing but the name is known. Among the exceptions is Colman Elo, who was ordained priest as a young man and more than once visited ◊ *St Columba* on Iona. For a time, about 590, he was at Connor in Antrim, but his name is chiefly associated with the monastery he founded at Lann Elo (Lynally), near Durrow in Meath. This Colman is credited with having written a little work called the *Alphabet of Devotion*; and when he suffered for a time from loss of memory it was said that this was a punishment for undue satisfaction with his own intellectual attainments.

Other saints of this name are *Colman of Dromore*, abbot-bishop at that place (later sixth century; f.d. 7 June); *Colman of Kilmacduagh*, abbot-bishop there (d. *c.* 632; f.d. 29 October); and *Colman of Cloyne*, a royal bard at Cashel who late in life founded the church of Cloyne (sixth century; f.d. 24 November).

COLMAN OF LINDISFARNE, bishop. B. in Ireland; d. on Inishbofin, 676: f.d. 18 February. He became a monk at Iona, and *c.* 661 succeeded ◊ *St Finan* as bishop of Lindisfarne. At that time the disagreement in Northumbria about the date of Easter and other Celtic ecclesiastical usages had reached a critical stage, and in 664 (or 663) a conference met at Whitby to settle the matter. St Colman upheld the Celtic customs, ◊ *St Wilfrid* those of Rome, and King Oswy accepted Wilfrid's arguments. Thereupon Colman resigned his bishopric and retired, first to Iona and then to Inishbofin off the Connacht coast. There went with him all his Irish monks and thirty of the English. But the two elements in this community disagreed among themselves (the English complained that all the harvest work was left to them), so Colman made a separate foundation for the English monks on the mainland, 'Mayo of the Saxons'. The first abbot of Mayo after Colman was an Englishman, *St Gerald*, who lived till 732 (f.d. 13 March). ◊ *Bede*, who was not in sympathy with the distinctively Celtic practices, gives a glowing account of the church of Lindisfarne under St Colman's short period of rule. He emphasizes the example of frugality and simplicity of living set by the bishop, and the complete devotion of his clergy to their proper business of imparting the word of God and ministering to their people.

COLUMBA, or COLMCILLE, abbot and missionary. B. in Donegal, *c.* 521; d. on Iona, 597; f.d. 9 June. This saint, equally famed in Ireland and Scotland, is said to have been directly descended from Niall of the Nine Hostages. From an early age he was intended for the priesthood; he was given in fosterage to a priest, and afterwards studied under one or more of the great teachers of his time. After ordination he seems to have passed some fifteen years preaching and teaching in Ireland, where he founded monasteries at Derry and Durrow. Then, probably in the year 563, he left his country. It was said later that this was an act of penance for some responsibility he had incurred for the bloody battle of Cooldrevne, fought two years earlier, but the matter is not at all clear; his biographer ◊ *St Adamnan* simply says that he wanted to be 'a pilgrim for Christ'. At this time the northern Picts in what we call Scotland were still heathen, but there were Irish immigrants in Argyll who were at least nominally Christian. Columba, with twelve companions, settled on the island of Iona, off the south-west corner of Mull.

From the Iona monastery, which was destined to play so important a part in the Christian history of northern England, through Lindisfarne, St Columba and his monks preached among the Picts, one of whose kings, Brude, and his people were greatly impressed by Columba's miracles. (These included the driving away of a water 'monster' from the river Ness by the sign of the cross.) He is credited with Brude's conversion. He made extensive journeys on the mainland, and made three or four other monastic settlements to accommodate the followers who joined him. One of these establishments was on the unidentified island of Hinba, to which he frequently retired. He was there when he was called on to carry out the sacring of Aidan, the Irish king of Argyll. But there are not many particulars known of the thirty-four years during which Columba was what Adamnan calls an 'island soldier'. Adamnan's Life of him was written nearly a century after Columba's death, and it owes something to the writer's imagination and more to unreliable sources; it is principally a narrative of supernatural happenings, of the saint's deeds of power and foretellings of future events. But it is a great tribute to one who in all his works was 'loving to every one, happy-faced, rejoicing in his inmost heart with the joy of the Holy Spirit'.

A. O. Anderson (tr.), *Adomnan's Life of St Columba* (1961); L. Menzies, *St Columba of Iona* (1920); W. D. Simpson, *The Historical St Columba* (1963).

COLUMBA OF CÓRDOVA, martyr. D. 853; f.d. 17 September. She was a Spanish girl who lived the life of a nun in a community organized by some of her relatives at Tabanos. When the community was dispersed by the Moors, she went to the Moorish magistrate in Córdova and openly defied him, affirming that Mohammed was a false prophet. For this she was beheaded, and her body thrown into the river Guadalquivir. These particulars were related by ◊ *St Eulogius of Córdova*, who was later a victim of the same persecution.

St Columba of Sens was another maiden martyr, venerated in France and elsewhere (f.d. 31 December), but the date and circumstances of her martyrdom are unknown. Her *passio* is a document that has no value as history.

COLUMBAN, abbot and missioner. B. in Leinster, *c.* 540; d. at Bobbio in Italy, 615; f.d. 23 November. Columban had been a monk from his youth when, at about the age of forty-five, he was given leave by the abbot of the Irish Bangor, ◊ *St Comgall*, to go over to the continent of Europe, where he proved himself the greatest and most influential of the monks from Ireland. He took a dozen companions with him, including ◊ *St Gall*, and before long had founded three monastic centres, at Annegray, Luxeuil, and Fontaine, in the Vosges. But after some time the inflexibility of Columban's rule and his defiant adherence to Irish ecclesiastical customs aroused criticism, and he had to defend himself in letters to the pope, ◊ *St Gregory I*. Then he incurred the enmity of Queen Brunhild by rebuking her grandson, Thierry II of Burgundy, for his loose-living. Finally, in 610, the abbot and those of his monks who were Irish-born were ordered to be deported home.

Circumstances enabled them to elude their captors and to carry on their mission in a number of places, eventually reaching Bregenz on Lake Constance. From here in 612 Columban made his way over the Alps into Lombardy. He was then at least seventy years old, but he was soon involved in lively ecclesiastical controversy, in the course of which he wrote a famous letter to Pope Boniface IV which combined deep respect with vehement plain-spokenness and an insufficient understanding of the issues involved. Having been given land between Genoa and Piacenza, he began the foundation of the great abbey of Bobbio in 614, and died there in the following year. The rule of life composed by St Columban for his monks was a severe one, drawn up no doubt on the basis of those of Bangor and other Irish houses; but the example of Luxeuil and Bobbio, and the activities of his disciples, gave it an extensive diffusion in France, Germany, and elsewhere, until it was eventually superseded by the more tractable provisions of ◊ *St Benedict*. The emblem of Columban is a bear.

G. Metlake, *Life and Writings of St Columban* (1914); F. MacManus, *St Columban* (1963).

COMGALL, abbot. B. in Ulster, 517; d. at Bangor, 603; f.d. 11 May. He is said to have been a warrior as a young man, but by the time he was about forty he had been ordained priest and settled at Bangor (Bennchor), on the south shore of Belfast Loch. Disciples gathered round him, of whom the best known is ◊ *St Columban*, and the Bangor monastery was one of the principal religious centres of Ireland till it was destroyed by the Danes in 823. Comgall went to Scotland for a time, where he lived in a monastery on the island of Tiree, and it is said that he accompanied ◊ *St Columba* on his expedition to the Picts of Inverness. The manuscript called the Bangor Antiphonary, written there less than a century after St Comgall's death, contains a long hymn in his praise. Two of his monks were prominent evangelists in Scotland, St Moluag of Lismore in Argyll and St Maelrubha of Applecross in Ross.

CONRAD OF PARZHAM ◊ under *Ignatius of Laconi*

CORNELIUS, pope and martyr. B. in Rome; d. at Civitavecchia, June 253; f.d. 26 September. After the martyrdom of St Fabian in 250 it was over a year before the Roman clergy and people were able to elect a bishop, Cornelius, in his place – a result of the continuance of persecution and of differences among Christians themselves. A party, led by the priest Novatian, claimed in effect that apostasy was an unforgivable sin, and that the church had no power to absolve and receive back people who had lapsed under persecution and then repented. Cornelius rejected this teaching, and Novatian set himself up as bishop of Rome in opposition. Cornelius was supported particularly by ◊ *St Cyprian* in Africa and ◊ *St Dionysius of Alexandria*, and Novatian and his teaching were condemned by councils of bishops at Carthage and Rome. Existing letters from Cyprian testify to the goodness and generosity of Cornelius, who when persecution flared up again was relegated to Centumcellae (Civitavecchia). He died soon afterwards and is traditionally venerated as a martyr; he may have succumbed to hardships in exile, but later statements that he was beheaded are not supported by any historical evidence.

COSMAS and DAMIAN, martyrs. Date unknown; f.d. 27 September. There is good evidence that there were two early martyrs bearing these names, who suffered at Cyrrhus in Syria; beyond that, nothing whatever is now known about them. From the fifth century their cultus became very extensive; the fame of few martyrs spread so far so quickly. They came to be called 'the holy moneyless ones' and invoked as patron saints of physicians, for the kernel of their legend is that they were twin brothers who practised medicine without charging fees, and during a persecution of Christians were put to death for their faith. The details of this legend – the torments inflicted, the miracles wrought – are of the most extravagant description. At one time earnest efforts were made to show that Cosmas and Damian never existed, that they were simply a christianized version of the heathen Dioscuri, the twin sons of Zeus. This is not so, though there is evidence that popular superstition sometimes approximated them to the Dioscuri. And a feature of their cultus was an adaptation of the heathen observance called 'incubation': a sick person slept in the saints' church, hoping to be favoured with a dream that would lead to his cure. Cf. ◊ *Florus and Laurus.*

CRISPIN and CRISPINIAN, martyrs. Date unknown; f.d. 25 October. These martyrs are particularly venerated at Soissons in France, where there was a church in their honour in the sixth century. Their legend, which is very late and quite worthless, says that they were missionaries from Rome in the third century who preached the gospel at Soissons, where they earned their living as shoemakers and were eventually martyred. The truth may well be that they were Roman martyrs whose relics were brought to Soissons and enshrined there. Crispin and Crispinian are the traditional patron saints of shoemakers and other workers in leather, and this ascription has not been wholly forgotten in England, either in the trade or more generally. A local tradition of unknown origin says that they fled from persecution to Faversham in Kent, where formerly there was an altar bearing their name in the parish church. Their emblem in art is a shoe or a last.

CRISPINA, martyr. B. in Numidia; d. there, 304; f.d. 5 December. She was a married woman of good position, with several children. During the persecution under Diocletian she was brought before the proconsul Anulinus at Thevaste on a charge of refusing to sacrifice to the gods on behalf of the emperor. The written Passion, which professes to give the discussion which ensued between Crispina and Anulinus, no doubt depends on an authentic document: he urged her not to be obstinate but to conform to the imperial edict; she was firm in her refusal: 'I do observe an edict: that of my Lord Jesus Christ.' Threats of death failing to move her, Anulinus lost patience: 'We cannot put up with this impious Crispina any longer.' The proceedings were read over, and she was sentenced to death by the sword. ◊ *St Augustine* several times refers to St Crispina as a well-known African martyr, worthy to be ranked with such as ◊ *St Agnes.*

CUBY, or CYBI, abbot. Sixth century; f.d. 8 November. Cuby is one of the few saints of Cornwall who seems to have been born there, perhaps the son of St Selevan ('St Levan'). Place names suggest he was an energetic missionary monk, who visited southeast Wales and made his way by sea up the west coast to Anglesey. Here the prince Maelgwn Gwynedd is said to have given him a ruined Roman fort for his headquarters, where the town of Holyhead now stands; it is still known in Welsh as Caer Gybi, Cybi's town. The existing Life of the saint dates only from the thirteenth century, and takes him on a fabulous pilgrimage to Jerusalem as well as narrating a long stay with ◊ *St Enda* on Aranmore; but there is no reason to suppose that St Cuby was ever in Ireland either. We are told that he was accompanied on Aran by an aged kinsman named Cungar, an elusive saint whose name is found in Wales, Brittany, and Somerset (Congresbury). Matthew Arnold in his poem 'East and West' narrates – but misunderstands – an Anglesey legend about St Cybi.

CUNEGUND ◊ under *Henry the Second*

CUTHBERT, bishop. B. *c.* 634; d. on Farne, 687; f.d. 20 March. In spite of lively claims made in the past on behalf of Ireland, it seems certain that St Cuthbert was, as his name suggests, a Northumbrian Englishman. As a lad tending sheep on the hills above Leader Water he had a vision, ◊ *Bede* tells us, of angels conducting the soul of ◊ *St Aidan* to Heaven, and later on he became a monk under St Eata at Melrose. The time came when he undertook long journeys, year after year, on horseback and on foot, into the remotest parts of the country between Berwick and Galloway, to minister to the scattered people and keep the spirit of Christianity alive among them. In 664 he accompanied St Eata to Lindisfarne and extended his work southward to the people of Northumberland and Durham. Yet he was by nature a solitary, and in 676 he retired to the desolate islet of Farne where he lived till 684, when he was called to be bishop of Hexham.

Almost at once Cuthbert exchanged his see with Eata for that of Lindisfarne, and as bishop there 'he continued to be the same man that he was before', one whom charity impelled to devote himself whole-heartedly to his flock, preaching, helping with alms and counsel, and visiting every part of his large diocese. St Cuthbert makes special appeal today as a keenly observant man, interested in the ways of birds and beasts; in his own time he was famed as a worker of miracles in God's name, on one occasion healing a woman's dying baby with a kiss. The ample sources for his life and character show a man of extraordinary charm and practical ability, who attracted people deeply by the beauty of holiness; it is not for nothing that Bede so often refers to him as 'the child of God'. His episcopate lasted for only two years, and when he felt the approach of death he withdrew to his retreat on Farne. He died there at night, and news was signalled to his community on Lindisfarne by the waving of torches from the cliff top. At Lindisfarne he was buried, but after the Viking raids began his remains were removed and found their final resting-place in Durham cathedral; bones discovered in 1827 beneath the site of the medieval shrine are probably his.

B. Colgrave (tr.), *Two Lives of St Cuthbert* (1940); H. Colgrave, *St Cuthbert of Durham* (1955); J. F. Webb, *Lives of the Saints* (Penguin).

CUTHBURGA ◊ under *Werburgh*

CUTHMAN. Ninth century (?); f.d. 8 February. St Cuthman's name occurs in several medieval calendars and the church at Steyning in Sussex seems formerly to have been dedicated in his honour. The story told about him is that he was a young shepherd in south-west England who on his father's death migrated to Steyning; he took his aged mother with him, trundling her in a handcart. At Steyning he undertook the building of a small church with the help of his neighbours, and there he lived out his life. The memory of this forgotten saint was revived by Christopher Fry in his one-act play *The Boy with a Cart* (1939).

CYNEBURGA ◊ under *Werburgh*

CYNEHELM ◊ *Kenelm*

CYPRIAN, bishop and martyr. B. in Tunisia, *c.* 200; d. at Carthage, 258; f.d. 16 September (B.C.P., 26). For most of his life Cyprian was a barrister and teacher of public speaking at Carthage, but when he was about forty-six he became a Christian, and only two years later was made bishop of Carthage. When Emperor Decius began to proceed against Christians in 249 Cyprian went into hiding, for which he was much criticized; but he was thus able to continue to look after his flock. After the death of Decius in 251, Cyprian took a leading part, with Pope Cornelius, in opposing the rigorism of Novatian (◊ *St Cornelius*), but later on he was to have a serious disagreement with Pope Stephen I. When heretics were reconciled to the church, it was the custom in Africa to re-baptize them; Stephen objected to this, since in the Roman church baptism given by heretics was recognized as valid, other things being equal. The tradition upheld by the pope eventually prevailed, but Cyprian did not live to see the end of the controversy. During the plague of 252 in Carthage he was unwearied in comforting the sufferers, but this did not prevent the heathen populace from blaming the 'impious Christians' and their leader for the epidemic. His flock loved him for his goodness, and he made it a rule not to come to decisions without consulting his clergy and gaining the people's approval. He wrote a number of treatises, of which the best known is concerned with the nature of the church's unity (Eng. trans. 1957). Cyprian did not always live up to the high ideal expressed in his sermon on the virtue of patience; on the other hand, he fulfilled his own *Exhortation to Martyrdom* to the letter.

When persecution began again in 258, under Emperor Valerian, St Cyprian was one of the first victims. There is an account of what happened compiled directly from contemporary documents. Cyprian was first examined by the proconsul, and on affirming his adherence to the one true God, and refusing to divulge the names of his priests, he was exiled to Curubis. When a new proconsul came into office, Cyprian was brought up for trial in Carthage. He again refused to sacrifice to the Roman gods, and was sentenced to death. Accompanied by a tumultuous crowd, he was led to the field of Sextus; there he knelt in prayer. He gave a generous gift to the executioner, blindfolded himself, and his head was struck off. In the two examinations of St Cyprian it is noticeable with what considerateness, almost deference, he was treated, and how courteous bishop and proconsuls were to one another; this contrasts sharply with the abuse and ranting so often set down in less authentic accounts of such occasions.

P. Hinchcliff, *Cyprian of Carthage* (1974).

CYPRIAN and JUSTINA, martyrs. No date; f.d. 26 September. The story of these two is simply a moral tale, already known in part in the fourth century and afterwards translated from Greek into many languages. It relates that Cyprian was a sorcerer of great attainments at Antioch, who used his powers to try and win the favour of a Christian maiden, Justina. When he failed, he first fell into melancholia and then, after being present at worship in a church, asked for baptism. Finally he and Justina were martyred at Nicodemia.

CYRIACUS THE RECLUSE. B. at Corinth, 449; d. near Bethlehem, 557; f.d. 29 September. An interesting Life of St Cyriacus, widely venerated in the East, was written by the contemporary Cyril of Scythopolis. When a young man, Cyriacus emigrated to Palestine, and was given the monastic habit by ◊ *St Euthymius the Great.* He then became a disciple of ◊ *St Gerasimus* near the Dead Sea for nine years. During his immensely long life St Cyriacus lived at several monasteries and hermitages in the Holy Land; his favourite home was St Chariton's Cave, in the wilderness of

Tekoa south-east of Bethlehem, a huge cavern with inner caves on different levels, very damp and cold. It was here that Cyriacus died. He was a gentle man, of prophetic spirit, and much attached to the daily psalmody; he was precentor of the Souka monastery, near the cave, for thirty years, during which, he said, he never ate before sun-down and was never overcome by anger. An incident, related by Cyril in the Life, of two followers of St Cyriacus meeting a woman recluse in the desert beyond Jordan, may well have been the starting point of the legend of ◊ *St Mary the Egyptian*.

The Roman martyr *Cyriacus* (f.d. 8 August) was buried on the Ostian road, but is otherwise unknown. His legend associates him with the martyrs Largus and Smaragdus and other historical characters, but it is a fictitious romance.

CYRICUS and JULITTA, martyrs. Date unknown; f.d. 16 June. Their legend relates that Cyricus (Quiricus) was a three-year-old boy whose mother, Julitta, was condemned as a Christian at Tarsus under Diocletian. When the child was taken from his mother, the governor, Alexander, tried to comfort him; but Cyricus lashed out, kicking and struggling, and scratched Alexander's face. The man in a rage threw Cyricus down the steps of the tribune, killing him outright. So far from being distressed, Julitta rejoiced at her son being a martyr, and went cheerfully to torture and death. There is some evidence for the existence of an unknown martyr named Cyricus at Antioch, and it may have been about him that this fictitious tale was evolved in several forms. In any case, as early as the sixth century the Acts of Cyricus and Julitta were rejected in a list of apocryphal documents (the list was formerly attributed to Pope Gelasius I). Cyricus is the Saint-Cyr found in several French place-names.

CYRIL and METHODIUS, missionaries. B. in Salonika *c.* 827, *c.* 815; d. 869, 885; f.d. 7 July. These two brothers are known as the 'apostles of the southern Slaves'. In earlier life the younger, Cyril (then called Constantine), taught with distinction in the imperial university at Constantinople, whilst St Methodius was governor of a province. They both became priests, and about 863 were sent to preach the gospel in Moravia, where they had considerable success, greatly helped by their knowledge of the Slavonic language; but the presence of German missionaries there brought about a religio-political collision. In 869 the brothers were in Rome, where Cyril died. Pope Adrian II consecrated Methodius bishop, but on his return to his mission he was consigned to prison at the instigation of German bishops. After two years Pope John VIII got him released, and he continued his work of evangelization until 879, when he was summoned to Rome to answer charges made by his opponents. He was able to clear himself, and John VIII confirmed him in his office as archbishop of Pannonia and Moravia, with permission for his clergy to celebrate the liturgy in Slavonic. But Methodius was still subjected to serious vexations, especially from Bishop Wiching of Nitra, who was so unscrupulous as to forge a papal letter in his own favour. St Methodius died, probably at Velehrad in modern Czechoslovakia, in 885, and Wiching drove out his principal followers, who took refuge in Bulgaria (◊ *St Clement Slovensky*).

In modern times there has been much discussion and disagreement about the exact history of SS. Cyril and Methodius; what is beyond question is that their memory is revered by Czechs and Croats, Serbs and Bulgars. St Cyril's working out of an alphabet, probably the one now called Glagolitic, for writing Slavonic enabled the brothers to translate the liturgy and much of the Bible, thus laying the foundation of Slavonic literature (the so-called Cyrillic alphabet is perhaps the work of their followers in Bulgaria, but Cyril may have invented both).

CYRIL OF ALEXANDRIA, bishop and theologian. B. at Alexandria, *c*. 380; d. there, 444; f.d. 9 February. He was a nephew of that Theophilus of Alexandria who engineered the deposition of ◊ *St John Chrysostom*, in which Cyril himself took part. In 412 he succeeded his uncle in the see of Alexandria, and was soon exercising authority with a hastiness and violence that led to much trouble. He shut the churches of the Novatianist schismatics, he drove out the Jews, he quarrelled with the imperial prefect, Orestes, and stirred up the monks against him. The Neoplatonist philosopher Hypatia, a woman of noble character and a friend of Orestes, was brutally murdered by a mob; it has not been established that Cyril was directly concerned in this crime, but it was nevertheless the work of those who looked to him as their leader. All this was an unpromising beginning to the career of one who rendered a signal service to Christianity by his learned and energetic defence of the unity of Christ's person, divine and human, against the teaching of Nestorius. Cyril took the lead at the general Council of Ephesus in 431, when the doctrine of Nestorius was condemned and he was removed from the see of Constantinople.

In the years after the council Cyril was moderate and conciliatory in seeking the reconciliation of the less extreme Nestorians, perhaps surprisingly so for a man of his character. He left a considerable number of writings, mostly scriptural or other expository works, or treatises arising out of the Nestorian controversy. He was indeed an outstanding theologian, and it is as a theologian rather than a bishop that his memory is held in honour. For the East he has long been the 'Seal of the Fathers'; in the West he has been numbered among the doctors of the church since Pope Leo XIII so named him in 1882.

CYRIL OF JERUSALEM, bishop. B. at Jerusalem, c. 315; d. there, 386; f.d. 18 March. This Cyril was made bishop of Jerusalem c. 349; it was the era of the troubles arising from Arianism, and of the approximately thirty-five years he was a bishop he spent nearly sixteen in exile from his see, on three separate occasions. The last time was from 367 to 378, he having been banished by the Arian emperor Valens; when he finally returned after Valens' death he was faced by a city sunk in corruption and disorder, and devoted his last years to its reclamation. Cyril is remembered principally for his *Catecheses*, eighteen instructional addresses given to candidates for baptism during Lent, and five given to the newly baptized after Easter. These last are called 'mystagogic', because they deal with the mysteries – sacraments – of baptism, confirmation and the eucharist; they are of great interest and value and have been published in English (1951). In the Roman Catholic church St Cyril of Jerusalem has been honoured as a doctor of the church since 1883.

CYRUS and JOHN, martyrs. D. c. 303; f.d. 31 January. There is little information available about these martyrs, and that little is unreliable. It is said that Cyrus, an Alexandrian, was first a physician and then a monk, and that John was an Arab and a soldier. Hearing that a Christian woman, Athanasia, and her three daughters were suffering greatly for their faith at Canopus, they went there to help and encourage them. But they were themselves arrested, and put to death a few days after the execution of Athanasia and her girls. In order to get rid of the worship of Isis that still lingered at Menuthis, near Canopus, St Cyril translated the relics of SS. Cyrus and John from Alexandria to the church at Menuthis as a counter-attraction. It became a much frequented shrine; but pre-Christian superstitions were not so easy to displace, for customs very like 'incubation' (◊ *Cosmos and Damian*) are recorded there. The relics of SS. Cyrus and John were eventually taken to Rome; Menuthis is now known as Abukir, meaning 'Father Cyrus', the scene of Nelson's victory in 1798.

D

DAMASUS THE FIRST, pope. B. in Rome, c. 304; d. there, 384; f.d. 11 December. He was a Roman deacon, son of a priest, perhaps of Spanish descent. When he was made bishop of Rome in

366 his election was violently opposed by the supporters of another candidate, Ursinus, and the civil power intervened on behalf of Damasus; the trouble continued for most of his pontificate, his opponents bringing vexatious charges of violence and evil-living against him. He had also to contend with Arianism and other heresies, but in 380 orthodox Christianity was recognized by the emperors Gratian and Theodosius I as the religion of the Roman state. The most important service St Damasus rendered the church was his encouragement of the biblical work of ◊ St Jerome, who was his secretary for a time; he is also specially remembered for his restoration of the catacombs and care for martyrs' burying-places. Damasus himself wrote epitaphs in verse for the tombs, and many of these inscriptions are extant; unfortunately they have little historical value, for the true histories of many Roman martyrs were already almost or quite forgotten.

DANIEL ◊ under *Berard*

DANIEL THE STYLITE. B. in Syria, 409, d. near Constantinople, 493; f.d. 11 December. He was the best-known of the disciples of ◊ St Simeon the Stylite (Gk. *stulos,* 'pillar'). His birthplace was Maratha, near Samosata, and until he was forty-two he was a monk near his home; during that time he twice visited Simeon on his pillar at Telanissus. He then removed to a hermitage near Constantinople, and on the death of St Simeon in 459 determined to carry on his way of life. The erection on which Daniel lived consisted of two conjoined pillars, on which was a railed platform supporting a shelter. Hereon he was ordained priest and celebrated the Eucharist, and came down once in thirty-three years, to reprove an erring emperor. He was often consulted by the emperors Leo I and Zeno and by the patriarchs of Constantinople, and people flocked to him, bringing their sick to be anointed and prayed over. There is a long contemporary account of St Daniel's life, in which he emerges as a shrewd 'uncomplicated' man, who gave practical advice and preached sermons to the crowd which were simple and to the point; he dwelt on the love of God, and care for the poor, and love for one another, and the wickedness of sin, 'without rhetoric or difficult ideas'. He lived to be eighty-four and was buried at the foot of his pillar.

E. Dawes and N. H. Baynes, *Three Byzantine Saints* (1948).

DAVID, or DEWI, abbot-bishop. Sixth century; f.d. 1 March. The name of the patron saint of Wales was Dewi, of which David is the English approximation. According to his legend he was son of a Cardigan chieftain, Sant, and a St Non; he founded twelve monasteries, from Croyland to Pembrokeshire; he went on pilgrimage to Jerusalem, and was there consecrated bishop; he took a principal part in two councils, at Brefi in Cardigan and at Caerleon; at the first of these he was recognized as primate of Wales in place of ◊ *St Dubricius*, and moved the see from Caerleon to Mynyw (Menevia, Saint David's), where he died. Most of this, and more, depends on a Life written *c.* 1090, whose author was concerned to uphold the claim of the Welsh bishopric to be independent of Canterbury; very little reliance can be put on the document.

St David may have been born at Henfynw in Cardigan; his principal monastery, where he presided as abbot-bishop, was certainly at the place now called Saint David's in Pembrokeshire. The community was extremely strict, and David was known traditionally as 'the Waterman', meaning perhaps that he and his monks were teetotallers. There are over fifty ancient David dedications and place names, all in South Wales and very numerous in the south-west corner; there are also dedications in Devon, Cornwall, and Brittany. Several Irish saints are stated to have been pupils of St David or to have visited Mynyw, and he seems to have had some influence on monastic developments in Ireland. The association of leeks with St David's day (e.g. in Shakespeare's *Henry V*, IV, 1) has not been satisfactorily explained; his emblem is a dove.

A. W. Wade-Evans, *Life of St David* (1923).

DAVID OF SCOTLAND ◊ under *Margaret of Scotland*

DEINIOL, abbot-bishop. Sixth century; f.d. 11 September. He was called 'of the Bangors', because to him was attributed the foundation of the monasteries of Bangor Fawr on the Menai strait and of Bangor Iscoed on the river Dee (whose monks were massacred by Ethelfrith of Northumbria *c.* 615). Deiniol's family is said to have been of Strathclyde origin, and his burial place was on Bardsey. The medieval cathedral of Bangor is dedicated in his honour.

DEMETRIUS, martyr. Date unknown; f.d. 8 October. He may have been a deacon, martyred at Sirmium (Mitrovica in Serbia), but the great centre of his cultus came to be Salonika. The story told there was that he was a local man who was killed without trial for preaching Christianity, in the time of Emperor Maximian. The legend grew, and Demetrius was represented as a proconsul and a famous warrior saint; like ◊ *St George, St Procopius*, and others, the soldier of Christ was thus transformed into a literal soldier, who suffered martyrdom. Salonika claimed to have his relics and he became famous all over the East.

DEMETRIUS OF ROSTOV, bishop. B. near Kiev, 1651; d. 1709; cd by Russian Orth. ch., 1757; f.d. 28 October. Demetrius (Dmitry) Tuptalo was son of a wealthy Cossack. He became a priest-monk and was head of two houses before being appointed bishop of Rostov on Don in 1702. He was an outspoken preacher who upheld the church's independence of state control, an active educationist, and a scholar, much of whose life was devoted to writing. He wrote notices of the saints based on Western critical models, religious drama in verse, memoirs, and a number of devotional and instructional works; these included the *Spiritual Alphabet*, insisting on the clergy's duties towards their flocks. St Demetrius himself preached at least a short homily whenever he celebrated the Eucharist, and was deeply beloved by his people. As a writer his warmth of style and approach makes him a noteworthy figure in Russian religious literature. He noted in his published *Diary* concerning monks who insisted on trying to write verse: 'God gives these versifiers printing-presses, money, enthusiasm, and leisure; but their output is of little use to the world.' In 1689 Demetrius accompanied to Moscow Ivan Stepanovich Mazeppa, the Cossack hetman of whom Lord Byron wrote in a romantic poem.

DENIS ◊ *Dionysius of Paris*

DESIDERIUS, bishop and martyr. D. at Saint-Didier-sur-Chalaronne, 607 (?); f.d. 23 May. Desiderius of Vienne was one of the bishops to whom ◊ *St Gregory* wrote recommending ◊ *St Augustine* to his kindness when Augustine was on his way to England from Rome. Another letter the pope addressed to Desiderius remonstrated with him for personally giving lessons in so profane a subject as grammar. A more serious accusation was in respect of a lady named Justa, a charge trumped up at the instigation of Thierry II of Burgundy and his grandmother, Queen Brunhilda. In consequence Desiderius was banished from his diocese for some years. On his return he was soon in trouble again, having rebuked King Thierry for his shameless life. While being taken to a place of detention he was set upon and killed by his escort, though apparently on the initiative of the soldiers rather than by order of Thierry. St Desiderius was venerated as a martyr, since he was put to death in the carrying out of his duty as a bishop. There are several other French saints of this name, called Didier or Dizier in France.

DEWI ◊ *David*

DIDACUS ◊ *Diego*

DIDIER ◊ *Desiderius*

DIEGO, Franciscan laybrother. B. near Seville, *c.* 1400; d. at Alcalá de Henares, 1463; cd 1588; f.d. 13 November. As a young man Diego (Didacus) lived for a time as a solitary, and then joined the Franciscan friars minor as a laybrother. He was sent to the Canary Islands and put in charge of the door at the Fuerteventura friary; here he did great work among the poor, and earned such a reputation for holiness that in 1445 he was chosen as superior of the house for a term. He passed the last thirteen years of his life in humble duties at various houses of his order in Spain.

Other Observant friars minor who attained outstanding holiness in leading the uneventful life of a laybrother are *St Charles of Sezze*, who died in Rome in 1670 (cd 1959; f.d. 7 January); *St Paschal Baylon*, a Spaniard, whose emblem in art is a monstrance, d. 1592 (cd 1690; f.d. 17 May); and *St Salvator of Horta*, another Spaniard, who died in Sardinia, 1567 (cd 1938; f.d. 18 March).

L. Perotti (tr.), *St Charles of Sezze: an Autobiography* (1963).

DIONYSIUS OF ALEXANDRIA, bishop. D. at Alexandria, *c.* 265; f.d. 17 November. He was a pupil of Origen in the Alexandrian catechetical school, of which he himself became the head, and which he directed for about fourteen years. In 247 he was made bishop of Alexandria. Persecution soon broke out there, and Dionysius was arrested; but he was enabled to escape, and directed his church from a hiding-place in the Libyan desert until the death of the persecuting Emperor Decius in 251. In the controversy that followed about those who had lapsed under persecution and then repented, Dionysius was a zealous supporter of lenient treatment for them. At the beginning of Valerian's persecution in 257, Dionysius was again arrested, and exiled from Alexandria. He returned in 261, to a city that was demoralized by civil strife, plague, and famine: it was as dangerous for a man to stay at home as to go out, wrote the bishop, easier to go from East to West than from one street in Alexandria to another. Despite all the disturbances of his seventeen years as a bishop, St Dionysius took an active part in church affairs and wrote extensively, but of his writings little has been preserved. He was a student of pagan as well as Christian literature. His virtues and learning were widely recognized, and he was sometimes referred to as Dionysius the Great.

DIONYSIUS, or DENIS, of PARIS, bishop and martyr. D. 258 (?); f.d. 9 October. This Dionysius, long popularly regarded as the patron saint of France, is better known by the French form of his name, Denys or Denis. It was said in the sixth century that he was a missionary sent into Gaul in the year 250, who a few years later was beheaded at the place in Paris now called Montmartre, 'Martyrs' Hill'. A priest, Rusticus, and a deacon, Eleutherius, are supposed to have suffered with him.

By the middle of the ninth century a very strange legend had grown up round St Dionysius, in which three different people, living in different ages, were made into one man. The original martyr was said to have been sent to Gaul by Pope ◊ *St Clement I* at the end of the first century; he was identified with Dionysius the Areopagite, mentioned in the Acts of the Apostles, xvii, 34; and consequently he was also identified with the unknown late fifth-century author of certain famous mystical writings, which were for long erroneously attributed to Dionysius the Areopagite. In addition to this farrago, St Dionysius was claimed as a *cephalophore*, 'head-carrier': that is, one of those martyrs who was fabled to have carried his severed head to his place of burial, in this case to the site of the abbey church of Saint-Denys.

DOMINIC, founder of the Order of Preachers. B. at Calaruega, 1170; d. at Bologna, 1221; cd 1234; f.d. 4 August. The founder of the Friars Preachers was born of a Castilian family, and his early years were uneventful. When he was about twenty-six he became one of the canons regular who formed the cathedral chapter at Osma; in 1206 the turning-point of his life came, when his bishop, Diego, became unofficial leader of a papal mission to the heretical Albigenses, who were firmly established in Languedoc. The bishop chose Dominic as his companion; they lived simply and in poverty, and undertook discussions with their opponents for which they prepared very carefully. These methods contrasted with the formality and display of the official missioners, and a house of nuns founded at Prouille became the centre of the new preachers. The death of Bishop Diego at the end of 1207 coincided with the murder of the papal legate Peter de Castelnau by the Albigenses, and Pope Innocent III ordered a military campaign against their leader, Count Raymund of Toulouse. There followed five years of bloody civil war, massacre, and savagery, during which Dominic and his few followers persevered in their mission of converting the Albigenses by persuasion addressed to the heart and mind.

In 1215 Dominic was able to establish his headquarters in Toulouse, and the idea of an order of preachers began to take shape: a body of highly trained priests on a monastic basis, bound by vows with emphasis on poverty, but devoted to the active work of preaching and teaching anywhere and everywhere. The enterprise was formally approved at Rome in 1216, and in the following year the founder sent eleven of his brothers, over half the then total, to the University of Paris and to Spain. He himself established friaries at Bologna and elsewhere in Italy, and travelled tirelessly to superintend the nascent order, preaching as he went. St Dominic always gave importance to the help of women in his work: one of his last undertakings was to install nuns at San Sisto in Rome; another was to send thirteen of his friars to Oxford.

All the evidence goes to show that St Dominic was a man of remarkable attractiveness of character and broadness of vision; he had the deepest compassion for every sort of human suffering; he saw the need to use all the resources of human learning in the service of Christ; his constant reading was St Matthew's gospel, St Paul's letters and the *Conferences* of St John Cassian. The order that he founded was a formative factor in the religious and intellectual life of later medieval Europe; its diffusion is now world-wide. This saint was the subject of the song 'Dominique' that was so popular in 1963–4; his emblems are a star and a dog with a torch in its mouth.

M. H. Vicaire, *St Dominic and his Times* (1964); B. Jarrett, *Life of St Dominic* (1924).

DOMINIC SAVIO ◊ under *John Bosco*

DOMITILLA ◊ under *Nereus and Achilleus*

DONATUS OF FIESOLE, bishop. D. *c.* 876; f.d. 22 October. It is the tradition of Fiesole, near Florence, that Donatus was one of the many Irishmen who journeyed on the continent of Europe in the earlier middle ages. Returning from Rome, he arrived at Fiesole just when the local bishop's see was vacant, and was miraculously indicated to fill it. He is said to have been a teacher in the service of the Frankish kings, and there is a record of his giving in 850 the church and hospice named St Brigid's at Piacenza to the abbey founded by ◊ *St Columban* at Bobbio. Long afterwards it was alleged that Donatus had an Irish travelling companion who became his archdeacon, St Andrew of Fiesole, but there is no satisfactory evidence for Andrew's existence.

DONNAN, martyr. D. on Eigg, 617; f.d. 17 April. Donnan was an Irishman who established a community of monks on the island of Eigg in the Inner Hebrides. While he was celebrating Mass one Easter eve a gang of armed men arrived; when Mass was over, they herded the monks into a building, set fire to it, and slew them all. It is said that the deed was prompted by the local chieftainess, who resented the monks' presence on the island; but it may simply have been a Viking raid. The monks were looked on as martyrs, and there are a number of dedications in St Donnan's name in Scotland.

DOROTHY, martyr. D. *c.* 303 (?); f.d. 6 February. The story of St Dorothy as it has come down to us is legendary. It tells that she was a maiden of Caesarea in Cappadocia, who was arrested during Diocletian's persecution of Christians. Two apostate women were sent to pervert her, but she reconverted them, and was thereupon sentenced to be beheaded. As she was being led to execution a lawyer named Theophilus mocked her, asking her to send him flowers and fruit from the heavenly garden. Miraculously a child appeared with a basket of apples and roses, which she sent to Theophilus; he became a Christian in consequence, and was martyred too. Although said to have been a Cappadocian, St Dorothy's name is unknown in Eastern calendars. Her emblem is a laden basket.

DUBRICIUS, or DYFRIG, bishop. Sixth century; f.d. 14 November. He was an important church leader in south-east Wales and western Herefordshire, where he had centres at Hentland and Moccas; he was associated with ◊ St Illtyd and St Samson, and with the island of Caldey. In later medieval legends he becomes the 'archbishop of Caerleon' and crowns 'King' Arthur, and the ecclesiastical politics of the twelfth century claimed him as founder of the Normans' see of Llandaff, where he was one of the four titular saints of the cathedral. The reputed relics of St Dubricius were translated from Bardsey to Llandaff in 1120. He is the 'Dubric the high saint, Chief of the church in Britain' of Tennyson's Coming of Arthur, and the place-name Saint Devereux in Herefordshire is a corruption of the saint's name.

G. H. Doble, St Dubricius (1943).

DUNSTAN, bishop. B. near Glastonbury, c. 909; d. at Canterbury, 988; f.d. 19 May. St Dunstan was born ten years after the death of King Alfred; the churchman, as well as the king, deserves the epithet 'great'. Little is known of his earlier years: he was related to the royal family of Wessex, received a good education at Glastonbury, and would perhaps have followed a secular career had not a dangerous illness turned his eyes to more direct service of God as monk and priest. About 943 King Edmund I commissioned him to restore monastic life at Glastonbury, and from that moment dates the revival of organized monasticism in England, which had ceased to exist since the Scandinavian invasions. ◊ St Ethelwold and St Oswald of Worcester were associated with Dunstan in this work, which was fully supported by King Edgar. After this prince came to power in 957 Dunstan founded or refounded many abbeys (Malmesbury, Westminster, Bath, and Exeter among them), and c. 970 a conference of bishops, abbots, and abbesses drew up a national code of monastic observance, the Regularis Concordia. It was in line with continental custom and the Rule of St Benedict but with its own features: the monasteries were to be integrated into the life of the people, and their influence was not to be confined within their own walls.

St Dunstan was a principal adviser to all the Wessex kings of his time; he was banished abroad during the reign of the youthful Edwy, but Edgar recalled him, and in 959 he was made archbishop of Canterbury. The present coronation rite of the English sovereign derives from that compiled and used by Dunstan for the sacring of Edgar as king of all England at Bath in 973. Yet the sacred ministry, monastic organization, reform of church life, and secular statesmanship do not exhaust the aspects of this many-sided man. He was credited with dexterity as a metal-worker and bell-founder, he seems also to have been a skilful scribe and draughtsman, and he played the harp and loved the music of the human voice: when he sang at the altar, wrote a contemporary, 'he seemed to be talking with the Lord face to face'. As an old man at Canterbury it was his delight to teach the boys of the cathedral school – a gentle master, it would appear, whose memory was cherished by his pupils. His emblem in art is a pair of tongs.

D. J. V. Fisher, *The Earliest Lives of St Dunstan, St Ethelwold and St Oswald*, in preparation: E. S. Duckett, *St Dunstan of Canterbury* (1955).

DYFRIG ◊ under *Dubricius*

DYMPNA, martyr. Date unknown; f.d. 15 May. It was perhaps the discovery in the early thirteenth century at Gheel, near Antwerp, of the bones of an unknown man and woman that led to their local cultus. The legend that grew up about them is a classic example of a folk-tale adapted as the life-story of a saint. It relates that Dympna (the name was found on a brick with the coffins) was the daughter of a heathen Irish prince who, when his Christian wife died, conceived a perverted passion for his daughter. With her chaplain, Gerebernus, she fled abroad and settled at Gheel. Her father found her there and, when she refused to return home with him, slew her and the priest. Whether Dympna was in fact an Irishwoman is as it may be, but the identification of her with the Irish St Damhnait cannot be sustained.

Many alleviations of mental disorder, epilepsy, and the like were attributed to St Dympna's intercession, and she was soon regarded as patroness of the insane; by the end of the thirteenth century there was a hospital for such afflicted persons at Gheel. That medieval foundation is still in being, and has grown into one of the largest and most efficient colonies for the mentally sick in the world. A feature of its system is the boarding-out of suitable patients in private houses throughout the neighbourhood, thus integrating them into normal human society.

E

EADBURH, EADGYTH, EADMUND ◊ under *Edburga*, *Edith*, *Edmund*

EDBURGA OF MINSTER, abbess. D. 751; f.d. 12 December. St Edburga (Eadburh) succeeded ◊ *St Mildred* as abbess of Minster in Thanet. She is known chiefly from St Boniface's letters to her, in which he thanks her for books and other 'tokens of affection' she had sent him and for the 'spiritual light' conveyed in her letters.

St Edburga of Winchester (d. 960; f.d. 15 June) was a granddaughter of King Alfred, and abbess of the nunnery founded by his widow at Winchester. She was specially venerated at Pershore in Worcestershire, where her relics were enshrined. There were one or more other English saints of this name, not easily identifiable. They must all be distinguished from King Offa's daughter Eadburh, of whom curious stories were told.

Another abbess with a local popular cultus in the Midlands is *St Osburga* (f.d. 30 March); she is said to have been abbess of a convent at Coventry and to have d. *c.*1016, but there is nothing certain except the honour paid to her memory.

EDELBURGE ◊ under *Ethelburga*

EDITH OF WILTON, nun. B. at Kemsing 961 (?); d. at Wilton, 984; f.d. 16 September. St. Edith (Eadgyth) was the natural daughter of King Edgar and Wulfrida. Her mother took her as a baby to the nunnery at Wilton, near Salisbury, and she lived there all her short life, 'knowing not the world rather than forsaking it'. She refused the abbacy of Wilton and other convents, preferring, we are told, 'to serve her sisters in the most humble capacities, like Martha herself'.

St Edith of Polesworth and *St Edith of Tamworth* (tenth century?; f.d. 15 or 19 July) were probably one person, another royal saint but difficult to identify. Associated with the name of Edith of Polesworth is that of *St Modwenna* (f.d. 5 July), formerly venerated at Burton-on-Trent; she is an equally obscure character, and has been confused with the Irish *St Moninne* (f.d. 6 July), abbess of Killeavy, who was said to have been veiled by ◊ *St Patrick* himself.

EDME ◊ under *Edmund of Abingdon*

EDMUND, king and martyr. B. 841; d. 869; f.d. 20 November. He is said to have been chosen king of the East Angles while still a youth. In 869 a great host of Danes took up quarters at Thetford in Norfolk, and Edmund led his troops against them. The Englishmen were defeated and Edmund slain, probably after he had been taken prisoner. A later account, professing to derive at secondhand from an eye-witness, says that the king was captured at Hoxne in Suffolk; he refused to share his Christian kingdom with the heathen invaders, whereupon he was tied to a tree and shot with arrows, till his body was 'like a thistle covered with prickles'; then his head was struck off. Edmund was speedily revered as a martyr, and his cultus was widespread in the middle ages. His body was enshrined at Bury St Edmunds (St Edmund's borough), where a great abbey was founded in 1020. In *Past and Present*, bk ii, ch. 16, Thomas Carlyle translates and comments on the passage from Jocelin of Brakelond's chronicle describing the moving of St Edmund's relics to a new shrine in 1198. The king's emblem is an arrow.

F. Hervey, *History of King Eadmund the Martyr* (1929).

EDMUND OF ABINGDON, bishop. B. *c.* 1170; d. near Pontigny, 1240; cd 1246; f.d. 16 November. Edmund Rich was born at Abingdon of a prosperous family and was educated at the universities of Oxford and Paris. He was ordained priest, taught theology at Oxford, and was soon reputed to be a man of very virtuous life who experienced heavenly visitations. There are no certain dates or details forthcoming for these earlier years, but in 1222 he was appointed treasurer of Salisbury cathedral, and in 1233 was elected archbishop of Canterbury after three other candidates had been rejected by Pope Gregory IX. Edmund was essentially a teacher and preacher, a man of study and prayer, but his brief episcopate of seven years was passed in a turmoil of public affairs, with which he dealt reluctantly but resolutely. To lighten the burden he chose as his chancellor Master Richard of Wich, known to after ages as ♢ *St Richard of Chichester.*

Immediately after his consecration St Edmund was successful in averting civil war in the Welsh marches, and he brought about a reorganization of the government. But he was soon in difficulties with King Henry III over discrepancies between church law and the English common law, and was involved in serious disputes with the monastic chapter at Canterbury. In 1238 Edmund carried his case against the monks to Rome in person, but he was not destined to see the trouble finally resolved. Fresh difficulties arose with the king, and in the autumn of 1240 Edmund left England, probably intending to make a second visit to Rome. But he got no further than Soisy near Pontigny in Burgundy, where he died. St Edmund was a learned and a holy man, and a good if not great bishop: on his deathbed he called God to witness, 'I have sought nothing else but you.' Very little of his writing has survived, but his *Mirror of Holy Church* makes it clear that he is entitled to an honourable place among the English medieval mystics; in that treatise he sets out at various levels the contemplative's way to God. He was buried in the abbey church at Pontigny, where his body still lies; locally there he is called St Edme.

C. H. Lawrence, *St Edmund of Abingdon* (1959).

EDWARD THE CONFESSOR, king. B. at Islip, *c.* 1004; d. at Westminster, 1066; cd 1161; f.d. 13 October. He was the son of

Ethelred II, king of the English, and Emma, sister of Duke Richard II of Normandy, and he lived in that country from about his tenth year till he was recalled to England in 1041. In the following year he succeeded to the throne, and in 1045 married Edith, daughter of the ambitious and powerful Earl Godwin. Edward's reign was outwardly peaceful and he was a peace-loving man; but he had to contend with Godwin's opposition and other grave difficulties, and he did so with a determination that hardly supports the common picture of him as a tame and ineffectual ruler. His anonymous contemporary biographer gives a convincing portrait of him in his old age that has obscured the evidence concerning his middle life. After his death, movingly described by the biographer, a religious cultus of the king was slow in developing until after his actual canonization.

The belief that Edward was a saint was supported by his general reputation for religious devotion and for generosity to the poor and infirm, by the relation of a number of miracles (he was the first sovereign reported to 'touch for the King's Evil', scrofula), and, too, by the assertion that he and his wife were so ascetic as always to have lived together as brother and sister. Edward and Edith were certainly childless; but that this was due to life-long voluntary abstinence is unlikely in the circumstances of their marriage and is not supported by adequate evidence. St Edward was buried in the church of the abbey of Westminster, a small existing monastery which he had refounded and endowed with princely munificence; with one uncertain and obscure exception, he is the only English saint whose bodily remains still rest in their medieval shrine, which was set up in its present position behind the high altar in 1268. He is called 'the Confessor', that is, one who bears witness to Christ by his life, to distinguish him from the King Edward who follows. His emblem is a finger ring.

The early anonymous *Life*, ed. and tr. by F. Barlow (1961); id., *Edward the Confessor* (1970).

EDWARD THE MARTYR, king. B. c. 962; d. at Corfe, 978; f.d. 18 March. He was the son of King Edgar of England by his first wife, and succeeded his father in 975. Three years later he was assassinated at Corfe in Dorset, and quietly buried at Wareham. It is said that he was on his way to visit his half-brother Ethelred, when he was set upon by Ethelred's retainers and stabbed before he could dismount from his horse. The murderers may well have acted on their own initiative in the interests of their young master; it was not till a century later that it was openly stated that the whole thing was plotted by Edward's stepmother Elfrida, to put her son Ethelred on the throne. Supernatural manifestations were alleged in support of the charge. A year later Edward's body was translated from Wareham to the nunnery church at Shaftesbury, where he came to be venerated as a saint and martyr. He had not in fact died for religion, and he provides a good example of the honour due to a martyr being given to one who had simply suffered an unjust death. He can have been only about fifteen or sixteen at the time.

EDWIN ◊ under *Paulinus of York*

EGWIN, bishop. D. at Evesham, *c.* 717; f.d. 30 December. St Egwin, perhaps a member of the Mercian royal house, was appointed bishop of Worcester *c.* 692. He is remembered chiefly as the founder of the monastery at Evesham, which, after its refounding *c.* 975, became one of the great Benedictine abbeys of England. The occasion of Egwin's foundation is said to have been a vision of the Virgin Mary, seen first by the herdsman Eof and then by Egwin himself, in a meadow by the Avon. It is further said that the bishop had previously had to go to Rome to clear himself of accusations provoked by his pastoral strictness.

ELIAS and his companions, martyrs. B. in Egypt; d. at Caesarea Maritima, 309; f.d. 16 February. The story of these martyrs is recorded by the historian Eusebius, who was living at Caesarea at the time. They were five Christians from Egypt who out of kindness had accompanied some of their brethren who had been sentenced to forced labour for their faith in the quarries of Cilicia. On their way back the Egyptians were stopped and questioned at the gates of Caesarea in Palestine. They gave their names as Elias, Jeremy, Isaias, Samuel, and Daniel, and their city as Jerusalem (meaning the Jerusalem that is above). The governor ordered them to be tortured to extort more precise information; but they remained mute and were beheaded.

ELIGIUS, or ELOI, artisan and bishop. B. near Limoges, *c.* 588; d. at Noyon, 660; f.d. 1 December. He came of a modest Gallo-Roman family, and was apprenticed to the master of the mint at Limoges. In due course, coming to the notice of King Chlotar II, he was appointed to a similar post at Marseilles; on Chlotar's death in 629, Dagobert I became his patron, and Eligius acquired considerable influence with the king. He had a great talent for engraving and smithing, and gained sufficient wealth to found a monastery at Solignac and a convent for women in Paris. In 641 Dagobert chose him to be bishop of Noyon and Tournai. He discharged this office with vigour, especially in the foundation of religious houses and in missionary work among the heathen Frisians. St Eligius was an outstanding churchman of his day, a friend and counsellor of ◊ *St Bathild*, and very generous to the poor. Numerous works of art, especially reliquaries, were attributed to his workmanship, some of which still exist. He is the patron saint of smiths, farriers, and all kinds of metalworkers.

ELIZABETH ✧ under *Zachary*

ELIZABETH OF HUNGARY, princess. B. at Bratislava, 1207; d. at Marburg, 1231; cd 1235; f.d. 19 November. She was the daughter of King Andrew II of Hungary, and at the age of fourteen married the landgrave of Thuringia, Ludwig IV. The marriage had been arranged for political reasons, but it was also a love match, and the couple lived in great content with one another for six years; their home was at the Wartburg castle, near Eisenach, and they had three children. Then, in 1227, Ludwig went to join the crusaders assembling in Apulia, and died suddenly at Otranto (in parts of Germany he is popularly called St Ludwig). We are told that when the news reached Elizabeth she ran through the castle shrieking crazily. What followed is a matter of some uncertainty. It is commonly said that, in the depth of winter, with a baby at her breast, she was turned out of Wartburg castle by her brother-in-law. In any case, having provided for her children, a few months later she formally renounced the world, put on the dress of the third order of St Francis, and devoted herself to the care of the poor and sick at Marburg in Hesse.

Elizabeth had also put herself wholly under the direction of her confessor, Master Conrad of Marburg, a learned and able man but, on the kindest and most simple showing, one of deplorable insensitivity. He overshadowed the closing years of St Elizabeth's short life. His treatment of her was ruthless, at times brutal, and she admitted how much she feared him. But his methods did not break her spirit: she was humble and obedient, and bowed before every storm; and after it had passed she straightened up, strong and unhurt, like grass after heavy rain (the comparison is her own). Until her health failed St Elizabeth was tireless in serving the wants of those in need: the princess who made garments for them went fishing to get them food – she has ever been one of the most loved saints of the German people.

J. Ancelet-Hustache, *St Elizabeth of Hungary* (1964).

ELIZABETH, or ISABEL, OF PORTUGAL, queen. B. 1271; d. at Estremoz, 1336; cd 1626; f.d. 8 July. She was daughter of King Peter III of Aragón, and was named after her great-aunt, ✧ *St Elizabeth of Hungary*. At the age of twelve she was married to King Denis of Portugal, and the first of their two children was born seven years later. Denis was a strong and effective ruler; his wife seconded him by such public benefactions as the establishment of a hospital, a 'rescue home' for women, and an orphanage for foundlings. But the good sovereign was a bad husband, and

Elizabeth suffered much and patiently from his neglect and infidelities. She worked hard for reconciliation when their son Alfonso led an armed revolt against his father; but Denis unjustly suspected her motives and banished her to a fortress for a time. On other occasions she was more immediately successful in averting or ending strife among her royal kinsfolk. After she became a widow, in 1325, St Elizabeth retired to a house at Coimbra, near a Poor Clare convent she had founded, and devoted herself wholly to the service of God and the needy people of the neighbourhood. In 1336 her son, by then King Alfonso IV, went to war with Alfonso XI of Castile, and Elizabeth followed the Portuguese army in the field on her last task of peacemaking. She was successful; but the ordeal was too much for her and she died before she could return home.

ELIZABETH OF SCHÖNAU ◊ under *Hildegard*

ELIZABETH BICHIER DES ÂGES, foundress. B. near Poitiers, 1773; d. at Le Puy, 1838; cd 1947; f.d. 26 August. She was born at the Château des Âges and was christened Joan Elizabeth Mary Lucy, but was commonly called by the second name. During the French revolution Elizabeth was living with her widowed mother at La Guimitière in Poitou; in the absence of a regular priest, she organized secret meetings for worship among the faithful, and it was thus that she came in contact with ◊ *St Andrew Fournet*. The eventual result of their meeting was the establishment of a community of sisters to look after the sick and teach girls in the neighbouring countryside. It grew at an amazing speed: between 1811 and 1830 over sixty small convents were opened in Poitou and in southern France of these Sisters of St Andrew the Apostle (officially, Daughters of the Cross). Mother Elizabeth was a gentle but resolute woman, involved in much travelling, undaunted by difficulties, concerned simply for the good of others: 'There are ruins to be rebuilt, ignorance to be remedied,' Fournet had said to her. When he died in 1834, she received much help from a Basque priest, *St Michael Garicoïts* (cd 1947; f.d. 14 May), whom she encouraged in the founding of the society of missioners called Priests of the Sacred Heart of Bétharram.

ELMO ◊ *Erasmus*

ELOI ◊ *Eligius*

ELPHEGE ◊ *Alphege*

ELZEAR, layman. B. in Provence, *c.* 1285; d. at Naples, 1323; cd 1369; f.d. 27 September. This young nobleman while still a youth was married to an equally young heiress, Delphine of Signe. At the age of twenty-three he inherited his father's estates, principally Sabran in Provence and Arialdo in Apulia, and the management of these occupied much of his time; but he also served as tutor to the son of King Robert of Naples, and was sent to Paris on a diplomatic mission. His wife expressed nervousness for him at the French court, but he replied that he had kept his virtue in Naples and so had nothing to fear in Paris. Delphine shared his deep religious devotion, and in a rough age he was notably forbearing towards his subjects and fellows; some, indeed, complained that he was more fit to be a monk than for his duties in the outside world. St Elzear was only thirty-eight when he died, and he was cd by Pope Urban V, who was his nephew and godson.

EMERIC ◊ under *Stephen of Hungary*

EMILY DE RODAT, foundress. B. near Rodez, 1787; d. at Villefranche, 1852; cd 1950; f.d. 19 September. Emily de Rodat was brought up by her grandmother at the Château de Ginals. From the age of seventeen she occupied herself with various works of charity, and three times entered different convents but failed to settle down. With the help and encouragement of Abbé A. Marty, she in 1815 opened a free school at Villefranche-de-Rouergue; despite some opposition it was a success, and from it developed the congregation of the Holy Family of Villefranche, whose establishments are now found in many lands. Mother Emily directed it for thirty years, seeing the beginning of its extension and the widening scope of its work. Throughout these years she had to contend with chronic personal suffering, both physical and moral, and from 1835 she was deprived by his death of the support of Abbé Marty. A life of intense prayer brought her inward serenity; outwardly she appeared at times somewhat dour and intractable: 'a saint, but a headstrong saint', said a contemporary of her. But things in St Emily that may have seemed unpalatable were often the ripe fruit of religious wisdom and experience.

EMILY DE VIALAR, foundress. B. near Albi, 1797; d. at Marseilles, 1856; cd 1951; f.d. 24 August. From the age of fifteen to thirty-five this Emily looked after her widowed, and cantankerous, father, and ministered to the children and the needy on his estate at Gaillac in Languedoc. Then, in 1832, she was left a large legacy, and she bought a house at Gaillac from which her charitable work could be carried on in an organized way. Others joined her, and in 1835 she was invited to make a second foundation, in Algeria. There her work prospered and grew, until trouble arose with the bishop of Algiers, Mgr Dupuch – the difficult prelate of a difficult diocese. In 1842 he excommunicated Mother Emily; she was vindicated, but she and her communities had to go back to France. During the next dozen years Mother Emily's congregation spread to many parts of the world (including Jerusalem and Australia), and she personally established a number of the convents. The sisters are known as Sisters of St Joseph 'of the Apparition' (cf. Matt. i, 18–20). The Algerian affair was not the only serious trial in their early days; but St Emily was a very determined character, shrewd and vigorous, inspired by a love that a cardinal at her canonization called 'wise, understanding, and very sensitive'. 'Quietly to trust in God', she wrote, 'is better than trying to safeguard material interests – I learned that by bitter experience.'

ENDA, abbot. D. at Killeany, c. 530; f.d. 21 March. It is said that St Enda learned the principles of monastic life at a place called Rosnat in Britain, probably ◊ St David's foundation in Pembrokeshire or ◊ St Ninian's in Galloway. He organized his own settlement on Aranmore in Galway Bay, which is regarded as the first Irish monastery in the strict sense, 'the capital of the Ireland of the saints'. The island was given him by King Oengus of Munster, and his most famous disciple there was ◊ St Ciaran of Clonmacnois. The stories told of the earlier life of St Enda and of his sister St Faenche are unhistorical.

ENGELBERT, bishop. B. c. 1185; d. near Schwelm, 1225; f.d. 7 November. While still a boy he received several ecclesiastical benefices through family influence, and was appointed archbishop of Cologne in 1217. Engelbert's life was chiefly taken up with secular affairs of state, and he would hardly have received a saint's cultus had it not been for the circumstances of his death. His kinsman Frederick of Isemberg having abused his trust as administrator for the nuns of Essen, Engelbert deprived him of the office. Frederick plotted with other aggrieved noblemen and brought about the archbishop's assassination while on a journey.

EPHRAEM, poet and theologian. B. at Nisibis, c. 306; d. at Edessa, 373; f.d. 18 June. He was a deacon all his life, which was passed in his native Mesopotamia. In 363 he migrated from Nisibis to Edessa (Urfa in Iraq), whose important theological school was famous. Ephraem's fame rests on his writings, above all on his metrical homilies, to be read aloud, and his hymns for singing. The latter in particular were designed for popular use and were didactic in character, often directed against various false doctrines then current. Compositions attributed to him are still much used in the Syrian churches, and his reputation spread to the Greek-speaking world before his death. The English hymns 'Receive, O Lord, in Heaven above/Our prayers' and 'Virgin, wholly marvellous' are translated from St Ephraem's Syriac. He wrote commentaries on a considerable number of books of the Bible, and a personal 'Testament' which seems to have been added to by a later hand. All St Ephraem's work is elevated in style, 'flowery' in expression, and full of imagery: even as a theologian he wrote as a poet. He has always been regarded as a great teacher in the Syrian churches and many of his works were early translated into Greek, Armenian, and Latin. In 1920 Pope Benedict XV proclaimed him a doctor of the church.

EPIPHANIUS OF SALAMIS, bishop. B. in Palestine, *c.* 315; d. at sea, 403; f.d. 12 May. He came of a hellenized Jewish family, and while still a young man founded a monastery at Eleutheropolis (Beit Jibrin), which he directed for thirty years. In 367 he was elected bishop of Salamis, the principal see in Cyprus, and as bishop made his mark as a controversialist. He was a man of some learning, conservative in temper, and a fiery defender of orthodoxy; his attacks on the teaching of Origen earned him the friendship of ◊ *St Jerome.* But Epiphanius, too, was immoderate in his zeal and unable to use tact and discretion in his polemics. When he was nearly eighty he went to Constantinople to support Archbishop Theophilus of Alexandria in his campaign against ◊ *St John Chrysostom.* But he soon realized he was in a false position and, disillusioned, took ship to return to Cyprus. He died on the voyage. Among the writings of St Epiphanius is *The Medicine Box,* in which he sets out to refute all heresies, real or imagined, from the earliest times; according to him there were eighty of them, corresponding to the 'fourscore concubines' of the Song of Songs (vi, 8). Another work of his was a sort of encyclopedia of the Bible.

ERASMUS or ELMO, martyr. D. *c.* 303 (?); f.d. 2 June. The cultus of St Erasmus is attested at Formiae in Campania in the sixth century. His spurious 'acts' state that he was a bishop in Syria who, persecuted from place to place under Diocletian, eventually came to Formiae, where he died from his sufferings. A later legend said he was put to death by having his intestines wound out of his body on a windlass. Perhaps because of the resemblance of the windlass to a capstan, Erasmus came to be honoured as a patron saint of sailors; the name 'St Elmo's fire', given to the electrical discharges sometimes seen at the masthead of ships, refers to him, Elmo being a derivation from the name Erasmus. The light was taken as a sign of his protection. His symbol in art is a windlass.

ERCONWALD, bishop. D. *c.* 693; f.d. 30 April or 13 May. In 675 ◊ *St Theodore of Canterbury* appointed Erconwald bishop of the East Saxons, with his see in London. His shrine in St Paul's cathedral was much resorted to in the middle ages, but little is known of his life except that he founded a monastery at Chertsey and a nunnery at Barking. He appointed his sister ◊ *St Ethelburga* abbess of the latter. Erconwald took some part in the reconciliation of St Theodore with ◊ *St Wilfrid*.

ERIC, king of Sweden. D. at Uppsala, *c*. 1160; f.d. 18 May. He became king of a considerable part of Sweden in 1150, and designed to conquer and to convert to Christianity the neighbouring Finns. He was killed when a Danish prince, reinforced by Swedish rebels, attacked Uppsala. To help consolidate his position, Eric's son Cnut encouraged the cultus of his father as a martyr, and Eric was venerated as the national saint of the Swedes. The ancient belief in a special heavenly destiny, Valhalla, for those killed in battle doubtless had a part in the idealization of Eric and other Scandinavian heroes.

ESKIL, bishop and martyr. D. at Strängnäs, *c*. 1080; f.d. 12 June. Eskil is said to have been an Englishman and a relative of ◊ *St Sigfrid*, whom he accompanied on his mission to Sweden. He preached the gospel with some success in Södermanland, until a heathen reaction took place. Then, having protested against an idolatrous festival, he was stoned to death by the people. St Eskil was formerly greatly honoured in Sweden, and the place where he was buried, Eskilstuna, was named after him.

ETHELBERT OF KENT, king. B. *c*. 560; d. at Canterbury, 616; f.d. 25 February. This was the king who welcomed ◊ *St Augustine of Canterbury* and his monks when they arrived in Kent in 597. Ethelbert's wife Bertha, a Frankish princess, was a Christian, and he was soon converted; unlike many other newly-baptized monarchs of that and later ages, Ethelbert did not try to compel his subjects to follow his example. Instead he gave the missionaries every help and encouragement in peaceable preaching of the gospel. He built St Andrew's cathedral in Rochester and was instrumental in the conversion of the neighbouring King Sabert of the East Saxons, in whose territory he built the first cathedral of St Paul in London. St Ethelbert was the most influential ruler of his time in southern England; his code of laws for Kent is the earliest known legal document written in a Germanic language.

During the middle ages there was a considerable cultus as a martyr of another *St Ethelbert*, king of the East Angles; he was murdered at Sutton Walls in Herefordshire, apparently for dynastic reasons (d. 794; f.d. 20 May). Hereford cathedral is dedicated in his honour, with St Mary. In the same way the names of the Kentish princes *Ethelbert* and *Ethelred*, who were assassinated *c*. 670, found their way into some church calendars, on 17 October, and there seems to have been competition for the possession of their relics.

ETHELBURGA OF BARKING, abbess. D. *c*. 676; f.d. 12 October. Ethelburga (Æthelburh) was the sister of ◊ *St Erconwald*, and, as abbess of Barking in Essex, writes Bede, 'she showed herself in every way worthy of her brother, in holiness of life and constant solicitude for those under her care, attested by miracles from above'. He then relates certain wonderful occurrences at the nunnery in Ethelburga's time.

Another *St Ethelburga*, sister of ◊ *St Etheldreda*, was abbess of Faremoutiers-en-Brie (d. 665; f.d. 7 July). She is sometimes called Edelburge or Aubierge in France.

ETHELDREDA, or AUDREY, abbess. B. at Exning, *c.* 630; d. at Ely, 679; f.d. 23 June (B.C.P., 17 October). Etheldreda (Æthelthryth) was a daughter of King Anna of the East Angles; she is honoured liturgically as a virgin, though she was twice married, on the first occasion being widowed after three years. It is said that this marriage was never consummated; the second, to Egfrid, son of King Oswy of Northumbria, certainly was not. The young man got tired of a brother-and-sister relationship, but Etheldreda would not alter it and was supported in her refusal by ◊ *St Wilfrid*. So Egfrid released his wife, who took the veil under Wilfrid's aunt at Coldingham. She then went to the Isle of Ely, where she had previously lived in retirement for a time, and *c.* 672 founded a double monastery at Ely over which she presided till her death. The present Ely cathedral stands on its site. Bede wrote a long hymn in praise of St Etheldreda who, judging from the number of churches dedicated in her honour and of calendars containing her name, must have been the most revered of all Anglo-Saxon women saints. This was no doubt in great part due to the many marvels attributed to her intercession, which made her shrine at Ely an important pilgrimage centre. Etheldreda was succeeded as abbess by her sister *St Sexburga*, who had founded and governed a convent at Minster-in-Sheppey after the death of her husband, King Erconbert of Kent (d. *c.* 699; f.d. 6 July).

ETHELRED ◊ under *Ethelbert of Kent*

ETHELWOLD, bishop. B. at Winchester, *c.* 908; d. at Beddington, 984; f.d. 1 August. He became a monk at Glastonbury under ◊ *St Dunstan*, with whom he was associated in the tenth-century renewal of the English church. About 954 Ethelwold was entrusted with the re-establishment of Abingdon abbey, and in 963 was consecrated bishop of Winchester, where he ejected the secular clergy from the cathedral and the New Minster, putting monks in their place. In the years that followed he founded or re-founded a number of monasteries, including Peterborough, Ely and Thorney. He was in touch with continental monasticism, and it was he who drew up the *Regularis Concordia* (cf. Dunstan). He translated books into English, among them the Rule

119

of St Benedict, for the benefit of nuns who had no Latin. St Ethelwold was a bishop of tireless energy, who carried out reforms whatever the opposition; he was merciless to the slack, full of sympathy for the good-willed and the unfortunate, and his work had a lasting effect.

For a Life, ◊ under *St Dunstan.*

EUCHERIUS OF LYONS, bishop. D. *c.* 450; f.d. 16 November. He was a Gallo-Roman of high rank, married to a lady named Galla; they had two sons, both of whom became bishops and were numbered among the saints. In middle life, *c.* 422, Eucherius became first a monk at Lérins and then a hermit on the adjoining isle of Sainte-Marguerite, off Cannes; but his reputation for wisdom and virtue was such that he was called away to be bishop of Lyons, *c.* 435. He left a few writings, which include a letter on the solitary life and an account of the martyrs of the Theban Legion. His letter to a relative on disdain for worldly things was translated into English by Henry Vaughan, 'the Silurist', in *Flores Solitudinis.*

EUGENIA, martyr. Date unknown; f.d. 25 December. There is good evidence that St Eugenia was a martyr at Rome in the early ages, buried in the cemetery of Apronian on the Via Latina. But when her true story was forgotten there became attached to her name a legend of the ◊ *Pelagia the Penitent* type. It relates that she put on male dress and became abbot of a monastery in Egypt; she was accused of misconduct and cleared herself by declaring her sex; she then went to Rome, and, after various fabulous occurrences, was beheaded for her faith. This tale had a great success and spread over the Christian world, gathering further imaginative details as it went.

EUGENIUS OF CARTHAGE, bishop. D. at Albi, 505; f.d. 13 July. Eugenius was chosen to be bishop of Carthage in 481, at a time when the North African provinces were in the hands of the Arian Vandals; the task of his episcopate was to protect his persecuted flock, but most of it was spent in exile. In 484 King Huneric summoned the orthodox bishops to a conference with the Arians, and when they were assembled took the opportunity to deport all the Catholic leaders. Eugenius passed three years of hardship at Telmin in Tunisia. He was then allowed back, but in 497 was banished again, to southern France, where he died. A contemporary historian, Victor of Vita, recorded the trials and faithfulness of St Eugenius, and ◊ *St Gregory of Tours* preserved the text of a letter written in exile, in which Eugenius encourages his people to hold fast to the faith of their baptism. – There is a considerable number of other saints, mostly obscure, named Eugenius.

EULALIA, martyr. D. at Merida, 304 (?); f.d. 10 December.

Eulalia was the most celebrated virgin martyr of Spain, but not much reliance can be placed on her story as it has come down to us. It says that she was a twelve-year-old girl at Merida, who during Maximian's persecution rebuked the local magistrate for his activities against Christians. He tried to induce her to show honour to the gods, and on her refusal she was tortured and burnt to death. The Spanish poet Prudentius tells that a white dove seemed to fly out of her mouth and a fall of snow covered her dead body. Veneration for St Eulalia spread from Spain to Africa, Gaul, and Italy, and in England she is mentioned by ◊ *St Aldhelm*, and by ◊ *St Bede* in his hymn to St Etheldreda: 'Scorched by fierce flame, Eulalia endures.' It is now generally agreed that the martyred Eulalia of Barcelona is only a fictional duplicate of Eulalia of Merida.

EULOGIUS OF ALEXANDRIA, bishop. D. 608; f.d. 13 September. A Syrian priest from Antioch, in 580 he was elected patriarch of Alexandria. There is little information about his life, except that he was by speech and writing an energetic but temperate upholder of orthodox Christianity, especially against Monophysism. His particular interest is that he was the recipient of letters from Pope ◊ *St Gregory the Great*, whom he had met in Constantinople. One of them records the initial success of the monk Augustine's (◊ *Augustine of Canterbury*) mission to the heathen English, 'the Angli, living in a corner (*angulus*) of the world'; this, Gregory adds, shows how much can be done by prayer, and it should be an encouragement to the Alexandrians. One passage in this letter seems to imply that St Eulogius himself had had something to do with the sending of the mission to England.

EULOGIUS OF CÓRDOVA, martyr. D. at Córdova, 859; f.d. 11 March. It is known from the short biography by his friend Alvarus that St Eulogius was a well-read priest, learned in the Scriptures, of candid and kindly disposition. In 850 the African Moslems then occupying Córdova began to persecute Christians. Eulogius was arrested, seemingly at the instance of a treacherous bishop, and from prison he wrote an eloquent letter of encouragement to ◊ *SS. Flora and Mary*, also in prison. After they had been put to death, Eulogius was set free. During the next seven years he kept a record of the sufferings and death of those who were slain, the *Memorandum of the Saints*, and wrote a vindication of them as true martyrs. There had been a good deal of anti-Moslem agitation, and a church council at Córdova had had to warn Christians against deliberately provocative behaviour. St Eulogius was chosen to fill the vacant archiepiscopal see of Toledo; but he could not be consecrated, for in 859 he was again arrested, having given shelter to a formerly Moslem girl, St

Leocritia. 'Had you asked me, I would gladly have done as much for you,' Eulogius told the magistrate. He refused to apostatize, and accordingly the historian of martyrs was himself martyred, being beheaded four days before Leocritia whom he had tried to save. Their bodies rest together in the cathedral of Oviedo.

EUNAN ◊ *Adamnan*

EUPHEMIA, martyr. D. at Chalcedon, 307 (?); f.d. 16 September. There are many references to St Euphemia by ancient writers and churches were dedicated in her honour in many places, including Chalcedon, where the Council of Chalcedon was held in 451. She seems to have been a maiden martyr there, probably during Diocletian's persecution. But her extant 'acts' are worthless: they consist chiefly of a catalogue of the tortures which she miraculously survived, until she was thrown to wild beasts.

EUPHRASIA, nun. B. in Constantinople, *c.* 382; d. in Egypt, *c.* 412; f.d. 13 March. When Euphrasia (Eupraxia) was seven years old her widowed mother took her to live at Tabbenisi, in middle Egypt. At the child's wish she was left for a time with a group of dedicated women, and in the event spent the rest of her life with them. After her mother's death Euphrasia broke off her engagement (she had been betrothed to a senator's son at the age of five), gave the property she had inherited to the poor, and cut herself off from 'the world' altogether. She got rid of temptations to return to it by undertaking the hardest domestic jobs for the community, and by inflicting on herself such penances as going without food for a week on end. This made some of the sisters jealous and they accused her of being conceited and hypocritical; but Euphrasia won them over by her gentleness and patience.

EUPHRASIA PELLETIER, foundress. B. 1796; d. at Angers, 1868; cd 1940; f.d. 24 April. Rose Virginia Pelletier was born on the island of Noirmoutier, off the coast of Vendée, of parents who were refugees from the Vendée wars. When she was eighteen she joined the Institute of our Lady of Charity and Refuge at Tours, was made superioress of the house in 1825, and soon after was sent to make a new foundation at Angers. Having done this successfully, Mother Euphrasia returned to Tours; but experience had suggested to her the desirability of radical changes in her congregation's organization and she had now to meet strong opposition. She was accused of innovation, ambition, and insubordination; however, as was said of her, 'she was capable of ruling a kingdom'. Modestly and determinedly she rode the storm, and in 1835 official approval was given to the Institute of the Good Shepherd at Angers. Like its parent body, this congregation does rescue work for women and those in moral danger. During the thirty-three years St Euphrasia Pelletier directed it, 110 convents were opened in four continents, and today it numbers some 10,000 sisters.

G. Bernoville, *St Mary Euphrasia* (1959).

EUPHROSYNE. No date; f.d. 25 September. The legend of this young woman is a variation of that of ◊ *St Pelagia the Penitent*: to avoid marriage, she dresses as a man, calls herself Smaragdus, and joins a monastery near her native Alexandria; her own father does not recognize her, and continues to come to her for religious counsel over a period of thirty-eight years; when she is dying she reveals herself to him, and he succeeds to her cell in the monastery. There appears to be no evidence that this Euphrosyne ever existed, but her memory has been much honoured in the East.

EUPHROSYNE OF POLOTSK, recluse. D. at Jerusalem, 1173; f.d. 23 May. She was a daughter of Duke Svyatoslav of Polotsk in Byelorussia, and lived as a solitary in her native town from an early age. Having learned to write, she copied books and sold them for the benefit of her charitable works. Soon after 1170 she went on a long pilgrimage. At Constantinople the patriarch, Michael III, gave her the *eikon* of the Blessed Virgin afterwards called 'of Korsun', and she was received by the crusader King Amaury I in the Holy Land. St Euphrosyne died in Jerusalem, and her body was taken back to Kiev for burial.

EUPRAXIA ◊ *Euphrasia*

EUSEBIUS OF VERCELLI, bishop. B. in Sardinia; d. at Vercelli, 370; f.d. 16 December. He was brought up in Rome, became a priest there, and *c.* 340 was named bishop of Vercelli in Piedmont. In the earlier years of his episcopate St Eusebius was able to devote himself to the care of his flock, living with his clergy in an organized community; he is said to have been the first bishop to do this, and is particularly honoured by canons regular in consequence. But he was also a strong upholder of orthodoxy against Arianism, and in 355 was banished by Emperor Constantius for refusing to sign the condemnation of ◊ *St Athanasius* by the Council of Milan. For six years Eusebius was an exile in Palestine, Asia Minor, and Egypt, suffering much ill-treatment from those in charge of him (on one occasion he went on 'hunger-strike' for four days in protest). After his release in 361 he visited Alexandria and Antioch in a fruitless attempt to compose ecclesiastical difficulties there, and then returned to Italy. Here he met ◊ *St Hilary of Poitiers* and they worked together for a time in fighting Arianism. His last years were apparently passed in peace. There is treasured at Vercelli a very ancient manuscript of the gospels whose Latin text is earlier than ◊ *St Jerome*'s version; it seems likely that this manuscript was written by the hand of

St Eusebius. There is a considerable number of other saints of this name.

EUSTACE, martyr. Date unknown; f.d. 20 September. The legend of St Eustace relates that he was a general under Trajan, and that while out hunting near Tivoli he was converted to Christianity by a vision of a stag having a luminous crucifix between its antlers. His conversion brought disgrace and penury on him but, after various misadventures with his family, he was reinstated and led his troops in a victorious campaign. When called on to join in thanksgiving to the gods, he refused, and was roasted to death together with his wife and two sons. Eustace is not listed among the Roman martyrs, and there is no evidence for an early cultus of him in either West or East. The episode of the stag is found in the legends of other saints (e.g. ◊ *Hubert*), and in one form or another a similar incident is told in the folk-tales of several Asiatic peoples. It is probable that St Eustace is a wholly fictitious character.

EUSTOCHIUM, dedicated virgin. B. in Rome, *c.* 368; d. at Bethlehem, *c.* 419; f.d. 28 September. St Eustochium was one of the daughters of ◊ *St Jerome*'s friend ◊ *St Paula*, and in 385 she accompanied her widowed mother to live near Jerome in Bethlehem. For over thirty-five years Eustochium was a favourite pupil of his in religious life and learning: she learned Greek and Hebrew, and assisted him in his biblical work. On the death of Paula in 404, Eustochium took charge of the company of dedicated maidens and widows at Bethlehem. She was at its head when their residence was pillaged and burnt by a rabble, and she did not long survive the shock. Her sudden death, wrote Jerome, 'has upset me terribly, and almost changed my way of life, for old age is telling on me'. It is chiefly from Jerome's letters that St Eustochium is known. The longest of them was addressed to her, when she was about sixteen; it is really an informal treatise on the life of virginity, and a celebrated document in the history of monastic ideals. She was, Jerome says elsewhere, a woman of great spirit in a little body, and he attributes the writing of many of his biblical commentaries to her encouragement.

EUTHYMIUS THE ENLIGHTENER ◊ under *John the Iberian*

EUTHYMIUS THE GREAT, abbot. B. at Melitene, 377; d. in Palestine, 473; f.d. 20 January. His birthplace was in Armenia, and there he became a priest and was made a supervisor of monastic settlements. When he was about thirty he migrated to Palestine, where he lived a solitary life in various places, usually in a cave, finally settling in the desolate country between Jerusalem and Jericho. A number of recluses gathered round him, whose direction he undertook without giving up his own solitary mode of life.

St Euthymius was one of the most revered of the early Palestinian monks. He gained influence among the Arabs by his healing of the paralytic son of an important sheikh, and was consulted by Empress Eudokia, widow of Theodosius II.

EUTHYMIUS THE YOUNGER, abbot. B. near Ankara, c. 824; d. on Hiera, 898; f.d. 15 October. After being married for only a year, this Euthymius left his wife and baby in order to become a monk on Mount Olympus in Bithynia. The community was very disturbed by the troubles between the patriarch Ignatius at Constantinople and his rival ◊ Photius, and in 859 Euthymius sought a quieter life on Mount Athos. Here he lived alone in a cave for three years. Afterwards he sought solitude in an empty tower near Salonika, but left it because of the crowds who came to hear him preach. In 870 he re-founded a monastery at Peristera, east of Salonika, and later a convent of women; when these houses were firmly established he put them in charge of his grandson and granddaughter respectively, and returned to Athos. St Euthymius was credited with miraculous powers and the gift of prophecy, as related by his biographer Basil, who was one of his monks at Peristera. He died on the island of Hiera near Mount Athos.

EVURTIUS, bishop. Fourth century (?); f.d. 7 September. The name of this early bishop of Orléans figures in the calendar of the Book of Common Prayer, but nothing certain is known about him. He is said to have been a subdeacon at Rome, who was miraculously designated to the Gallic bishopric.

EWALD ◊ Hewald

EXPEDITUS. No date; f.d. 19 April. The name Expeditus has found its way into a few martyrologies and calendars, but there is good reason to believe that no such martyr ever existed. The invocation of the supposed saint as one to be called on in moments of urgency undoubtedly arose from a play on the word *expedite*, 'expeditiously' (there are many other examples of the same process). On the other hand, it is not true that the name Expeditus originated in the nineteenth century, when the word *spedito*, 'sent off', on the cover of a box of relics sent from Rome to a convent in Paris, was mistaken for the name of the saint whose relics were enclosed. Quite apart from the unlikelihood of this explanation, it is disproved by the fact that already in the eighteenth century 'St Expeditus' was invoked in Germany and Sicily in cases of pressing emergency.

EYSTEIN, bishop. B. in Norway; d. at Trondheim, 1188; f.d. 26 January. Eystein (Augustine) Erlendsson was the second archbishop of Nidaros, now called Trondheim. He was appointed in 1157, and during his long and energetic episcopate he sought to free the Norwegian church from the control of the nobility and to strengthen its relations with Rome. He was made papal legate by Pope Alexander III, and was instrumental in the enacting of equitable legislation and the establishment of houses of clergy living in common. St Eystein inevitably played an active part in the political affairs of his country, and because of his support of King Magnus V against his rival Sverre he had in 1181 to take refuge in England. He stayed at the abbey of St Edmundsbury, and it was probably there that he wrote his account of ◊ *St Olaf*, of which a manuscript was discovered in England. It is probable, too, that he visited the shrine of ◊ *St Thomas of Canterbury*, to whose memory he was very devoted. Eystein returned to Norway in 1183, and was reconciled with King Sverre. He died a few years later and his body was enshrined in Nidaros cathedral; in 1229 the Norwegian bishops in council declared him to have been a saint.

F

FABIOLA, Roman matron. D. in Rome, 399; f.d. 27 December. She was a member of the patrician family of the Fabii, and married a husband whose debaucheries provoked her to obtain a civil divorce. She then took another consort, contrary to the ordinances of the church, thus gravely scandalizing her fellow Christians in Rome. But both men died before long, and Fabiola was re-admitted to the church's communion after she had done public penance. She then completely forsook her luxurious way of life, devoted her wealth to good works, and in 395 travelled to Bethlehem to see ◊ *St Jerome*; she hoped to settle down there in a house of her own and share in the biblical work of Jerome's assistants. But she did not find the quiet life she was seeking, for which in any case she seems to have been temperamentally unsuited, since Jerome says that her idea of the solitude of the stable of Bethlehem was that it should not be cut off from the crowded inn. There were dissensions among the leading Palestinian Christians, and the Huns were threatening the country. With Jerome and his group she fled to Jaffa, and from there she went back to Rome.

Together with ◊ *St Paula*'s widowed son-in-law, ◊ *St Pammachius*, Fabiola threw herself with characteristic vigour into the establishing of a large hospice for sick and needy travellers at Porto. It was the first institution of the kind, and its fame spread rapidly. But it was not enough to occupy all St Fabiola's lively enthusiasm, and she seems at the time of her death to have been intending some new enterprise that would take her abroad.

FAITH, martyr. Date unknown; f.d. 6 October. Veneration of St

Faith was widespread in the middle ages, especially in England and France (Foi, Foy). She was perhaps a martyr at Agen in Aquitaine, at an unknown date, but the accounts of her passion are late and quite untrustworthy. A chapel in the crypt of St Paul's cathedral bearing her name commemorates the former parish-church of St Faith on the same site.

Another *St Faith* figures as the sister of *SS. Hope* and *Charity* (whose mother was St Wisdom (◊ *Sophia*)), all said to have been martyred in Rome under Hadrian (f.d. 1 August). This family is duplicated in the East. The concatenation of names is itself suspicious, and there is no good evidence that these martyrs had any but a legendary existence.

FARE ◊ under *Faro*

FARO, bishop. D. *c.* 672; f.d. 28 October. He was the son of a Burgundian nobleman, and for some years filled the office of chancellor to King Dagobert. When approaching middle age his sister persuaded him to receive holy orders, and by the year 637 he was bishop of Meaux. Faro's episcopate was a long one but little is known of it, or indeed of his life in general; Bede says that he gave hospitality to ◊ *St Adrian of Canterbury* when he was on his way from Rome to England.

St Faro's brother and sister are also venerated as saints. The brother, *St Cagnoald* (d. *c.* 635; f.d. 6 September), was a monk under ◊ *St Columban* at Luxeuil, and became bishop of Laon. The sister, *St Burgundofara* or *Fare* (d. *c.* 660; f.d. 3 April), took the veil after strong family opposition; the nunnery which she founded *c.* 627 and presided over for many years was afterwards well known, under the name of Faremoutiers. A reference made to Fare by Bede led long afterwards to the mistaken idea that she died in England.

FEBRONIA, martyr. No date; f.d. 25 June. Febronia is the heroine of a tale which relates that she was a dedicated maiden of extraordinary beauty at Nisibis in Mesopotamia. During Diocletian's persecution the prefect Selenus offered her freedom if she would renounce her religion and marry his nephew Lysimachus, a young man suspected of inclining towards Christianity. When Febronia refused she was tortured, mutilated, and battered to death; whereupon Selenus went mad and killed himself. Lysimachus and many of the spectators were converted and baptized. This story, which gained immense popularity, is not heard of before the seventh century and there is nothing to suggest that Febronia was more than a character in fiction.

FELICITY, martyr. Date unknown; f.d. 23 November. Felicity was a Roman martyr, put to death on 23 November in an unknown year, and buried in the cemetery of Maximus on the Salarian

127

Way; her story is lost. The traditional account asserts that she was a rich widow, with seven sons, all Christians. During the reign of Antoninus Pius they were arrested, and the sons followed their mother's example in refusing to sacrifice to the gods. They were then brought before four different judges and sentenced to die in differing ways, the mother last of all. The names of St Felicity's sons are given as *Felix, Philip, Martial, Vitalis,* ◊ *Alexander, Silvanus,* and *Januarius.* These were authentic martyrs, all on 10 July in a year or years unknown, buried at four different cemeteries in Rome; but there is nothing to connect them with one another or with St Felicity. The story above appears to be a fictional adaptation of that of the seven faithful Jewish brothers and their mother in II Maccabees, vii. The account of *St Symphorosa* and her seven sons (f.d. 18 July), martyrs in Rome, is so like that of Felicity that it may well be a doublet of it.

FELICITY ◊ *Perpetua and Felicity*

FELIX. Saints of this name are exceedingly numerous: sixty-seven are mentioned in the Roman Martyrology. Most of them are very obscure, and the few particulars recorded are often unreliable ◊ under *Gervase and Protase; Felicity.*

FELIX and ADAUCTUS, martyrs. Date unknown; f.d. 30 August. These two Roman martyrs were buried in the cemetery of Commodilla on the Ostian Way. We are told that, when the priest Felix was on his way to execution, a man in the crowd shouted that he too was a Christian and would die for Jesus Christ; he was seized and put to death with Felix. The second man's name was not known, so he was dubbed Adauctus, 'the additional one'. This story forms part of the legend about these martyrs that was worked up from their uninformative epitaph written by Pope ◊ *St Damasus.*

FELIX OF CANTALICE ◊ under *Ignatius of Laconi*

FELIX OF DUNWICH, missionary. B. in Burgundy; d. in England, 648; f.d. 8 March. This saint gives its name to the town of Felixstowe. He was a Burgundian bishop who was sent by ◊ *St Honorius of Canterbury* to preach the gospel in East Anglia. In 631 Felix established his see at Dunwich, a town on the Suffolk coast which has been almost wholly washed away by the sea. He laboured with much success for seventeen years. With the help of the king of the East Angles, Sigebert, he established a school for boys, obtaining teachers from the school at Canterbury. St Felix was buried at Dunwich, but later on his shrine was at Ramsey abbey.

FELIX OF NOLA, priest. B. at Nola; d. there *c.* 260; f.d. 14 January. This Felix was a priest, the son of a soldier, of Syrian origin, who lived in retirement at Nola, near Naples. In the year

250 Emperor Decius began to persecute Christians, and Felix attracted attention by his pastoral activity; he was arrested and treated with much brutality, but escaped from prison, miraculously, it was said. He then went in search of the bishop of Nola, Maximus, who had gone into hiding; he found him alone, ill and helpless, and carried him on his back to a house where he could be looked after. An attempt was made to arrest Felix again, but he eluded capture by hiding in a ruined building, where a spider's web spun across the entrance deceived the pursuers. On the death of Maximus the people wanted Felix to be their bishop, but he refused the office and lived out his life as a simple priest, revered for his goodness and his sufferings under persecution. The little that is known about St Felix derives chiefly from the poems of another saint of Nola, ◊ *Paulinus*, who wrote over a hundred years later, and built a new church in his honour; at that time crowds of people came from distant parts to visit the burial place of Felix.

FELIX OF THIBIUCA, bishop and martyr. D. at Carthage, 15 July 303; f.d. 24 October. The bishop of Thibiuca in north Africa was one of the earliest victims of the measures taken by Emperor Diocletian in restraint of Christianity. The first edict ordered, among other things, the destruction of all Christian writings, and Bishop Felix was told to hand in the sacred books to the authorities. He refused, and maintained his refusal before the proconsul at Carthage: 'It is better that I should be burned,' he said, 'than that the holy Scriptures should be treated thus; it is better to obey God rather than men.' He was executed for his disobedience, and buried at Carthage. The early account of the passion of St Felix was later interpolated with a story that he was handed over by the proconsul to the praetorian prefect, who conveyed him to Italy. There Felix repeated his refusal, and was beheaded at Venosa in Apulia. This addition is wholly fictitious.

FELIX OF VALOIS ◊ under *John of Matha*

FERDINAND III OF CASTILE, king. B. near Salamanca, 1199; d. at Seville, 1252; cd 1671; f.d. 30 May. He was the son of King Alfonso IX of León and Berengaria of Castile, who was a granddaughter of Henry II of England; by his second wife, Joan of Ponthieu, Ferdinand had a daughter, Eleanor, who married Edward I of England. He became king of Castile in 1217 and of León in 1230, a union of kingdoms that was henceforth unbroken. His reign was of the greatest importance in Spanish history, for he undertook the campaigns which wrested the greater part of Andalusía from the Moors and incorporated it in the Christian state. Ferdinand founded the university of Salamanca, and perhaps had a part in the beginning of that of Valladolid. At his death he was popularly acclaimed a saint, but he was not formally recognized as such till over four hundred years later. His emblem in art is a greyhound.

FERGAL ◊ *Virgil*

FIACRE, hermit. Seventh century; f.d. in Ireland, 1 September. The original name of this saint is undetermined but it was probably Fiachra, a name known in Ireland, where he is said to have been born. Coming into France, he was kindly received by ◊ *St Faro* at Meaux, who gave him a piece of land on which to build a hermitage; the town of Saint-Fiacre-en-Brie now stands on the site of the adjoining hospice for travellers which Fiacre established. He was very strict in excluding women from his own enclosure, and stories are told of the misfortunes that befell those who trespassed, even after his death. His chapel and his shrine, eventually at Meaux, were much resorted to by the sick for many centuries; his intercession was invoked especially by persons suffering from haemorrhoids. On the other hand Fiacre is also looked on as a patron saint of gardeners, because of the fine vegetables he grew around his hermitage. When cabs for hire first appeared on the streets of Paris in 1620 their stand was close by the Hôtel Saint-Fiacre: hence the name *fiacre* for the French four-wheeler. St Fiacre's emblem in art is a spade.

FILUMENA ◊ *Philomena*

FINAN, missionary. D. in Northumbria, 661; f.d. 17 February. An Irish monk of Iona, who succeeded ◊ *St Aidan* as bishop of Lindisfarne in 651 and carried on his missionary work sucessfully south of the Humber. In particular he baptized the king of the Middle Angles, Peada, son of the obstinately heathen Penda, and the king of the East Saxons, Sigebert, sending Diuma, an Irishman, and St Cedd to spread the faith among their respective peoples. St Finan upheld the Celtic dating of Easter and strongly resisted those, from Kent or abroad, who were to him innovators in this matter.

FINBARR, abbot-bishop. D. *c.* 633; f.d. 25 September. St Finbarr, or Barr, was probably a native of Connacht but was active in Munster, and he is venerated as the founder of the monastery and episcopal see of Cork. His name is associated with that of ◊ *St David*, whom he is supposed to have visited in south Wales, but it is very unlikely that they really made a pilgrimage to Rome together. The accounts of Finbarr include several preposterous wonders, as that he crossed the Irish Sea on horseback. He is said to have died at Cloyne, but his body was taken to Cork for burial.

FINNIAN OF CLONARD, abbot-bishop. D. *c.* 549; f.d. 12 December. This Finnian was outstanding among the saints of Ireland in the era after ◊ *St Patrick*, and was the traditional initiator of the monastic movement in the stricter sense in that country. He had close relations with the British church, and developed his monastery at Clonard, in Meath, in the light of the teaching of ◊ *St Cadoc* and *St Gildas*. It soon became famous as a school of religious life and learning: its founder was 'the master', 'the teacher of saints', and disciples gathered round him in large numbers, including some who in turn were to become celebrated religious leaders, such as ◊ *St Ciaran of Clonmacnois*, *St Columba of Iona*, and *St Brendan the Voyager*. It is not known beyond doubt whether St Finnian was a bishop, as well as abbot. He died of the 'yellow plague' during the epidemic in the middle of the sixth century. The contemporary collection of regulations for penitents, ascribed to one Vinnianus, was probably not drawn up by this Finnian but perhaps by the one that follows below.

FINNIAN OF MOVILLE, abbot-bishop. D. *c.* 579; f.d. 10 September. He is said to have done part of his training at the monastery founded by ◊ *St Ninian* in Galloway, and to have left there because of complications over a Pictish girl who had fallen in love with him. He is supposed then to have gone to Rome, where he was ordained priest. Eventually he formed a community at Moville in his native Ulster, where a great school grew up. There are several references to Finnian's love for books, and he is credited with bringing a new Latin biblical text from Rome; but the story of his quarrel with ◊ *St Columba* over an unauthorized transcription may well be fictitious.

St Finnian of Moville is sometimes identified with *St Frigidian* or *Frediano* (f.d. 18 March), who is venerated at Lucca in Italy. He was a sixth-century bishop there and is reputed to have been an Irishman from Ulster, but that the two men were one has not been established.

FINTAN OF CLONEENAGH, abbot. D. 603; f.d. 17 February. The high repute of this Irish abbot was due above all to the poverty and austerity of his life and that of his monks at Cloneenagh, near Maryborough in Leix. Their most luxurious food was vegetables (Fintan himself subsisted on stale barley bread and muddy water), and their husbandry was carried on with the simplest tools, without the use of any animal. Some neighbouring monks were moved to protest against such rigour; but Fintan answered them with all the courtesy and gentleness that seem to have marked his dealings with people. ◊ *St Columba of Iona* had a great regard for him, and is said to have described his physical appearance: a handsome holy-looking man, with ruddy cheeks and shining eyes, his hair flecked with white.

Other saints of this name are *Fintan*, or *Munnu*, of Taghmon

(d. 635; f.d. 21 October), who was for a time on Iona and then founded a monastery at Taghmon in Co. Wexford; and *St Fintan of Rheinau* (d. 878; f.d. 15 November): when a youth he was carried off from Leinster by raiders, became a wandering pilgrim on the continent, and spent his later years with some hermits at Rheinau, near Schaffhausen on the Rhine.

FLAVIAN OF CONSTANTINOPLE, bishop. D. in Lydia, 449; f.d. 18 February. Flavian was made archbishop of Constantinople in 446, and at once fell out with the imperial chamberlain, Chrysaphius, who sought by intrigue to get him removed from office. At a council held by Flavian in 448 the abbot Eutyches (godfather of Chrysaphius) was degraded from the priesthood for his erroneous teaching about the person of Christ. Eutyches appealed to Rome, and Pope ◊ *St Leo the Great* addressed a letter to Flavian setting out orthodox doctrine on the matter, a letter famous in history as the 'Tome of Leo'. The emperor, Theodosius II, summoned a council to deal with the dispute. It met at Ephesus in 449, under the presidency of Archbishop Dioscorus of Alexandria, and its proceedings were so disorderly that Pope Leo dubbed it 'the robber council', a name which has stuck. Dioscorus supported Eutyches; Flavian was ill-treated and deposed, and died very soon after in prison at Hypepe in Lydia. He is sometimes called a martyr, on the ground, apparently mistaken, that his death was the immediate and direct result of being beaten up by the emperor's soldiers at Ephesus. St Flavian was vindicated at the Council of Chalcedon in 451, and the date of his feast commemorates the bringing of his body to Constantinople by ◊ *St Pulcheria* in that year.

FLORA and MARY, martyrs. D. at Córdova, 851; f.d. 24 November. It was to these young women that ◊ *St Eulogius of Córdova* addressed his 'Exhortation to Martyrdom' during the persecution in Spain under the African Moslem ruler Abd ar-Rahman II. Flora was denounced by her Moslem brother; she was whipped, and handed back for him to keep in order. But she escaped from home and, with a girl named Mary, defiantly gave herself up to the magistrate. He shut them in a cell, threatening to sell them into prostitution if they would not apostatize: 'They threaten you with a shameful slavery,' Eulogius wrote to them, 'but do not fear: no harm can touch your souls whatever infamy is inflicted on your bodies.' They remained firm and were beheaded together. Their story is known from the account written by St Eulogius.

FLORUS and LAURUS, martyrs. Date unknown; f.d. 18 August. It is very doubtful whether these martyrs ever existed; or they may, with their two companions, be doublets of the ◊ *Four*

Crowned Martyrs. They are heroes of a Greek tale, according to which they were twin brothers, both of them stonemasons by trade. They were employed in the building of a heathen temple in Illyricum; but, having been converted to Christianity, they cast down the idolatrous images and handed over the building for Christian worship. Thereupon Emperor Licinius ordered them to be put to death, and with their employers Proculus and Maximus they were drowned in a well.

An attempt has been made to show that the veneration of Florus and Laurus, and of certain other saints, is a survival of the worship of the Dioscuri, Castor and Pollux, the sons of Zeus. This theory was demolished by H. Delehaye in his *Legends of the Saints* (London, 1962). Cf. ◊ *Cosmas and Damian*.

FOI ◊ *Faith*

FOILLAN, abbot. B. in Ireland; d. near Nivelles, 655; f.d. 31 October. Among the brothers of ◊ *St Fursey* were St Foillan and *St Ultan* (d. 686; f.d. 1 May), who came with Fursey to England and were missionary monks under him among the East Angles. When Fursey departed to Gaul, Foillan succeeded him as abbot, but the depredations of the Mercians drove him and Ultan to follow their brother across the sea. Abbess Itta of Nivelles gave Foillan land at Fosses, where he set up a monastery and did missionary work among the people of the surrounding country, on whom he made a lasting impression. He kept up close relations with ◊ *St Gertrude*'s establishment at Nivelles, and this was the occasion of his untimely end: it was when returning from a visit to Nivelles that he was set on by robbers in the forest of Seneffe and murdered, with three companions. Their bodies were not found till nearly three months later. Ultan succeeded Foillan as abbot of Fosses, and he too was revered there as a saint.

FORTY MARTYRS, THE. D. at Sebastea, 320; f.d. 9 or 10 March. When in the year 320 Emperor Licinius suddenly commanded all Christians in the East to repudiate their religion on pain of death, there were among those who refused forty soldiers of the twelfth, 'Thunder-struck', legion. They were of several nationalities, and at the time were stationed at Sebastea in Armenia (now Sivas in Turkey). Efforts to win them over by persuasion having failed, it was ordered that they should be stripped naked, herded on to a frozen pond, and kept there; to help break down their resistance a fire was kindled and warm baths prepared where they could see them. By the next day most of them were dead; those who were not were then killed, including the youngest, Melito, whose widowed mother encouraged him to the last. Only one of the forty failed in the atrocious ordeal, and we are told that his place was taken by another soldier, who was moved by his comrades' example, and by a dream of angels, to declare himself a Christian. But doubts can be cast on this story.

The term The Forty Martyrs is also used of a group of the many English and Welsh Roman Catholics who suffered death for conscience's sake during the 16th and 17th centuries; these forty were canonized in 1970. They include Edmund Gessings, John Kemble, Cuthbert Mayne, John Southworth (priests); Ambrose Barlow, John Houghton, John Roberts (monks); John Wall, John Stone (friars); Edmund Arrowsmith, Edmund Campion, David Lewis, Robert Southwell (Jesuits); Margaret Clitherow, Richard Gwyn, Philip Howard, Ann Line, Swithun Wells (lay people).

R. Challoner, *Memoirs of Missionary Priests* (1924 ed.); E. Waugh, *Edmund Campion* (1935); C. Devlin, *Robert Southwell* (1967); ed. F. W. Steer, *Life of St Philip Howard* (1970).

FOUR CROWNED ONES, THE, martyrs. D. at Sirmium, 306 (?); f.d. 8 November. Much has been written about the puzzle of the saints in whose honour is dedicated the church of the Quattro Coronati on the Caelian Hill at Rome: two irreconcilable groups, with different names and in different places, seem to be involved. The most convincing explanation is that they were five men who were martyred in Pannonia, one of whom, Simplicius, was un-accountably omitted; some time after their relics had been brought to Rome and interred on the Via Labicana, a legend was fabricated in which four Roman soldiers were represented as having been martyred under Diocletian for refusing divine honours to an image of Aesculapius in the Baths of Trajan.

According to the Pannonian account, the five men, named Simpronian, Claudius, Nicostratus Castorius, and Simplicius, were all very skilled stone-carvers. At Sirmium (Mitrovica), hav-ing refused to carry out the Emperor Diocletian's order to supply a statue of Aesculapius, they were commanded to offer sacrifice to the Sun-god. At their refusal they were put to death, by being shut up alive in leaden boxes and thrown into the river. The late fourth-century account of them is of special interest for what it tells about the imperial quarries and workshops in the moun-tains near Sirmium; and also because it gives a more human picture of Diocletian than that of the bloodthirsty tyrant com-monly presented in the passions of martyrs. Working masons of the middle ages held the Four Crowned Ones in special honour, and this has been perpetuated in English Freemasonry; there is a Quatuor Coronati lodge in London which for seventy-five years has published its annual volume of 'transactions' under the title of *Ars Quatuor Coronatorum*. There was already a chapel of the Four Crowned Martyrs in Canterbury in the year 619.

FOY ▷ Faith

FRANCES OF ROME, laywoman and foundress. B. in Rome, 1384; d. there, 1440; cd 1608; f.d. 9 March. St Francesca Romana was a daughter of the Roman aristocracy, and at the age of thirteen married Lorenzo de' Ponziani; they had several children, two at least of whom died young. From an early age Frances was of an ascetic disposition, with a strong feeling for the sufferings of others, and recurring epidemics of plague and civil war gave ample scope for her charitable activities. The Ponziano mansion was pillaged by the troops of Ladislas of Naples in 1409, and Lorenzo had soon to seek refuge elsewhere, leaving Frances in charge; when at length he could return from exile in 1414 he was a broken man, whose care was cheerfully added to his wife's other responsibilities. A number of Roman ladies shared her ideal of a life of self-denial and good works 'in the world', and these she organized into a society in 1425. Eight years later she established a community, in association with the Benedictine monks of Monte Oliveto; its members came to be known as the Oblates of Tor de' Specchi, from the house in which they lived.

In 1436 Lorenzo died, after a married life of forty years without a quarrel. St Frances was now without family ties, and she withdrew to the Tor de' Specchi, where she directed the community for her remaining four years. Her biographers record many particulars of her life – mystical experiences, revelations, angelic visitations – some of which pose historical and theological problems of no little difficulty. She had unquestionably been a religious power in Rome, and Pope Eugenius IV in particular had great respect for her. The community which she founded still flourishes and the former Palazzo Ponziano is a place of pilgrimage.

F. P. Keyes, in *Three Ways of Love* (1964).

FRANCES CABRINI, foundress. B. at Sant' Angelo Lodigiano, 1850; d. at Chicago, 1917; cd 1946; f.d. 13 November. Frances Xavier Cabrini (christened Francesca Maria) was the youngest of the thirteen children of a substantial farmer in Lombardy. After qualifying as a school-teacher she applied for admission to two convents, but was refused by both on the ground of insufficiently good health. She was then given charge of a small orphanage at Codogno, and in 1880 founded the Missionary Sisters of the Sacred Heart, which soon had other convents in northern Italy. Mother Cabrini had always wanted to work in China, but her attention became directed to the urgent needs of Italian immigrants in America; in 1889 she landed in New York, with six of her sisters, and established their first American convent and orphanage in face of tiresome obstacles.

Mother Cabrini found English a difficult language to learn; she was ignorant of Protestants and at first prejudiced in their

135

regard; her inflexibility sometimes led her into untenable positions; many of the American Italians were in a deplorable state, and very unpopular. But she rose above all handicaps, personal or external. In the course of twenty-eight years she opened schools and charitable establishments across the United States, including four great hospitals; she introduced her sisters into several countries of South America and into France, Spain, and England; and six times she had to revisit Italy. The troubles and opposition attendant on these foundations were heavy, and the amount of travelling involved was not the least of her trials – since a childhood accident she had had a fear of water. Her attitude to every difficulty was: 'Who is doing this? We? – or our Lord?' But she cultivated the efficiency of herself and her sisters to the utmost, and her determination and business acumen in the cause of charity won the respect of the most hard-headed and hard-hearted Americans. The work begun for Italian immigrants was carried on for all without distinction (including the convicts in Sing-Sing prison), and she herself became a naturalized American at Seattle. St Frances Cabrini was the first citizen of the United States to be canonized as a saint, and in 1950 Pope Pius XII named her patroness of all emigrants, sixty-three years after Leo XIII had pointed out the way to her: 'Do not go to the East, but to the West.'

A Stanbrook nun, *Frances Xavier Cabrini* (1944).

FRANCIS OF ASSISI, founder of the Friars Minor. B. at Assisi, *c*. 1181; d. at Porziuncola, 1226; cd 1228; f.d. 4 October. Francesco Bernardone was the son of a wealthy merchant draper, and as a youth led a frivolous, carefree life with other young sparks. Experience of sickness and civil warfare steadied him; and then one day in the church of San Damiano he seemed to hear an image of Christ say to him: 'Francis, repair my falling house.' He, characteristically, took the words literally, selling a bale of goods taken from his father's warehouse to pay for repairing San Damiano. The upshot was that his father disinherited and disowned him, and Francis went away penniless 'to wed Lady Poverty'. Three years later, in 1210, Pope Innocent III authorized him and eleven companions to be roving preachers of Christ in simplicity and lowliness. Thus began the Friars Minor, 'Lesser Brothers'. Their headquarters was the Porziuncola chapel at Santa Maria degli Angeli, near Assisi, recruits flocked in, and another friary was begun at Bologna. Up and down Italy the brothers called the people, high and low, to faith and penitence; they refused even corporate ownership of property, human learning, and ecclesiastical preferment: at first but few of them were in holy orders (St Francis himself was never a priest). In 1212 he founded with ◊ *St Clare* the first community of Poor Ladies, and twice at this time he made abortive attempts to become a missionary among the Moslems. This desire had some measure of fulfilment in 1219 when he accompanied the crusaders of Gautier de Brienne to Egypt; he made appeal in person to Sultan Malek al-Kamel, but had no success with either Saracens or crusaders, and after visiting the Holy Land he came back to Italy.

Already in 1217 the new movement was beginning to develop into a religious order; it had so many members that it was divided into provinces, and groups of friars were sent to countries outside Italy, including England. Soon after his return from the East, Francis resigned his headship. But during his absence there had been certain innovations among the brothers; accordingly, with the support of his good friend Cardinal Ugolino, he in 1221 produced a revised version of the rule, which reiterated the poverty, humbleness, and evangelical freedom of which he had always set the example. But before being finally approved this rule had to be somewhat modified and formalized, to meet varying opinions in the order. In 1224, while he was praying on Monte La Verna in the Apennines, there appeared on St Francis's body scars corresponding to the five wounds of the crucified Christ (the phenomenon called 'stigmatization'). They never left him, and were one of the sources of the physical pain and weakness he suffered increasingly until he welcomed 'Sister Death' two years later.

During the past hundred years, in particular, admiration of St Francis has been widespread and spontaneous among Christians of all communions and among others too: he has, indeed, often been acclaimed for reasons that would have startled him and moved him to protest, and he has been made the hero of a spurious romanticism. There is a compelling appeal in his *Canticle of the Sun* and in what we are told about him by the *Little Flowers of St Francis* (Penguin edn) and the *Mirror of Perfection*; in his simplicity, directness, and single-mindedness; and in the lyrical qualities of his life. But he was something more and other than an inspired individualist: he was a man of tremendous spiritual insight and power, whose consuming love for Jesus Christ and redeemed creation found expression in all he said and did. St Francis is often shown in art with the stigmata.

L. Sherley-Price, *St Francis of Assisi: his Life and Writings as recorded by his Contemporaries* (1959); Fr Cuthbert, *Life of St Francis* (1948); books by J. R. H. Moorman (1950); G. K. Chesterton (1951); J. Holland Smith (1972).

FRANCIS OF CAMPOROSSO ◊ under *Ignatius of Laconi*

FRANCIS OF PAOLA, founder. B. at Paola, in 1436 (?); d. at Plessis-lez-Tours, 1507; cd 1519; f.d. 2 April. For a short time as a youth this Francis was with the Friars Minor, but left them to live a hermit's life in a cave by the sea, near his birthplace, Paola in Calabria. As time passed he was joined by others, a regular religious house was opened, and the community developed into an order of friars, called Minims (*Minimi fratres*, the 'least brethren'). Their rule of life was notably austere, and their founder became known for his spiritual powers, especially his gift of reading minds. His reputation spread to France, and in 1482 he was summoned to Plessis-lez-Tours to succour King Louis XI, who was facing death in a state of superstitious terror. Francis lived in France for the rest of his life, establishing his order at Plessis, Amboise, Paris, and elsewhere, with the help of Louis's son, Charles VIII. The order of Minims still exists; but, unlike his namesake of Assisi, St Francis of Paola made no strong mark on his own or subsequent ages.

FRANCIS BORGIA, Jesuit. B. at Gandia, 1510; d. in Rome, 1572; cd 1671; f.d. 10 October. The name of Borgia (Borja) is understandably ill-sounding: this Francis was outstanding among those who brought honour to it. He was a great-grandson of the man who became Pope Alexander VI of unhappy memory, and his father was duke of Gandia in the Spanish province of Valencia. Francis married Eleanor de Castro, by whom he had eight children, and in 1539 he was appointed imperial viceroy in Catalonia. He proved a model governor; but he was not acceptable to everybody, on account of his determined efforts to suppress corrupt administration of justice by the nobility and magistrates. His wife died in 1546, and in the following year he was received privately into the Society of Jesus; having made over his titles and estates to his eldest son, and provided for his other children, he was ordained priest in 1551. He did all he could to make men forget his exalted origins, but his abilities could not be hidden; he preached successfully in Spain and Portugal, and in 1554 ◊ St Ignatius Loyola made him commissary for those countries. In this office Francis popularized the then little-known Society of Jesus, founding numerous houses and colleges, and attracting many good recruits.

In 1561 Francis Borgia was summoned to Rome and four years later was appointed father general of the Jesuits. The order made great progress during his short rule; he has, indeed, been called its second founder. He was particularly concerned with the improvement of the Roman College (now the Gregorian University), which he had already partially endowed. In 1571 Pope ◊ St Pius V chose St Francis to accompany a mission to several European capitals; his reputation had preceded him, and crowds gathered, shouting: 'We want to see the saint' and clamouring to hear him preach. But the fatigue entailed aggravated his failing health, and he died a few days after getting back to Rome. In his last moments, as his brother Thomas rehearsed their names, Francis pronounced a blessing on each of his children and grand-children. He was typical of the patrician saints, self-effacing, determined, enterprising, winning people of all ranks by his kindness and courtesy.

M. Yeo, *The Greatest of the Borgias* (1936).

FRANCIS CARACCIOLO ◊ under *Cajetan*

FRANCIS DI GIROLAMO, Jesuit. B. near Taranto, 1642; d. at Naples, 1716; cd 1839; f.d. 11 May. He was ordained a priest among the parochial clergy of Naples, but at the age of twenty-eight offered himself to the Society of Jesus. He was duly pro-fessed, and from 1676 till his death worked in Naples and as a rural missioner in the surrounding country. His very effective preaching was marked by brevity and vigour: he was, it was said, 'a lamb when he talks and a lion when he preaches'. In search of sinners he penetrated into the prisons, the brothels, and the galleys, and continued his mission in hamlets, back lanes, and at street corners. He converted a number of Moorish and Turkish prisoners to Christianity; but his most spectacular peni-tent was a Frenchwoman who had murdered her own father and then disguised herself as a man and served in the Spanish army. He rescued many children from dangerous surroundings, opened a charitable pawnshop, and organized an association of working-men to help the Jesuit fathers in their labours. Many miraculous cures were attributed to St Francis, and at his funeral all the poor of Naples thronged round the coffin.

FRANCIS DE SALES, bishop and writer. B. near Annecy, 1567; d. at Lyons, 29 December 1622; cd 1655; f.d. 29 January. This great bishop was a Savoyard, born in the Château de Sales at Thorens; he studied at Annecy, Paris, and the university of Padua and in 1593, after some opposition from his father, he was ordained priest. His first mission, a hard and even physically dangerous one, was to the people of his native Chablais country, who had gone over to Calvinism. The spirit in which Francis went to them is shown by his own saying, that whoever preaches with love preaches effectively; by the end of four years most of the people had returned to the Roman Catholic church. In 1602 Francis became bishop of Geneva, and threw himself into the reform and reorganization of this very difficult diocese. He preached inde-fatigably; it was during a Lenten course at Dijon in 1604 that he first met ◊ *St Jane de Chantal*, with whom he founded the Order of the Visitation six years later. It was at the Visitation convent of Bellecour at Lyons that he died, at a comparatively early age. A Calvinist minister in Geneva said of him, 'If we honoured any man as a saint, I know no one since the days of the apostles more worthy of it than this man.'

St Francis de Sales once declared: 'I hate duplicity as I hate death.' In controversy he was a model of good manners; he was sensitive for others, moderate in judgement, clear in expression, dignified and modest: 'I must be bishop of Geneva in public, but Francis de Sales in private.' His writings were called forth by the requirements of his work, especially as a religious adviser of individual persons. Psychologist and humanist as he was, he set himself to show how ordinary life 'in the world' can be made holy, and that without singularity or exaggeration: 'Religious devotion', he wrote, 'does not destroy: it perfects'; 'It is a mistake, a heresy, to want to exclude devoutness of life from among soldiers, from shops and offices, from royal courts, from the homes of the married.' Though in fact they were written primarily for those living a life of privileged leisure, his devotional writings are still widely read. Both the *Introduction to the Devout Life* and the informal treatise on *The Love of God* have recently been retranslated into English. The first of them was appreciated by such diverse characters as King James I and John Wesley; the second, as it were the story of love for God in men's hearts and lives, is the greatest of Francis's writings. His concern for the sciences and arts and the French language prompted him to found the Académie Florimontane at Annecy, thirty years before the Académie Française was established. In the Roman Catholic church St Francis de Sales is honoured as a doctor of the church, and Pope Pius XI declared him to be the patron saint of journalists and other writers; in his earlier days he had written many fugitive pieces, 'tracts', when working among the Calvinists.

A. J. M. Hamon, *Life of St Francis de Sales* (2 vols., 1925–29); other Lives by E. K. Sanders (1928) and M. de la Bedoyère; M. Henry-Couannier, *Francis de Sales and his Friends* (1964).

FRANCIS SOLANO, missionary. B. in Andalusía, 1549; d. at Lima, 1610; cd 1726; f.d. 13 July. He was a Franciscan friar, sent from Spain in 1589 to do mission work in Peru. The ship on which he sailed had to be abandoned in a storm; Francis insisted on staying aboard with some Negro slaves who had been left to their fate, and with his help most of them were saved. Francis made numerous converts to Christianity among the Indians in various parts of South America; unlike some of the European clergy he took much trouble to learn the local dialects, which gave rise to the idea that he had a supernatural gift of tongues. In 1604, while warden of the friary at Lima, he preached in the marketplace against the corruption of the city so powerfully that the inhabitants were panic-stricken. The civil authorities, alarmed for public order, complained to the archbishop, ◊ *St Toribio*. Whereupon St Francis had to calm the people by explaining that his vivid pictures of the wrath to come were not a prophecy of material catastrophes but a warning of the personal fate awaiting the wicked. At the time of his death he had laboured among Indians and Spanish colonists for twenty years.

FRANCIS XAVIER, missionary. B. near Pamplona, 1506; d. on Shangchwan, 1552; cd 1622; f.d. 3 December. The great pioneer missionary to the East Indies and Japan belonged to a good Basque family of Spanish Navarre. While studying at the University of Paris he came under the influence of ◊ *St Ignatius Loyola*, and was one of the first seven Jesuits who dedicated themselves to God at Montmartre in 1534. In 1541 he was sent with two companions to Portuguese India. After a voyage of thirteen months they landed at Goa, and for the next seven years Xavier laboured in that city, among the Paravas in the extreme south of India, in Ceylon, in the Malay peninsula and the Molucca islands, visiting his headquarters at Goa from time to time. The sufferings of the native peoples, both from one another and from the Portuguese, made, he said, 'a permanent bruise on my soul'. The oppressive exploitation by Europeans and the evil living of so many of them were among the missionaries' biggest obstacles, a subject on which Xavier wrote very outspokenly to the king of Portugal. The numbers he baptized have sometimes been greatly exaggerated, as were the miracles attributed to him; but he made numerous conversions among the low-caste peoples, though he had no understanding of or sympathy with Indian religions and had no success with Brahmans.

St Francis left Malacca for Japan in 1549. After learning a little of the Japanese language at Kagoshima, he made his way with his companions (three of whom were Japanese Christians) to Kyoto and Yamaguchi where, as representative of the Portuguese king, he was given a good reception and had leave to teach. After two years in Japan he left his converts in charge of a Portuguese priest and revisited his Indian mission. Then, in 1552, he set out for China, a country at that time closed to foreigners. He was landed from a Portuguese ship on the island of Shangchwan, near the mouth of the Canton river. While waiting there for a Chinese junk whose master had agreed to put him ashore secretly on the mainland, he was taken ill; in a fortnight he died, alone in a hut but for a young Chinese Christian who had accompanied him from Goa. He was only forty-six. His body was taken back to Goa, where it is still enshrined. One of the primary sources for St Francis Xavier's life is his letters, of which many have been preserved, some of them very long and detailed; they give a living picture of the man and of the conditions in which he worked so unassumingly and selflessly. He is a patron saint of Roman Catholic missionaries in foreign parts.

Lives by E. A. Stewart (1917) and J. Brodrick (1952).

FREDIANO ◊ under *Finnian of Moville*

FRÉVISSE ◊ *Frideswide*

FRIDESWIDE, abbess. D. *c*. 735; f.d. 19 October. Though she is the patron saint of the city and university of Oxford little can be said for certain about St Frideswide: the earliest account of her dates only from the twelfth century. This says that she was a princess who, to avoid marriage, fled from home and lay in hiding for three years; when her suitor was struck blind and gave up his quest, she established a nunnery at Oxford and lived therein in peace for the rest of her days. It may at any rate be supposed that Frideswide was foundress and abbess of a religious house at Oxford in the eighth century; her shrine was in the church of a monastery there in 1004, on the site of Christ Church. It is unexplained how this obscure saint, under the name of Frévisse, came to have a cultus at the village of Bomy in the middle of Artois.

F. M. Stenton, in *Oxoniensia*, vol. i (1936).

FRIGIDIAN ◊ under *Finnian of Moville*

FRUCTUOSUS OF TARRAGONA, bishop and martyr. D. at Tarragona, 259; f.d. 21 January. All that is known of this bishop of Tarragona in Spain is that he was martyred, with his deacons SS. Augurius and Eulogius, during the reign of Valerian and Gallienus. Their authentic 'acts' relate that they were arrested just as they were going to bed, and a few days later were brought before the governor. Their examination was short and to the point: the prisoners affirmed their worship of one only God, and were sentenced to be burnt. Officers were posted to prevent any demonstration; but at the gate of the amphitheatre some of the Christians were able to get close, and one asked the bishop for his prayers: Fructuosus replied so that all could hear, 'I am bound to bear in mind the whole universal church from East to West,' and added words of comfort to his flock. As the flames enveloped them, say the 'acts', 'they stretched out their arms in token of the Lord's victory, praying to him till they gave up their souls'.

St Fructuosus of Braga established monasteries and community refuges for whole families of Romano-Hispanic people in Visigothic Spain. He died archbishop of Braga in 665 (?); his feast day is 16 April.

FRUMENTIUS, bishop. D. *c*. 380; f.d. 27 October. He is venerated as the first evangelizer of Ethiopia. According to Rufinus, who was a contemporary, Frumentius and Aedesius were the young travelling-companions of a Tyrian philosopher, Meropius. In Ethiopia Meropius was murdered, but the youths attained positions of trust at the court of the king at Axum. In the following reign Frumentius obtained permission for Greek merchants to open chapels in Ethiopia, and he also did mission work on his own. In due course Aedesius returned to Tyre, where Rufinus met him; but Frumentius made his way to Alexandria and explained the Ethiopian situation to ◊ *St Athanasius*, asking that a bishop should be sent to Axum. Athanasius chose Frumentius himself and sent him back to plant the Christian church in Ethiopia: 'Apostolic signs accompanied his ministry, and great numbers of heathen were won to the faith'. Whatever the exact details of the Tyrian youths' adventures, there is strong confirmation of the presence in Ethiopia of a bishop named Frumentius, consecrated by St Athanasius about the middle of the fourth century.

FULGENTIUS OF RUSPE, bishop. B. at Thelepte, *c.* 467; d. at Ruspe, 533; f.d. 3 January. He came of a family of senatorial rank in North Africa, was given an excellent education, and appointed procurator of his native town; but he soon gave up this post to be a monk. In 507 he was elected bishop of Ruspe, in modern Tunisia. The Arian Vandals were in occupation of North Africa at this time, and Fulgentius had hardly taken over his see when with many other orthodox bishops he was banished to Sardinia. He devoted himself to study and writing at Cagliari, and thereby attracted the notice of the Vandal king, Thrasimund, who in 515 had him brought to Carthage for discussions with the Arian clergy. But the influence of Fulgentius on them was too powerful, and in 518 he was sent back to Sardinia. Thrasimund's successor, Hilderic, finally let all the bishops return in 523. Thus nearly half of the episcopate of St Fulgentius was passed in exile. He was so beloved by his flock that they prevented him from passing his last years in seclusion in a monastery. Fulgentius was a theological writer, especially against Arianism, of some importance but little originality; some of his opinions (e.g. concerning the destiny of unbaptized children) are found shocking today, but were not uncommon in his time and place.

FURSEY, abbot. B. in Ireland; d. in France, 648; f.d. 16 January. After ◊ *St Columban*, St Fursey (Fursa) is perhaps the best known of the Irish monastic missioners abroad in the earlier middle ages. With his brothers SS. ◊ *Foillan* and *Ultan* he came first to England, sometime after 630, and was welcomed by King Sigebert of the East Angles, who was encouraging the work of ◊ *St Felix of Dunwich* at just this time. Fursey established a monastery, probably at Burgh Castle, near Yarmouth, ministered from there for some ten years, and then passed over into Gaul. Given land by Erchinoald (into whose household ◊ *St Bathild* had recently been sold), he founded a monastery at Lagny, near Paris, *c.* 644. He died at Mézerolles while on a journey, and was buried at Péronne, where his tomb became a place of pilgrimage and the monastery there an Irish centre.

Fursey, says Bede, was 'renowned for his words and works, outstanding in goodness', and it is Bede who relates the visions of the unseen world of spirits, good and evil, which account for much of Fursey's fame. From time to time he fell into a trance-like state of considerable duration, when he saw such things as the fires of falsehood, covetousness, discord, and injustice lying in wait to consume the world. Together with those of the English Drithelm (also recorded by Bede), St Fursey's visions had considerable influence in the religious thought of western Europe in the later middle ages, notably as expressed in Dante's *Divine Comedy*.

G

GABRIEL THE ARCHANGEL ◊ under *Michael the Archangel*

GABRIEL LALEMANT, martyr. B. in Paris, 1610; d. in Canada, 17 March 1649; cd 1930; f.d. 26 September. He became a Jesuit in 1630 and offered himself for the foreign missions, but his health was so poor that it was not till sixteen years later that he was sent to Canada. After ministering in Quebec for two years he was allowed to join ◊ *St John de Brébeuf* on the Huron mission. Six months later there was an attack by the Iroquois; the two priests were captured and taken to the village of Saint-Ignace, and there were tortured so abominably that the sturdy Father Brébeuf died in a few hours. But the delicate and nervous Lalemant survived torment for a whole night, till he was killed by a blow on the head from a tomahawk. A contemporary wrote: 'There was no part of his body that was not burnt, even his eyes, for the villains had forced burning embers into the sockets.'

GABRIEL POSSENTI ◊ under *Gemma Galgani*

GAETANO ◊ *Cajetan*

GAIANA ◊ *Rhipsime and Gaiana*

GALL, monk. B. in Ireland; d. near Bregenz, *c.* 640; f.d. 16 October. He was one of the twelve monks who accompanied ◊ *St Columban* to the European continent, and was with him till 612 when Columban went into Italy. According to one story they disagreed because Columban suspected Gall of malingering, and imposed on him the penance, which Gall faithfully observed, of not celebrating Mass during the continuance of Columban's life. With a few companions he settled in a waste place to the west of Bregenz, near the Lake of Constance, in what is now Switzerland. In later times many legends grew up about him which had little basis in fact. He was not, for instance, the founder of the renowned monastery which bore his name; this was inaugurated about a century after his death, on the site of his settlement, and is now represented by the cathedral at Sankt Gallen and the very famous monastic library there.

M. Joynt (tr.), *The Life of St Gall* (1927).

GAUDENTIUS OF BRESCIA, bishop. D. *c.* 410; f.d. 25 October. This bishop of Brescia in northern Italy, who was a friend of ◊ *St Ambrose*, is remembered chiefly in connexion with ◊ *St John Chrysostom*. After Chrysostom was banished for the second time in 404, the Western emperor, Honorius, wrote on his behalf to Emperor Arcadius at Constantinople. The letter, with another from Pope St Innocent I, was carried by a deputation, of which Gaudentius was a principal member. They were stopped by officials outside Constantinople and ordered to give up the letters, and when they refused to deliver them to anyone but Arcadius in person they were taken from them by force. Then a vain attempt was made to bribe the deputation to recognize Chrysostom's intruded successor as archbishop. Gaudentius saw that their mission was hopeless, and at his request they were eventually allowed to go back home. They were shipped on a vessel so unseaworthy that it had to be left at Lampsacus. Chrysostom sent a letter of thanks for their efforts to St Gaudentius and the others, a rather stiff and cool missive which suggests it was written by a secretary rather than by the warm-hearted John. Rufinus had a high opinion of St Gaudentius as a teacher, but only a few of his homilies have survived.

GELASIUS I, pope. D. 496; f.d. 21 November. It is said that St Gelasius was an African, but he appears at least to have been born in Rome and to have been one of the Roman clergy. He was elected pope in 492, during a difficult period of the church's history in both West and East and of Rome's relations with Constantinople. During a pontificate of only four and a half years Gelasius showed himself a vigorously active and capable leader, a firm upholder of the primacy of the Roman see and of the subordination of the temporal to the spiritual power. A collection of his letters and some other writings have survived, but the two best-known documents that bear his name are not his: the Massbook called the *Gelasian Sacramentary* doubtless incorporates certain of his liturgical reforms, but he seems to have had nothing to do with the composite document called the *Gelasian Decree*.

GEMMA GALGANI, laywoman. B. at Camigliano, 1878; d. at Lucca, 1903; cd 1940; f.d. 11 April. Gemma was the child of poor parents, and on becoming an orphan at nineteen she went into domestic service at Lucca. She wished to be a Passionist nun, but was prevented by spinal tuberculosis, of which she believed herself to have been cured by the intercession of St Gabriel Possenti, who had himself died of consumption. She was of remarkably fervent religious disposition, and from 1899 underwent many extraordinary experiences, which were carefully investigated by her confessor, Father Germano. For over eighteen months the marks, *stigmata*, of Christ's crucifixion appeared intermittently on her hands and feet (cf. ◊ *St Francis of Assisi*), as well as other marks of his passion; and she had frequent ecstasies and visions. Gemma was quiet and unexcitable, and she bore the trials of bad health with the utmost patience: on the other hand she occasionally behaved in a way that she attributed to diabolical possession. The intense veneration shown for Gemma after her early death led to canonization proceedings, which were opposed by some because of the very strange character of some of the phenomena connected with her. Accordingly it had to be pointed out authoritatively that she was recommended for canonization solely because of the holiness of her life, and that no official judgement was made (or ever is in such cases) about the nature and cause of her experiences.

St Gabriel Possenti, referred to above, was a young Italian cleric in the Passionist Congregation (1838–62; cd 1920; f.d. 27 February). His devoted life was as 'ordinary' and uneventful as St Gemma's was exceptional.

GENÈS ◊ *Genesius of Arles*

GENESIUS THE ACTOR, martyr. No date (?); f.d. 25 August. The story told of him is that, in the course of an entertainment given to Diocletian in Rome, he played the part of a candidate in a mocking representation of Christian baptism. But the grace of God touched him, and when afterwards he was presented to the emperor he declared that he had suddenly been converted to Christ during the performance. He was therefore put to the torture; but he would not recant, and so his head was struck off. The same or a similar story is told of three other actor martyrs (Ardalio, Gelasius of Heliopolis, and a Porphyry), and in every case it is probably fictitious. Whether there ever was a martyr named Genesius at Rome has not been decided for certain. Tne legend has attracted and been turned to account by several dramatists and musicians, among them Lope de Vega, Jean de Rotrou, Karl Löwe, Felix Weingartner, and Henri Ghéon.

GENESIUS OF ARLES, martyr. D. 250 (?); f.d. 25 August. According to his ancient acts this Genesius (Genès), a catechumen, was an official shorthand-writer at Arles in Gaul. When one day it was his duty to take down an imperial edict (that of Decius?) against Christians, he threw down his tablets in disgust, declaring he would not do it as he was himself a Christian. He then left the court to seek a place of refuge. He was pursued, arrested, and beheaded on the banks of the Rhône, and thus 'attained the glory of martyrdom, being baptized in his own blood'. His cultus became widespread, and the church of his name in Rome may ultimately have prompted the legend of ◊ *St Genesius the Actor*. The church of the parish of Saint Gennys in north-east Cornwall is now esteemed to be dedicated in honour of Genesius of Arles; but this may be a mistake, or a medieval alteration, for an unidentified local Gennys.

GENEVIÈVE, patroness of Paris. B. at Nanterre, *c.* 420; d. at Paris, *c.* 500; f.d. 3 January. We are told that when on his way to Britain in 429 ◊ *St Germanus of Auxerre* met at Nanterre, near Paris, a little girl named Geneviève (Genovefa). She confided to him that she wanted to live only for God. Germanus encouraged her good will, and when she was fifteen Geneviève received from a bishop the veil of a dedicated virgin. When her parents died she went to live with her godmother in Paris; she devoted her days to prayer and charitable works, but she encountered opposition and malicious criticism, even after St Germanus had visited her again. This detraction reached its height during the advance of the Huns in 451; but Germanus's archdeacon succeeded in persuading the panic-stricken people that Geneviève was not a prophetess of doom, and to listen to her counsel not to abandon their homes. Attila's turning off to Orleans was attributed to Geneviève's prayers. When the Franks blockaded Paris, she led a convoy to run the blockade up the Seine to Troyes, to bring back food for the starving citizens. The Frankish leader Childeric listened favourably to her pleas on behalf of prisoners of war, and later on King Clovis liberated captives and was lenient to malefactors at her urging. Parisians saw the hand of their protectress at work long after her death, particularly when in 1129 an epidemic of ergot-poisoning, 'burning sickness', was suddenly stayed when her relics were carried in public procession; this event is still commemorated annually in the churches of Paris. Most of the information about St Geneviève derives from a Life that claims to be by a contemporary; its authenticity and value are the subject of much discussion. The idea that she was a shepherdess is recent and without authority; the evidence suggests that she came from a family of good position.

GENNARO ◊ *Januarius*

GEOFFREY OF AMIENS ▷ *Godfrey*

GEORGE, martyr. Third–fourth century; f.d. 23 April. St George, patron saint of the kingdom of England, of soldiers, of boy-scouts, and titular saint of numerous churches throughout the world, was one of the most famous of the early martyrs, and his reputation is still alive, especially in the East. But no historical particulars of his life have survived; and such are the vagaries of his legend that earnest endeavours have been made to prove that he never existed, or that he was somebody else, or that he represents a christianized version of one or other of the pagan myths. These endeavours are more remarkable for their ingenuity than for their cogency. Veneration for St George as a soldier saint was widespread from early times, and its centre was in Palestine, at Diospolis, now Lydda. St George was probably martyred there, at the end of the third or the beginning of the fourth century. That is all that can be reasonably surmised about him; as early as the beginning of the sixth century he was referred to as a good man 'whose deeds are known only to God'.

Legends of St George exist in a large variety of forms, in which scholars have not been able to detect a single reliable detail. The story popularized by the book called the *Golden Legend* in the later middle ages represents him as a 'knight' from Cappadocia, who at Silene in Libya rescued a maiden from a dragon, which led to the baptism of thousands of persons. Then, after a number of crude miraculous happenings, George fell a victim to Diocletian's persecution, being tortured and beheaded at Nicomedia for his Christian faith. The thing everybody knows about St George, the killing of the dragon, has been much used in the efforts to show that the saint was no more than a myth; it is therefore of importance that this incident does not figure in any of the earlier versions of the legend: it was a late medieval addition.

How St George came to be adopted as the protector of England is not altogether clear. His name was known in England (and Ireland) long before the Norman conquest, and it is probable that returning crusaders did much to establish his popularity. He may have been named the national patron when King Edward III founded the order of the Garter under his patronage, *c.* 1348. In 1415 his day was made a festival of the highest rank in England. In 1970 the annual feast of the saint in Roman Catholic churches was made optional; but in England and other places where St George is specially honoured his feast retains its old solemnity. The badge embodied in St George's flag, a red cross on a white ground, was known in the fourteenth century, and perhaps earlier.

GERALD ▷ under *Colman of Lindisfarne*

GERALD OF AURILLAC, layman. B. *c.* 855; d. at Saint-Cirgues, 909; f.d. 13 October. Having succeeded his father as count of Aurillac, in Auvergne, and as owner of considerable estates, he was distinguished for the justice and efficiency with which he discharged the duties of a wealthy nobleman. His personal life was no less virtuous, and markedly well-ordered and religious. But it is possible he would not have become well-known had he not, *c.* 890, founded a monastery at Aurillac: this abbey was taken over by the Cluniac order, and ◊ *St Odo of Cluny* wrote a Life of St Gerald which made him celebrated in medieval France. A later member of St Gerald of Aurillac's family was *St Robert of Chaise-Dieu* (d. 1087; cd *c.* 1095; f.d. 17 April), who founded the great abbey of that name in Auvergne.

G. Sitwell (tr.), *Lives of Odo of Cluny . . . and Gerald of Aurillac* (1958).

GERARD OF BROGNE, abbot. B. near Fosses, *c.* 895; d. at Brogne, 959; cd 1131; f.d. 3 October. He built and endowed a monastery on his estate at Brogne, near Namur, and himself became its abbot. Under his rule the life and discipline of this house was so exemplary that in 931 Duke Gislebert of Lorraine commissioned Gerard to reform the abbey of Saint-Ghislain, near Mons. There followed similar undertakings at several important monasteries in Flanders, and the movement was extended to Normandy, including Mont-Saint-Michel. St Gerard carried out his reforms on the lines and in the spirit of St Benedict of Aniane, but he did not attempt to join the abbeys in a confederation. All his efforts were not equally successful: some foreign monks who arrived in Bath during his time are said to have left Saint-Bertin at Ghent because they were discontented with his strictness. After twenty-two years thus devoted to the restoration of Benedictine monasticism St Gerard retired to Brogne, and died there a few years later.

GERARD OF CSANAD, bishop and martyr. B. at Venice, *c.* 980; d. in Hungary, 1046; f.d. 24 September. While a monk of San Giorgio Maggiore at Venice this St Gerard studied in the schools of Bologna; his one existing writing shows evidence of his wide reading, and he became abbot of the monastery. He gave up this office, intending to live as a solitary in the Holy Land, but on the way there bad weather drove him ashore on the Dalmatian coast. Here he fell in with an abbot from Hungary who induced him to settle in that country. About 1020 King ◊ *St Stephen* appointed Gerard tutor to his son Emeric, and later on he lived for seven years in a hermitage in the forest of Bakony; when King Stephen set up the see of Csanad in 1030 Gerard was made its first bishop and he was an energetic missionary in the Mako country. In the disorders and recrudescence of heathenism that followed Stephen's death St Gerard incurred the rage of the insurgents. While journeying from Csanad to Szekesfehervar he was set upon and killed, his body being hurled from a height into the Danube. He was venerated as a martyr, and in 1333 his relics were translated to his native Venice; there he is known as St Gerard Sagredo, though there is no reason to believe that he belonged to that family.

GERARD MAJELLA, Redemptorist laybrother. B. at Muro Lucano in Italy, 1726; d. at Caposele, 1755; cd 1904; f.d. 16 October. He was apprenticed to his father's trade of tailoring and was then manservant to the bishop of Lacedonia, a cantankerous master who treated him badly. In 1749 Gerard was accepted as a laybrother in the Redemptorist congregation, where his quality was recognized by ◊ St Alphonsus Liguori. For three years Gerard's life was marked by a series of phenomena of very various kinds: ecstasies, being apparently seen in two places at once ('bilocation'), healing, prophecy, the ability to read consciences. Though not a priest, his religious direction and advice were sought by clergy and by communities of nuns, to which he gave conferences. When on one occasion he was slandered by a young woman he did not deny her charges, and his puzzled superiors put him under surveillance and excluded him from communion for months, until the girl admitted that she had lied. When asked by St Alphonsus why he had kept silence in such circumstances, Gerard replied that he thought that was what was required in face of unjust accusations. His last months were passed as porter in the Redemptorist house at Caposele, in that kingdom of Naples where he had lived all his life.

J. Carr, St Gerard Majella (1946).

GERARD SAGREDO ◊ Gerard of Csanad

GERASIMUS, abbot. B. in Lycia; d. in Palestine, 475; f.d. 5 March. He left his home in Asia Minor to visit the desert monks in Egypt and Palestine, and settled near the Dead Sea. Having been led astray theologically, he was put on the right path by ◊ St Euthymius the Great, and the two became firm friends. About 455 he began the establishment of a laura near Jericho, which attracted many disciples; a communal monastery was organized near by for the training of aspirants to the more solitary way of living. In a celebrated book called The Spiritual Meadow John Moschus (d. 619) gives a long account of St Gerasimus drawing a thorn from a lion's paw and then training the grateful animal, which he named 'Jordan', to fetch and carry for the monks. When Gerasimus died Jordan was disconsolate, and lay down on his master's grave and died too. This recalls the tale of Androcles and the lion, and probably is the origin of the lion shown in pictures of ◊ *St Jerome*, his name in Latin, Hieronymus, being confused with Gerasimus. A lion is the emblem of St Gerasimus.

GEREON, martyr. Date unknown; f.d. 10 October. From the fourth century certain martyrs, now unknown, were venerated on the site of the church of St Gereon at Cologne. Late in the sixth century they were said to have been a detached party of fifty men from the Theban Legion (the ◊ *martyrs of Agaunum*); in later medieval times they grew in number to 318, 'relics' of them were found, and a spurious account of them written. There were similar stories and happenings at Bonn and Xanten. Gereon was the name given to the leader of the Cologne martyrs, whom it is impossible to identify. With reference to them and to ◊ *St Ursula* and her maidens Father H. Delehaye writes, 'It is surely superfluous to recall that at Cologne the imagination of hagiographers was liable to exaggerate things to perhaps an unexampled degree' (*Les Origines du culte des martyrs*, p. 360).

GERMAINE OF PIBRAC, shepherdess. B. at Pibrac, *c*. 1579; d. there, 1601; cd 1867; f.d. 15 June. Germaine Cousin was born on a farm in a village near Toulouse; she was an unhealthy child, scrofulous, with a withered hand. She lived at home and was badly treated by her stepmother (or perhaps by her half-brother's wife): she was fed on scraps, slept in the stable or in a cupboard under the stairs, and from nine years old was sent out daily to look after the sheep. The neighbours laughed at her religious devotion and called her 'the little bigot'; Germaine took it all in good part and was always ready to lend a hand to anybody. But people began to take a different view of her when it was reported that one winter's day her stepmother accused her of taking a loaf of bread to give to a beggar; Germaine opened her apron and it was full of spring flowers. Not long after, she was found dead, under the stairs. From 1644 miracles of healing were said to take place at her grave, which has been a place of pilgrimage from that day to this. Happenings similar to that of St Germaine and the flowers are related also of ◊ *St Elizabeth of Hungary*, *St Elizabeth of Portugal*, and St Rose of Viterbo.

GERMANUS OF AUXERRE, bishop. B. at Auxerre, *c*. 378; d. at Ravenna, 448; f.d. 31 July. Germanus, born of Gallo-Roman parents, practised as an advocate in Rome and, having returned to Gaul and married, was appointed to a high official post. No doubt he carried out his duties with distinction, for in 418 he was elected bishop of Auxerre, much against his will. He at once made radical changes in his mode of life, and proved to be a bishop of exceptional ability. Germanus was twice sent to the island of Britain, where the church was being disturbed by the Pelagian heresy. Deputed by Pope ◊ *St Celestine I*, he in 429–430 not only vanquished the false teachers but also, it is said, vitally helped the Britons to defeat a raid of Picts and Saxons in battle (the 'Alleluia Victory'); before returning home he gave God thanks for his successes at the tomb of ◊ *St Alban*. The second visit was fourteen years later, when there was a revival of Pelagianism which alarmed the British bishops. This time Germanus was able to get the troublesome teachers banished, and henceforward, says Bede, 'the faith was maintained uncorrupted in these parts for a long time'. St Germanus died at Ravenna, where he had gone in his old age to plead with the emperor the cause of the people of Armorica (now Brittany), who were in conflict with the imperial viceroy in Gaul.

The Life of St Germanus by Constantius, trans. in F. R. Hoare, *The Western Fathers* (1954).

GERMANUS OF CONSTANTINOPLE, bishop. B. *c.* 634; d. at Platonium, *c.* 733; f.d. 12 May. He was promoted from the see of Cyzicus to be patriarch of Constantinople in 715, and ten years later Emperor Leo III published the first edict against the public veneration of sacred images, an enactment prompted by political as well as religious considerations. It is for his firm opposition to the emperor in this matter that St Germanus is chiefly remembered: 'When we show reverence to representations of Jesus Christ,' he wrote in a letter, 'we do not worship paint laid on wood: we worship the invisible God in spirit and in truth.' In 730 Germanus was in effect deposed, and soon after died in retirement at a very great age. A few of his writings have survived, among them six homilies on the Virgin Mary and some hymns, including the one translated as 'A great and mighty wonder,/A full and holy cure!'

GERMANUS OF PARIS, bishop. B. near Autun, *c.* 496; d. in Paris, 576; f.d. 28 May. This Germanus, abbot of St Symphorian's at Autun, was made bishop of Paris *c.* 556. He was unwearying and fearless in his endeavours to put a stop to civil strife and to curb the viciousness of the Frankish kings, but with little effect. It was to him that ◊ *St Radegund* appealed successfully for protection against her brutal husband, Chlotar I. St Germanus founded a monastery in Paris in whose church he was buried; it afterwards became very famous under his name, Saint-Germain-des-Prés.

GERTRUDE OF HELFTA, mystic. B. *c.* 1256; d. at Helfta, 1302; f.d. 16 November. This St Gertrude is often called 'the Great'. At the age of five she was entrusted to the nuns of Helfta in Saxony to be brought up, and seems never to have left the convent; her mentor and friend there was ◊ *St Mechtilde*. Gertrude was given an excellent education, but she never held office in the community and her life was externally uneventful. She committed herself wholeheartedly to the contemplative life when she was twenty-five, in consequence of a vision of Christ; thereafter she lost interest in secular studies and gave all her attention to the Bible, the writings of the Fathers, and the liturgy. Her life became a succession of spiritual experiences, many of which are described in the collection of writings called the *Revelations of Gertrude and Mechtilde* wherein *The Herald of God's Loving-Kindness* is mostly written from her notes or dictation but in part by herself. It forms an important contribution to medieval mysticism; in later times it has had a special interest because of St Gertrude's adumbrations of devotion to the sacred heart of Jesus, now so widespread among Roman Catholics. This Gertrude has sometimes been confused with Gertrude of Hackeborn, who was abbess of Helfta when she was brought there as a child.

G. Dolan, *Gertrude the Great* (1912).

GERTRUDE OF NIVELLES, abbess. B. at Landen, 626; d. at Nivelles, 659; f.d. 17 March. Both her parents, Pepin of Landen and Itta, were revered for their holy lives, and her sister Begga is numbered among the saints. On her husband's death in 640 Itta founded a monastery at Nivelles, and appointed Gertrude its abbess when she was judged old enough. She was still very young, but she carried her responsibilities well, with her mother's assistance, and followed her in giving encouragement and help to monks, particularly Irish ones, to do missionary work in the neighbourhood (cf. ◊ St Foillan). She was only thirty when she resigned her office to her niece, and she died soon afterwards. The cultus of St Gertrude became widely spread in the Lowlands and neighbouring countries, and a considerable body of folklore gathered round her name.

Her sister *St Begga* (d. 693; f.d. 17 December) married a son of ◊ *St Arnulf of Metz* and became the mother of Pepin of Herstal. Begga's name had nothing to do with the naming of the sisterhoods called *béguines* five hundred years later. Gertrude's emblem is a pastoral staff with a mouse running up it.

GERVASE and PROTASE, martyrs. Date unknown; f.d. 19 June. In the year 386 human remains were found in Milan which purported to be those of two apparently forgotten martyrs. Their discovery was the result of a search ordered by ◊ *St Ambrose* in consequence of what he refers to as a 'presentiment'; but ◊ *St Augustine* and other contemporaries call it a dream, vision, or revelation. The cultus of the martyrs, Gervase and Protase, became popular and widespread, but nothing whatever is known about their history. Attempts have been made to connect them with the Dioscuri (cf. ◊ *SS. Florus and Laurus*).

The remains of two other unknown martyrs were found and

153

enshrined by St Ambrose in 395, namely, *SS. Nazarius* and *Celsus* (f.d. 28 July); they had been buried in a garden outside Milan. The accounts of both these happenings are somewhat inconsistent and there has been considerable speculation about them.

The relics of Gervase and Protase were found in a church near the tomb of *SS. Nabor* and *Felix* (f.d. 12 July), martyrs who were certainly venerated in Milan at an early date, together with *St. Victor* (8 May).

GILBERT OF SEMPRINGHAM, founder. B. at Sempringham, *c.* 1085; d. there, 1189; cd 1202; f.d. 4 February. The founder of the only specifically English religious order. Being regarded as unfit for ordinary feudal life, he became parson of Sempringham in Lincolnshire, where his father was lord of the manor. In 1131 Gilbert organized a group of young women of his parish into a religious community, under the Benedictine rule. Lay sisters and brothers were added, a second house was founded, and in 1148 Gilbert provided chaplains for his nuns by establishing a body of canons following the Augustinian rule. This order grew rapidly, having men's and women's houses side by side and also monasteries of canons only, with leper hospitals and orphanages. As master general of it, St Gilbert set an admirable example of abstemious and devoted living, but the later years of his long life were seriously disturbed. When he was about eighty he was arrested and charged with sending help to ◊ *St Thomas of Canterbury*, who had taken refuge abroad from King Henry II; eventually the charge was dropped, although Gilbert refused to deny it on oath. Later still there was a revolt among his laybrothers, who grievously slandered the old man; the case was taken to Rome, where it was decided in his favour. St Gilbert lived to be over a hundred and passed his last years nearly blind, as a simple member of the order he had founded and governed. The Gilbertine Order came to an end when all its houses, over twenty in number, were suppressed by King Henry VIII.

R. Graham, *St Gilbert of Sempringham and the Gilbertines* (1901).

GILDAS, called 'the Wise'. B. *c.* 500; d. *c.* 570; f.d. 29 January. Gildas is famous as the author of the work called *De excidio et conquestu Britanniae*, 'Concerning the Ruin and Conquest of Britain'; in it warning lessons are drawn from the history of Britain under the Romans, and five contemporary kings, with their people and clergy, are violently denounced for their iniquities. The history of Gildas himself is obscure. He is said to have been born in lower Clydeside and to have studied under ◊ *St Illtyd* in South Wales; the author of the *De excidio* was certainly a well-educated man, with a wide knowledge of the Bible, and a master of fierce invective prompted by sincere moral indignation. It is also said that Gildas was for a time a solitary on an island in the Bristol Channel, and that he visited Ireland; he seems to have had considerable influence on the development of the Irish church. According to Breton tradition St Gildas spent much of his later life in Brittany, founding a monastery in Rhuys and dying on the isle of Houat; the reliability of these particulars has been called in question. Furthermore, some scholars now incline to the belief that the *De excidio* was not wholly written by Gildas, but that part of it is a forgery of just after his time.

GILES, hermit. Date unknown; f.d. 1 September. Giles (in Latin, Aegidius) was one of the most popular saints of western Europe in the later middle ages, and also one about whom very little is known. The centre of his cultus was at Saint-Gilles, near Arles, and he may have been a hermit in that neighbourhood before the ninth century. A Life of him for the edification of pilgrims to his shrine was composed in the tenth century; it includes some startling wonders and anachronisms and one celebrated incident. The hermit had a pet hind, which one day was hunted in the woods by the hounds of the Visigothic king Wamba. An arrow was loosed into the undergrowth, and when the king rode into a clearing there was Giles, himself wounded by the arrow, protecting the hind in his arms, and the hounds rooted motionless by an invisible power. Variations of this tale are related of several other saints. St Giles was looked on as a patron of cripples and the indigent, and in Great Britain alone over 150 churches were dedicated in his honour, among them St Giles Cripplegate in London and the high kirk in Edinburgh. St Giles's emblem is an arrow.
F. Brittain, *St Giles* (1928).

GLEB ◊ *Boris and Gleb*

GODEHARD ◊ *Gothard*

GODELIVE, laywoman. B. near Boulogne, *c*. 1045; d. at Ghistelles, 1070; f.d. 6 July. She provides an example of an innocent sufferer being popularly venerated locally as a martyr. When about eighteen Godelive (Godeleine) married a Flemish nobleman, Bertulf of Ghistelles; he deserted her almost at once, leaving her to be outrageously treated by her mother-in-law. Under pressure from Godelive's father and the bishop of Tournai-Noyon, Bertulf returned to his wife, but eventually resolved to get rid of her. While he was away from home, two retainers at his command murdered Godelive by a combination of strangling and drowning, while trying to give an appearance of natural death. Bertulf was never convicted of the crime, but local indignation and reports of miracles at her intercession led to Godelive's cultus as a saint in Flanders. These happenings are known from an account written by a contemporary, Drogo of Bergues.

155

GODFREY, or GEOFFREY, OF AMIENS, bishop. B. near Soissons, 1065; d. at Soissons, 1115; f.d. 8 November. He was so effective in restoring a decayed monastic community at Nogent-sous-Coucy that, having refused the great abbacy of Saint-Remi at Rheims, he was made bishop of Amiens in 1104. He was a most zealous reformer, putting down simony, enforcing clerical celibacy, and supporting the organization of communes. But he was rigorous even to excess and provoked discouraging opposition, so that in 1114 he withdrew to the monastery of the Grande-Chartreuse. A council ordered him to return to his diocese, but he died in the following year at St Crispin's abbey in Soissons, where he was buried. His name is not found in calendars before the sixteenth century.

GODRIC, hermit. B. at Walpole, 1065 (?); d. at Finchale, 1170; f.d. 21 May. From being a pedlar around his birthplace near King's Lynn, Godric took to the sea and became a prosperous trader. His voyages were many and long, and then and later he made several pilgrimages, to Saint Andrews in Scotland, Jerusalem, Compostela, and elsewhere; on a second visit to Rome he was accompanied by his aged mother, who walked barefoot with him half across Europe. In 1102 he helped King Baldwin I of Jerusalem to escape after the battle of Ramleh; in recording this a contemporary chronicler refers to Godric as 'a pirate'. Then, in middle age, he took to modest booklearning at Durham, and lived for a time with an old recluse near Bishop Auckland. From about 1110 till the end of his long life he lived at Finchale, in a hut on a wooded bend of the river Wear, three miles from Durham.

Godric was a powerfully-built man, blue-eyed and long-haired, and on his own showing, as reported by Reginald of Durham who knew him well, his earlier life had been disorderly and his business methods dishonest. As a hermit he sought with equal vigour to make amends; his self-inflicted penances were fearsome, and he was full of salutary counsel for all who sought it of him. Knowledge of future and distant events was attributed to him, and his love of and power over wild creatures was very remarkable: it extended even to vipers, which he treated as domestic pets until they distracted him at his prayers. But perhaps the most remarkable thing about St Godric is that he was apparently the earliest known lyrical poet in English: his biographers have preserved four fragments of verse, including a stanza addressed to ◊ St Nicholas, patron of sailors. Furthermore, the extant melodies of these hymns are ascribed to Godric as well, which would make him also the author of the earliest known musical settings of English words. He is described as being wholly ignorant of music, and his own explanation was that both words and melodies were taught him in vision by the Virgin Mary and his dead sister.

GOTHARD, bishop. B. at Reichersdorf, *c.* 960; d. at Hildesheim, 1038; cd 1131; f.d. 4 May. In the year 996 Gothard (Godehard) became abbot of Nieder Altaich, near his birthplace in Bavaria, where the Rule of St Benedict had recently been reintroduced. Under his direction the house kept such a good religious discipline that the emperor, ◊ *St Henry II*, entrusted him with the reform of several other monasteries, and when ◊ *St Bernward* died in 1022 Gothard was made bishop of Hildesheim in his place. He carried his reforming activities into the diocese with vigour, showing particular care for the cathedral school; among his foundations was a large 'home' for the poor at Sankt Moritz near Hildesheim. The pass and railway tunnel from Switzerland into Italy takes its name from this St Gothard, in whose honour the neighbouring hospice for travellers and its chapel were dedicated.

GREGORY THE ENLIGHTENER, bishop. B. *c.* 240; d. in Armenia, *c.* 326; f.d. 1 October. This Gregory is called 'the Enlightener' because he brought the light of Christ to the people of Armenia; but the beginnings of Christianity in that land are uncertain, and Gregory's own life is seriously obscured by extravagant legend. He is said to have been the son of a Parthian who murdered King Khosrov I of Armenia. The baby Gregory was taken for safety to Caesarea in Cappadocia, where he was baptized and brought up. There he married and had two sons; then he returned to Armenia, and succeeded in converting King Tiridates (Tradt) III to Christianity. Gregory was ordained bishop at Caesarea, and devoted the remainder of his life to preaching the gospel and organizing the church in Armenia. Very possibly he was ill-treated by Tiridates before the conversion of that monarch, but the stories of the twelve torments he suffered, and of other matters, are obviously sheer romance. Shortly before his death St Gregory retired into solitude, having first appointed his son Aristakes to be chief bishop (*katholikos*) of the Armenian church in his place.

GREGORY THE GREAT, pope and doctor. B. in Rome, *c.* 540; d. there, 604; f.d. 12 March. The first and greatest of the sixteen popes named Gregory came of a patrician family, and he was for some years chief civil magistrate of the city of Rome. Having devoted some of his wealth to the foundation of a monastery in Rome and half-a-dozen others in Sicily, he became a monk himself when he was about thirty-five. From 579 to 585 he was papal agent (*apocrisiarius*) at Constantinople; and five years after his return to his monastery he was elected pope, the first monk to be chosen for that office. St Gregory's epoch-making pontificate lasted fourteen years, at a time of great difficulty and disorder. When the Lombards were devastating northern Italy in 592 he negotiated treaties with them; he reformed the administration of the estates of the Roman church, and from their income spent large sums on the relief of sufferers from war, pestilence, and famine, and to ransom prisoners; he maintained the church's independence of the civil power, and himself provided for the discharge of duties in which the secular authorities were neglectful or inefficient; by cultivating good relations with the Lombards, Franks, and Visigoths he strengthened the church's position in northern Italy, France, and Spain; and the experience gained at Constantinople enabled him to strengthen the authority of the Roman see in the East as well as the West. One of Gregory's most far-reaching actions, prompted, it is said, by the sight of fair-haired Anglo-Saxon youths exposed for sale in the Roman slave-market, was to send missionaries to England. ◊ St Augustine of Canterbury and the forty other monks were from the pope's own monastery of St Andrew on the Caelian Hill, and he took the keenest interest in the progress of this mission.

St Gregory was not only a great bishop and statesman: he is accounted the fourth of the great Latin doctors of the church, and his writings are directed towards the fostering of Christian life and the formation of pastors. The *Regula pastoralis*, 'Pastoral Care', on the office and duties of a bishop came to be used throughout Christendom and was translated into English by King Alfred (modern trans., 1950). The *Moralia* is a long and practical commentary on the book of Job; while the *Dialogues*, which has been specially influential, relates the miraculous doings and visions of holy people in Italy, most of whom are otherwise quite unknown. Unfortunately Gregory was not exempt from the credulity of his time and was ready to believe all that he was told in this connexion. Over 800 of his letters and a number of sermons have survived; and he was responsible for considerable work on the public worship of the Western church, but its exact extent is uncertain. St Gregory's life and ideals were for centuries the inspiration and guide of the best among the clergy of the West, and he was a power in European history: he was the father of the medieval papacy, without which the early middle ages would have been much longer in emerging from a chaos of lawlessness and strife. It is significant of St Gregory's conception of religious authority that he called himself 'the servant of the servants of God', a designation used by the popes ever since.

F. H. Dudden, *Gregory the Great* (2 vols., 1905), P. Batiffol, *St Gregory the Great* (1929).

GREGORY THE SEVENTH, pope. B. at Rovaco in Tuscany, c. 1020; d. at Salerno, 1085; cd 1606; f.d. 25 May. Gregory VII, often called by his previous name, Hildebrand, probably a man of humble origin, had already played an influential part in the troubled affairs of the Roman church, when he was elected pope in 1073; at that time he was a cardinal in deacon's orders. He energetically carried on the reforms in the church already begun, and in 1075 decided to enforce the forbiddance of lay investiture. This was the investing of bishops and abbots elect with the symbols of their offices by lay princes, a practice which led to serious abuses and harm to religion. The decision precipitated a struggle with Emperor Henry IV that dominated Gregory's pontificate. Secular as well as ecclesiastical politics were involved, and the emperor resorted to armed force; the pope excommunicated him, and in 1077 Henry submitted, or seemed to submit, at Canossa. But the conflict went on. Henry besieged Rome and took it in 1084. It was retaken for Gregory by the Norman Robert Guiscard; but so dreadful was the conduct of Guiscard's troops that the pope had to flee before the fury of the Roman citizens, and he died in the following year at Salerno. His last words have become proverbial: 'I have loved righteousness and hated iniquity: that is why I die in exile.' He had indeed fought singlemindedly and without personal ambition to free the church from harmful influences and dependence on secular powers. But he pushed the claims of the papacy in respect of civil governors to unexampled lengths and with unexampled vigour, and appeared to put too much reliance on secular and legal means to attain religious ends. Gregory's personal integrity and his strength in adversity cannot be questioned, and his name is deservedly given to a whole era of ecclesiastical reform and development; but he was never the object of a widespread cultus, and was not enrolled among the saints till five hundred years after his death.

A. J. M. Macdonald, *Hildebrand* (1932).

GREGORY THE WONDERWORKER, missionary. B. at Neocaesarea, c. 213; d. there, c. 270; f.d. 17 November. He was a son of pagan parents of rank, and had a good education in letters and law. In 233, with his brother Athenodorus, he went to Caesarea in Palestine, where they came under Origen's influence and were baptized. They studied under Origen for five years, and then Gregory returned to Pontus as a missionary. Soon after 238 he was, in spite of his youth, made bishop of Neocaesarea, and in the course of some thirty years he is said to have converted practically the whole population of the city. His apostolic work was carried on in heartbreaking conditions of war, plague, and persecution; not much is known about it, but he is the first missionary of whom

159

it is related that he popularized Christian observances by adding secular attractions to religious festivals. St Gregory left a number of theological and other writings and he has always been highly regarded in the Greek church. The reason for his more popular fame is indicated by the epithet given to him, *Thaumaturgus*, 'the Wonderworker': extraordinary marvels were attributed to him, which were written down a century after his time by ◊ *St Basil* and *St Gregory of Nyssa*. On the testimony of the last named, he was the first recorded person to whom the ◊ *Virgin Mary* appeared in vision; with her, we are told, appeared ◊ *St John the Evangelist*, and they communicated to Gregory a statement of doctrine on the Blessed Trinity.

GREGORY OF NAZIANZUS, theologian. B. at Arianzus, 329; d. near there, 389; f.d. 9 May. This Gregory is one of the four great Greek doctors of the church, associated with the other two 'Cappadocian fathers', ◊ *St Basil the Great* and *St Gregory of Nyssa*, in the final defeat of the Arian heresy. His father, also named Gregory, was bishop of Nazianzus in Cappadocia, and the younger Gregory was given a good education, ending at Athens, where he cemented his friendship with a fellow student, St Basil. He was ordained priest by his father *c.* 362; but it was against his will – he wanted to be a monk – and he went to join Basil in his retreat at Annesi. About 372 he was, again unwillingly, made a bishop, by St Basil; but instead of going to his diocese (Sasima) he acted as auxiliary to his father at Nazianzus. Then, after some years in a monastery at Seleucia, he in 379 accepted charge of the orthodox community at Constantinople, where his eloquent preaching did much towards the renewed rejection of Arianism by the general council there in 381. Five of his discourses on the true doctrine of the Trinity were so impressive that they earned him the title of 'the Theologian'. Gregory was acclaimed bishop of the city in 380, but the difficulties he at once encountered were so grievous that he resigned within a few weeks, and soon after withdrew to end his days in contemplation near his birthplace.

As these particulars suggest, St Gregory of Nazianzus was a man of sensitive, retiring disposition, little fitted for the public life and affairs which he disliked. His sermons and other speeches show him to have been one of the finest orators of his time, and he was a poet as well. His numerous surviving letters throw further light on the character and friends of a very attractive personality, as does a long autobiographical poem from his pen. The unhappy difference with St Basil caused by his appointment of Gregory to the see of Sasima was ended by Basil's death in 379; and three years later Gregory preached a great panegyric of his friend, invoking memories of their days together in 'golden Athens'.

GREGORY OF NYSSA, theologian. B. at Caesarea in Cappadocia, c. 335; d. c. 395; f.d. 9 March. He was a younger brother of ◊ St Basil the Great. As a young man he was a teacher of rhetoric, married to a woman named Theosebeia. ◊ St Gregory of Nazianzus had a high opinion of both man and wife, and eventually prevailed on his namesake to devote his abilities to the service of the church. About 371 Gregory was consecrated bishop of Nyssa by his brother Basil. The beginnings of his episcopate were difficult, for, as Basil complained, he was too easy-going and unwary, and lacking in tact. For two years he was excluded from his see on a false charge of wasting church property; but after Basil's death in 379 he came to the fore as an opponent of Arianism and was hailed as 'a pillar of orthodoxy' by the general council at Constantinople in 381. Important missions were entrusted to him, and he was a greatly respected figure in the Eastern church by the time that he died. A good many of St Gregory's writings are extant, in which he surpasses the other Cappadocian fathers in the depth and richness of his philosophy and theology and the appeal of his ascetical works. On the Soul and the Resurrection is in the form of a dialogue with his sister ◊ St Macrina, and another dialogue, called Against Fate, shows what a hold astrology had on people's minds. One of his letters has a special interest in that it shows that the custom of religious pilgrimage was already being seriously abused at the end of the fourth century. A selection of translated texts from Gregory's mystical writings, under the title From Glory to Glory, was published in 1963.

GREGORY OF SINAI, mystic. B. near Smyrna, c. 1290; d. in Bulgaria, 1346; cd by the Orth. ch.; f.d. 27 November. After being carried off from his home in a raid by Seljuk Turks, and ransomed by his neighbours, this Gregory joined the monks of Mount Sinai. In consequence of disagreements he left there, and while in Crete learned the practice of mental prayer from another monk. Coming to Mount Athos, he was disappointed to find its inhabitants knew little of 'true silence and contemplation', so he set about teaching his ideas on prayer to the monks and solitaries. Then another piratical raid drove him away from Athos. At length, about 1325, he established a monastery on Mount Paroria, near Sozopol on the west coast of the Black Sea; he lived there for the rest of his life, though not without further disturbance from the Turks. Gregory wrote little, but his teaching had considerable influence in the Orthodox church. He emphasized the importance of physical aids (e.g. rhythmical breathing) to perfect concentration in mental prayer, which was part of the technique of Palamite Hesychasm (cf. ◊ *St Gregory Falamas*).

GREGORY OF TOURS, bishop and historian. B. at Clermont-Ferrand, *c.* 538; d. at Tours, *c.* 594; f.d. 17 November. Gregory of Tours is remembered chiefly as an historian, but his feast day as a saint is celebrated at Tours and in some other French dioceses. He belonged to an important Gallo-Roman family of Auvergne, and was appointed to the see of Tours in 573. He was an influential, energetic, and much-travelled bishop, whose difficulties were greatly increased by civil disturbances and political fluctuations; his faithfulness to his religious office made enemies, among them the notorious Queen Fredegund, for him in high places. Of Gregory's extensive writings the most valuable is the *History of the Franks*, a source book for the dark ages in western Europe, written with verve and enthusiasm to show his Frankish contemporaries the error of their ways. His hagiographical works, the *Glory of the Martyrs*, the *Glory of the Confessors*, the *Life of the* (Gallic) *Fathers,* and others, are less Lives of saints than collections of wonders related of them. Gregory formed a library from which Venantius Fortunatus did not disdain to borrow; all his writing was done after he became a bishop, a sufficiently remarkable performance seeing that bad health was added to his episcopal labours.

GREGORY OF UTRECHT, missionary. B. near Trier, *c.* 707; d. at Maastricht, *c.* 775; f.d. 25 August. He was a Frank who as a youth attracted the notice of ◊ *St Boniface of Crediton*, whose disciple and helper he became. He was given charge of a religious house at Utrecht, where several English missionaries were trained, as well as ◊ *St Ludger*, who wrote a biography of him. After the martyrdom of Boniface in 754 Gregory directed the Frisian mission for twenty years; he is sometimes called a bishop of Utrecht but seems not to have been so. When called on to assign a sentence on the murderers of his two half-brothers, Gregory refused to do so, ordering them to be released after he had given them a salutary admonition.

GREGORY PALAMAS, mystic and theologian. B. at Constantinople (?), *c.* 1296; d. at Salonika, 1359; çd by the Orth. ch., 1368; f.d. 14 November. Gregory Palamas was the foremost exponent and upholder of an ascetical and mystical theory that caused great controversy in the Orthodox church during the fourteenth century: it is called Hesychasm, or sometimes, after Gregory, Palamism. He was a monk on Mount Athos, and in 1333 his teaching involved him in a controversy with an able Greek monk from southern Italy, Barlaam. Hesychasm was a doctrine, practice and technique which its supporters claimed could lead contemplatives to a vision of the 'uncreated light' of God; its opponents objected that Gregory's teaching about it violated God's unity and transcendence. Gregory had the powerful support of the Athonite monks and the controversy went on for ten years; his numerous writings were then condemned and he was excommunicated. But when John Cantacuzenus seized the imperial throne in 1347 he sought to gain the support of the monks of Athos, whose influence among the people was immense; he therefore had Gregory restored and appointed archbishop of Salonika. The Hesychast controversy then reopened. Finally Gregory's cause triumphed and his teaching was declared to be orthodox by the church of Constantinople in 1351; but by then he was worn out and his health seriously impaired. Eight years after his death a council at Constantinople canonized Gregory Palamas as a doctor of the Orthodox church. In recent years there has been a revival of interest in Hesychasm and it has been the subject of considerable study in both East and West. As well as being a speculative theologian of importance, St Gregory Palamas was a devoted teacher and pastor.

J. Meyendorff, *A Study of Gregory Palamas* (1964).

GUDULA, laywoman. Seventh century; f.d. 8 January. Every visitor to Brussels is familiar with the great church of Sainte-Gudule, but very little is known about the saint in whose honour it is dedicated. She was a daughter of Count Witger and his wife *St Amalburga* (d. *c.* 690; f.d. 10 July) and was brought up at the convent of Nivelles. She then lived with her parents at Ham, near Alost, apparently spending all her days in religious devotion and good works for her neighbours. St Gudula's sister *Raineld* is also venerated as a saint (f.d. 16 July); she was killed in a raid at Saintes, near Hal, *c.* 680.

GUÉNOLÉ ◊ *Winwaloe*

GUIGNER ◊ *Gwinear*

GUTHLAC, hermit. B. in Mercia, *c.* 673; d. at Crowland, 714; f.d. 11 April. As a youth Guthlac fought in the army of King Ethelred of Mercia, but when he was about twenty-four he entered the monastery of Repton. There his austere habits, especially his refusal of all intoxicating drink, were the subject of unfavourable comment, but he lived down the criticism and gained his brethren's respect. After some time he left the monastery and settled at a hermitage on a bend of the river Welland in the Fens. Here he lived for the rest of his life. Sometimes he was troubled by the depredations of local inhabitants, but much more by spiritual trials and temptations, which his biographer relates in terms reminiscent of the lives of the Desert Fathers.

Like them and other solitaries, St Guthlac cultivated close relations with the birds and beasts; he did not complain of the thieving habits of crows and magpies, 'for men ought to set an example of patience even to wild creatures.' When he was dying Guthlac sent for his sister, *St Pega* (f.d. 8 January), who was a hermitess in the same neighbourhood (Peakirk = Pega's church); she is said afterwards to have gone on pilgrimage to Rome and to have died there, about 719. A monastery was established at the site of St Guthlac's hermitage, which developed into the great abbey of Crowland.

B. Colgrave (tr.), *The Life of St Guthlac by Felix* (1956).

GUY OF ANDERLECHT, layman. B. in Brabant, *c.*950; d. at Anderlecht, 1012 (?); f.d. 12 September. According to the fanciful account compiled some hundred years after his death, Guy was a peasant who was made sacristan of the church at Laeken, near Brussels. After some years he was induced to invest his small savings in a commercial venture. The venture failed, and having lost both his money and his job, Guy spent seven years wandering from shrine to shrine, even so far as Jerusalem. Then he returned home, and soon after died and was buried at Anderlecht. Some considerable time later, in circumstances that seem not to have been free from superstition, a cultus of him began at his grave, and it continued to increase locally for centuries. Much folklore gathered round his name and shrine, particularly associated with horses; an annual pilgrimage of Brussels cab-drivers to Anderlecht continued till 1914.

GWENFREWI ◊ *Winifred*

GWINEAR, martyr. Sixth century (?); f.d. 23 March. The medieval Life of St Gwinear, written some eight centuries after his time, relates that he was the leader of a band of Irish missionaries who landed in Cornwall at the mouth of the Hayle river. Gwinear and some of his companions were killed by the heathen local ruler, Teudar; others of them escaped and gave their names to churches from Saint Ives to Porthleven; these events were accompanied by fantastic marvels. There is no certainty that Gwinear and his fellows were Irish or missionaries, or that there was a massacre by a 'hateful tyrant'. There is evidence which suggests that he really came from Wales, with another local saint, ◊ *Meriadoc*, and afterwards went to Brittany. Gwinear is venerated there, as St Guigner at Pluvigner, where his legend was adapted to local conditions.

H

HADRIAN ⟡ *Adrian*

HALLVARD, martyr. D. 1043; f.d. 15 May. The traditional story of this young man or youth recounts nothing of his life but only his death. He was the son of a landowner at Husaby in Norway. One day when about to cross the Drammenfjord in a boat he was appealed to by a woman, probably a bondwoman; she had been falsely accused of stealing, and was in fear of her life. Hallvard took her aboard, but was unable to get clear before the woman's pursuers arrived. They called on him to give her up, but he would not, for the woman swore she was innocent. At this, one of the pursuers shot at Hallvard and the woman with a bow, killing them both. Hallvard was revered by the people as a martyr because he had died in defence of innocence; his body was later enshrined at Christ church in Oslo, and he is still looked on as patron saint of the city.

HARVEY, abbot. Sixth century; f.d. 17 June. St Harvey (Hervé) is venerated all over Brittany but reliable particulars of him are very few. According to his late medieval Life he was the son of a British bard, but was born in Brittany, and was blind from birth. After being a hermit he became abbot of Plouvien, but eventually settled with his community at Lanhourneau in Finistère, where he died. The legend represents him as a wandering monk and minstrel, and relates many fanciful popular tales about him. He was never a priest, but he is said to have taken part in the solemn anathematizing of the tyrannical ruler Conomor, *c.* 550. Hervé is one of the most popular names for boys in Brittany and, as Harvey, is a common English surname; but the saint seems never to have had any cultus on this side of the Channel. Until the Revolution, a chapel (now destroyed) near Cleder in Finistère claimed a most uncommon saint's relic, namely, the cradle in which St Hervé was rocked.

HEDDA ⟡ under *Birinus*

HEDWIG, laywoman. B. in Bavaria, 1174; d. in Silesia, 1243; cd 1267; f.d. 16 October. St Hedwig was daughter of Count Berthold III of Andechs, and through a sister was aunt to ⟡ *St Elizabeth of Hungary*. She married the duke of Silesia, Henry I the Bearded, a man of religious disposition who encouraged and helped his wife's numerous charitable enterprises. The first and best known of these was the abbey of Cistercian nuns at Trebnitz, a little north of Breslau (now Wroclaw). The couple had six children, some of whom were the cause of considerable distress to their parents from time to time; but she outlived them all except the daughter Gertrude, who was abbess of Trebnitz. St Hedwig's favourite residence was near by and, after her husband's death in 1238, she lived within the convent itself, but without formally becoming a nun. Henceforth she devoted herself to the welfare, spiritual and temporal, of the people round about, using her fortune for the alleviation of poverty and suffering. The policies and foundations of Duke Henry and St Hedwig were important in Silesian history through the increase of German influence they brought to the country.

HELEN, empress. B. *c.* 255; d. at Nicomedia, *c.* 330; f.d. 18 August. It was long believed that the mother of Constantine the Great was a native of Britain; there is no historical justification for this belief: she was almost certainly born at Drepanum (Helenopolis) in Asia Minor, of lowly parentage. The emperor Constantius Chlorus made her his wife, and Constantine was born to them in 274; but in 292 Constantius repudiated Helen for political reasons. It is not certain when she became a Christian; but her son on becoming emperor (proclaimed by the Roman army at York in 306) treated his mother with the greatest honour, and when toleration was extended to Christianity after 312 Helen devoted all her influence to its promotion. In old age she made a lengthy visit to the Holy Land, where she expended large sums in relief of the poor and other good works, and helped in the founding of churches on sacred sites.

St Helen's name is particularly connected with the finding, buried close to the hillock of Calvary, of the cross on which the Saviour suffered. Such a discovery was certainly claimed about this time, but the earliest writers do not mention St Helen as having anything to do with it: she may, indeed, have been dead before it happened, but since the end of the fourth century it is with this discovery that St Helen is always associated. Whether the wood that was found was in fact that of the true cross is another and different question, and one that is now impossible of solution. The cross is St Helen's emblem in art.

HELIER, martyr. Sixth century (?); f.d. 16 July. This saint gives its name to the town of Saint Helier in Jersey, but he is known only from a corrupt version of a medieval account of him. According to this, he was born at Tongres in Belgium, and his education was entrusted to one Cunibert, who converted the youth to Christianity. In consequence his heathen father killed Cunibert, and Helier fled from home. He settled in the island of Jersey, and lived there as a hermit for fifteen years with a man named Romard. Helier was murdered by sea-rovers, and subsequently venerated as a martyr.

HENRY THE SECOND, emperor. B. in Bavaria, 973; d. near Göttingen, 1024; cd 1146; f.d. 15 July. He succeeded his father in the dukedom of Bavaria in 995, was elected king of the Romans at Mainz in 1002, and crowned Holy Roman emperor in 1014: his career as successor to Otto III is a matter of general history. Henry's chief concerns were the consolidation of the power of the German monarchy, and reform and reorganization in the church, the second in subordination to the first. His tutor as a youth had been ◊ *St Wolfgang* of Regensburg, and ◊ *St Odilo* of Cluny and Richard of Saint-Vanne were among his friends; but that he himself wanted to be a monk and the story of his 'celibate marriage' were rumours encouraged after his death by the emperor's partisans and seem clearly to have had no foundation in fact: St Henry was a layman and a sovereign, and his religious ways were not those of the cloister. His most important ecclesiastical foundation was the see of Bamberg, which became an educational and cultural centre. It was in Bamberg cathedral that he was buried, as was his wife *Cunegund*, who also was canonized (d. 1033; cd 1200; f.d. 3 March). She passed her years of widowhood in the nunnery she had founded at Kaufungen in Hesse; both husband and wife were zealous supporters of Benedictine monasticism.

HENRY OF UPPSALA, bishop and martyr. D. in Finland, *c.* 1160; f.d. 19 January. The patron saint of Finland was an Englishman who was appointed bishop of Uppsala in Sweden, *c.* 1152. He accompanied the Swedish king, ◊ *St Eric*, on an expedition against the Finns, and stayed on among them at Turku to do missionary work. But his tact appears to have been less than his zeal; in any case the warlike circumstances of his coming were not a recommendation, and he came to a violent end. His assassin is generally said to have been a peasant on whom the bishop had imposed penance for another murder.

The title Saint was often given to a Dane named Henry who lived in a hermitage on the island of Cocket, on the Northumberland coast, and died there in 1127; but there is no evidence for any public cultus of him.

HERIBERT, or HERBERT, OF COLOGNE, bishop. B. at Worms, *c.* 970; d. near Cologne, 1021; f.d. 16 March. Heribert was an outstanding German bishop of his era; but, like so many prelates of those times, he was actively engaged also in secular public affairs and not much is known of his personal life. He was a trusted counsellor and official of Otto III, but at first opposed his imperial successor ◊ *St Henry II*, and for a time was imprisoned by him; the two saints were afterwards reconciled. Heribert founded the abbey of Deutz, outside Cologne, and was a model bishop: generous to the needy, a good disciplinarian, and a man of peace. Already during his lifetime he was looked on as a saint; but the bull of formal canonization, attributed to Pope ◊ *St Gregory VII*, is now known to be a forgery, produced in the seventeenth century.

Another *St Herbert* (d. 687; f.d. 20 March) was venerated in the Lake District of England, and is still not wholly forgotten there. He was a disciple and friend of ◊ *St Cuthbert*, living a hermit's life on the island in Lake Derwentwater which bears his name.

HERMES, martyr. Date unknown; f.d. 28 August. The chief saint of this name was a martyr of Greek origin (perhaps a slave or freedman), buried in the cemetery of Basilla on the Old Salarian Way at Rome. Pope ◊ *St Damasus* wrote an inscription for his tomb, of which fragments have been found. The legend of St Hermes makes him a prefect of Rome, who became a Christian and was martyred under the emperor Hadrian; but these particulars are worthless, being derived from the spurious *passio* of the second-century Pope St Alexander I. In consequence of a transfer of relics, Hermes had a certain cultus in France and Germany in the middle ages.

G. H. Doble, *St Hermes* (1935).

HERMES ⍟ under *Philip of Heraclea*

HERVÉ ◊ *Harvey*

HEWALDS, THE TWO, martyrs. B. in Northumbria; d. in Westphalia, 695; f.d. 3 October. Among the missionaries who followed ◊ *St Willibrord* into Frisia were two named Hewald (Ewald), distinguished from one another as 'the Dark' and 'the Fair'; they were both Englishmen, but had lived for a time in Ireland. They preached the gospel among the continental Saxons, and were eventually martyred, their hearers fearing lest their old religion and customs should be changed. The fair Hewald was killed outright, but the dark one was first put to slow torture; their bodies were thrown into the river and, Bede tells us, heavenly portents followed. The bodies were recovered, and the Frankish Pepin of Herstal had them honourably buried at Cologne. The traditional place of the martyrdom is on a tributary of the Rhine at Aplerbeke, near Dortmund in Westphalia, of which province the Hewalds are the patron saints.

HILARION, hermit. B. near Gaza, *c.* 291; d. in Cyprus, *c.* 371; f.d. 21 October. The first recorded solitary in Palestine is known chiefly through the biography of him written by ◊ *St Jerome*. Having been educated at Alexandria, Hilarion was inspired by ◊ *St Antony* in person, and *c.* 307 he withdrew to a desolate spot near Maiuma, the port of Gaza. He lived there for more than fifty years, with a mud-brick hut for shelter, eating only figs and vegetables, bread and oil, working with his hands to support life and overcoming all temptations to abandon so austere an existence. Many heathen were converted to Christianity by his exhortations and example, and by the miracles attributed to him: of these, his enabling one Italicus to win a chariot race must have made a special appeal to the backers of Italicus. From *c.* 329 disciples began to gather round Hilarion; monastic settlements looking to him sprang up in other parts of Palestine, and he was besieged with visitors: he could not bear these disturbances, and *c.* 360 he left Maiuma for Egypt.

The remaining years of St Hilarion's life were a pathetic – and perhaps somewhat neurotic – quest for solitude. He was harassed in Egypt and, Julian the Apostate having ordered his arrest, he had to flee to the Libyan desert, from whence he soon made his way to Sicily. Here, earning his bread by collecting and selling firewood, the old man was found by one of his early disciples, Hesychius. Hilarion soon became restless again, and Hesychius tried to satisfy him by taking him to Epidaurus (Dubrovnik) on the Dalmatian coast, where no one had heard of Hilarion. Once again he attracted public attention; so he stole away by night with Hesychius and took ship to Cyprus. There his journeying ended, for after a few years he died peacefully, not far from Paphos, at the age of eighty. His body was smuggled away by Hesychius, to be buried at Maiuma.

HILARY OF ARLES, bishop. B. *c.* 400; d. 449; f.d. 5 May. This Hilary was a monk of Lérins and was hardly thirty when he succeeded his relative ◊ *St Honoratus* as bishop of Arles. He was an energetic and devoted prelate; but his zeal outran his discretion, and he was twice in trouble with Pope ◊ *St Leo I* for exceeding his episcopal powers. But after his death the same pope wrote of him as 'Hilary of sacred memory'. He is chiefly remembered for the discourse he delivered on the life of St Honoratus, of which the text has survived (tr. by F. R. Hoare in *The Western Fathers*, 1954).

HILARY OF POITIERS, bishop and theologian. B. at Poitiers, *c.* 315; d. there, *c.* 367; f.d. 13 or 14 January. He belonged to a well-off pagan family, was a highly cultivated man, and in due course became a Christian. At the age of about thirty-five, his wife being still living, he was elected bishop of his native city of Poitiers. Hilary was the most outstanding opponent of Arianism in the West. Though coming to the controversy only in middle age, he pursued it with unswerving vigour, and in 356 he was banished to Phrygia by the Arian emperor Constantius II. But he continued his campaign there, making a deep study of Greek theological thought, and in 360 the Arians had him sent back to Gaul, as a 'mischief-maker' who was a nuisance to them in the

East. The victory of orthodoxy over Arianism had become the bishop's one aim in life, and he fought for it as long as he lived: he was the 'Athanasius of the West' (◊ *St Athanasius*). St. Hilary's extensive writings, notably the work *On the Trinity*, were in the main called forth by the conflict in which he was engaged. But in dealing with the theologians and emperors and councils he did not neglect the needs of his own flock at Poitiers; before ◊ *St Ambrose* – but without Ambrose's success – he made use of metrical hymns for the teaching of Christian doctrine, a practice he had learnt in the East, and he wrote commentaries on St Matthew's gospel and the Psalms. Though so inveterate and vigorous a controversialist he seems to have been a sympathetic and friendly man; among those who came under his personal influence was ◊ *St Martin of Tours*. St Hilary of Poitiers was proclaimed a doctor of the church in 1851. In England he gives its name to the 'Hilary term' of universities and courts of law which begins on or about his feast day.

HILDA, abbess. B. in Northumbria, 614; d. at Whitby, 680; f.d. 17 November. Hilda (Hild) was a grand-niece of King Edwin of Northumbria; with him she was christened by ◊ *St Paulinus* at York in 627, when she was thirteen. It was not till twenty years later that she decided to be a nun, and in 649 ◊ *St Aidan* made her abbess of a convent at Hartlepool. After some years St Hilda made a foundation at Whitby, which she governed for the rest of her life. It was a double monastery, women and men in adjoining quarters, and among her subjects were ◊ *St John of Beverley* and the herdsman Caedmon, the first English religious poet. At the conference held at Whitby abbey to decide between Celtic and Roman ecclesiastical customs, St Hilda supported the Celtic party. Bede is enthusiastic in his praise of Abbess Hilda: she was the adviser of rulers as well as of ordinary folk; she insisted on the study of Holy Scripture and on proper preparation for the priesthood; the influence of her example of peace and charity extended beyond the walls of her monastery; 'all who knew her called her Mother, such were her wonderful godliness and grace.'

HILDEBRAND ◊ *Gregory VII*

HILDEGARD, the 'Sibyl of the Rhine'. B. at Bermersheim, 1098; d. at Rupertsberg, 1179; f.d. 17 September. Having been educated by a well-known recluse named Jutta at Diessenberg, she entered the neighbouring Benedictine convent, of which she became superioress in 1136. Although she lived to be eighty, Hildegard's health was always poor and she was of a rather excitable temperament; from an early age she claimed unusual spiritual experiences, and was credited with foreseeing the future. She lived during a troubled time for the Western church – Frederick Bar-

barossa was emperor – and in this turmoil she, like some other religious women of the middle ages, played the part of a sort of prophetess. She corresponded at length with four popes, two emperors, King Henry II of England, such eminent ecclesiastics as ◊ *St Bernard* of Clairvaux, and many other people. About 1147 she moved her community to Rupertsberg, near Bingen, and there built a large convent, from which she promulgated her 'oracles' and 'revelations'; these were highly coloured and often no less highly mysterious, so that while many hung on her words, others disparaged her as being a fraud or deceived.

From 1141 Hildegard composed numerous writings, which she dictated to monks who turned them into Latin. The longest and most studied of them is called *Scivias*, an apocalyptic work full, among other things, of denunciations of wickedness and warnings of the wrath to come expressed in symbolic and allegorical terms. She also wrote expository works on the gospels and the Rule of St Benedict, a book of natural science and another on the human body and its ailments (both giving evidence of careful observation), Lives of local saints, poems and hymns and music for them. In her lighter moments St Hildegard invented a language, which was really a mixture of German and Latin with an idiosyncratic alphabet. With all these labours she found time to visit many places in Germany to deliver the fruits of her visions in person to the clergy and others. St Hildegard was one of the most remarkable women of the middle ages, and certain traits in her writings have led to comparisons with Dante and William Blake. Among her friends was *St Elizabeth of Schönau* (d. 1164; f.d. 18 June), another visionary, who contributed, apparently inculpably, to the further elaboration of the legend of ◊ *St Ursula*.
F. M. Steele, *The Life and Visions of St Hildegarde* (1914).

HILDEGUND OF SCHÖNAU ◊ under *Marina*

HIPPARCHUS and PHILOTHEUS, martyrs. D. at Samosata, 297 (?); f.d. 9 December. According to their Syriac *passio*, it was when Emperor Galerius was in Samosata, on the Euphrates, that these two Christian magistrates of the city absented themselves from the sacrifice of thanksgiving for the emperor's victory over the Persians. They were therefore scourged and imprisoned for six weeks, but nothing would induce them to conform; so they were condemned to be crucified, together with five young men whom they had converted to Christ. There seems to have been no little sympathy among the people of Samosata for Hipparchus and his fellows. He was very bald, and when given a last chance to sacrifice he replied, 'No: not until hair again grows on my head': whereat the emperor held him up to ridicule by having a goat's skin tied over his head. The sentence was carried out on all together. It is possible that this martyrdom took place, not under Galerius, but under Maximinus Daia, *c.* 308.

HIPPOLYTUS OF ROME, theologian and martyr. D. in Sardinia, *c.* 235; f.d. 13 August. The particulars of his life and work are surrounded with uncertainty, but there is no doubt that he was a very learned man and the most important writer of the church at Rome in the third century (he wrote in Greek and may have been a native of the East). It is generally held that Hippolytus strongly attacked the bishops of Rome, St Zephryinus and ◊ *St Callistus I,* on doctrinal, disciplinary and personal grounds, and was set up by a party as rival to Callistus, thus being the first 'antipope'; that in the persecution by Maximinus Thrax he was banished to the quarries of Sardinia with Pope St Pontian, with whom he was there reconciled; that he died in captivity; and that his body was brought to Rome for burial with the honours of a martyr.

The most celebrated writing of Hippolytus is the *Philosophoumena,* in which he sets out to refute a number of heretical Gnostic teachings, deriving them from pagan sources. He wrote the oldest known work of biblical exegesis, a commentary on the book of Daniel; and it was a scholar in England, Dom Hugh Connolly, who finally showed that Hippolytus was the author of the work previously called th*e Egyptian Church Order* and now known as the *Apostolic Tradition.* It is a most valuable source for the worship, discipline, and customs of Christians in early third-century Rome (Eng. trans. 1934).

Two other saints of the same name have been confused with this St Hippolytus from time to time: one was erroneously said to be a bishop martyred at Porto; the other is a doubtless fictitious character associated with the martyrdom of ◊ *St Lawrence.* The form of death alleged of the second of these is reminiscent of that of Hippolytus, son of Theseus, in Greek mythology who was dragged to death by the bolting horses of his chariot.

HOMOBONUS, layman. D. at Cremona, 1197; cd 1199; f.d. 13 November. At his baptism Homobonus Tucingo was prophetically named: Uomobuono, 'good man'. He was the son of a well-to-do merchant of Cremona in Lombardy, and inherited his father's business, which he conducted successfully. He devoted a large part of his profits to the relief of those in want, some of whom he looked after in his own house: these activities, however, did not easily win the wholehearted support of his wife. Morning and evening Homobonus was to be found in his parish church, and it was at Mass that death suddenly took him. The people of Cremona clamoured for his canonization, which was decreed two years later by Pope Innocent III.

HONORATUS OF AMIENS ◊ under *Honorius of Canterbury*

HONORATUS OF ARLES, bishop. B. at Trier (?), *c.* 350; d. at Arles, 429; f.d. 16 January. He came of a Gallo-Roman family of consular rank and was a convert to Christianity. After a pilgrimage to Greece and Rome he established himself, *c.* 410, on a desert island off Cannes, where he was joined by, among others, ◊ *St Lupus of Troyes, St Eucherius of Lyons,* and *St Hilary of Arles.* This was the beginning of the celebrated monastery of Lérins, whose history lasted for nearly 1,400 years. His relative Hilary (◊ above) in a panegyric of St Honoratus speaks of the trouble taken by the saint that no one in this island community should be dispirited or overworked or idle; and 'it is astonishing how much work he got through himself, of poor health as he was'. Many visitors found their way to the island (including ◊ *St John Cassian*), and no one left it 'without a perfectly carefree mind'. In 427 St Honoratus was elected to the important see of Arles, but he died very soon after.

The account of Honoratus by Hilary is trans. in F. R. Hoare, *The Western Fathers* (1954).

HONORIUS OF CANTERBURY, bishop. D. at Canterbury, 653; f.d. 30 September. ◊ *St Gregory I* sent him as a missionary to the English, but whether actually with ◊ *St Augustine of Canterbury* is not known. About 627 he became the fifth archbishop of Canterbury. Nothing is known of his personal life and character, and little of his long episcopate. But it was marked by two events of importance: the sending of *St Felix of Dunwich* to evangelize the East Angles, and the appointment in 644 of the first Englishman to be a bishop, the Kentish Ithamar of Rochester. Ithamar in turn consecrated the first English archbishop of Canterbury, Frithona (Deusdedit), in 655.

The Faubourg and Rue Saint-Honoré in Paris are named from the *St Honorius* who was bishop of Amiens in the sixth century (f.d. 16 May). He is sometimes called Honoratus.

HOPE ◊ under *Faith*

HORMIDZ, martyr. D. in Persia, *c.* 422; f.d. 8 August. This young man was the Christian son of a city governor; his name suggests that he was a convert from Zoroastrianism. In the persecution under the Sassanian king Bahram IV – originally provoked by the violent conduct of a Christian priest – Hormidz was called on to renounce Christ. On his refusal he was deprived of his rank and property, and condemned to be a camel-driver in the army, treatment which failed to shake his constancy. The place and manner of his eventual martyrdom are not known. St Hormidz is the titular saint of a congregation of monks in Iraq and Persia.

HUBERT, bishop. D. at Tervueren, 30 May 727; f.d. 3 November. Nothing reliable is known about St Hubert before he became a cleric under ◊ *St Lambert*, whom he succeeded as bishop of Tongres-Maestricht. He was an active missionary in the great forest area of Ardenne, where idolatry had not yet wholly disappeared. In 726, while fishing from a boat in the Meuse, he met with an accident that caused him much suffering, and he died fifteen months later. St Hubert came to be regarded as patron saint of hunters and trappers in Ardenne; by the fifteenth century this led to the attribution to him also of the legend related of ◊ *St Eustace* : that, hunting in the forest on a Good Friday when a young man, he was converted to a better life by coming upon a stag which displayed a crucifix between its antlers. This stag is his emblem.

HUGH, LITTLE SAINT ◊ under *William of Norwich*

HUGH OF CLUNY, abbot. B. at Semur, 1024; d. at Cluny, 1109; cd 1120; f.d. 29 April. Though he was the eldest son of an important Burgundian nobleman, Hugh was allowed to be professed a monk of Cluny in Burgundy at an early age, and was elected to the abbacy when only twenty-five. The office carried with it the headship of the influential Benedictine confederation that depended on Cluny, and throughout his life Hugh was prominent in councils and other ecclesiastical affairs. He was a wholehearted reformer; pope after pope, from Leo IX to Paschal II, turned to him for advice and help, and entrusted him with responsible missions to places ranging from Aquitaine to Hungary. He was a man of great psychological insight and diplomatic ability. His integrity and generosity were known to all; when ◊ *St Anselm* fell out with King William II of England it was to St Hugh at Cluny that he first went for counsel, and the saintliness of Hugh's life impressed such various men as ◊ *St Peter Damian, St Gregory VII*, and William the Conqueror. He continued ◊ *St Odilo*'s policy of bringing the constituent monasteries of the Cluniac congregation into closer dependence on the mother house; during the sixty years of his abbacy Cluny reached the highest point of power and international influence in its long history, though not perhaps without some diminution of its spiritual fervour. It was in 1077 that the Cluniac reform was first introduced into England, at Lewes in Sussex.

HUGH OF GRENOBLE, bishop. B. near Valence, 1053; d. at Grenoble, 1132; cd 1134; f.d. 1 April. Good looks and a diffident manner, added to his abilities, seem to have helped this Hugh's swift rise in ecclesiastical office; he was only twenty-seven when he was made bishop of Grenoble. He would have preferred to be a monk, but proved the vigorous reforming prelate that the diocese needed so badly. After a discouraging start, he carried on his duties for fifty-two years; he was unpopular with the nobility, whose depredations on church property the bishop dealt with very firmly. As a youth St Hugh had been a pupil of ◊ *St Bruno* at Rheims, and one of his early and most beneficent actions as bishop was the establishing in 1084 of Bruno and the first Carthusian monks at the Grande Chartreuse in his diocese. Among his activities were the founding of a hospital at Grenoble and the provision of a stone bridge over the Isère. The Life by his friend the Carthusian Gigues brings out the attractiveness of Hugh's character; it was written by order of Pope Innocent II, who canonized him only two years after his death.

HUGH OF LINCOLN, bishop. B. at Avalon in Burgundy, 1135 (?); d. in London, 1200; cd 1220; f.d. 17 November. About 1178 King Henry II founded a Carthusian monastery ('charterhouse') at Witham in Somerset, between Bruton and Frome; he sent to France for the monk Hugh of Avalon to take charge of it. Hugh had already been a Carthusian for seventeen years, and he spent six years at Witham, leading the same uneventful life of worship and work. Sometimes he was called away on the affairs of his house, especially by his royal patron; and in dealing with that very able and overbearing man Hugh used good temper and steady firmness. He began by refusing to undertake the office of prior of Witham until the king had given alternative accommodation and compensation – 'to the last penny,' he insisted – to the people who had been turned out of their homes to make room for the monastery. After interviewing his earthly sovereign, he would hurry back to his prayers and his pets (his tame swan was famous; it became his emblem in art).

In 1186 Hugh had to leave the quiet life of Selwood to be bishop of the largest diocese in England, Lincoln. The see had been vacant for nearly sixteen years and the work to be done was tremendous; he proved as good a bishop as he was a monk. With all his burdens and spiritual earnestness he was full of liveliness and gaiety, but he was easily roused to anger, especially by injustice in any form. He vigorously supported the common people against the king's foresters, who enforced the savage forest laws in the vast royal hunting-grounds. At Lincoln, and again at Northampton, he stood up alone to rioting mobs incensed against the Jews, and from such scenes would go to play with children, or to tend the neglected sick or visit the outlying parts of his huge diocese. It was he who began the rebuilding of Lincoln cathedral that ultimately resulted in the building we see today.

Hugh said of himself that he was 'peppery'; his admirers said of him that 'he was a good man, fearless as a lion in any danger', and his bravery was without bluster. He calmed the rage of the fierce Henry II with a joke – a daring joke at the king's expense; he calmed the rage of the fierce Richard I with a kiss – and still refused to pay taxes to finance the king's war in France: an early case of the refusal of a money-grant demanded directly by the Crown. He died at Lincoln's Inn in London, worn out with his fourteen years of work as a bishop. St Hugh is one of the most attractive characters of medieval England: John Ruskin found him 'The most beautiful sacerdotal figure known to me in history'.

The contemporary Life, ed. and tr. by D. L. Douie and H. Farmer, *Magna Vita Sancti Hugonis* (2 vols., 1961–2); modern biographies by an anon. Carthusian (ed. H. Thurston, 1898) and R. M. Woolley (1927).

HYACINTH ◊ *Protus and Hyacinth*

HYACINTH OF CRACOW, Dominican friar. B. in Silesia, 1185; d. at Cracow, 1257; cd 1594; f.d. 17 August. Hyacinth was already a priest when he joined the Order of Preachers in Rome, and in 1221 he was sent to Cracow, where he established the first Polish house of his order. He later founded a friary at Danzig, and another, which did not last long, in Kiev. His later movements and activities are unknown. But his biographers made the most of his reputation as a wonderworker, and in the sixteenth century he was credited as well with very extensive missionary journeys for which there is no good evidence. One of these writers even altered his name, which was really Jacko or Jacek, a Polish diminutive of Jacob: this was transformed into *Jacinthus*, 'Hyacinth.' – There were several Hyacinths among the early martyrs, including the one associated with ◊ *St Protus*.

I

IA ◊ under *Ivo*
IDE ◊ *Ita*
IGNATIUS OF ANTIOCH, bishop and martyr. D. at Rome, *c.*107; f.d. 1 February. This very early martyr, also called *Theophoros*, 'God-bearer', is celebrated for seven letters that he wrote, whose text has come down to us. Little is known of his life. He was probably of Syrian origin, and legend identified him with the child whom Christ set down among his disciples (Matt. xviii, 1–6); more reliable sources say he was a disciple of ◊ *St Peter* and *St Paul*, or of ◊ *St John*. In any case he became the second or third bishop of the great Christian centre of Antioch in Syria. Here, when an oldish man, he was sentenced to death, and was sent to Rome to be thrown to wild beasts at the public 'games'. It was during this journey that he wrote his letters, in one of which he says he is in charge of a squad of soldiers ('ten leo-

pards'), whose 'behaviour gets worse the better they are treated'. They stopped for a time at Smyrna, where Ignatius was met by ◊ St Polycarp, then a young man. Here the first four letters were written, to the Christians at Ephesus, Magnesia, Tralles, and Rome. Then at Lystra, before crossing into Europe, he wrote three more, to the Christians at Philadelphia and Smyrna, and a farewell letter of advice to Bishop Polycarp.

These letters (Eng. trans., 1934 and others) are of the greatest value and interest for the light they throw on Christian belief and practice less than a century after Christ's ascension. Ignatius continually urges his readers to maintain unity amongst themselves, meeting together in the Eucharist under the presidency of their bishop. The best-known letter is the one sent in advance to the Roman Christians. In it he implores them not to try to get him reprieved. It reveals a patient, gentle man, so passionately devoted to Christ that he could not bear to miss the chance of dying a violent death for his sake: 'Let me follow the example of the suffering of my God.' In due course St Ignatius was thrown to the beasts in Rome, quite probably in the amphitheatre now known as the Colosseum; no further particulars of his life and martyrdom are known. Certain later accounts profess to tell us more, but they have no historical value.

IGNATIUS OF CONSTANTINOPLE ◊ under *Photius*

IGNATIUS OF LACONI, Capuchin laybrother. B. at Laconi, 1701; d. at Cagliari, 1781; cd 1951; f.d. 12 May. Ignatius Vincent Peis belonged to a family of poor village folk in Sardinia, where he passed the whole of his life. When he was twenty he was accepted as a laybrother by the Capuchin Franciscans; at forty he was entrusted with the work of going round to beg alms for the friars' support, and that was his main occupation for another forty years. The particulars that have survived of Brother Ignatius's Christ-centred life and determined, gentle character read like something out of the *Little Flowers of St Francis*.

Other Capuchin laybrothers who have been canonized are *St Conrad of Parzham*, who died in Bavaria in 1894 (cd 1934; f.d. 22 April); *St. Felix of Cantalice*, d. in Rome in 1587 (cd 1712; f.d. 18 May); *St Francis of Camporosso*, d. at Genoa, 1866 (cd 1962; f.d. 25 September); and *St Serafino*, also an Italian, d. 1604 (cd 1767; f.d. 12 October). The lives of all these bear the same mark of Franciscan simplicity.

IGNATIUS OF LOYOLA, founder of the Society of Jesus. B. at Loyola, *c.* 1491; d. in Rome, 1556; cd 1622; f.d. 31 July. The founder of the Jesuits was the youngest son of a Basque nobleman of ancient family. As a young man he was a soldier, and was wounded at the siege of Pamplona by the French; during a long convalescence he did much reading, of the life of Christ and of the saints, and at length determined to give his life wholly to God's service. After a year's retirement at Manresa in Catalonia, which influenced his whole life, he went on pilgrimage to Jerusalem, and then from 1524 to 1534 gave himself to study, beginning with Latin grammar among the schoolboys of Barcelona and ending with his graduation as master of arts in the University of Paris. From time to time he did evangelical work among the people, an activity by a layman that roused suspicion among Spanish church authorities.

In Paris Ignatius (Iñigo) became the inspiration of a group of seven students (one of them was ◊ *St Francis Xavier*), who in 1534 bound themselves by vow to be missionaries to the Moslems in Palestine. Three years later this group, increased to ten, met in Venice and, finding that war made the journey to Palestine impossible, offered their services to Pope Paul III in any capacity. Ignatius, now forty-seven years old, and others of them were then ordained to the priesthood, and various tasks were assigned to the members of the group. Soon it was proposed that they should be organized into a regular religious order, with the usual vows, and an additional one of being at the pope's disposal at any time anywhere. In 1540 Paul III gave his formal approval, and thus the Society (or Company) of Jesus came to birth. For the remaining fifteen years of his life St Ignatius directed his order from Rome and amplified its constitutions, seeing it grow from ten members to a thousand, spreading from country to country in Europe and overseas to distant lands. From the first it was active in the mission field, and in 1547 began its work of education in schools and universities; it began, too, to meet the challenge of the Protestant Reformation, a concern in which Ignatius insisted that an example of charity and moderation be given, 'without hard words or contempt for people's errors'.

St Ignatius of Loyola, a man of compelling personality with a notable gift for friendship, was above all a man of prayer, who received deep religious illumination. He left one famous book, the *Spiritual Exercises* (latest Eng. trans. 1963) which was begun at Manresa and finally published in 1548. The influence of this work during the past four hundred years has been incalculable, and not confined to Roman Catholics. A volume in English of his *Letters to Women* was published in 1960.

J. Brodrick, *St Ignatius Loyola: the Pilgrim Years* (1956); other biographies by H. D. Sedgwick (1923), P. van Dyke (1926), P. Dudon (1949).

ILDEFONSUS, bishop. B. at Toledo, *c.* 606; d. there, 667; f.d. 23 January. He was the abbot of a monastery at Toledo, who in 657 was made archbishop of that city. His successor in the see gave high praise to his virtues and abilities, but St Ildefonsus lived to govern it for only nine years. He was also a musician and a writer: the best known of his four extant writings is a treatise on the Virgin Mary, the first document of the kind emanating from the Spanish church. It is a work of enthusiasm rather than of sober thought, and its style is very repetitious.

A. Braegelmann, *Life and Writings of St Ildephonsus* (1942).

ILLTYD, abbot. Fifth-sixth century; f.d. 6 November. Illtyd (Illtud, Iltut, and other forms) was clearly an outstanding figure among the Welsh saints, the chief area of his labours being the south-eastern part of the country. A Life of him was written about 1140 and has no historical value; but the Life of St Samson, written perhaps over five hundred years earlier, has some important references. It calls Illtyd 'the most learned of the Britons in both Testaments and in all kinds of knowledge', and speaks of his great monastic school. This establishment was Llanilltyd Fawr (Llantwit Major in Glamorgan), and other prominent saints besides ◊ *Samson* are said to have been Illtyd's pupils there. The author of Samson's Life also describes Illtyd's death, in illustration of the saint's power of prophecy. The passage is an impressive one, but it does not state where or when the death took place. The monastery at Llantwit survived in one form or another up to the Norman conquest.

G. H. Doble, *St Iltut* (1944).

ILTUT ◊ *Illtyd*

IMRE ◊ under *Stephen of Hungary*

INNOCENTS, THE HOLY. Feast day on 28 December. This name is given to the children of Bethlehem, 'from two years old and under', who were killed by order of King Herod in an attempt to get rid of the child Jesus, whom he had heard of as a possible rival (Matt. ii, 1–3, 16–18). They have been venerated as martyrs from early times. It is the custom in Bethlehem for Christian children to gather in the church of the Nativity every afternoon and sing a hymn in memory of the 'flowers of martyrdom': those 'young warriors', as the English Aelfric wrote in the tenth century, who bore witness to the Saviour whom as yet they did not know. There have been some highly exaggerated estimates of their number; it is unlikely that there were more than about twenty of them at the most.

IRENAEUS OF LYONS, theologian. B. at Smyrna (?), *c.* 130; d. at Lyons, *c.* 202; f.d. 3 July. This father of the church was one of the most important theologians of the second century. In his youth he was strongly influenced by ◊ *St Polycarp*, whose teaching he treasured 'not on paper but in my heart, for the things we learnt in childhood are part of our soul'. But he left Asia Minor and at the time of the persecution under Marcus Aurelius he was a priest at Lyons. On returning from a mission to Rome he succeeded the martyred ◊ *St Pothinus* as bishop of Lyons. A later tradition asserts that St Irenaeus himself ended his life as a martyr, but the evidence in support of this is far from decisive. His principal writing is a treatise against the false teachings of the Gnostics (*Adversus haereses*). The *Presentation of the Apostolic Preaching* has been preserved through an Armenian translation of the Greek text. Little is known of St Irenaeus' life; but he was clearly a very conscientious bishop, who became a writer because the duties of his pastoral ministry required it.

IRENE ◊ *Agape, Chionia, and Irene*

ISAAC THE GREAT, bishop. B. *c.* 347; d. 438; f.d. 9 September. Isaac (Sahak) was the son of ◊ *St Narses I*, and like him an outstanding figure in the early Armenian church. Of his varied activities as the head of that church for half a century one of the most far-reaching was the encouragement he gave to the beginnings of Armenian literature; it began with a translation of the Bible, in which he had the help of ◊ *St Mesrop*. St Isaac's opposition to Nestorianism and his contacts with the imperial court at Constantinople led to his being driven from his see by the Persians in 427, and he had thenceforth to administer his church amid much ecclesiastical turmoil and disorder.

ISAAC JOGUES, martyr. B. at Orléans, 1607; d. at Ossernenon, 18 October 1646; cd 1930; f.d. 26 September. He entered the Society of Jesus in 1624 and twelve years later was sent as a missionary to Canada. He took the gospel to the Mohawks and in the course of his labours penetrated to the eastern entrance of Lake Superior, one thousand miles inland – the first European to do so. In 1642 Father Jogues was captured (with ◊ *St René Goupil*) by Iroquois, being kept prisoner for a year and so cruelly tortured that he lost the use of his hands. The Dutch at Fort Orange helped him to escape; less than three years later he was back at his place of captivity (Ossernenon, now Auriesville, N.Y.), this time as a missionary there. But the Bear clan, believing him to be a sorcerer, blamed him for an outbreak of sickness and the failure of their crops, and one afternoon he was seized, together with St John Lalande. They were beaten and slashed with knives and that evening Isaac Jogues was tomahawked. The next day Lalande was killed in the same way. Their heads were struck off and impaled on the settlement palisade, and their trunks thrown into the Mohawk river.

ISABEL ◊ *Elizabeth of Portugal*

ISIDORE THE FARM-SERVANT, layman, B. at Madrid, *c.* 1070; d. there, 1130; cd 1622; f.d. 10 May (in U.S.A. 25 October). He spent all his life in the service of the same employer, working on a farm at Torrelaguna outside Madrid, the city of which he is now the patron saint. A biography of him written 150 years after his death is not very trustworthy: it consists largely of wonders associated with Isidore's name. But clearly he was a model worker, a kind neighbour, and a most devout Christian. His wife Mary resembled him in character, and she also is popularly looked on as a saint in Spain. Isidore was canonized at the instance of King Philip III, who attributed recovery from a serious illness to his intercession. In art, St Isidore's emblem is a sickle.

ISIDORE OF SEVILLE, scholar. B. at Cartagena, *c.* 560; d. at Seville, 636; f.d. 4 April. He succeeded his elder brother ◊ *St Leander* as bishop of Seville *c.* 600, and during a long episcopate strengthened the Spanish church by organizing councils, establishing schools and religious houses, and continuing to turn the Visigoths from Arianism. He also sought to convert the local Jews, but by highly questionable methods. It is, however, through his writings that Isidore acquired fame: he was a writer of astonishing industry on religious, historical, and scientific subjects. His last and most extensive work, called *Etymologies* or *Origins*, which is an encyclopedia of the knowledge of his time, continued to be used throughout the middle ages; but his history of the Goths and Vandals is more valuable today. St Isidore was not an original or critical writer, but because of his ecclesiastical works he was declared a doctor of the church by Pope Innocent XIII in 1722. His great influence during the middle ages is attested by the very large number of the manuscripts of his writings; Dante mentions him in the *Paradiso* (x, 130), in the company of the Venerable ◊ *Bede* and the Scottish Richard of Saint-Victor.

ITA, abbess. D. *c.* 570; f.d. 15 January. Ita (Ide) was for many years the head of a community of dedicated women at Killeedy in County Limerick, where she seems to have had a school for little boys who were taught 'Faith in God with purity of heart; simplicity of life with religion; generosity with love'. Among her pupils is said to have been ◊ *St Brendan* (The Voyager) of Clonfert. St Ita's legend stresses her physical austerities and relates a number of miracles, some of them absurd.

Ide Ni Riain, *St Ita* (1964).

IVO, bishop. No date; f.d. 24 April. The patron of the town of Saint Ives in Huntingdonshire and the village of Saint Ive (pron. Eve) in east Cornwall derives his origins from the finding, at Slepe near Ramsey abbey *c.* 1001, of some bones and bishop's insignia to which a name and legend became attached: St Ivo probably had no historical existence. Saint Ives in west Cornwall, on the other hand, was formerly called Porth Ia. According to late medieval legend *St Ia* was a holy maiden who came from Ireland – sailing on a leaf that grew to accommodate her – and landed and settled where Saint Ives now stands (f.d. 3 February).

IVO OF CHARTRES, bishop. B. near Beauvais, *c.* 1014; d. at Chartres, 1116; f.d. 24 May. He studied under Lanfranc at Bec, joined a community of canons regular, and in 1090 was made bishop of Chartres. When King Philip I of France repudiated his wife Bertha and carried off the wife of Fulk of Anjou, Ivo refused to recognize the new queen; whereupon Philip imprisoned the bishop and seized his property. Pope Urban II got him released, and excommunicated the king. St Ivo was a learned and important canonist, and a moderating influence in the disputes over the lay investiture of bishops, not failing to denounce the exactions of Roman curial officials.

IVO OF KERMARTIN ◊ *Yves*

J

JAMES ◊ *Marian and James*

JAMES THE GREATER, apostle. D. at Jerusalem, 44; f.d. 25 July. He was the brother of and fellow fisherman with ◊ *St John*, and is called 'the Greater' to distinguish him from the other apostle ◊ *James*, '*the Less*'. With ◊ *Peter* and John he was chosen by Christ to be a witness of his transfiguration and his agony in the garden (Matt xvii, 1–9; xxvi, 36–46), and with these two had a certain precedence among the twelve. He was the first of the apostles to be martyred, being put to the sword by order of King Herod Agrippa I to please the Jewish opponents of Christianity (Acts xii, 1–2). An early story relates that his accuser suddenly repented, declared himself a Christian, and was beheaded with him. According to Spanish tradition St James visited Spain and preached the gospel there. The story is first heard of only in the seventh century, and the evidence against it is so weighty that it is now quite discredited outside Spain. It was further claimed that after his martyrdom the body of St James was brought from Jerusalem to Spain. In the later middle ages its shrine at Santiago de Compostela was one of the greatest centres of pilgrimage in Christendom, and it is still much resorted to; there is, however, no evidence whatever as to the identity of the relics discovered in Galicia early in the ninth century and claimed to be those of St James. James himself is often represented in art as a pilgrim, with a cockle shell.

T. D. Kendrick, *St James in Spain* (1960).

JAMES THE LESS, apostle. D. at Jerusalem, 62 (?); f.d. 1 May, with ◊ *St Philip* (in R.C.ch., 11 May). James, the son of Alphaeus, is listed among Christ's twelve apostles in the gospels; he is sometimes said to be the same as James, 'the Lord's brother', referred to several times in the New Testament. If this identification is right (about which there is much doubt), it was James the Less who eventually presided over the Christian community at Jerusalem and was there martyred. The contemporary Jewish historian Josephus records that the bishop James was stoned to death; a century later a converted Jew, Hegesippus, says that James was first taken to the pinnacle of the Temple and implored to dissuade the assembled people from belief in Christ. He spoke to the contrary effect, and was thereupon thrown down from the pinnacle and stoned and beaten to death as he lay there. The Epistle of St James in the New Testament is commonly attributed to James, the Lord's brother.

JAMES OF THE MARCH ◊ under *John of Capistrano*

JAMES OF NISIBIS, bishop. D. at Nisibis, 338 (?); f.d. 15 July. This James was the first bishop of Nisibis (Nusaybin) in Mesopotamia, which soon became a very important Christian centre. Little is known about his life except that he was a teacher of ◊ *St Ephraem* and attended the first general council at Nicaea; but his memory is highly honoured in the East, especially in the Syrian churches, and legends have gathered round his name. A number of writings were formerly attributed to him in error.

JANE FRANCES DE CHANTAL, foundress. B. at Dijon, 1572; d. at Moulins, 13 December 1641; cd 1767; f.d. 21 August. Jeanne-Françoise Frémyot married at twenty Baron Christophe de Rabutin-Chantal. The marriage was a very happy one, but after only eight years Jane Frances was left a widow with four children. For some years she was forced to live with her father-in-law, who treated her with indignity, but in 1604 she met ◊ *St Francis de Sales*, who agreed to be her spiritual director. There ensued a friendship between them which is one of the most perfect in the annals of the saints. In 1607 Francis disclosed his plan for a new religious order of women, and Mme de Chantal agreed to cooperate; in 1610, after a melodramatic scene with her only son, Celse-Bénigne (who became the father of Mme de Sévigné), she took charge of the first of its convents, at Annecy in Savoy. At first the aspirants were easy to guide; but later, when daughters of noble families were coming in, Mme de Chantal's skill and tact were thoroughly tried: so many of them were over-refined, touchy, and ignorant. The Order of the Visitation was designed for single women and widows who, because of age or other reasons, were unfitted for the more severe life of other orders, and it evoked much tiresome criticism. St Jane Frances was fully capable of dealing with this, and proceeded to establish other convents; before her death there were over eighty Visitation houses. She combined a deep religious life with great administrative ability and strength of character. St Francis de Sales died in 1622 and her son was killed in battle against the English five years later; but she overcame these and other bereavements, as well as her religious trials, and was active to the end. Her own death came while she was returning from a visit to Ann of Austria in Paris. ◊ *St Vincent de Paul*, who knew her personally and well, said of Jane Frances de Chantal: she was 'one of the holiest people I have ever met on this earth'.

E. Stopp, *Madame de Chantal* (1962); M. Henry-Couannier, *Francis de Sales and his Friends* (1964).

JANUARIUS, bishop and martyr. D. 305 (?); f.d. 19 September. Traditionally Januarius (Gennaro) was a bishop of Benevento who was martyred with six companions at Pozzuoli, but his exact identity has not been established. There is preserved in the cathedral at Naples a glass phial containing a substance said to be the dried blood of St Januarius. This relic is shown in public eighteen times a year, when, after a varying interval of time, the substance liquefies. This phenomenon has been carefully examined and seems unquestionably to take place; so far no fully satisfactory explanation of it is forthcoming. The happening has been recorded for the past 500 years, but there is no known mention of the supposed blood relic before 1389, over 1,000 years after the presumed date of St Januarius's death.

A similar phenomenon is attributed to blood relics of other martyrs in other places; these are nearly all in southern Italy and some of the relics are manifestly spurious, e.g. those of ◊ *St John the Baptist* and *St Stephen*. On the other hand from time to time for two centuries after his death in 1616 the phenomenon was observed in authentic blood relics of *St Bernardine Realino*. He was a Jesuit, the whole of whose long ministry was passed in Naples and at Lecce in Apulia (cd 1947; f.d. 3 July).

JANUARIUS ◊ under *Felicity*

JAPAN, MARTYRS IN. D. at Nagasaki, 1597; cd 1862; f.d. 5 February. Of the numerous Christian martyrs in Japan the canonization of twenty-six has been completed, of whom six were European Franciscan missionaries, led by the Spanish St Peter Baptist. Among the others were a Japanese Jesuit priest, St Paul Miki, and a Korean layman, St Leo Karasuma. The remainder were Japanese laymen, of whom three were young boys. They were killed simultaneously by a sort of crucifixion, being raised on crosses and then stabbed with spears. The persecution had been touched off by the irresponsible and boastful talk of a Spanish sea-captain, the Japanese 'shogun' Hideyoshi having already been provoked to fury by the success of the Christian missionaries.

JARLATH OF TUAM, abbot-bishop. D. *c.* 550; f.d. 6 June. He is said to have been a disciple of ◊ *St Enda.* He founded a monastery at Cluain Fois, near Tuam, and is venerated in Ireland as the originator of that see. – An earlier St Jarlath was converted by ◊ *St Patrick* and became the third bishop of Armagh.

JEANNE ◊ *Jane, Joan*

JEROME, doctor of the church. B. at Strido in Dalmatia, *c.* 342; d. at Bethlehem, 420; f.d. 30 September. St Jerome (Eusebius Hieronymus) was the most learned of the Latin fathers of the church and among the greatest of biblical scholars. He was brought up a Christian and studied for eight years in Rome, but was not baptized till he was more than eighteen. About 374 he went to Syria and spent some years among the hermits in the desert east of Antioch; here he learnt Hebrew from a rabbi, and afterwards in Constantinople 'sat under' ◊ *St Gregory of Nazianzus.* At Antioch he was ordained priest; but it was against his express wishes, and he did not exercise the priestly office, which he believed to be incompatible with his own vocation. From 382 to 385 he acted as secretary to Pope ◊ *St Damasus* in Rome, who directed him to revise the Latin version of the New Testament. Jerome also became the leader of a group of Roman ladies who were drawn to an ascetic and studious life. But his rigorist spirit and his irascibility made him disliked by many, and on the death of Damasus he returned to the East, followed by ◊ *St Paula, St Eustochium,* and others of his disciples. In 386 they settled at Bethlehem, Paula's fortune paying for the provision of buildings wherein men and women respectively could lead an ordered and peaceful religious life. A hospice was opened for travellers, and a free school in which Jerome taught Greek and Latin to the local children.

From time to time their quiet was disturbed by Jerome's controversies, about celibacy, about Pelagianism, in particular about the teachings of Origen, which led to a bitter quarrel with his boyhood's friend Rufinus. These involved him in much writing of letters and polemical treatises, and there were other writings as well; but year after year, with the help of his devoted amanuenses, his biblical work went on. Practically the whole of the Latin Bible – known since the thirteenth century as 'the Vulgate' – was either translated from Hebrew and Greek or worked over by St Jerome. The task was finished *c.* 404, and soon afterwards the Bethlehem retreat began to be disturbed by external events: refugees from Rome when it was sacked by Alaric, local raids by Huns and Isaurians, attacks on Jerome's religious houses by sectaries.

'Now', he wrote, 'we have to translate the words of Scripture into deeds; instead of talking of holy things we must enact them.'

St Jerome was in some ways a contradictory character. His religious ideals were pitched very high; he held the affection of his friends and followers; he was considerate to the weak and lowly. On the other hand there were his intemperateness in controversy, his contempt for opponents, the virulence of his tongue and pen, his savage and insulting invective. To attribute these things simply to too close a following of classical rhetorical models is perhaps a little naïve. The remark attributed to Pope Sixtus V seems more to the point: looking at a picture which showed Jerome beating his breast with a stone, Sixtus is said to have observed, 'You do well thus to use that stone: without it you would never have been numbered among the saints.' But St Jerome's place as a biblical scholar among the four great Latin doctors is undisputed. A first volume of translations into English of his entrancing letters has been published in the Ancient Christian Writers series. In art Jerome, accompanied by a lion, is often represented with a cardinal's hat, because of his services to Pope Damasus.

F. X. Murphy (ed.), *A Monument to St Jerome* (1952); J. Steinmann, *St Jerome* (1959); J. N. D. Kelly, *Jerome, His Life and Writings* (1973).

JEROME EMILIANI ◊ under *Cajetan*

JOACHIM and ANN. F.d. 16 August, 26 July. Nothing whatever is known about the parents of the Virgin Mary, to whom these names are traditionally given. They derive from an early apocryphal writing called the *Protevangelium of James*, which professes to give an account of Mary's coming into the world (and other things besides). This story bears a strong resemblance to the biblical narrative (I Samuel i) of the childless Hannah's bearing of Samuel (Ann, Anna, is the same name as Hannah).

JOAQUINA, foundress. B. at Barcelona, 1783; d. at Vich, 1854; cd 1959; f.d. 28 August. Joaquina de Vedruna at the age of sixteen married a lawyer, Theodore de Mas. The marriage was a happy one, and eight children were born; but, by the time she was thirty-three, Joaquina was already a widow. Ten years later, after providing for her children, she began the establishment of a community at Vich in Catalonia for nursing and teaching; they were called the Carmelites of Charity. With the help of, among others, ◊ *St Antony Claret* the foundation prospered and spread, and provided nurses for both sides in the Carlist wars. About 1850 Mother Joaquina was attacked by a slow paralysis, which forced her to give up the direction of her congregation; the disease eventually rendered her helpless and speechless: but it failed to quench her spirit and religious trust. She died of cholera at the age of seventy.

JOAN ✧ under *Jane*

JOAN OF ARC, the Maid of Orléans. B. at Domrémy, *c.* 1412; d. at Rouen, 1431; cd 1920; f.d. 30 May. Jeanne la Pucelle, 'Joan the Maid', called Joan of Arc in England, was an illiterate and highly intelligent peasant girl from Champagne. The dauphin Charles of France was at war with the combined forces of England and Burgundy, and from about the age of thirteen Joan experienced inward promptings, her 'voices', urging her to save France from the aggressors. Early in 1429 she obtained an audience with the dauphin, whom she won over; after a searching examination by churchmen, she was provided with a suit of armour and a staff of attendants, and joined the army at Blois, which ten days later routed the English besieging Orléans. This was followed by another victory at Patay; Troyes surrendered; and Joan persuaded the dauphin to be crowned at Rheims, as King Charles VII. The effect of this triumph of Joan's moral leadership was tremendous; but the French did not press home their advantage, so in 1430 Joan went off on her own to relieve the beleagured town of Compiègne. There the Burgundians captured her when leading a sortie, and sold her to the English. King Charles left her to her fate.

After nine months of brutal confinement Joan was arraigned before the court of the bishop of Beauvais, Peter Cauchon, on charges of witchcraft and heresy. During fifteen sessions she stood up to her learned accusers, fearlessly and good-humouredly, with native shrewdness, always refusing to betray her conscience, her heavenly 'voices'. She was found guilty, and the University of Paris confirmed the verdict. For a short time Joan wavered before imminent and hideous death, and then stood firm again. She was handed over to the civil authorities and burned in the market-place of Rouen. She was less than twenty years old.

St Joan of Arc was convicted by a tribunal of churchmen which unscrupulously served the political designs of its English masters. To strengthen his own position King Charles VII twice took steps to have the verdict set aside; but it was Pope Callistus III who appointed a commission which in 1456 declared the condemnation to have been obtained by fraud and deceit, and fully rehabilitated the memory of its victim. Four and a half centuries later Joan was canonized: not for her patriotism or military valour, but for the virtue of her life and her faithfulness to the prompting of God's grace.

A Lang, *The Maid of France* (1908); studies by V. Sackville West (Penguin), E. Robo (1960), W. S. Scott (1975) and others; R. Pernoud, *Joan of Arc* (1965). George Bernard Shaw's play *Saint Joan* (1923) provoked a certain amount of controversy and was the author's greatest box-office success.

JOAN OF FRANCE, queen. B. 1464; d. at Bourges, 1505; cd 1950; f.d. 4 February. Joan of Valois was daughter to King Louis XI of France by Charlotte of Savoy. She was physically ill-favoured, hunchbacked and pock-marked; her father disliked her, and in 1476 married her off to Louis, duke of Orléans. The marriage was forced on him and never consummated, but it was not till he became king in 1498 and wanted to marry Ann of Brittany that he applied for a declaration of nullity, which was granted. Joan accepted the situation with patience – patience in adversity was the mark of her life – and passed her remaining years in good works at Bourges, the capital of her duchy of Berry. With the help of a Franciscan friar, Gabriel (Gilbert) Nicolas, she founded a small religious order of women, the 'Annonciades', and established a confraternity to pray and work for concord between enemies.

A. M. C. Forster, *St Joan of France* (1950).

JOAN BICHIER ◊ *Elizabeth Bichier*

JOAN DE LESTONNAC, foundress. B. at Bordeaux, 1556; d. there, 1640; cd 1949; f.d. 2 February. She was a niece of the essayist Montaigne, and in 1573 married Gaston de Montferrant, by whom she had four children. Joan was widowed in 1597, and some years later began the foundation of the Sisters of Notre Dame of Bordeaux, for the education of girls. At one period she was the victim of a conspiracy by two of her nuns: she was deposed from her office of superioress and treated with contumely. She bore this with great forbearance for three years, and then was vindicated. St Joan was ninety-six at her death.

JOAN THOURET, foundress. B. near Besançon, 1765; d. at Naples, 1826; cd 1934; f.d. 24 August. Joan Antida Thouret was the daughter of a tanner; when she was twenty-two she joined the Sisters of Charity of St Vincent de Paul in Paris. At the revolution this community was forcibly dispersed, so Joan returned to her native Sancey and ran the village school. In 1799 she opened a school at Besançon; she had four helpers, and this was the beginning of the congregation of Sisters of Charity under St Vincent's Protection. It grew rapidly, spreading to Switzerland and Savoy, and in 1810 Joan was invited to take charge of a large hospital in Naples. There she spent most of the rest of her life, opening many educational and other establishments in Italy. Her last years were troubled by the archbishop of Besançon, who precipitated a disagreement about ecclesiastical jurisdiction over her convents in France; but St Joan was not discouraged and continued her work to the end.

JOANNICIUS, monk. B. in Bithynia, *c.* 754; d. at Antidium, 846; f.d. 4 February. For twenty years he was a soldier in the Byzantine army, seeing active service against the Bulgars. Repenting of his disorderly ways, he left the service at forty and became a monk and then a hermit on the Bithynian Olympus. While at a monastery near Brusa the second iconoclast controversy began in 818; Joannicius, who had formerly favoured the iconoclasts, now showed himself a vigorous opponent of them. He was greatly respected among the prophetical figures of his time, and both ◊ St Theodore the Studite and St Methodius of Constantinople consulted him. He counselled moderation in their treatment of iconoclasts – unusual enough advice from a monk in that struggle. St Joannicius was over ninety when he died at the monastery of Antidium.

JOHN. There is a very large number of Johns among the saints (sixty-four in the Roman Martyrology alone). The following are the principal ones:

JOHN, apostle and evangelist, called 'the Divine', i.e. the Theologian. D. at Ephesus (?), c. 100; f.d. 27 December. He was a Galilean fisherman, and he and his brother ◊ St James the Greater, the sons of Zebedee, were called from mending their nets to follow Jesus Christ (Mark i, 19–20). The brothers apparently had an excitable and quick-tempered side to their character (Mark x, 35–41; Luke ix, 54–56), and Jesus nicknamed them 'sons of thunder'; on the other hand he chose them, with ◊ Peter, to be with him on the momentous occasions of his transfiguration and his agony in Gethsemane. Moreover, tradition has always identified John with the unnamed 'disciple whom Jesus loved', who leaned on his Master's breast at the Last Supper; to whom Jesus on the cross confided the care of his mother; who ran before Peter to the tomb on the morning of the resurrection and, seeing it empty, believed; and who first recognized the risen Lord by the Sea of Tiberias. In the Acts of the Apostles John is again found associated with Peter, at the healing of the lame man in the Temple, sharing his imprisonment, and going with him to the converts in Samaria. St Paul names John with Peter and James as pillars of the church in Jerusalem (Gal. ii, 9).

In later years John was exiled to the island of Patmos, 'because I had preached God's word and borne my testimony to Jesus' (Rev. i, 9). John is said to have passed his last years at Ephesus, and to have died there at a great age. ◊ St Jerome wrote that, when he was too old to preach, John would simply say to the assembled people: 'Love one another. That is the Lord's command: and if you keep it, that by itself is enough.' The story that he came to Rome and there emerged unharmed when thrown into a cauldron of boiling oil is apocryphal. The feast of St John 'at the Latin Gate' (6 May), which in later times was referred to this

189

event, was expunged from the general calendar of the Roman church in 1960.

The Fourth Gospel, three biblical epistles, and the book of Revelation (The Apocalypse) traditionally bear the name of St John as their author. In modern times the authorship and historical value of these works have been the subject of serious debate among biblical scholars, some of whom deny that it is possible to know who wrote them. But the traditional attributions have by no means been wholly discredited. John's symbol in art is an eagle.

A. H. N. Green-Armytage, *John who Saw* (1952).

JOHN ◊ *Cyrus and John*

JOHN and PAUL, martyrs. Date unknown; f.d. 26 June. These early martyrs are among those mentioned in the canon of the Roman Mass, but all historical particulars of them have long been lost. Their existing *passio* is simply an adaptation of the story of *SS. Juventinus and Maximinus* (f.d. 25 January), army officers who were martyred at Antioch under Julian the Apostate in 363. The legend says that John and Paul were put to death in a private house, but the remains of a third–fourth century house found under the church of SS. John and Paul in Rome throw no light on the question (◊ *Pammachius*).

JOHN THE ALMSGIVER, bishop. B. at Amathus in Cyprus, *c.* 560; d. there 11 November 619; f.d. 23 January. The greater part of this John's life is unknown, except that he lived with his wife and family in Cyprus or Egypt, probably engaged in public affairs. When about fifty, while still a layman, he was chosen to be patriarch of Alexandria. This church had been very greatly reduced by the monophysite heresy, and John set himself to commend orthodoxy by an example of virtuous living and most liberal almsgiving. He founded and endowed lying-in and other hospitals (with a 'maternity benefit'), homes for the aged and infirm, and lodgings for travellers. He helped the poor, 'my masters', by regulating weights and measures and making individual gifts, and taxed his clergy to help pay for it all. One of his beneficiaries was a trader who had fallen on hard times: John provided him with a ship and a cargo of corn which the man bartered for tin in the island of Britain. Twice a week John adjudicated disputes among his people and dispensed advice, and nothing and nobody was too insignificant for his attention. When the Persians sacked Jerusalem in 614 he succoured the refugees and sent large amounts of money and food for the relief of the city. Five years later the invaders were threatening Egypt, and John retired to Cyprus, where he died soon after. In his last will and testament he said that he had found the treasury of his church full and left it empty: 'I have done my best to render to God the things that were God's.' John the Almsgiver was the original patron saint of the Order of St John at Jerusalem (later, Knights of Malta).

E. Dawes and N. H. Baynes, *Three Byzantine Saints* (1948).

JOHN THE BAPTIST. D. *c.* 29; f.d. 24 June. The forerunner and herald of Jesus Christ, of whom Christ himself said: 'Among those who are born of women there is not a greater prophet ...' (Luke vii, 28). John's parents were a priest of Jerusalem, Zachary, and Elizabeth, a kinswoman of the Virgin Mary; his birth in their old age was foretold by an angel in remarkable circumstances (ibid. i, 5–23). About the year 27 John appeared as an itinerant preacher, announcing: 'Repent, for the Kingdom of Heaven is at hand', and those who confessed their sins he washed in the river Jordan. He gained many followers, including several who were to be chosen apostles of Christ, and Jesus himself came to be baptized by him; from then on John pointed Jesus out as 'the Lamb of God who takes away the sin of the world' (John i, 29–36). Soon after, John was thrown into prison: he had rebuked Herod Antipas for taking Herodias, his half-brother's wife. From prison he was able to follow Jesus's ministry, and sent messengers to ask him questions (Luke vii, 19–29). But Herod in a moment of folly promised to give Herodias's daughter, Salome, whatever she wanted; and Herodias told the girl to ask for John the Baptist's head. It was given her (Matt. xiv, 1–12). Thus, as St Augustine says, an oath that was rashly taken was criminally kept. There is a good possibility that John spent some time with the community whose documents and buildings have since 1947 been discovered at Qumran, near the Dead Sea. Contrary to the usual custom, the principal feast of St John the Baptist commemorates his birth; but his death by beheading is also observed, on 29 August.

J. Steinmann, *St John the Baptist and the Desert Tradition* (1958); G. C. Darton, *St John the Baptist* (1961); C. H. H. Scobie, *John the Baptist* (1964).

JOHN OF THE CROSS, mystical theologian and poet. B. near Avila 1542; d. at Ubeda, 14 December 1591; cd 1726; f.d. 24 November. John de Yepes, a Spaniard of good family in reduced circumstances, was a Carmelite friar; he got to know ◊ *St Teresa* of Ávila, and in 1568 joined the first of the reformed houses of men of the order, at Duruelo. He laboured outstandingly to spread the reform, and in 1577 was imprisoned at Toledo by order of the Carmelite prior general, being subjected to most brutal and oppressive treatment. It was then that he wrote his first poems. Escaping after nine months, he was appointed to various offices among the reformed friars, and continued to write. When disagreement emerged in the ranks of the reformed, John supported the moderate party; the extremists obtaining authority, he was removed from office and sent to a remote friary at La Peñuela. He fell ill and was removed to Ubeda, where again he was treated with inhumanity, till within three months of his death. Only after he was gone did John of the Cross receive the recognition due to the co-founder of the reformed ('discalced') Carmelites and one of the most attractive of Christian mystics.

St John wrote of divine things from the depths of his own experience, and with a literary beauty all his own. His chief works are three poems with their corresponding commentaries, *The Dark Night of the Soul, The Spiritual Canticle,* and *The Living Flame of Love,* with a second commentary on the first of them, *The Ascent of Mount Carmel.* All his writings have been translated into English by David Lewis (1906) and again by E. A. Peers (1953); they have made no little appeal even to some who make no profession of Christianity. Roy Campbell's translation of the poems is published as a Penguin. St John of the Cross was named a doctor of the church by Pope Pius XI in 1926.

B. Frost, *St John of the Cross* (1937); E. A. Peers, *Spirit of Flame* (1943); Lives by Fr Bruno (1932), Fr Crisogono (1958) and G. Brenan (1973).

JOHN THE EGYPTIAN, hermit. B. at Asyut, *c.* 304; d. near there, 394; f.d. 27 March. He was a carpenter at Asyut (Lycopolis) who in middle age took up a solitary life on a neighbouring mountain. His reputation for holiness is said to have been only less than that of ◊ *St Antony,* and his gift for foretelling the future was such that he was twice consulted by Emperor Theodosius I. In old age he was visited by the monastic historian Palladius, the text of whose account of their meeting still exists.

JOHN OF GOD, founder. B. in Portugal, 1495; d. at Granada, 1550; cd 1690; f.d. 8 March. When he was about forty, having led an irregular life as a soldier and as an estate servant in Spain, this John repented of his ways; but his conversion was manifested in such extreme forms that he was confined for a time as a lunatic. In 1539 he determined to devote himself to the sick and destitute, while earning his living as a wood-merchant. With the help of the archbishop of Granada, he took a house, and for ten years gave shelter and care to those in need, not excluding prostitutes and vagabonds, for his help to whom he was sometimes criticized. But he had the support of more enlightened people, and became greatly respected in Granada for his modest character and devoted work. It was not till after John's death that his followers were organized into an order of hospitallers, the Brothers of St John of God, whose work has spread far and wide. He is a patron saint of nurses and the sick.

JOHN THE IBERIAN, abbot. D. on Mount Athos, *c.* 1002; f.d. 12 July. In early middle life he gave up his post in the service of the ruler of Iberia (Georgia) and entered a monastery in eastern Asia Minor, afterwards migrating to Mount Athos with his son Euthymius. Here they were joined by John's brother-in-law, a retired military man named Thornikios who had amassed a fortune, and together they set about establishing a monastery for Iberian monks. It was called Iviron and still exists, though its members are now Greek. John did not like the responsibilities and worries of being abbot and tried to get away to Spain; but he was persuaded to come back, and died peacefully at his post: 'a man dear to God and deserving of all reverence'.

St John was succeeded as abbot of Iviron by his son, *St Euthymius the Enlightener* (d. 1028; f.d. 13 May). He was of great service to his church through his translations from Greek into Iberian (Karthvelian), some sixty writings of the fathers, biblical commentaries, Lives of the saints and liturgical books. Euthymius had eventually to visit Constantinople, where he met with a street-accident that caused his death.

JOHN OF BEVERLEY, bishop. B. at Harpham; d. at Beverley, 721; f.d. 25 October. He was a student at the Canterbury school under ◊ *St Adrian*, and entered the double monastery at Whitby while ◊ *St Hilda* was abbess there. About 687 he was made bishop of Hexham (he ordained ◊ *Bede* priest *c.* 703) and in 705 was translated to York. John was a persevering teacher, much drawn to solitude. Little information has survived about his life, but in times past his memory was widely honoured in England; in one of her 'shewings' Dame Julian of Norwich refers to him as 'a dearworthy servant to God ... a full high saint in Heaven in his sight, and a blissful'. St John resigned his see in 717 and withdrew to the religious house he had founded at the place now called Beverley.

JOHN OF BRIDLINGTON, canon regular. B. at Thwing; d. at Bridlington, 1379; cd 1401; f.d. 21 October. He studied at Oxford and joined the Austin canons at Bridlington near his birthplace, ultimately becoming their prior. His external life seems to have been uneventful. The miracles reported at his shrine doubtless facilitated his canonization.

JOHN OF CAPESTRANO, missioner. B. at Capestrano, 1386; d. at Villach, 23 October 1456; cd 1724; f.d. 28 March. Although he was governor of Perugia and married, at the age of thirty John felt called to become a Franciscan friar; this he did, having first been dispensed from his matrimonial ties. For thirty years after his ordination in 1420 he was a very successful mission preacher up and down Italy; he played an influential part in the efforts to heal the divisions in the Franciscan order, and he was entrusted with missions abroad on behalf of the popes. In 1451 he was sent to deal with the Hussites in the Austrian dominions, where his methods with the obstinate were such as to incur the reprobation of later times. Finally John was called on to preach a crusade against the Turks, who in 1453 had captured Constantinople. He accompanied the Hungarian general Hunyadi in the field, his presence encouraging the troops at the great victory at Belgrade in 1456. Within a few months both he and Hunyadi were dead of plague.

St John of Capestrano worked in Italy in close association with ◊ *St Bernardine of Siena*, and also with *St James of the March* of Ancona (d. 1476; cd 1726; f.d. 28 November), another mission preacher. He too combined compassion for the poor and oppressed with excessive severity towards those whom he regarded as being culpably in error.

J. Hofer, *St John Capistran, Reformer* (1943).

JOHN OF DAMASCUS, theologian and hymn-writer. B. at Damascus, *c.* 675; d. near Jerusalem, *c.* 749; f.d. 27 March. The last of the Eastern fathers was the son of an important Christian official at the court of the khalif Abdul Malek at Damascus; he is said to have been educated by a Greek monk from Calabria whom the Moslems had taken prisoner. John, also called Mansur, succeeded to his father's post and filled it for some years. When Emperor Leo III ordered the destruction of sacred images, the protection of the Moslem Arab ruler enabled John to write and publish in their defence with impunity and great effect. It was probably before this that John became a monk and priest at the monastery of Mar Saba, in the mountain wilderness between Jerusalem and the Dead Sea; he lived there till his death. The most important of St John's writings is the *Fount of Knowledge*, of which the third part, *The Orthodox Faith*, is a digest of Christian doctrine as expounded by the Greek fathers; it was much used and influential in the West in the middle ages. Three of his sermons are concerned with the bodily assumption of the Virgin Mary into Heaven after her death. His hymns are still sung in the Greek liturgy, though the number attributed to him has doubtless been exaggerated; two of them are well known in English: 'Come, ye faithful, raise the strain' and 'The day of Resurrection! Earth, tell it out abroad!' In 1890 Pope Leo XIII declared St John of Damascus a doctor of the church.

JOHN OF KANTI, priest. B. near Oswiecim, 1390; d. at Cracow, 24 December 1473; cd 1767; f.d. 20 October. This saint, sometimes called John Cantius, is greatly revered in his native Poland. With an interval as a parish priest – forced on him, it is said, by academic jealousy – he appears to have spent his life teaching in the University of Cracow, latterly as professor of sacred Scripture.

He impressed on his students the need for moderation and good manners in controversy, and he was noted for his boundless generosity to the poor of the city.

JOHN OF MATHA, founder. B. in Provence; d. at Rome, 17 December 1213; f.d. 8 February. He was founder of the order of Trinitarian friars, whose work was originally to ransom prisoners from the hands of the Moslems. Nothing else is known about him, his biographies being based on records that have been proved spurious. With John of Matha in his foundation there has been coupled the name of *St Felix of Valois* (f.d. 20 November); the evidence available points to his having been a purely imaginary character.

JOHN OF NEPOMUK, martyr. B. at Nepomuk in Bohemia, *c.* 1345; d. at Prague, 20 March 1393; cd 1729; f.d. 16 May. This priest was a canon of Prague, and it is commonly said that he was murdered by order of King Wenceslas IV for refusing to divulge the confessions of the king's wife. Earlier evidence shows that the murder was in fact an incident in a series of violent disagreements between Wenceslas and the archbishop of Prague: John of Nepomuk supported his archbishop and thus incurred the king's enmity. He was thrown, bound and gagged, into the river Vltava. The falsity of the 'confession story' was officially recognized in Rome in 1961.

JOHN OF RILA, abbot. B. in Bulgaria; d. at Rila, 946; f.d. 19 October. He was one of the earliest native Bulgarian monks, and spent sixty years of his life in the Rhodope mountains south of Sofia. Here he founded the great monastery of Rila, which survived through the ages until the buildings were turned into a meteorological station by the communist government in 1947.

JOHN OF ROCHESTER, bishop and martyr. B. at Beverley, 1469; d. in London, 22 June 1535; cd 1935; f.d. 9 July, with ◊ *St Thomas More*. John Fisher was equally distinguished as a humanistic scholar, a fosterer of sound learning in others, and a faithful bishop. His father was a Yorkshire mercer, and John was educated at Michaelhouse at Cambridge, of which college he became master, and in 1501 was vice-chancellor of the university. He was closely associated with Lady Margaret Beaufort's benefactions to Cambridge, and himself endowed scholarships, provided for Greek and Hebrew in the curriculum, and engaged Erasmus as professor of divinity and Greek. In 1504 Fisher was made chancellor at Cambridge and bishop of Rochester, and he was as devoted to the welfare of his diocese as of his university. He fully realized the urgent need of reform in the church, from popes and bishops downwards, but was opposed to Lutheran ideas of reform and wrote against them, while preferring prayer and example before controversy.

From 1527 Bishop Fisher actively upheld the validity of Katherine of Aragon's marriage with Henry VIII, and was consistently opposed to the king's claim to be head of the church in England. Unlike the other English bishops, Fisher refused to take the oath appurtenant to the Act of Succession, on the ground that it constituted a repudiation of the pope: 'Not that I condemn any other men's conscience,' he wrote; 'their conscience may save them, and mine must save me.' In April 1534 he was imprisoned in the Tower and while he was there Pope Paul III named him a cardinal. King Henry was furious, and within a month Fisher was brought to trial in Westminster Hall, charged with treason in that he had denied the king's ecclesiastical supremacy; he was found guilty and sentenced to death. He had been in bad health for some time, and was so frail that he had to be carried in a chair to the place of execution on Tower Hill. While waiting at the Tower gate he opened his New Testament for the last time and his eyes fell on St John's words in his gospel xvii, 3-5. 'There is enough learning in that', he observed, 'to last me to the end of my life.' Half an hour later he was beheaded. His friend Thomas More wrote of St John of Rochester: 'I reckon in this realm no one man, in wisdom, learning and long approved virtue together, meet to be matched and compared with him.'

Contemporary Life, ed. by P. Hughes (1935); E. E. Reynolds, *St John Fisher* (1955). E. L. Surtz. *Works and Days of John Fisher* (1967).

JOHN OF SAHAGUN, Austin friar. B. at Sahagun in Spain; d. at Salamanca, 1479; cd 1690; f.d. 12 June. As a young priest he held five benefices at the same time until, repenting of such pluralism, he gave them up, went to the University of Salamanca, and then ministered in a parish there. In 1463 he became an Augustinian friar in the same city. At Alba de Tormes his life was attempted because of his public denunciation of oppressive landlords, and it is said that his death was hastened by poisoning, brought about by a woman whose paramour he had reformed.

JOHN BERCHMANS ◊ under *Aloysius Gonzaga*

JOHN BOSCO, founder. B. in Piedmont, 1815; d. at Turin, 1888; cd 1934; f.d. 31 January. John Bosco was brought up in a peasant family by his widowed mother; from an early age he was drawn to work among boys and young men – work which he began soon after his ordination as a priest in 1841. He settled in the Valdocco suburb of Turin, where in time he had hundreds of youths attending his chapel and his evening classes. With his mother as housekeeper, he opened a boarding-house for apprentices, followed by workshops for the teaching of tailoring, shoemaking, and other trades. These activities grew, and led to the foundation from 1854 of a congregation to carry on the work;

Don Bosco had a great admiration for the spirit of ◊ *St Francis de Sales*, and he called his helpers 'Salesians'. From Turin they have spread over the world, their establishments including general schools of all grades, agricultural and trade schools, and even hospitals and foreign missions. Nor were the needs of girls overlooked. In 1872, together with a peasant woman from near Genoa, *St Mary Mazzarello* (d. 1881; cd 1951; f.d. 14 May), Don Bosco began a new congregation for similar work among girls; he called them the Daughters of Mary, Help of Christians, and their success was immediate too.

St John Bosco, who once wrote that he did not remember ever having formally to punish a boy (and some of his protégés were what are now called 'juvenile delinquents'), was an outstanding figure in the efflorescence of heroic sanctity in north Italy in the nineteenth century. His work was beset by many difficulties, some of them gratuitously put in his way by both anti-clerical civil authorities and unsympathetic ecclesiastics: what he achieved is the index to his life and character. His genius with boys was partly inborn, partly the fruit of experience; he disclaimed having any system of education, while emphasizing that his methods were preventive as opposed to repressive. He sought to make things attractive, whether school subjects or religious practice, and in several directions he was an enlightened innovator. A large number of seemingly miraculous events – e.g. multiplication of food – are recorded of Don Bosco, some of them very well attested. 'God will help us', he reiterated, and his faith was not in vain. He was an effective preacher, quiet and restrained in manner, but his writings were few; among them are biographies of *St Joseph Cafasso* (d. 1860; cd 1947; f.d. 23 June) and of *St Dominic Savio* (d. 1857; cd 1954; f.d. 9 March). Don Cafasso, a priest of Turin, was Don Bosco's teacher, adviser, and religious guide for over twenty years and a decisive influence in his life, as well as in the lives of many young clergymen whom he taught in the Institute of St Francis at Turin. Dominic Savio was one of the pupils whom St John Bosco hoped to train to be a helper in his work; but the boy died when only fifteen years old. None doubted his remarkable goodness, but the canonization of one so extremely young was not uncontested; young martyrs apart, the case seems to be unique.

L. C. Sheppard, *Don Bosco* (1957).

JOHN DE BRÉBEUF, martyr. B. in Normandy, 1593; d. in Canada, 16 March 1649; cd 1930; f.d. 26 September. He was one of the first three Jesuits to be sent from France to Canada in 1625, and the first to proclaim the gospel among the Huron Indians, for a time wholly unsuccessfully. His second mission began in 1633 and lasted for fifteen years under most adverse and trying conditions; but just when an impression was at last being made on the Hurons, raids by the Iroquois were intensified. St John de Brébeuf and ◊ *St Gabriel Lalemant* were captured, and at the village of Saint-Ignace in Ontario they were subjected to torments among the most horrible in the records of martyrdom and inhuman cruelty. Brébeuf, a man of powerful body and great endurance, survived only a few hours.

JOHN DE BRITTO, martyr. B. in Lisbon, 1647; d. in India, 1693; cd 1947; f.d. 4 February. A Portuguese Jesuit, he went to India as a missionary in 1673 and was given charge of the Madura mission in Madras. He adapted himself so far as possible to the manners and customs of the people among whom he lived, but the success of his mission eventually led to his death. A convert to Christianity in the Marava country, having been a polygamist, put away his wives, and one of them complained of this to her uncle, the raja of Marava, putting the blame on Father de Britto. The raja thereupon began a persecution of Christians, and John de Britto was beheaded at Oriur for subverting the religion of the country. A moving letter he wrote to his fellow missionaries on the eve of his execution is extant.

JOHN CANTIUS ◊ *John of Kanti*

JOHN CASSIAN, abbot. B. *c.* 360; d. at Marseilles, *c.* 435; f.d. 23 July. Cassian was probably born in what is now Rumania. He was a monk at Bethlehem and in Egypt before being ordained deacon at Constantinople, from where in 404 he was sent to Rome to defend the cause of ◊ *St John Chrysostom*. He seems to have spent the rest of his life in the West. He was made priest, and settled at Marseilles, where *c.* 415 he established two monasteries, one for men and one for women. Cassian's writings on monastic life, the *Institutes* and the *Conferences*, have been very influential in the Western church, as well as in the East, notably on ◊ *St Benedict*, who prescribed the Conferences as one of the books to be read aloud to his monks after supper.

O. Chadwick, *John Cassian* (1950).

JOHN CHRYSOSTOM, bishop and doctor. B. at Antioch, *c.* 347; d. at Comana in Pontus, 14 September 407; f.d. 27 January. John Chrysostom ('Golden Mouth') was the only son of a general officer in the imperial army, and was brought up a Christian (though not baptized till manhood) by his widowed mother. He was intended for the law and was a student under the celebrated pagan orator Libanius. But after being an ascetic in the mountains for some years, in 381 John joined the clergy of Antioch. Here he gained an ever-increasing reputation as a preacher for twelve years, and in 398 he was elected archbishop of Constantinople.

Chrysostom was a whole-hearted reformer, very outspoken and rather tactless, and he soon incurred enmity from two directions, which combined against him. His attacks on the misuse of wealth and on other wickedness antagonized the rich and powerful, in particular the spiteful Eudoxia, wife of the emperor Arcadius; and the archbishop of Alexandria, Theophilus, found ecclesiastical and personal grounds for opposition to him. In 403 the intrigues of Theophilus brought about a gathering of disaffected Egyptian and Syrian bishops at The Oak, outside Constantinople; they considered a number of charges, mostly frivolous, against John, and declared him deposed from his see. The emperor sent him into exile, only to recall him at once; but less than a year later his enemies procured his definitive banishment to Cucusus in Armenia. Chrysostom's letters tell us much about his hard three years there, during which his supporters were fruitlessly active on his behalf. For greater security it was ordered in the summer of 407 that he he moved further away, to Pityus, in Iberia: he died from exhaustion on the road.

St John Chrysostom is honoured as one of the four great Greek doctors of the church, and above all as a preacher. In his homilies he expounds books of the Old and New Testaments, particularly St Paul's epistles, and there are many sermons for special occasions, such as panegyrics on the martyrs and the famous series 'on the Statues', called forth by a dangerous riot in Antioch. Chrysostom's preaching was very eloquent, and lengthy, but straightforward and thoroughly practical. His aim was to expound the Bible in such a way that his hearers, ordinary people, might know and understand its teaching and its practical application. In his moral exhortations he appeals, he threatens, he sympathizes, he caricatures, dealing in concrete, topical instances rather than ineffective abstractions: passage after passage in his sermons and letters is as relevant to the twentieth century as to the fifth. Many of his works have been translated into English, most recently the *Baptismal Instructions* (1963). In an analysis of his character Cardinal Newman declared Chrysostom's charm to lie 'in his intimate sympathy and compassionateness for the whole world, not only in its strength but in its weakness; in the lively regard with which he views everything that comes before him. . . .'

C. Baur, *John Chrysostom and his Time* (2 vols., 1960–61); D. Attwater, *St John Chrysostom* (1959).

JOHN CLIMACUS, monk. D. at Mount Sinai, *c.* 649. *Klimax* is the Greek word for 'ladder', and this John has his second name from the book he wrote called the *Ladder to Paradise*. It treats of the attainment of moral perfection, to be reached by the thirty 'rungs' into which the book is divided. It has been exceedingly popular and influential among monks and others in the West as well as the East; an English translation was published in 1959 under the title *The Ladder of Divine Ascent*. It also gave rise to a new theme in Byzantine iconography, the ladder to Heaven, which is seen at Mount Athos and elsewhere. Little is known about the author, except that he was a monk and abbot of the monastery at Mount Sinai, famed as a holy man throughout Palestine and Arabia.

JOHN DAMASCENE ◊ *John of Damascus*

JOHN EUDES, founder. B. at Ri in Normandy, 1601; d. at Caen, 1680; cd 1925; f.d. 19 August. For twenty years St John Eudes was a priest of the French Oratory, distinguishing himself as a missioner and by his work for the sick during two epidemics. In 1643 he left the Oratory and founded a congregation of priests (the 'Eudists') to conduct seminaries; this was reconstituted after the French Revolution. He had already organized a group of Visitation nuns to care for women reclaimed from a disorderly life, and from this group there developed the congregation of the Sisters of our Lady of Charity and Refuge. It was Eudes who took the first steps towards bringing devotion to the heart of Jesus, as representing his love, into the public worship of the Roman Catholic church.

P. Herambourg, *St John Eudes* (1960).

JOHN FISHER ◊ *John of Rochester*

JOHN GUALBERTO, abbot. B. at Florence; d. at Passignano, 1073; cd 1193; f.d. 12 July. He was the founder, at Vallombrosa in Tuscany, of a community following an adaptation of the Rule of St Benedict; it developed into the mother house of a group of monasteries (now very small) bearing its name. The story goes that John, the son of a Florentine nobleman, having the murderer of his brother at his mercy, was moved by the thought of Christ on the cross and spared the man's life. This was the turning-point of John's life and he became a monk.

JOHN LALAND ◊ under *René Goupil*

JOHN-BAPTIST DE LA SALLE, educationist and founder. B. at Rheims, 1651; d. at Rouen, 7 April 1719; cd 1900; f.d. 15 May. He was given a canonry at Rheims eleven years before he was ordained priest in 1678, but gave up a life of dignified ease to devote himself to the education of the sons of the poor. After a false start, he realized that the first problem was the provision of teachers; he resigned his canonry and private fortune, and set about training a group of young men, the first Brothers of the Christian Schools. It was ultimately decided that they should all be in fact laybrothers and not priests. This work went on side by side with the opening of schools. La Salle took over a free school in Paris in 1688, where he also introduced Sunday-schools, and he was later invited by the exiled King James II of England to provide education for the sons of the gentry in his entourage; in 1700 the brothers opened a school in Rome. The successful growth of the new congregation provoked violent opposition from professional schoolmasters and others, and in 1702 the archbishop of Paris refused to recognize La Salle as its head, but he was not in fact displaced. It continued to expand its activities, and today numbers over 17,000 brothers in all parts of the world, their establishments ranging from primary schools to teachers' training and university colleges.

St John-Baptist de La Salle was the first to set up teachers' training colleges as such, and he sought to inspire his teachers with 'a father's love for their pupils, ready to devote all their time and energies to them, as concerned to save them from wickedness as to dispel their ignorance. There were no such teachers for the poor'. His system of education, outlined in *The Conduct of Christian Schools* (English trans., 1935), was a milestone in the schooling of the young, with its use of the 'simultaneous method' and its teaching through the mother tongue rather than Latin. Matthew Arnold said of this book that later works on the subject hardly improved on its precepts and had none of its religious feeling. La Salle, who had studied at Saint-Sulpice under Louis Tronson, also wrote several works of value on prayer and meditation.

W. J. Battersby, *De La Salle* (3 vols., 1945–52); id. a single-volume biography, 1957.

JOHN LEONARDI ◊ under *Cajetan*

JOHN MARK ◊ under *Mark*

JOHN REGIS, missioner. B. near Narbonne, 1597; d. at La Louvesc, 30 December 1640; cd 1737; f.d. 16 June. John Francis Regis, son of a well-to-do merchant, was during the last ten years of his short life one of the great French Jesuit home missioners of the seventeenth century. The field of his activity was Auvergne and Languedoc, where he worked in often desperate conditions among the poorer and more neglected people, sometimes with scant encouragement from nervous superiors. He died at La Louvesc in Dauphiné, and his tomb there is still visited by many thousands of pilgrims every year.

JOHN-BAPTIST VIANNEY, the Curé of Ars. B. at Dardilly, near Lyons, 1786; d. at Ars, 1859; cd 1925; f.d. 8 August. John Vianney was the son of a peasant farmer. His studies for the priesthood lasted from 1806 till 1815, interrupted for fourteen months when he was in hiding to avoid military service; his progress was very slow and unpromising, and eventually he was ordained more on account of his devoutness and good will than for any other qualifications. In 1818 he was sent as parish priest to Ars-en-Dombes, a lonely and neglected village; he remained there for forty years until his death, devoted heart and soul to his parishioners and their needs. But not to them only. He became known as a preacher and confessor, strange tales were heard of this country priest's gifts and powers, and the isolated village became a place of pilgrimage. Tens of thousands of people came there from France and beyond, and for year after year Abbé Vianney had to spend anything up to eighteen hours a day in the confessional. Some of his fellow clergy misjudged him: he was, they said, over-zealous, ignorant, a charlatan, even mentally deranged. Their bishop, Mgr Devie, answered them: 'I wish, gentlemen, that all my clergy had a touch of the same madness.'

Especially in the earlier part of his ministry, Abbé Vianney was very strict and rigorously 'puritanical'; but his severity in the pulpit was matched by his extraordinary insight and power of conversion in the confessional; the most impressive examples of his unusual gifts are those evinced in relation to his penitents – knowledge of distant or future events, for instance. On the other hand the manifestations which he himself regarded as attacks by Satan in person provide a difficult problem. St John Vianney's personal simplicity was illustrated in all that he did, in the short, pithy advice given to those who consulted him, in his discouragement of fussy piety, in his straightforward preaching: 'There were no affected attitudes, no "ohs!" and "ahs!" about him; when he was most deeply moved he simply smiled – or wept.' The turmoil of pilgrimages, the constant call on his energies, the burdens of his office, and the austerity of his personal life gradually wore him out. At least three times he left Ars, meaning to hide himself in a monastery; each time he was induced to come back, and he died still in harness. In 1929 Pope Pius XI named St John Vianney as the patron of parish clergy.

A contemporary of Abbé Vianney, who knew him personally and encouraged him, was *St Peter Eymard* (d. 1868; cd 1962; f.d. 3 August). After serving in the parochial ministry and as a member of the Marist congregation, in 1856 he founded the Priests of the Blessed Sacrament in Paris; other organizations, for sisters and for lay people, followed.

F. Trochu, *The Curé d'Ars* (1957); L. C. Sheppard, *The Curé d'Ars: Portrait of a Parish Priest* (1963).

JONAH and BERIKJESU, martyrs. D. in Persia, 327; f.d. 29 March. These martyrs, called in the West Jonas and Barachisius, were among the many victims of the persecution by the Sassanian king

Shapur II. They were arrested for giving encouragement to imprisoned Christians, but neither by torture nor trickery could they be induced to perform an act of idolatry. So Jonah was dismembered and crushed to death in a press, and Berikjesu was killed by having burning pitch poured down his throat.

JOSAPHAT ◊ *Barlaam and Josaphat*

JOSAPHAT OF POLOTSK, bishop and martyr. B. at Vladimir, *c.* 1580; d. at Vitebsk, 1623; cd 1867; f.d. 14 November. After being abbot of a monastery in Vilna, Josaphat Kunsevich became bishop of Polotsk in Byelorussia in 1617. This and other Orthodox dioceses of the province of Kiev had in 1595 come into communion with the see of Rome, and Josaphat devoted himself to upholding and spreading this union. His virtues and reasonableness gained him much support; but the situation was very difficult, for secular interests were involved, and there was much bitterness and violence on both sides. While on a pastoral visit to Vitebsk, St Josaphat was murdered by a mob amid cries of 'Kill the papist!'

In 1657 his activities in the same cause led to the death of a Polish Jesuit, *St Andrew Bobola* (cd 1938; f.d. 16 May); at Janov, near Pinsk, he was killed by Cossacks in circumstances of revolting barbarity.

JOSEPH, husband of the Virgin Mary. F.d. 19 March, 1 May. All that is known about the foster-father of Jesus Christ is found in the gospels. He was of the house of David, a carpenter or builder by trade, an 'upright man', and there is no reason to suppose that he was other than a young man when he became betrothed to Mary. His distress at finding her with child was dispelled by an angelic vision, and he took her to wife. After the birth of Jesus at Bethlehem, Joseph was warned from Heaven in a dream, first to flee with Mary and the Child to Egypt in order to escape Herod, and afterwards, when Herod was dead, to return to the land of Israel. But he feared Herod's successor in Judaea, and went on to Galilee, where they took up their abode at Nazareth (Matt. i, 18–25; ii, 13–23). The episode of the twelve-year-old Jesus being lost on the way back from the Passover at Jerusalem (Luke ii, 41–48) again shows Joseph faithful in his capacity as guardian and helpmate. It is not known when he died, but clearly it was before the crucifixion of Jesus (cf. John xix, 26–27). The few biblical particulars give an impression of a just, kind, dignified and level-headed man, prompt in action but self-effacing. This was not enough for the writers of apocryphal narratives, several of whose wilder fictions are concerned with St Joseph. It was due to these writers that he has been so long depicted by artists as an old man. The cultus of St Joseph appears to have begun in Egypt; in the West it was late in beginning but is now intense.

F. L. Filas, *The Man Nearest to Christ* (1944); H. Rondet, *St Joseph* (1956).

JOSEPH OF ARIMATHAEA. First century, f.d. 17 March. The disciple who after the crucifixion begged Jesus's body from Pilate and 'laid it in his own new tomb'. Nothing is known of Joseph beyond what is said in the gospels, but already in the fourth century legendary tales of him were in circulation. It was not until about the middle of the thirteenth century that there first appears the legend that the apostle ◊ *Philip* sent Joseph from Gaul to be a missionary in the island of Britain, whose first church he founded, at Glastonbury. He was also associated with the romance of the Holy Grail and King Arthur. These stories obtained wide credence, but they are devoid of any historical foundation.

J. Armitage Robinson, *Two Glastonbury Legends* (1926).

JOSEPH OF COPERTINO, ecstatic. B. at Copertino, 1603; d. at Osimo, 1663; cd 1767; f.d. 18 September. Joseph Desa was born near Brindisi of very poor parents, and as a youth was sickly and slow-witted (he was nicknamed 'the gaper'). However, he became stable-boy at a Conventual Franciscan house at La Grottella, and so improved that he was admitted among the friars. From his ordination in 1628 his life was marked externally by a long succession of extraordinary happenings: ecstasies, healing of diseases, and, in particular, levitations (suspensions or flights in the air). These are specially remarkable in Father Joseph's case because the evidence adduced for some of the strangest of them is of considerable weight. St Joseph was treated with no little severity by his ecclesiastical superiors and excluded from much of the daily life of his order because of the disturbance caused by his raptures; but he bore it all humbly and obediently, living as one whose 'conversation was in Heaven' rather than on earth. During his last ten years he was moved from one friary to another, and ended his days in seclusion at Osimo in the March of Ancona.

JOSEPH OF VOLOKOLAMSK, abbot. B. *c.* 1439; d. 1515; cd by the Russ. Orth. ch., 1578; f.d. 9 September. Joseph Sanin was of Lithuanian origin, and a man of imposing personality and intellectual ability, who in 1477 was made abbot of Borovsk. But his strict discipline discontented his monks, and he left them in order to found a new community near Volokolamsk. St Joseph was no less a sincere seeker of reform in the Russian church than ◊ *St Nilus of Sora*, but their ideas and methods were opposed. Joseph's conception of the role of monasticism in the church made it necessary that monasteries should hold a good deal of communal property (e.g. for social works); he also had a much less independent attitude than Nilus towards the civil power. The two were brought face to face at a church council held in Moscow in 1503, and Joseph won over a majority to support the 'possessors'. The controversy went deeper than such questions as that of church property, and its ultimate resolution in favour of the 'Josephites' was very important for the future of the Russian church.

JOSEPH CAFASSO ◊ under *John Bosco*

JOSEPH CALASANZ, educationist and founder. B. at Peralta de la Sal, *c.* 1557; d. in Rome, 1648; cd 1767; f.d. 27 August. In the history of primary schools Joseph Calasanz was the forerunner of ◊ *St John-Baptist de La Salle* (notice the coincidence of the name of Joseph's birthplace in Aragón). After studying in three Spanish universities and graduating in law and divinity he was ordained priest in 1583, and later went to Rome. Here he was shocked by the ignorance and moral and physical squalor of the common people, and in 1597 started a free school in a slum district, across the Tiber. It grew rapidly, other priests joined the work, and in 1617 they were organized as the Clerks Regular of the Religious Schools (colloquially, 'Piarists'), the first priests to teach in elementary schools.

St Joseph Calasanz aimed at a full system of primary and secondary schools; his curricula were carefully organized, and he adumbrated the 'simultaneous method' of tuition. He wanted children to *love* goodness: 'if from the first', he wrote, 'a child is instructed in religion and letters it can reasonably be hoped that his life will be happy.' Piarist schools were established in Spain, Bohemia, and Poland as well as Italy; but the founder's last years were clouded by serious trials due to the ambitions of a subordinate. He bore them 'with the fortitude of another Job' (the phrase is Pope Benedict XIV's), but the credit of his order was not restored till after his death, which did not take place until he was over ninety.

JOSEPH COTTOLENGO. founder. B. at Brà in Piedmont, 1786; d. at Chieri near Turin, 1842; cd 1934; f.d. 30 April. In 1827 a canon of a collegiate church in Turin, Joseph Cottolengo, established a small free hospital in hired rooms; after the cholera epidemic of 1831 he transferred it to Valdocco, then on the outskirts of the city. From this modest beginning there developed the Little House of Divine Providence, an institution, or series of institutions, to care for the sick and afflicted of all kinds, the helpless aged, orphans – every sort of distressed person. To carry on the work in all its aspects Canon Cottolengo organized several religious societies of men and women. His outstanding personal characteristic was an absolute trust that God would provide for the continuance of what had been begun: he invested no funds, he kept no accounts; when money came in it was thankfully received and spent, when it did not he waited patiently without worrying (a hundred and fifty years earlier ◊ *St John-Baptist de La Salle* had been told: 'If you endow, you will be sunk'). Today the Little House at Turin, with its thousands of beneficiaries, is one of the most impressive places in Europe: here can be seen on a huge scale human suffering in its most horrifying forms side by side with human selflessness and love raised to a supernatural degree by a Power beyond itself. St Joseph Cottolengo's example was one of the inspirations of ◊ *St John Bosco*, who in the earlier years of his priesthood helped from time to time at the Little House.

JOSEPHA ROSSELLO, foundress. B. at Albisola Marina, 1811; d. at Savona, 7 December 1880; cd 1949; f.d. 3 October. She was one of the nine children of a potter, and from childhood showed an enterprising and masterful disposition. In 1837 she volunteered to the bishop of Savona in Liguria for work among girls and young women; it began in a very small way, and developed into the congregation of Daughters of our Lady of Mercy, with rescue-homes, hospitals, and schools. In 1875 a first house was opened in the Americas, at Buenos Aires. The trust and respect in which Mother Josepha was held is shown by the fact that the bishop of Savona, against the strong opposition of many of his clergy, allowed her to organize a house for the encouragement of vocations to the priesthood.

JUDE, apostle. First century; f.d. 28 October, with ◊ *St Simon*. The apostle of this name who was 'not Iscariot'; he is also called Thaddaeus or Lebbaeus (John xiv, 22; Matt. x, 3). He is traditionally identified with Jude, 'brother of James', the writer of the Epistle of Jude in the New Testament, but this is not altogether certain. An apocryphal document alleges that Jude the apostle preached the gospel and was martyred in Persia with his fellow apostle Simon; as St Thaddaeus he has been confused with ◊ *St Addai* in Mesopotamia. St Jude enjoys great popularity as a powerful intercessor for those in desperate straits, as students of the publicity columns of *The Times* newspaper are aware.

JULIAN THE HOSPITALLER, or 'the Poor Man'. No date; f.d. 12 February. Of the many churches, hospitals, and other charitable establishments in western Europe which bore, or bear, the name of St Julian, the large majority no doubt commemorate the hero of a romance, for whose historical existence there is no evidence whatever. According to the version familiar to our ancestors from the *Golden Legend*, Julian was a nobleman who through a mistake of identity killed his own father and mother. To expiate his unwitting crime he went with his wife to live by a ford across a river, where they gave help to travellers and built a refuge for poor people. One day they succoured a man almost dead with cold, who before he disappeared in glory told Julian that Jesus Christ had accepted his penance; 'And a while after St Julian and his wife rendered unto God their souls and departed out of this world.'

There are many saints named Julian, whose stories have in some cases got mixed up with the tale of the Hospitaller and *vice versa*. He has been honoured as the patron of ferrymen, innkeepers, circus people, and others.

JULIAN OF ANTIOCH, martyr. Date unknown; f.d. 16 March. He is sometimes called 'of Anazarbus' from his native place in Cilicia. After many sufferings he was tied in a sack and drowned in the sea, it is not known where. Antioch claimed to have his relics, and ◊ *St John Chrysostom* preached a homily there in his honour.

Another of the many early martyrs of this name is *St Julian of Brioude* (f.d. 28 August), who suffered in Auvergne at an uncertain date and was much venerated in France.

JULIAN OF TOLEDO, bishop. D. at Toledo, 690; f.d. 8 March. An able and learned man, he was important as a bishop and writer in the history of the Spanish church, which during his episcopate was centralized for the first time at Toledo. He had a strong influence on the development of the Mozarabic rites of public worship, formerly proper to Spain but now all but extinct. Julian is said to have been of Jewish descent, but he presided at a council whose legislation in respect of Jews was ruthless and unjust in the extreme.

JULIANA FALCONIERI, foundress. B. at Florence, 1270; d. there 1341; cd 1737; f.d. 19 June. Juliana was the only child of the wealthy couple who paid for the church called the Annunziata at Florence. Having refused marriage, she was enrolled as a tertiary of the Servite order, of which her uncle, St Alexis Falconieri, was one of the ◊ *Seven Founders*. For nearly twenty years she lived a devout and useful life at home; then, in 1304, she formed a community of tertiary sisters ('Mantellate'), who gave themselves to prayer and good works in Florence. From this circumstance St Juliana is regarded as the foundress of Servite nuns.

JULIUS OF DUROSTORUM, martyr. D. *c.* 302 (?); f.d. 27 May. He was a veteran soldier in the Roman army, one of a small group of comrades all beheaded about the same time for pertinaciously adhering to the Christian faith, at Durostorum in

Lower Moesia (near Silistria in Bulgaria). The authenticity of the surviving simple account of St Julius' death has not been questioned.

JUSTIN, martyr. B. at Nablus, *c.* 100; d. in Rome, *c.* 165; f.d. 14 April. Though born at the place anciently called Shechem in Palestine, Justin belonged to a pagan Greek family. Having studied one system of philosophy after another, he at length came to Christianity by way of Platonism, when he was about thirty-three. He remained a layman, but 'it is our duty', he said, 'to make our teaching known', and he travelled from place to place proclaiming the gospel. He was the most important Christian 'apologist', i.e. vindicator, of the second century and the first of whose written works notable parts are extant: they are the two *Apologies*, setting forth the moral values of Christianity, and the *Dialogue*, demonstrating its truth to the Jewish Trypho. These writings are valuable for the information they give about Christian faith and practice at that time, and they have been translated into English. Justin twice stayed in Rome; on the second occasion he was denounced as a Christian, and was put to death by beheading, together with five other men and a woman. The contemporary account of their examination by the prefect of Rome, Rusticus, is a genuine historical document. When finally ordered to sacrifice to the gods, St Justin replied, 'No right-minded man forsakes truth for falsehood', and the rest spoke to the same effect: 'Do with us as you will. We are Christians, and we cannot sacrifice to idols.'
L. W. Barnard, *Justin Martyr* (1967).

JUSTINA, martyr. Date unknown; f.d. 7 October. This maiden martyr was greatly revered at Padua, where a church was built in her honour in the sixth century. But the document which states that she was baptized by a disciple of ◊ *St Feter* and was martyred under Nero is a forgery of the middle ages.

JUSTINA ◊ *Cyprian and Justina*

JUSTUS OF BEAUVAIS, martyr. Date unknown; f.d. 18 October. According to his legend this Justus was a young boy killed by Roman soldiers for concealing the hiding-place of two other Christians; this is supposed to have happened between Beauvais and Senlis during Diocletian's persecution, at a place now called Saint-Just-en-Chaussée. There used to be a considerable cultus of St Justus in France; the story is without historical value, but there may have been a Gallo-Roman martyr of this name.

JUSTUS OF CANTERBURY, bishop. D. *c.* 627; f.d. 10 November. He came to England with the second band of Roman missionaries, and in 604 was made the first bishop of Rochester. He fled to Gaul with ◊ *St Mellitus* during the heathen reaction after King

Ethelbert's death, but soon returned, and in 624 became the fourth archbishop of Canterbury. When sending him the pall, the badge of his new office, Pope Boniface V wrote of Justus's known constancy and vigilance in the cause of Christ's gospel. – The St Just whose name occurs in two Cornish parishes has not been identified.

JUSTUS OF LYONS, bishop. B. near Viviers; d. in Egypt, *c.* 390; f.d. 14 October. While bishop of Lyons, his conscience was disturbed by the fear that an action of his had been instrumental in bringing about a man's violent death at the hands of a mob. In consequence he left his see by stealth, *c.* 382, and sought peace of mind in a monastery in Egypt. His hiding-place was discovered by chance, but he resolutely refused to leave it. After his death St Justus's body was taken back to Lyons, together with that of one of his clergy, *St Viator* (f.d. 21 October), who had been with him in his retirement.

JUTTA, laywoman. B. at Sangerhausen; d. at Kulmsee, 1260; f.d. 5 May. The written life of this young noblewoman, a native of Thuringia, bears a very curious resemblance to that of ◊ *St Elizabeth of Hungary*, who was almost her contemporary. Jutta too was happily married, with a family of children; she was prostrated by the loss of her husband, who died on a pilgrimage to the Holy Land; she divested herself of her property, and passed her few remaining years in religious retirement and care for the poor. In Jutta's case this was in the territory of the Teutonic Knights, whose grand-master was a relative of hers. After her death at her hermitage near Kulmsee a strong local cultus of her grew up in Prussia.

JUVENTINUS and MAXIMINUS ◊ under *John and Paul*

K

KATHERINE OF ALEXANDRIA, martyr. No date; f.d. 25 November. The legend of this saint is one of the most famous and most preposterous of its kind. It relates that Katherine was a high-born, learned, and beautiful maiden of Alexandria, who publicly protested to the emperor, called Maxentius, against the worship of idols. Confronted by fifty philosophers, she demolished their arguments, and they were burnt alive for their failure to answer her; she refused to deny her faith and marry the emperor, who then had her beaten for two hours on end and imprisoned. In her cell she was fed by a dove, and Christ appeared to her in a vision. An attempt was made to break her on a spiked wheel (the 'catherine-wheel'), but it fell to pieces and she was unhurt, while some of the spectators were killed by flying splinters. Her constancy brought about the conversion of two hundred soldiers, who were straightway beheaded. Finally Katherine too was beheaded, as she called down blessings on all who should remember her; from her severed veins there flowed not blood but milk. Her body was carried ('by angels') to Mount Sinai, where the Orthodox monastery is now called St Katherine's and her shrine is shown.

Such in very brief outline is the tale which was the starting-point of the great cultus of St Katherine, of which the ramifications were many and curious in both East and West. There is no trace of her name in early martyr records, nor any other positive evidence that she ever existed outside the mind of some Greek writer who first composed what he intended to be simply an edifying romance. Her emblem in art is a wheel.

KATHERINE OF BOLOGNA, abbess. B. at Bologna, 1413; d. there, 1463; cd 1712; f.d. 9 March. As a child Katherine de' Vigri was a maid of honour at the ducal court of Nicholas III d'Este at Ferrara, where she was given a good education. Then she joined a group of Franciscan tertiaries, who later became Poor Clare nuns, and in 1456 was sent back to Bologna as abbess of a new convent there. From an early age Katherine was subject to visions, some of which from their nature and effects she judged to be diabolical temptations, while others were consolatory and for her good. She was an effective novice-mistress and superioress, and had a talent for calligraphy and miniature-painting; a breviary written out and ornamented by her still exists at the Bologna convent. St Katherine left a number of writings in prose and verse, most of which are unpublished.

KATHERINE OF GENOA, mystic. B. at Genoa, 1447; d. there, 1510; cd 1737; f.d. 15 September. At the age of sixteen Katherine Fieschi married a young man named Julian, of the wealthy Adorni family: it was a marriage of family convenience. Julian was quick-tempered, dissipated, and unfaithful to his wife; she was sensitive and serious – perhaps rather humourless – and her efforts to find compensation in the gay life of Genoese society were a failure. Then suddenly, in 1473, she underwent what may be called a conversion, and a few years later her changed way of life changed her husband too. For twenty years they devoted themselves to nursing the sick in the Pammatone hospital, eventually going to live on the premises, where Katherine was matron from 1490 to 1496. During that time her devotion to the plague-stricken nearly cost her her life. She survived Julian for thirteen years, for the last nine of which she suffered from a disease that became more and more agonizing.

From the time of her conversion St Katherine led an intense inner life and was raised to high mystical states. Her religious practice was idiosyncratic – for instance; she went to communion every day, when to do so was most unusual – and for years she made extraordinarily long fasts without abating her charitable activities. She was one of the many examples of the religious contemplative who combines 'other-worldliness' with competence in handling human affairs; yet what she feared above all was 'the contagion of the world's slow stain', whose power to separate man from God she had experienced in the earlier years of her marriage. The writings that bear St Katherine's name were inspired by rather than actually written by her, but they contain the essence of her influential religious thought; the *Treatise on Purgatory* and the *Spiritual Dialogue* have been published in English (1934).

F. von Hügel, *The Mystical Element of Religion* (2 vols., 1961).

KATHERINE OF SIENA, mystic. B. at Siena, 1347 (?); d. in Rome, 1380; cd 1461; f.d. 30 April. Katherine Benincasa was the youngest of the many children of a Sienese dyer. She was a lively, good-looking girl, but resisted her parents' efforts, not always gentle, to get her to marry; about 1367 she became a tertiary sister of the Dominican order, living at home and spending much time in prayer. A long succession of raptures and other spiritual experiences are recorded of her, culminating later in the pain of the *stigmata* (cf. ◊ *St Francis of Assisi*), but without visible lesions. She attracted the attention of Siena, and a group of people gathered round her, priests and laity, noble and simple, young and old, including an Austin friar from England, William Flete. These were her 'family' or 'fine troop', the 'Caterinati', members of which accompanied her on her subsequent travels and with her were the occasion of some spectacular conversions of evil-doers.

Katherine's concern in wider public affairs began in 1375, when she sought to mediate in the armed conflict between Florence and other communes and the papal government. This took her to Avignon and Pope Gregory XI, whom she implored to carry out his wish to leave France and return to Rome. He did so, but at his death in 1378 his successor, Urban VI, was at once opposed by a rival pope. This began the 'great schism' that rent western Christendom for forty years. Katherine threw herself into the struggle on behalf of Urban, tirelessly dictating (she had never learned to write) fiery and intransigent appeals for his cause to churchmen and civil leaders everywhere. Urban called her to Rome and often consulted her; but there was no support for her impassioned advice, even from the members of her 'family', and amidst the general turmoil she died.

St Katherine of Siena was in the line of ◊ *St Hildegard*, and of *St Bridget of Sweden* (with close associates of whom she was in touch), but there has perhaps been a tendency to exaggerate the importance of her political and social activities. Her greatness ultimately resided in her personal faith and holiness, and in her passionate concern for the salvation of all mankind. Many of her letters survive, throwing much light on her spirited and candid character; those to Pope Gregory are a curious mixture of respectfulness and outspoken familiarity. Among her correspondents was that free-lance soldier from Essex, Sir John Hawkwood. Her dictated *Dialogue*, a rather unsystematic work dealing with man's religious and moral problems and duties, is an Italian classic (Eng. trans., 1898). St Katherine was named a doctor of the Church in 1970.

Raymund of Capua's contemporary Life, tr. G. Lamb (1960); modern Lives by E. G. Gardner (1907), J. Joergensen (1938), M. de la Bedoyère (1947), A. Curtayne (1957).

KATHERINE OF VADSTENA, or 'of Sweden' ◊ under *Bridget*

KATHERINE LABOURÉ, visionary. B. in the Côte d'Or, 1806; d. in Paris, 31 December 1876; cd 1947; f.d. 28 November. From 1831 until her death she led a life that was outwardly wholly uneventful as a Sister of Charity of St Vincent de Paul in Paris, discharging modest duties and waiting on the sick. She was an exemplary nun, matter-of-fact and unemotional by temperament. During her noviceship she had had certain visions of the Virgin Mary; the form taken by one of these provided the design of what is known as the 'miraculous medal', because of the circumstances of its origin. It is an oval medallion, bearing an image of the Virgin on one side and certain religious symbols on the other. The holiness of Sister Katherine was spontaneously recognized by all who knew her.

KATHERINE DEI RICCI, visionary. B. at Florence, 1522; d. at Prato, 1590; cd 1747; f.d. 13 February. This Katherine was a nun of a Dominican convent at Prato in Tuscany, where she discharged the offices of novice-mistress and prioress with good sense and efficiency. The very remarkable religious experiences recorded of her have aroused much discussion; for example, the long ecstasy into which she fell at the same time every week, in which she as it were relived Christ's passion. This phenomenon took place regularly for twelve years. Katherine's influence was not confined within the walls of her convent. She was greatly preoccupied by the need for reform in the church, as is apparent from her letters, many of them addressed to highly-placed persons; this accounts, too, for her reverence for the memory of Savonarola, who had defied the evil-living Pope Alexander VI and been hanged at Florence at 1498. St Katherine was in touch with such contemporary reformers as ◊ *St Philip Neri, St Charles Borromeo,* and *St Pius V.*

KENELM, prince. D. after 811; f.d. 17 July. The feast of St Kenelm (Cynehelm), 'martyr', was kept in many churches of southern and western England during the middle ages. It was then believed that, succeeding his father King Coenwulf of Mercia at the age of seven, he had at once been murdered at the instigation of his ambitious sister Quoenthryth. These three are historical persons; but Kenelm probably died before his father, and he certainly lived at least into adolescence. He may have been killed in battle. His shrine was at Winchcombe in Gloucestershire.

KENNETH ◊ *Canice*

KENTIGERN, or **MUNGO**, bishop. D. *c.* 612 (?); f.d. 14 January. He is said to have been a native of Lothian, and there is reason to believe that he was founder of the church at Glasgow and a missionary in Cumbria generally. It is further related of him that he was driven by persecution into Wales, where he founded the monastery at Llanelwy, being succeeded as abbot there by ◊ *St Asaph* when he was recalled to the north by the Christian king Rederech; but the evidence for these particulars is altogether insufficient. 'Mungo' (Munghu) is a Celtic nickname commonly used for Kentigern; it is usually explained as meaning 'most dear', but this is questionable. The ring and fish displayed on the heraldic arms of the city of Glasgow refer to a legend about St Kentigern, in which he miraculously saves an unfaithful wife from the anger of her royal husband.

KEVIN, abbot. B. in Leinster; d. at Glendalough, 618; f.d. 3 June. St Kevin (Coemgen) was the founder of the monastery at Glendalough, the Valley of the Two Lakes, in Wicklow, famed alike for its school and the beauty of its situation. Many disciples flocked to him, and many stories were told of him; they are recorded in medieval accounts and are full of the keen feeling for wild nature that distinguishes the lives of so many Irish saints.

KEYNE. Sixth century (?); f.d. 8 October. The only unassailable statements that can be made about St Keyne appear to be that her name is associated with South Wales and western Herefordshire, and that Robert Southey wrote a humorous poem about her holy well near Liskeard in Cornwall. The legend recorded in the fourteenth century makes her a maiden who was both a recluse and an itinerant evangelist, from Brecknock to St Michael's Mount.

KIERAN ◊ *Ciaran*

KÜMMERNIS ◊ *Wilgefortis*

L

LADISLAS THE FIRST, king of Hungary. B. 1040; d. at Nitra in Bohemia, 1095; f.d. 27 June. Ladislas (Laszlo), of the house of Arpad, became king of Hungary in 1077 and followed in the footsteps of ◊ *St Stephen I (of Hungary)*. He developed the power of his young kingdom, extended its boundaries by the annexation of Croatia and Dalmatia, repulsed Cuman invaders from the east and fostered Christianity within his dominions. He was distinguished personally for the justness of his rule and the virtue of his life. In a sentence, Ladislas was the ideal national hero, and in 1192 his relics were enshrined as those of a saint in the cathedral he had founded at Nagyvarad.

LAMBERT OF MAASTRICHT, bishop and martyr. B. at Maastricht, *c.* 635; d. at Liège, *c.* 705; f.d 17 September. He was a zealous missionary bishop for some thirty years, of which seven were spent in exile at Stavelot because of the enmity of the powerful West Frankish magnate, Ebroin. His murder at Liège (then only a hamlet) was at first attributed to personal revenge on the part of the murderer; later it was said that the responsibility rested with Pepin of Herstal, the East Frankish mayor of the palace whom Lambert had rebuked for adultery with his wife's sister. In any case Lambert was venerated as a martyr and great evangelizer; many churches in the Low Countries, especially Belgium, are dedicated in his honour.

LASZLO ◊ *Ladislas*

LAWRENCE, martyr. D. at Rome, 258; f.d. 10 August. It has been said of the traditional stories about St Lawrence that they portray, not the man, but the 'typical figure of a martyr'. It is known that he was one of the seven deacons of Rome, and that he was martyred there four days after Pope ◊ *St Sixtus II* in 258, and was buried in the cemetery on the road to Tivoli, where the church of St Lawrence-outside-the-Walls now stands. According to tradition, when ordered by the city prefect to hand over the church's valuables, he assembled the poor and sick and presented them to the prefect: 'Here,' he said, 'is the church's treasure.' Thereupon he was put to death by being roasted on a grid. It is more likely that in fact he was beheaded, as St Sixtus was. Scholars are not wholly in agreement about how much credence can be given to such particulars about St Lawrence as are given by ◊ *St Ambrose*, the poet Prudentius, and others. But it is unquestionable that from the fourth century he was venerated as one of the most famous martyrs of the city of Rome. With St Sixtus he is named in the canon of the Roman Mass. His emblem is a gridiron.

LAWRENCE OF BRINDISI, theologian and missioner. B. at Brindisi, 1559; d. at Lisbon, 1619; cd 1881; f.d. 21 July. This Lawrence (Cesare de' Rossi) joined the Capuchin Franciscans and studied at the University of Padua, where he acquired half-a-dozen languages and a remarkable knowledge of the Bible. His life was one of great activity: he preached in many European countries, particularly among Jews and Lutherans, filled responsible offices in his order, and was entrusted with diplomatic and political missions. In 1601, during warfare against the Turks in Hungary, he played a part similar to that of ◊ St John of Capestrano, advising the generals and leading the troops into battle, armed with a crucifix. St Lawrence left a large body of writings, including many sermons, works of controversy (with notes in Hebrew and Greek), and commentaries on Genesis and Ezekiel. In the Roman Catholic church St Lawrence of Brindisi has been venerated as a doctor of the church since 1959.

LAWRENCE OF CANTERBURY, bishop. D. at Canterbury, 619; f.d. 3 February. He was one of the first band of monks sent to England by Pope ◊ St Gregory I, and ◊ St Augustine of Canterbury's most trusted helper. Before his death Augustine consecrated Lawrence bishop, to be his first successor in the see of Canterbury, an irregular proceeding which none the less took effect. Equally with his predecessor, Lawrence failed to come to terms with the Christian Britons in the west. During the heathen reaction under King Eadbald, St Lawrence remained at his post; this is said to have been in consequence of a vision of ◊ St Peter, and that the occurrence led to Eadbald's conversion.

LAWRENCE GIUSTINIANI, bishop. B. in Venice, 1381; d. there, 8 January 1455; cd 1690; f.d. 5 September. The Giustiniani were a patrician family of Venice, but Lawrence rejected a secular career and became a canon of the chapter of St George on the island of Alga. He used to go about with a sack on his shoulder, begging food for the community. In 1433 he was made bishop of Castello. He was impatient of the temporal administration of his diocese, and delegated the work to others that he might be free personally to look after his flock, instead of 'casting up farthings'. Much against his will, in 1451 St Lawrence was moved to Venice (with the honorific title of patriarch), where he set about necessary work of reform with much energy. In public life he was a zealous and generous prelate, in private a self-denying and humble priest, who wrote several ascetical works of value; they are practical and unspeculative, aimed at raising the standard of the clergy.

LAWRENCE O'TOOLE, bishop. B. near Castledermot, c. 1128; d. at Eu in Normandy, 1180; cd 1226; f.d. 14 November. Lorcan ua

Tuathail was the son of a Leinster chieftain and spent part of his childhood as a hostage in the hands of a rival family, the MacMurroughs. He afterwards became a monk and abbot of Glendalough, from whence he was taken in 1161 to be archbishop of Dublin. Nine years later the Earl of Pembroke's ('Strongbow') Anglo-Norman adventurers landed in Ireland, and the rest of Lawrence's episcopate was conditioned by the events that followed, in the politics of which he was heavily involved. He took part in the church council of Cashel in 1172, and negotiated on behalf of the king of Connacht, Rory O'Connor, with Henry II of England. When in Rome for the general council held there in 1179 he was appointed papal legate in Ireland; this helped to provoke Henry against him and he was forbidden to return home. He went to the king, who was in Normandy, and induced him to lift this ban, but Lawrence had scarcely started on his journey back to Dublin when death overtook him, at Eu near the mouth of the Bresle. St Lawrence O'Toole was deeply devoted to his people; in his private life he kept the simplicity and austerity of a monk, living in community with his cathedral clergy and returning every Lent to Glendalough for a period of quiet and solitude. His memory is still honoured in the French diocese of Rouen, within which the place of his death, Eu, is situated.

LAZARUS ◊ under *Marys, The Three*

LEANDER, bishop. B. at Cartagena; d. at Seville, *c.* 600; f.d. 27 February. He was the elder brother of ◊ *St Isidore*, whom he preceded in the see of Seville. His principal work was the conversion of King Recared and many of the Visigoths from Arianism. While on a mission to Constantinople in 583 Leander met the future pope ◊ *Gregory the Great*, with whom he continued in touch by correspondence. Of St Leander's writings only a monastic rule for woman, written for his sister, and a homily survive.

LEBBAEUS ◊ *Jude*

LEBUIN ◊ under *Ludger*

LEGER, bishop. B. *c.* 616; d. near Arras, 679; f.d. 2 October. Leger (Leodegar) was appointed to the see of Autun in 663 and had the reputation of being a very strict bishop. After 670 he became involved in the political struggle against the ambitious West Frankish mayor of the palace, Ebroin, into the hands of whose troops he eventually fell. His eyes were put out, and later, after more mutilation, a court of bishops declared him deposed from his see. Finally his enemies had him killed. There still exists the text of a letter written by Leger to his mother on the death of his brother Gerin (also murdered). These two unfortunate men were revered as martyrs by their supporters; their opponents claimed that they had plotted the death of King Childeric II, Ebroin's nominee.

LEO THE GREAT, pope. B. in Rome (?); d. there 10 November 461; f.d. 11 April. Leo I, a man of the noblest character and great ability, was elected bishop of Rome in 440, at a time of crisis both in church and empire. In 451 the fourth general council met at Chalcedon to consider the teaching of Eutyches (Monophysism), and Leo's doctrinal letter ('tome') on the subject was acclaimed as the basis of the council's declaration of orthodox doctrine on Christ's two natures. In the next year Leo in person went to confront the invading Huns at the river Mincio, and induced Attila – for a consideration – to withdraw beyond the Danube; he could not stop the Vandals occupying Rome in 455, but at least was able to prevent a massacre. Such actions are representative of Pope Leo's determination to meet the demands of his day firmly and authoritatively. He saw the need to strengthen and extend the influence of the Roman church; he exerted his authority as pope in Spain, in Gaul, in Illyricum, and in North Africa, and he refused to recognize the canon of the Council of Chalcedon which, by giving the see of Constantinople a dignity above that of Alexandria and Antioch, threatened to disrupt an ancient traditional order.

He was typical of the best Roman character, energetic, magnanimous, consistent and unswerving in duty, his religion firmly anchored in the central Christian mystery of the Incarnation of the Word. The learned Pope Benedict XIV in 1754 added St Leo's name to those of the doctors of the church, but of written works there are only some letters and sermons in existence, remarkable for their precision and clear expression. In them the primacy of ◊ *St Peter*'s successor and his teaching authority are repeatedly emphasized; his was an important influence in the early history of the papacy.

T. G. Jalland, *Life and Times of St Leo the Great* (1941).

LEO THE NINTH, pope. B. in Alsace, 1002; d. in Rome, 1054; f.d. 19 April. The choice of the bishop of Toul, then called Bruno, as pope in 1048 marked the end of a deplorable period in the history of the papacy, and his vigorous reforming spirit began the movement that was to be carried farther by Pope ◊ *St Gregory VII*. Leo IX sought to free the church from the power of ambitious and unscrupulous lay nobles and he took strong measures against the associated evil of simony; he fought widespread abuses among the clergy, including the neglect of preaching; he encouraged the ideals of the Cluniac and other monks and of the canons regular; and he prepared the way for future popes to be elected by the cardinals of the Roman church alone. On the other hand Leo incurred the sharp criticism of ◊ *St Peter Damian* and others for himself leading troops against the Normans, who in 1053 were harrying papal territory in southern Italy (in the event the papal army was defeated). It was just at this time that the patriarch of Constantinople, Cerularius, impugned certain customs of the Western church; Leo sent legates to Constantinople with a lengthy reply, but before the matter came to a head he was dead.

Other popes of this name mentioned in the Roman Martyrology are *St Leo II* (d. 683; f.d. 3 July), *St Leo III* (d. 816; f.d. 12 June), and *St Leo IV* (d. 855; f.d. 17 July).

LEOBA ◊ *Lioba*

LEOCRITIA ◊ under *Eulogius of Córdova*

LEODEGAR ◊ *Leger*

LEONARD, hermit. Date unknown; f.d. 6 November. During the later middle ages St Leonard was greatly revered in France, England and Germany, but nothing certain is known about him; the eleventh-century Life in which he is first mentioned is historically worthless. This tells us, among other things, that he was a hermit, who founded a monastery at Noblac (now Saint-Léonard), near Limoges, in the sixth century. Doubtless his popularity was due to the very large number of miracles and aids attributed to his intercession, and to the enthusiasm of returning crusaders, who looked on him as the patron saint of prisoners.

LEONARD OF PORTO MAURIZIO, missioner. B. at Porto Maurizio, 1676; d. at Rome, 1751; cd 1867; f.d. 26 November. Paul Jerome Casanuova, said the contemporary ◊ *St Alphonsus de' Liguori*, was the finest missioner of his age. Son of a master-mariner, he became a Franciscan friar, and for over forty years preached up and down Italy with unwearying devotion and effectiveness, his most difficult and disappointing field being Corsica, where he was sent on a special mission in 1774. In addition, his printed works, mostly letters and sermons, fill a dozen volumes. The popularity of the service called the Stations of the Cross is largely due to the impetus he gave to its use. St Leonard was for a time the religious adviser of Clementina Sobieska, wife of the 'Old Pretender', whose son, Cardinal Henry of York, promoted the friar's canonization.

LEOPOLD OF AUSTRIA, prince. B. at Melk, 1073; d. at Vienna, 1136; cd 1485; f.d. 15 November. Little is known about Leopold III, margrave of Austria from 1095, except that he was a capable and beloved ruler and a munificent benefactor of the church. Three of his religious foundations still exist: the abbeys of Mariazell (Benedictines), Heiligenkreuz (Cistercians), and Klosterneuburg (Austin canons). He was notably free from ambition, for in 1125 he refused to be nominated as candidate for the imperial crown. The chronicler Otto of Freising was one of St Leopold's eighteen children.

LIAFWINE ◊ under *Ludger*

LIBERATA ◊ *Wilgefortis*

LINUS ◊ under *Clement I*

LIOBA, abbess. B. in Wessex, *c.* 700; d. near Mainz, 780; f.d. 28 September. In 748, at the request of ◊ *St Boniface of Crediton*, Abbess Tetta of Wimborne sent thirty of her nuns to help him in his missionary work in Germany; their leader was Lioba (Leoba), with whom Boniface had already been in correspondence (the charming text of her first letter to him still exists). They were installed at Bischofsheim in Franconia, and rapidly became a force in the German mission: a community of well-domesticated, hard-working women, who had as well to be able to read and write and know some Latin, so as to give informed support to the missionary priests. Abbess Lioba, we are told, was beautiful in person, always pleasant and smiling; nothing ruffled her patience, and her intelligence was as large as her generosity: 'the Scriptures were never out of her hand'. She was known far and wide: her neighbours came to her in every need and danger, bishops and men of affairs asked her advice, and Hildegard, wife of the future emperor Charlemagne, was a close friend in old age. In 776 St Lioba retired to another nunnery, at Schönersheim, and there died; she was buried close to St Boniface at Fulda.

An early Life trans. in C. H. Talbot, *The Anglo-Saxon Missionaries in Germany* (1954).

LIUDGER ◊ *Ludger*

LIVRADE ◊ *Wilgefortis*

LOUIS OF FRANCE, king. B. at Poissy, 1214; d. at Tunis, 1270; cd 1297; f.d. 25 August. Louis IX became king of France at the age of twelve, and seven years later married Margaret of Provence, elder sister of Eleanor, wife of Henry III of England; they had eleven children. His other associations with England were marked by his defeat of Henry's army at the battle of Taillebourg in 1242, and by the generous treaty he made with the same Henry in 1259. From the time when in 1235 he took over the government of his kingdom from the regency of his mother, the able but jealous Blanche of Castile, Louis was an ideal monarch. He was sincerely religious, but no bigot; impartial and merciful in administering justice, insisting on each man's rights, from king to peasant; an acute and trustworthy statesman; a man of peace and an efficient soldier. Like ◊ *St Joan of Arc* after him, one of his characteristics was his detestation of profane or blasphemous language; he never used it himself and would not tolerate it in others. In his Testament, his last advice to his eldest son, he sets out the principles he had kept before his eyes, and an extremely wise and impressive document it is.

The part of Louis' life that has principally caught popular imagination is the crusade that he led to the East in 1248. Damietta in Egypt was easily taken, but in 1250 the crusaders were heavily defeated at Mansurah, and Louis himself taken prisoner. After his release he withdrew the remnants of his troops to Akka in Palestine; but little could be done there, and he returned to France after an absence of six years. The dynamism of the Crusades was spent; nevertheless in 1270 Louis again sailed with an army, mobilized after much difficulty: eight weeks later he died of dysentery at Tunis. St Louis personified the highest ideals of a medieval Christian ruler, and the Life of him written by John of Joinville, his personal friend and companion on the crusade, is one of the most entrancing documents of the middle ages. Louis' title to sainthood can be summed up in one word, integrity – the quality on which he set so much value and which he possessed in a superlative degree.

John of Joinville, *Life of St Louis* (tr. R. Hague, 1955); *ib.* tr. M. R. B. Shaw in *Chronicles of the Crusades* (Penguin).

LOUIS BERTRAND, Dominican friar. B. at Valencia in Spain, 1526; d. there, 1581; cd 1671; f.d. 9 October. The greater part of the life of this Dominican, whose name is Luis Beltrán in Spanish, was passed in his native land; but from 1562 to 1568 he was a missionary in Colombia, Panama, and the Lesser Antilles. He was credited with making very large numbers of converts during this time: but either the numbers were greatly exaggerated or the conversions were very superficial, for he had to communicate with the Indians through an interpreter. It was claimed for him later that he had the gift of tongues and other supernatural powers. St Louis was one of the earliest missionaries to raise his voice against the rapacity and bad example in general of his countrymen in America; he was also one of those persons consulted by ◊ *St Teresa* about her projects for reform in the Carmelite order.

LOUIS GRIGNION, missioner and founder. B. at Montfort in Brittany, 1673; d. at Saint-Laurent-sur-Sèvre, 1716; cd 1947; f.d. 28 April. During his relatively short life as a missioner, especially among the poor, this St Louis had to overcome considerable setbacks and opposition. Two years after ordination he founded the Daughters of Wisdom at Poitiers, to nurse the sick poor and conduct free schools, but he was soon inhibited in that diocese; and his somewhat flamboyant missionary methods aroused official criticism in some other places. But he was well received by the people, his labours bore fruit, and before his death he was able to establish a society of priests, the Company of Mary, to carry on his work. His book on *True Devotion to the Blessed Virgin* has been widely diffused in many languages.

LOUISE DE MARILLAC, foundress. B. in Auvergne, 1591; d. in Paris, 1660; cd 1934; f.d. 15 March. She married an official of the royal court, Antony Le Gras, and after his death in 1625 was an active supporter of the charitable work of ◊ St Vincent de Paul, who came to put more and more reliance on her. Mademoiselle Le Gras, as she was known, became the co-founder with him of the Daughters of Charity, whose 'convent is the sick-room, their chapel the parish church, their cloister the city streets'; it was she who drew up the first draft of their rule of life. Her clear intelligence and wide sympathy played a big part in the beginnings of the congregation, whose aspirants she trained and whose rapid growth involved responsibilities which largely fell on her. At the time of her death there were already over forty houses of the sisters in France, the sick poor were looked after at home in twenty-six Parisian parishes, hundreds of women were given shelter, and there were other undertakings as well. St Louise was not physically robust, but she had great powers of endurance, and her selfless devotion was a source of incalculable help and encouragement to Monsieur Vincent.

J Calvet, *Louise de Marillac* (1959).

LOUP ◊ *Lupus*

LUCIAN OF ANTIOCH, martyr. B. at Samosata; d. at Nicomedia, 312; f.d. 7 January. This celebrated martyr, a priest of Antioch, was head of the theological school there and himself revised the text of the Greek version of the Old Testament and that of the four gospels. Being at Nicomedia when Diocletian's persecution began, he was imprisoned there for nine years; he was twice brought up for examination, when he defended himself ably and refused to renounce Christ. He was either starved to death or, more probably, killed by the sword, and was buried at Drepanum near by. Later on it was said that he had been drowned in the sea and that his body had been brought to land by a dolphin. How this piece of pagan folklore came to be attached to St Lucian is not known.

Another martyred *Lucian* was a priest put to death at Beauvais at an early date. No reliable particulars of him are known, but his name nevertheless occurs in the calendar of the Book of Common Prayer under 8 January.

LUCIUS, 'king'. No date; f.d. 3 December. This person apparently had no public cultus in England, but his name occurs in the Roman Martyrology, wherein he is connected with Chur in

Switzerland as well as with Britain. The *Liber Pontificalis, c.* 530 or later, states that a British king called Lucius wrote to Pope Eleutherius (*c.* 180), asking him in effect to send teachers. Bede repeats this, adding that missionaries came and converted the Britons. The story was expanded and embroidered in both England and Wales. There is no evidence for its authenticity, and it is now generally rejected as a fable. The suggestion has been well received that it originated in confusion between 'Britain' and 'Britium' (Birtha) in Mesopotamia, where there was a second-century Christian king named Lucius Abgarus.

LUCIUS ✧ *Montanus and Lucius.*

LUCY, virgin martyr. D. *c.* 304 (?); f.d. 13 December. There is no doubt that St Lucy was a martyr at Syracuse in Sicily, probably in Diocletian's persecution. Her memory was venerated at an early date, and she was named in the canon of the Roman Mass. But no confidence can be put in the story that she was denounced as a Christian by her rejected suitor, and miraculously saved from exposure in a brothel and from death by fire; that she was finally killed by a sword thrust in the throat is likely enough. St Lucy's name, suggestive of light, was perhaps the reason why she was popularly invoked against disease of the eyes; in art she is often represented holding two eyes in a dish.

LUDGER, missionary. B. near Utrecht, *c.* 744; d. at Billerbeck in Westphalia, 809; f.d. 26 March. As a young man Ludger (Liudger) came to England and studied for some years under Alcuin at York. He was sent in 775 to revive the work begun by St Lebuin at Deventer, and then was stationed at Dokkum, from whence he evangelized the Frieslanders for some years. Then he was driven out, and he spent his next two years in retirement at Monte Cassino. In 785 he returned to his missionary work in Friesland. Charlemagne then entrusted to him the evangelization of the Saxons in Westphalia. Ludger made his headquarters at the place now called Münster, 'monastery', from the community of clergy he organized there in 795. His preaching of the gospel had more success than Charlemagne's coercive methods, and *c.* 803 he was consecrated bishop of Münster. This great missionary died while on a preaching tour, and he was buried at the Benedictine monastery of Werden, on the Ruhr, which he had founded. Before going to York, St Ludger had been a pupil of ◊ *St Gregory (of Utrecht)* at Utrecht, and he wrote a Life of his master.

The *St Lebuin* (Liafwine) mentioned above was an Englishman, a monk of Ripon; he went into Friesland as a missionary and established the first church at Deventer (d. *c.* 773; f.d. 12 November).

LUDMILLA ◊ under *Wenceslas*

LUKE, evangelist. First century; f.d. 18 October. He was a gentile, a Greek, perhaps born in Antioch, and a medical man by profession – ◊ *St Paul* speaks of him as 'our beloved Luke, the physician' (Col. iv, 14). He was the author of the gospel that bears his name and of its continuation called The Acts of the Apostles. Certain passages in the latter, written in the first person plural, are usually held to show that the writer was with St Paul on parts of his second and third missionary journeys and on the voyage to Italy, when the ship was wrecked off Malta. In his letters, Paul thrice refers to Luke's presence in Rome, writing to Timothy, 'Luke is my only companion'. A writer of perhaps as early as the late second century declares that, having served the Lord constantly and written his gospel there, Luke died, unmarried, in Greece at the age of eighty-four, 'full of the Holy Spirit'. He is said to have been martyred, but it is very doubtful. St Luke is the patron saint of physicians and surgeons, and also of painters of pictures. He was himself a great artist in words, and his narratives have inspired many masterpieces of art; but the existing pictures of the Blessed Virgin which he is said actually to have painted are all works of a much later date. This evangelist's symbol is a winged ox.

A. H. N. Green-Armytage, *Portrait of St Luke* (1955).

LULL, bishop. B. in England; d. at Hersfeld, 786; f.d. 16 October. Lull was probably a Wessex man, as he was educated at Malmesbury. He went to Germany and became a highly trusted helper of *St Boniface of Crediton*, whom he succeeded in the bishopric of Mainz. He was a most worthy successor, a good pastor and zealous missionary. Letters to and from him show that he was anxious to form a good library, and he in turn was asked to send books to other people. Unhappily his episcopate was disturbed by a long dispute over jurisdiction with the abbot of Fulda, ◊ *St Sturm*; this led c. 768 to Lull's refounding of the abbey of Hersfeld in Hesse, and he established another monastery at Bleidenstadt in Nassau.

LUPUS OF TROYES, bishop. B. at Toul, c. 383; d. at Troyes, 479; f.d. 29 July. Lupus (Loup) married a sister of ◊ *St Hilary of Arles*, but seven years later, in 426, became a monk at Lérins; he was made bishop of Troyes soon afterwards. It was said that when the Huns overran Gaul in 451 he took a decisive part in saving his province from the invaders, but the story is almost certainly a fabrication; he is commonly identified with the Lupus who accompanied ◊ *St Germanus of Auxerre* on his first visit to Britain.

LUTGARD, mystic. B. at Tongres, 1182; d. at Aywières, 1246; f.d.

16 June. She was a young boarder at a nunnery at Saint-Trond in Belgium, who, in consequence of a vision of Christ calling her, became a nun in the same house; in 1208 she migrated to the more austere life of the Cistercian nuns at Aywières, near Brussels. Many more visions and mystical experiences are recorded of her, but her almost contemporary biographer was somewhat credulous. St Lutgard was a particularly attractive personality, who for the last eleven years of her life was afflicted with total blindness.

T. Merton, *What are these Wounds?* (1950).

LYONS, THE MARTYRS OF. D. 177; f.d. 2 June. The martyrdom of Christians at Lyons and Vienne under Marcus Aurelius is narrated in a letter sent by those two churches to the churches in Asia and Phrygia; it is preserved in the pages of Eusebius and is one of the most precious documents of Christian antiquity. The names of forty-eight of these martyrs are recorded, many of them Greek. Among them were the slave girl ◊ *Blandina*, the bishop ◊ *Pothinus*, Sanctus, a deacon, the newly baptized Maturus, Attalus, 'a man of repute', and a fifteen-year-old boy, Ponticus. The persecution was carried on deliberately and unscrupulously, torture was used, and the mob was excited against the Christians by charges of infamous crimes; some of the victims were vilified and denounced by their own servants. Many died in prison from ill treatment; those who were Roman citizens were beheaded; the rest were killed by wild beasts in the arena. 'We cannot describe in writing the greatness of the tribulation here or the heathens' fury against the saints or all that the blessed martyrs suffered' (from the letter).

M

MACARIUS THE ELDER, desert monk. B. in Upper Egypt, *c.* 300; d. in Sketis, *c.* 390; f.d. 15 January. He was one of the fathers of Egyptian monasticism. Following the example of ◊ *St Antony*, he withdrew into the wilderness of Sketis when he was about thirty and lived there some sixty years, famed for his austere life and his wisdom. There was recorded of him, whether truly or not, a happening that seems exactly to parallel the stigmatization of ◊ *St Francis of Assisi* nearly 900 years later. A considerable number of writings have been ascribed to him, most probably erroneously. There has been much confusion between this Macarius and his contemporary namesake, *St Macarius of Alexandria* or *The Younger* (f.d. 2 January); he also was a desert monk, in the same neighbourhood as his fellow.

MACCUL ◊ *Maughold*

MACLOVIUS ◊ *Malo*

MACRINA THE YOUNGER, dedicated maiden. B. at Caesarea in Cappadocia, *c.* 327; d. in Pontus, 379; f.d. 19 July. She was early betrothed to a young lawyer, upon whose early death she devoted herself to her family and exercised a strong influence over her younger brothers, ◊ *SS. Basil, Gregory of Nyssa,* and Peter of Sebastea. She succeeded her widowed mother, St Emmelia, as head of the little community on the river Iris in Pontus. Accounts of her life and conversation were written by her brother Gregory, who was with her when she died. This Macrina is called 'the Younger' to distinguish her from her paternal grandmother, *St Macrina the Elder* (f.d. 14 January), who with her husband suffered much during the persecution under Galerius.

The account by her brother St Gregory of Nyssa, tr. by W. K. L. Clarke (1916).

MADELEINE SOPHIE, foundress. B. at Joigny, 1779; d. in Paris, 1865; cd 1925; f.d. 25 May. Madeleine Sophie was the daughter of Jacques Barat, a cooper by trade; she was given a good education in an atmosphere of strict discipline by her brother Louis, eleven years her senior, who was in holy orders. Madeleine supplemented this by private study, and developed into a young woman of charm and ability, with a desire to serve God in the modest capacity of a Carmelite laysister. But the call came from elsewhere. At the request of the superior of the Sacred Heart fathers, Joseph Varin (afterwards a Jesuit), she went in 1801 to teach in a convent school at Amiens, where she was soon made superioress of the small community. This was the first house of the Society of the Sacred Heart, for the education of girls, which Mother Barat was to direct for sixty-three years, during which it became established in twelve countries of Europe and America. In its early stages it was nearly wrecked by the ambition of the chaplain at Amiens; but the patience and tact of Mother Barat and Father Varin prevailed, and together they drew up the rules of the society which were finally adopted in 1815. Mother Barat led a life of extraordinary laboriousness, travelling all over France and beyond to oversee new foundations (she was in England in 1844) and organizing the life and work of an ever-growing congregation, which became one of the best-known and most efficient educational institutes under the auspices of the Roman Catholic church. The secret of her endurance and determination was the religious spirit which inspired all her undertakings; she was endowed with wisdom and insight to a remarkable degree, joined with endearing modesty and attractiveness.

M. Williams, *St Madeleine Sophie* (1965).

MADELGAIRE, abbot. B. at Strépy, *c.* 615; d. at Soignies, *c.* 677;

f.d. 14 July. He was the husband of ◊ *St Waudru*. He founded two monasteries and, some time after the birth of his fourth child, retired to one of them, at Hautmont; later he moved to the other, at Soignies, where he was abbot. Some centuries after his death, a life of St Madelgaire was compiled, which is an extreme example of the not-uncommon medieval practice of borrowing from the biographies of other saints when writing of one about whom information was deficient. In this example there are plagiarisms from over a dozen saints' Lives, and six chapters from the Life of Madelgaire's wife are reproduced word for word. This saint is also known as Vincent of Soignies.

MAEDOC ◊ *Aidan of Ferns*

MAEL MAEDOC ◊ *Malachy*

MAGNUS OF ORKNEY. D. on Egilsay, 1116; f.d. 16 April. This Magnus was a son of Erling, joint ruler of the Orkney islands. When King Magnus Barefoot of Norway invaded the Orkneys, Magnus Erlingsson took refuge with Malcolm III of Scotland and is said to have lived for a time in the house of a bishop. After Magnus Barefoot's death he returned to the Orkneys, where his cousin Haakon was in possession; at length Haakon treacherously killed him, on the island called Egilsay. Magnus was eventually buried in Kirkwall cathedral, which is dedicated in his honour, and other churches bear his name; he was thus honoured because of his repute for virtue and piety, but there appears no reason why he should have been called a martyr. There is a number of other saints named Magnus, mostly martyrs, but little is known about any of them.

J. Mooney, *St Magnus, Earl of Orkney* (1935).

MAIOLUS ◊ *Mayeul*

MALACHY, bishop. B. at Armagh, *c.* 1094; d. at Clairvaux, 1148; cd 1190; f.d. 3 November. St Malachy (Mael Maedoc ua Morgair), a priest of the clergy of Armagh, was in 1123 commissioned to revive the abbey of Bangor in Down and in the following year was made bishop of the neglected diocese of Connor as well. He pursued both tasks vigorously, till in 1127 war drove him out. In 1129 he was nominated to the archbishopric of Armagh, but for some time was unable to take full possession of his see; he was violently opposed by representatives of the family in which the monastery and church of Armagh had been hereditary for generations, and he was more than once in danger of his life. When at length he had broken this and other abuses, and restored peace and order to the church, St Malachy resigned Armagh to the abbot of Derry in 1137. In 1139 he went to Rome to obtain the archiepiscopal pall for the sees of Armagh and Cashel; in this he was unsuccessful, but Pope Innocent II appointed him papal legate for Ireland. On both his outward and inward journeys he visited ◊ *St Bernard* at Clairvaux, leaving four of his companions there to be trained; with these monks and others he in 1142 founded the abbey of Mellifont in Louth, the first Cistercian house in Ireland. He also introduced canons regular into that country. For eight years Malachy was active in the exercise of his legatine authority, and then in 1148 set out again for Rome in quest of the palls. On the way he was taken ill at Clairvaux and died in St Bernard's arms. Bernard said of him that 'his first and greatest miracle was himself. His inward beauty, strength, and purity are proved by his life; there was nothing in his behaviour that could offend anyone.' He was buried in the abbey church at Clairvaux, and St Bernard wrote his Life. The so-called Prophecies of St Malachy, characterizing future popes, are a sixteenth-century forgery.

H. J. Lawlor (tr.), *St Malachy of Armagh*, by St Bernard (1920).

MALO, missionary monk. D. *c.* 640; f.d. 15 November. The port of Saint-Malo takes its name from this Malo (Maclovius or, wrongly, Machutus), who ministered and made foundations from the islet in the estuary of the Rance or from the neighbouring Aleth (Saint-Servan). He may have been an emigrant from south-west Wales. He is said to have been driven from Aleth by his enemies and to have settled at Saintes, dying near by at Archingeay.

MAMAS, martyr. D. *c.* 274; f.d. 17 August. He was a shepherd who was martyred at Caesarea in Cappadocia during the reign of Aurelian, and was much venerated in the East. Nothing else is now known about him; various stories grew up later, as that wild animals in the arena refused to touch him, or that he was stoned to death while still a boy.

MARCELLA, Roman matron. B. in Rome. 325; d. there, 410; f.d. 31 January. On the death of her husband very soon after marriage St Marcella organized a sort of religious sisterhood at her mansion on the Aventine Hill. She welcomed ◊ *St Jerome* on his arrival in Rome, and he guided the group in religion and learning: it was the beginning of his famous following of cultivated Roman ladies. Marcella was a woman of intellectual ability, and not afraid to stand up to the masterful Jerome. When Alaric the Goth sacked Rome she was subjected to personal violence to extort the whereabouts of her wealth, and she died from the effects of this ordeal.

MARCELLIAN ◊ *Mark and Marcellian*

MARCELLINUS and PETER, martyrs. D. in Rome, *c.* 304; f.d. 2 June. These martyrs, of whom the first was a priest, suffered during the persecution under Diocletian and were buried on the

Via Labicana 'at the two laurels'; but no reliance can be put on the details contained in their legend. Pope ◊ St Damasus, who when a boy had talked with their executioner about them, wrote an epitaph for their tomb, and they are named in the canon of the Roman Mass.

MARCELLUS THE CENTURION, martyr. D. at Tangier, 298; f.d. 30 October. During the festivities held by a Roman legion in celebration of Emperor Maximian's birthday the centurion Marcellus, regarding such festivities as idolatrous, threw off his military belt. 'I serve only the eternal king, Jesus Christ,' he declared. Brought before the deputy prefect at Tangier, Marcellus pleaded guilty to repudiating his allegiance to an earthly leader, and was put to death.

It was afterwards said that the official shorthand-writer, St Cassian (f.d. 3 December), was so indignant at the sentence that he refused to report the proceedings, and that he too was executed in consequence. In all probability this is a fictitious addition to the authentic account of St Marcellus, though there seems to have been a martyr at Tangier named Cassian.

MARCELLUS THE RIGHTEOUS, abbot. B. at Apamea in Syria; d. near Constantinople, c. 485; f.d. 29 December. He became abbot of the Eirenaion monastery near Constantinople, whose monks were known as Akoimetoi, 'sleepless' monks, because they were organized in groups who took it in turn to sing God's praises in church throughout the twenty-four hours. Marcellus put special emphasis on the need for poverty and manual work, and under his direction the Eirenaion became the most influential of such houses. He took part in the Council of Chalcedon in 451. There is a number of other saints named Marcellus or Marcellinus, about most of whom little or nothing is known.

MARGARET, virgin martyr. No date; f.d. 20 July. Margaret (called Marina in the East) was one of the most popular saints in the later middle ages in the West, but there is no positive evidence that she ever existed. Her story is simply a fictitious romance. It relates that in the reign of Diocletian a pagan priest at Antioch in Pisidia had a Christian daughter, Margaret. She rejected the advances of the prefect Olybrius, who thereupon denounced her as a Christian. The ordeals she then suffered are of the most fabulous description (including being swallowed by Satan in the form of a dragon); finally she was beheaded. This farrago professes to have been written by an eye-witness, Margaret's attendant, Theotimus. There are points of resemblance between the cultus of this Margaret and of ◊ Katherine of Alexandria; in the middle ages they were sometimes represented together. Margaret's emblem is a dragon.

Another *St Margaret* (f.d. 8 October), to whom the name Reparata was given, belongs to the Pelagia group of legends (◊ *Pelagia the Penitent*); fleeing from marriage, she disguises herself as a monk and is accused of seducing a nun; she is vindicated only by death (cf. *St Marina*).

MARGARET MARY, visionary. B. at L'Hautecour in Burgundy, 1647; d. at Paray-le-Monial, 1690; cd 1920; f.d. 17 October. She was the daughter of a notary, Claud Alacoque, and after an ailing and rather unhappy childhood she entered the Visitation convent at Paray-le-Monial in 1671; she was an exemplary but perhaps rather humourless nun, who was entrusted with responsible offices in her community. Between 1673 and 1675 Sister Margaret Mary experienced four visions of Jesus Christ, concerning devotion towards his heart as symbolizing his love for mankind, which men so often reject. She was charged to promote this devotion. These revelations accidentally became known to the other nuns, some of whom looked on them as delusions, and Sister Margaret Mary had much to suffer, not least when, in 1677, she told them with fear and trembling that Christ had twice asked her to be a willing victim to expiate their shortcomings. But she had the support of a holy and experienced Jesuit, Claud La Colombière, and by the time of her death opposition in her community was at an end. Her patience and trust under these and other trials contributed not a little to St Margaret Mary's canonization. Her visions and teaching have had considerable influence on the devotional life and habits of Roman Catholics, especially since the feast of the Sacred Heart of Jesus was made general in 1856. She left a short and touching autobiography.

Autobiography, tr. V. Kerns (1961).

MARGARET OF CORTONA, penitent. B. at Laviano, 1247; d. at Cortona, 1297; cd 1728; f.d. 22 February. This Margaret was the handsome daughter of a Tuscan peasant. From her eighteenth to her twenty-seventh year she was the mistress of a young nobleman near Montepulciano, to whom she bore a son. After her lover's death by violence in 1273 she and the child were given a home by a family in Cortona, and gradually her life became as self-denying as it had formerly been self-indulgent. She enrolled herself among the Franciscan tertiaries, and until her son grew up occupied herself in making a living and in works of charity. But some people doubted the sincerity of her repentance, and she and her friends did not escape slanderous gossip. Margaret became more and more of a recluse, though not wholly cutting herself off from the public life around her. Many conversions of sinners were brought about by her prayers and counsel, and many supernatural communications are recorded by her confessor, Friar Giunta. Her last years were passed in almost complete seclusion.

Fr Cuthbert, *A Tuscan Penitent* (1907); F. Mauriac, *Margaret of Cortona* (1948).

MARGARET OF HUNGARY, nun. B. in 1242; d. in Budapest, 1270; cd 1943; f.d. 18 January. Margaret's father was Bela IV, king of Hungary, who built a convent for Dominican nuns at Budapest, which his daughter entered as a girl; she refused to leave it even to marry the king of Bohemia. The rest of her life was equally determined. Particulars of it are recorded in the existing depositions of witnesses taken in 1277. Some of her self-imposed penances and hardships, like those of certain other saints, are no less than horrifying, striking the reader today as perverse and squalid: 'one gets the impression that Margaret's love of God and desire of self-immolation were associated with a certain element of wilfulness.' But it was not all like that; a maid-servant testified, 'She was kind and good, and much more humble than we serving-maids.'

MARGARET OF SCOTLAND, queen. B. *c.* 1045; d. in Edinburgh, 1093; cd 1250; f.d. in Scotland, 16 November. Granddaughter of Edmund Ironside, king of the English, she was probably born in Hungary, in exile, of a German mother, but was brought to England in 1057. After the Norman conquest she found refuge in Scotland, and in 1070 married King Malcolm III (Canmore). They had six sons and two daughters, and Margaret's biographer (probably her confessor, Turgot), emphasizes her good influence over her husband. She had always been deeply religious, and as queen she used her influence to bring certain customs of the Scottish church into line with the general discipline of the West. Her whole influence – and she was a strong-willed woman, every inch a queen – was directed towards encouraging, or imposing, a strong infusion of Anglo-Norman manners and institutions into a rather isolated Scotland. She brought up her children admirably, and was particularly noted for her solicitude for orphans and poor people. She died four days after her husband had been treacherously killed near Alnwick, and was buried at Dunfermline abbey, which she had founded with him in 1072. St Margaret's son *David*, one of the best of Scottish kings, was also revered as a saint by his people (d. 1153; f.d. 24 May); through the marriage of her daughter Matilda with Henry I of England Margaret was an ancestress of the present British royal house.

L. Menzies, *St Margaret, Queen of Scotland* (1925).

MARI ◊ *Addai and Mari*

MARIAN and JAMES, martyrs. D. in Africa, 259; f.d. 30 April. Marian, a church reader, and James, a deacon, were cast into prison at Cirta (Constantine in Algeria) during the persecution by Valerian. They were both tortured in order to make them apostatize, but each was strengthened by a dream of his triumphant martyrdom to come. They were put to death at the military town of Lambaesis, with other victims so numerous that they were drawn up in rows and the executioner passed down the ranks striking off head after head, 'in a rush of fury' – a feat of swordsmanship indeed. Marian and James are known from an account written by a man who shared their imprisonment but was himself released.

MARIANA OF QUITO ◊ under *Rose of Lima*

MARINA, woman monk. No date; f.d. 12 February. Marina's father became a monk in Bithynia and kept her with him, disguised as a boy. On his death she went on living undetected in the monastery. She was accused of fathering the child of an innkeeper's daughter, but was received back into the monastery after five years of expiation. At her death her sex and consequent innocence were discovered. This tale is simply a literary amplification of the legend of ◊ *St Pelagia the Penitent* (✪ under *Margaret, virgin martyr*).

On the other hand it appears to be true that a young woman entered the monastery of Schönau in disguise and lived there as a novice, undetected until her death in 1188. She was popularly called *St Hildegund* in Germany, but there seems to have been no public cultus.

MARINUS, martyr. D. *c.* 262; f.d. 3 March. He was a soldier, stationed at Caesarea in Palestine. When he was about to be promoted centurion he was denounced as a Christian by a jealous rival. Encouraged by Bishop Theotecnus, Marinus chose the gospel rather than the sword, and was accordingly put to death. A Roman senator, Astyrius, gave the body honourable burial, and he too is honoured as a martyr, but on inadequate evidence.

The Italian republic of San Marino takes its name from another St Marinus (fourth century (?); f.d. 4 September); but his story – that he was a stonemason who fled to a hermit's cell on Monte Titano to escape a woman who falsely claimed to be his wife – is historically worthless.

MARIUS and MARTHA ◊ under *Valentine*

MARK, evangelist. First century; f.d. 25 April. The author of the gospel according to Mark, the man named Mark who is referred to in the New Testament epistles as being with ◊ *St Peter* and *St Paul*, and the John Mark mentioned in the Acts of the Apostles are usually regarded as having been all the same person (identical too, it is sometimes said, with the young man who ran away naked when Christ was arrested in Gethsemane). If these identifications are correct we learn from the New Testament that St Mark was the son of a woman householder in Jerusalem named Mary (Acts xii, 12). He went with St Paul and ◊ *St Barnabas* (Mark's cousin) on their first missionary journey, but turned back alone at Perga (ibid. xii, 25, xiii, 13). In consequence, Paul later refused to take him on the second missionary journey, and Mark went with Barnabas to continue the evangelization of Cyprus (ibid xv, 37–39). The breach with Paul having been healed, Mark was with him in Rome (Col. iv, 10), where he probably wrote his gospel. Papias, writing *c.* 140, said that Mark was the interpreter of St Peter. That he afterwards went to Alexandria and preached the gospel there is possible, but the tradition that he was first bishop of that church and was martyred during the reign of the emperor Trajan lacks reliable support. St Mark's name is commonly associated with the city of Venice because in 829 what purported to be his relics were brought there from Alexandria, and enshrined in the original church of San Marco. His symbol is a winged lion.

MARK and MARCELLIAN, martyrs. Date unknown; f.d. 18 June. Two Roman martyrs, they were buried in the cemetery of Balbina, where the remains of their tomb have been found. An account of them is given in the spurious 'acts' of St Sebastian, in which they are described as twins of high rank who resisted the appeals of their wives and families to save their lives by apostasy, and were beheaded. Their true story is not known.

MARK OF ARETHUSA ◊ under *Cassian of Imola*

MARO, hermit. D. 433; f.d. 14 February. He was a hermit near Cyrrhus in Syria whose gifts and virtues brought him many disciples. Among his friends was ◊ *St John Chrysostom*, one of whose letters to him has survived. He was buried at a place between Apamea and Emesa (Homs), where a monastery grew up around his tomb; the people in Lebanon called Maronites are said to get their name from this monastery, Bait-Marun, and look on St Maro as their patriarch and patron saint.

MARTHA. First century; f.d. 29 July. The sister of Lazarus and Mary of Bethany (John xi). Martha was solicitous in ministering to Jesus Christ (Luke x, 38–42; John xii, 1–2), and is looked on as a pattern and patroness for those actively engaged in the service of the needy. It was to her that Jesus declared: 'I am the resurrection and the life ...', evoking her confession of faith, 'I believe that thou art the Christ, the Son of God. ...' (Cf. ◊ *Mary Magdalen* and *Marys, The Three.*)

MARTHA ◊◊ under *Valentine*

MARTIAL ◊ under *Felicity*

MARTIAL OF LIMOGES, bishop. Third century (?); f.d. 30 June.

He was said to be one of six bishops sent with St Denis of Paris (◊ *Dionysius of Paris*) from Rome to Gaul *c.* 250, where he evangelized Aquitaine from his see at Limoges. During the middle ages there grew up a highly extravagant legend to the effect that St Martial had been a personal disciple of Jesus Christ and should be numbered among the apostles; that he was sent from Rome into Gaul by ◊ *St Peter*; and that for nearly forty years his missionary labours were accompanied by the most astounding marvels.

MARTIN THE FIRST, pope and martyr. B. at Todi in Umbria; d. in the Crimea, 16 September 655; f.d. 12 November. The death of Pope Martin I in exile, which led to his being honoured as a martyr, was brought about by his refusal to countenance a religious aspect of the politics of the Byzantine emperor, Constans II. In the year he was elected pope, 649, Martin presided at a council in Rome which condemned the monothelite heresy and two imperial decrees for favouring it. Constans ordered him to be brought to Constantinople, and in 653–4 he was taken there, being imprisoned on the island of Naxos on the way. He arrived suffering from harsh treatment and illness, and was taken to jail on a stretcher. 'For forty-seven days', he wrote, 'I have not been given water to wash in. I am frozen through and wasting away with dysentery. The food I get makes me vomit. But God sees all things and I trust in him.' After suffering more cruelty and indignities St Martin was banished in 655 to Kherson in the Crimea, and there shortly afterwards he died, the last bishop of Rome so far to be venerated as a martyr.

MARTIN OF BRAGA, bishop. B. *c.* 515; d. at Braga, 580; f.d. 20 March. The place of origin and early history of this Martin are rather uncertain, but *c.* 550 he was in the north-west of the Iberian peninsula, Galicia, where he introduced communal monasticism. His principal foundation was the abbey of Dumium (Mondoñedo), and before 572 he was appointed archbishop of Braga. He was an active and successful missionary among the Arian Suevians, whose king he converted. St Martin was a writer of some importance, his works including a sermon which gives interesting particulars of rural superstitions that he encountered.

MARTIN OF TOURS, bishop. B. at Sabaria in Pannonia, 315 (?); d. at Candes near Tours, 397; f.d. 11 November. St Martin, a soldier's son, was born in what is now Hungary and brought up in Italy, at Pavia. As a young officer at Amiens he gave half his cloak to a naked beggar, in whom he was led to recognize Christ, and soon afterwards he was baptized. About 339 he asked for discharge from the army, for, he said, 'I am Christ's soldier; I am not allowed to fight'. Accused of cowardice, he retorted by offering to stand unarmed between the opposing lines. However, he was given his discharge, and for some time was in Italy and Dalmatia before living as a recluse on an island off the Ligurian coast. In 360 he became one of ◊ *St Hilary*'s clergy at Poitiers, and founded a semi-eremitical religious community at Ligugé, the first monastery in Gaul. Upon being made bishop of Tours in 370 or 371 he lived at a solitary place near by, which soon developed into another monastery, Marmoutier. His example and encouragement led to the establishment of other communities elsewhere.

St Martin was an extremely active missionary, his preaching being reinforced by his reputation as a wonderworker; he penetrated into the remotest parts of his diocese and beyond its borders, on foot, on donkey-back, or by water. He was not averse to the forcible destruction of heathen shrines; on the other hand, with Pope St Siricius and ◊ *St Ambrose*, he stood out against the condemnation to death (ostensibly for practising magic) by Emperor Maximus of Priscillian and other heterodox Spaniards. Martin encountered a good deal of opposition in his later years, one of his chief critics being ◊ *St Brice*; but his awe-inspiring spiritual power was too much for the 'unspeakably bloody ferocity' of Count Avitian, who refrained from intended barbarities in Tours.

As an evangelizer of rural Gaul and the father of monasticism in France St Martin of Tours was a figure of great importance, and his fame spread far and wide, not least through the biography and three long letters about him written by his friend Sulpicius Severus. He was one of the first holy men who was not a martyr to be publicly venerated as a saint, and his influence was felt from Ireland to Africa and the East. In England many churches were dedicated in his honour, of which St Martin's at Canterbury is the oldest and St Martin-in-the-Fields in London perhaps the best-known today; his name occurs twice in the calendar of the Book of Common Prayer, on 11 November and on 4 July, the anniversary of his episcopal consecration, of the translation of his relics, and of the dedication of his church at Tours.

Contemporary Life by Sulpicius Severus, tr. in F. R. Hoare, *The Western Fathers* (1954); P. Monceaux, *St Martin of Tours* (1928); E. I. Watkin, in *Neglected Saints* (1955).

MARTIN DE PORRES, Dominican laybrother. B. at Lima in Peru, 1579; d. there, 1639; cd 1962; f.d. 3 November. Brother Martin was a mulatto, the natural son of a Spanish *hidalgo* and an Indian woman from Panama. As a youth he was accepted as a laybrother in the Dominican friary at Lima, and there he spent his life, as barber, farm-labourer, almoner, infirmarian, and the like. He was devoted to the sick and the beggars who thronged the friary gate and had a great concern for animals, including vermin, about which engaging tales are told. But he also had aptitude for more delicate affairs, solving his sister's marriage difficulties, raising a dowry for his niece, and being consulted on private matters by persons of consequence in Lima. It was inevitable that he should be credited with supernatural powers, and at his death all Lima acclaimed his holiness, but his canonization met with setbacks and long delays. In the United States Martin de Porres has been adopted as patron saint of work for interracial justice and harmony.

G. Cavallini, *St Martin de Porres* (1963).

MARTINA ◊ under *Tatiana*

MARY, THE BLESSED VIRGIN, Principal f.d. 15 August. The mother of Jesus was a Jewish maiden, called Miriam in Hebrew, traditionally of the family of King David; nothing sure is known about her parentage or the place of her birth. St Luke's gospel (i, 26–38) relates that, having been betrothed to ◊ *Joseph*, she was living at Nazareth when an angel appeared to her and announced that the Holy Spirit would come upon her, and that by his power she would bear a son, Jesus, to be known as the Son of God. Mary accepted the humanly unbelievable, in the words 'Behold the handmaid of the Lord! Be it unto me according to thy word.' The angel had told her that her aged relative Elizabeth was with child (◊ *John the Baptist*), and Mary went to visit Elizabeth, who greeted her as the angel had done: 'Blessed art thou among women! And blessed is the fruit of thy womb!' And Mary gave voice to a song of praise and thanksgiving, 'My soul doth magnify the Lord . . .' (ibid. i, 39–56). Joseph took her to wife; and when they had to visit Bethlehem for a census, Jesus was born there. After the various events related in the gospels, of which St Luke says that 'Mary kept all these things and pondered them in her heart', they settled down with the child in Nazareth.

During the public ministry of Jesus his mother is heard of only occasionally, e.g. at the wedding-feast in Cana; but at the consummation of his mission she reappears for a brief, significant moment: 'Now there stood by the cross of Jesus his mother . . . When Jesus therefore saw his mother, and the disciple standing by whom he loved, he saith unto his mother, "Woman, behold thy son!" Then saith he to the disciple, "Behold thy mother!" And from that hour that disciple took her unto his own home' (John xix, 25–27). After Christ's ascension Mary was with the apostles and the others, watching and praying in the upper room, until they were filled with the Holy Spirit at Pentecost. This is the last reference to Mary in the New Testament, and nothing whatever is known of her closing years, not even where she died: both Jerusalem and Ephesus assert their claims.

That Mary was the virgin mother of the divine Christ is made plain in the Bible (Matt i, 18–23; Luke i, 34–35, iii, 23); and from the beginning Christians have believed that she remained virgin throughout her life, as church fathers and councils testify. In the Roman Catholic church it is an article of faith that God preserved Mary from the taint of 'original sin' from the first moment of her conception in her mother's womb (her 'immaculate conception'); and also, without denying her natural death, that at the end of her earthly life he took her to Heaven in both soul and body (her 'assumption'). The second of these beliefs is commonly held also by the Christians of the ancient churches of the East. In very early times attempts were made to supplement the biblical narrative from other sources, where the Virgin Mary and the early life of Jesus are concerned. These apocryphal writings are quite unreliable, sometimes puerile and fantastic, and contain little of value, except to scholars; but some of their statements have passed into the common stock of pious belief, such as Mary's sojourning in the Temple as a child and the legend of how Joseph was chosen to be her husband.

J. Guitton, *The Blessed Virgin* (1952); E. L. Mascall and H. S. Box (eds.), *The Blessed Virgin Mary* (1963); M. Thurian, *Mary, Mother of the Lord* (1964).

MARY ✧ *Flora and Mary*

MARY THE EGYPTIAN, penitent. Fifth century (?); f.d. 2 April. She was a harlot at Alexandria who, being suddenly converted while in Jerusalem, crossed the river Jordan and lived a solitary life of penitence in the wilderness for the rest of her days. This is the simple core of a story which in its developed and far less credible form was known all over Christendom in the middle ages.

MARY GORETTI, martyr. B. near Ancona, 1890; d. near Nettuno, 1902; cd 1950; f.d. 6 July. This Mary was the daughter of a poor peasant family, well known to her neighbours for her cheerful unselfishness and religious disposition. When she was twelve she began to be pestered by the overtures of a young man, whom she repulsed. Eventually he attempted to ravish her, threatening to kill her if she resisted. Resist she did, and in a frenzy he stabbed her repeatedly with a knife, so that she died twenty-four hours later. Mary Goretti was canonized as a martyr, not for the Christian faith but for Christian life. At the time of that canonization her assailant was still living: after eight years of unrepentant imprisonment he underwent a change of heart; at the end of twenty-seven years he was released, a changed man, and on Christmas day 1937 received communion side by side with Mary's widowed mother. He has been cited as an example by those who advocate the abolition of capital punishment.

MARY MAGDALEN. First century; f.d. 22 July. Mary of Magdala, whom Jesus had healed of 'seven devils', was one of the women who followed and ministered to him in Galilee (Luke viii, 1–2). She was present at his crucifixion : with two others she went to his tomb and found it empty; and St Mark (xvi, 9) states that it was to her that the risen Christ first appeared, to which St John (xx, 11–18) adds in his moving account that the Master gave her a message to deliver to the brethren.

Among other women mentioned in the gospels are the unnamed woman 'who was a sinner' (Luke vii, 37–50), and Mary of Bethany, Martha's sister (Luke x, 38–42). These are not further identified, and in Eastern tradition they and the Magdalen are usually treated as three different persons. But the West, following ◊ St Gregory the Great, regarded them as one and the same, though weighty voices from ◊ St Ambrose onwards preferred to leave the question undecided. This western tradition resulted in St Mary Magdalen being looked on as an outstanding type of the penitent and the contemplative. The Eastern tradition has now been adopted in the new Roman calendar (1969).

In the West, later medieval cultus of the saint owed much to romantic legends (◊ Marys, The Three), as that she had been betrothed to St John the Apostle. Her emblem is an ointment jar.

MARY-MAGDALEN DEI PAZZI, mystic. B. at Florence, 1566; d. there, 1607; cd 1669; f.d. 29 May. She became a Carmelite nun in her native city when she was seventeen and at first suffered acute inward trials and difficulties, which then gave place to deep spiritual consolations. She found her vocation in prayer and penance for the reform of 'all states of life in the church' and for the conversion of all men. She dictated a number of writings, which bear the imprint of the natural beauty of the surroundings of her life.

MARY-MAGDALEN POSTEL, foundress B. at Barfleur, 1756; d. at Saint-Sauveur-le-Vicomte, 1846; cd 1925; f.d. 16 July. In 1774 Julie Postel opened a school for girls at Barfleur in Normandy, which during the revolution was a centre for the 'underground' religious activities of those who refused to recognize the 'constitutional' clergy imposed by the state. During that time she was (like other women elsewhere under abnormal conditions) given charge of the reserved eucharist and allowed to minister it to the sick. When the storm was past Julie continued her teaching and other good works, and it was not till she was fifty-one that she took vows and began the foundation of the Sisters of the Christian Schools of Mercy. Their earlier years were discouraging, but Sister Mary-Magdalen (as she now was) would not give up: in 1830 she acquired as headquarters a derelict monastery at Saint-Sauveur-le-Vicomte, near Coutances, and the congregation was formally recognized seven years later. The devoted foundress continued to direct it until her ninetieth and last year. ✧ *Madeleine Sophie.*

MARY MAZZARELLO ✧ under *John Bosco*

MARY DI ROSA, foundress. B. at Brescia, 1813; d. there, 1855; cd 1954; f.d. 15 December. From the age of seventeen Mary di Rosa was engaged in social work for girls, among factory workers, in hospitals, for the deaf and dumb. She was herself physically delicate but mentally very alert, and her idea of living for Christ in his suffering brethren did not stop short at elementary and 'ready-made' duties. In 1840 she began to organize the Handmaids of Charity of Brescia, with the object of ministering to the religious and material needs of those in sickness and affliction; there was wide scope and to spare for them in war-ridden northern Italy, with the ruthless punishment of Brescia by the Austrians in 1849 and the cholera epidemic three years after. Mother Mary wore herself out, and died when only forty-two.

MARYS, THE THREE. First century; f.d. 25 May. The feast of this name observed in Camargue at the mouth of the Rhône (and elsewhere) has reference to ✧ *Mary Magdalen*, Mary the wife of Cleophas (John xix, 25), and Mary the mother of James (Mark xv, 40). It is associated with the legend that these three Marys, together with Lazarus, whom Jesus raised from the tomb, his sister ✧ *Martha*, who had been 'cumbered about much serving', and other persons, driven out of Palestine, arrived at Marseilles and proceeded to evangelize Provence. The beginnings of this baseless story are first found only in the eleventh century, in connexion with the alleged relics of St Mary Magdalen at Vézelay in Burgundy: but it is still popularly believed in Provence and other places.

MATILDA, queen. B. at Engern in Westphalia, *c.* 895; d. at Quedlinburg, 968; f.d. 14 March. Matilda was the wife of the German king Henry I the Fowler and mother of, among others, Emperor Otto I and the St Bruno who was archbishop of Cologne (✧ under *Bruno*). She was a widow for thirty-two years, during which she suffered ill treatment from Otto, provoked by her favouring of another son, Henry, called 'the Quarrelsome'. But Henry too showed himself ungrateful to her. Both complained among other things of their mother's liberality to the poor and to the church. She bore with them patiently, and died with a great reputation for goodness among the people.

MATILDA ✧ *Mechtilde*

MATTHEW, apostle and evangelist. First century; f.d. 21 September. He was a farmer of taxes for the Roman government at Capernaum, and Christ called him from his desk to be an apostle (Matt. ix, 9); the gospels of Mark and Luke call him Levi, and he may well have had both names. The authorship of the First Gospel is traditionally ascribed to him, but nothing else is known of his subsequent career. Eusebius says that he proclaimed Christianity to his fellow Jews. Various references state that he was eventually martyred in Ethiopia, in Persia, or elsewhere, but no reliance can be placed on any of them. In art his symbol is a man with wings.

MATTHIAS, apostle. First century; f.d. 24 February. After Christ's ascension, Matthias was chosen by lot to fill the place among the twelve apostles left vacant by Judas Iscariot (Acts i, 15–26). Later accounts of his activities and martyrdom by crucifixion cannot be relied on, and there seems to have been confusion between him and ◊ St Matthew in some of these writings. A fictitious gospel, now lost, was put out under his name.

MAUGHOLD, bishop. Fifth century; 27 April. This saint (also called Maccul) was venerated in the Isle of Man, where topographical features bear his name. He is said to have been a robber who was converted by ◊ St Patrick in Ireland; he went to Man as a missionary and was made bishop there. To him was attributed, very anachronistically, the division of the island into parishes.

MAURICE OF AGAUNUM ◊ Agaunum, Martyrs of

MAURUS, monk. Sixth century; f.d. 5 October. ◊ St Gregory the Great in his Dialogues relates that as a boy Maurus was confided to the care of ◊ St Benedict to be brought up; he became Benedict's assistant at the Subiaco monastery, and on one occasion saved the young ◊ St Placid from drowning, apparently in miraculous circumstances. Later, c. 860, a Life of St Maurus was produced at the abbey of Glanfeuil, between Tours and Nantes, claiming that Maurus had been sent by St Benedict to Gaul, had founded that abbey, and had died and been buried there. Glanfeuil may have been founded by a monk named Maurus: but there is no sound evidence for the identification of that monk with St Benedict's disciple. The saint gave its name to the French Benedictine Congregation of Saint-Maur (1621–1818), famous for the learning and scholarship of its monks.

MAWES ◊ under Budoc

MAXIMILIAN, martyr. D. in North Africa, 295; f.d. 12 March. Maximilian, the twenty-one-year-old son of a veteran in the Roman army, was brought before a court and ordered to be enrolled as a soldier. On the ground that he was a Christian he refused to accept the military badge, and the dialogue that ensued

239

between him and the proconsul Dio has come down to us. When in the course of it Maximilian declared: 'My army is the army of God, and I cannot fight for this world', it was pointed out to him that there were Christian soldiers serving the emperors; to which he replied, 'That is their business. I am a Christian too, and I cannot serve.' His father, told to correct his son, said, 'He knows what he believes, and he won't change his mind.' Threatened with death if he were obstinate, Maximilian answered, 'I shall not die. When I leave this earth I shall live with Christ, my Lord.' He was sentenced accordingly, and when he had taken farewell of his father and friends he was beheaded. The father, we are told, 'went home happily, thanking God for having allowed him to send such a gift to Heaven'. The place of St Maximilian's death is given as Theveste (Tebessa) in Numidia, but it may have been nearer Carthage, where his body was taken for burial.

MAXIMUS ◊ under *Cecily*

MAXIMUS THE CONFESSOR, abbot. B. at Constantinople, *c.* 580; d. near Batum, 662; f.d. 13 August. Maximus belonged to a noble family of Constantinople, and was appointed chief secretary to Emperor Heraclius; but after a time he resigned this post in order to become a monk at Chrysopolis (Skutari). He was elected abbot of the community, but in 626 it broke up before the advancing Persians, and he fled to Alexandria, later to Carthage, and then to Rome. Here he actively supported Pope ◊ *St Martin I* in his opposition to the unorthodox doctrine called Monothelism and a compromise decree of Emperor Constans II. Like Martin, Maximus was eventually taken to Constantinople as a prisoner; after years of ill-treatment, badgering and exile he was sentenced to be flogged, to lose his tongue and right hand, and to perpetual imprisonment, for defying the emperor. This ferocious sentence was carried out, and the old man (he was about eighty-two) was carried off to Skhemaris, a lonely fortress at the far end of the Black Sea. Here he died soon after. St Maximus the Confessor was an important theologian and mystic, and he is remembered today particularly for his mystical and ascetical writings. One of them, the *Four Centuries of Charity*, consisting of short aphorisms and reflections, has been called 'one of the most profound and beautiful works in all Christian writing'. There are two English translations of it.

MAYEUL, or MAIOLUS, abbot. B. at Avignon, *c.* 906; d. at Souvigny, 994; f.d. 11 May. While still a young man he was made archdeacon of Mâcon, but to escape advancement to a bishopric he entered the monastery of Cluny. In 954 the blind Abbot Aymard chose him as assistant abbot and in 965 he succeeded to the full office, much against his will. Mayeul was a man of distinguished presence, devoted to learning and the monastic life of religion, a worthy successor of ◊ *St Odo*; under his guidance Cluniac influence continued to extend, through example and help rather than by taking over other houses. St Mayeul had the respect and trust of Emperors Otto I and II, of whom the second wanted to put him forward for the papacy after the murder of Benedict VI; but the man who had through humbleness and prudence refused the see of Besançon would not be a candidate for that of Rome. St Mayeul died while on his way to make a visitation of the abbey of Saint-Denis at Paris at the request of King Hugh Capet.

MECHTILDE OF HACKEBORN, mystic. B. *c.* 1241; d. at Helfta, 1298; f.d. 19 November. She was mistress in charge of the school at the monastery of Helfta when her sister was abbess there; it thus fell to her to train the child who was to become ◊ *St Gertrude the Great*, who wrote of her mistress, 'There has never before been anyone like her in our monastery, and I fear there never will be again.' With another nun Gertrude wrote an account of Mechtilde's spiritual teaching and experiences, *The Book of Special Grace*, which was made public after her death. This Mechtilde must be distinguished from the contemporary Mechtilde of Magdeburg, another mystical writer associated with Helfta.

MECHTILDE ◊ *Matilda*

MÉEN, abbot. Sixth century (?); f.d. 21 June. Traditionally St Méen (Mewan) followed ◊ *St Samson* from Wales to Brittany. There he evangelized the Brocéliande district which figures in the Arthurian romances, and founded near Paimpont the monastery afterwards called Saint-Méen. He was accompanied by *St Austol* (f.d. 28 June), said to have been his godson. In Cornwall there are adjoining parishes called Saint Mewan and Saint Austell.

MEINRAD, hermit. D. at Einsiedeln, 861; f.d. 21 January. This saint's name is familiar from the abbey of St Meinrad at Einsiedeln, near the Lake of Zurich in Switzerland – a great monastery and pilgrimage centre that has an unbroken history of over a thousand years. Meinrad was a monk of Reichenau, who *c.* 836 came to live as a solitary at the place where the abbey now stands. In 861 he was murdered by robbers and, being a holy man, he was regarded as a martyr. A succession of hermits occupied his hermitage (which is what the name Einsiedeln means), and eventually a regular Benedictine monastery was established there. The statue of the Blessed Virgin in the huge church is said to have belonged to St Meinrad himself.

MELANIA THE YOUNGER, laywoman. B. in Rome, *c.* 383; d. at
Jerusalem, 439; f.d. 31 December. This Melania was the daughter
of a very wealthy patrician father, and against her will was married to a young relative, Valerius Pinianus. Her religious devotion
and austere way of living provoked much family opposition; but,
after the birth and early death of two children, her widowed
mother and, more slowly, her husband were won over. The resulting sales of property for the benefit of the poor and the
church, and the large-scale emancipation of slaves, led to a family
appeal to the Emperor Honorius, who took Melania's part. During the Visigothic invasion she fled with Pinian to Thagaste in
Africa, where she had estates, and from there in 417 they went
to Jerusalem and continued their beneficent life in Palestine.
After the death of her husband in 432, Melania established a
community of dedicated women on the Mount of Olives (she had
already endowed two such houses, for men and for women, in
Africa); she shared their life of prayer and good works, employ-
ing herself particularly in the copying of books. St Melania's
life brought her into contact with ◊ *St Paulinus of Nola, St
Augustine,* and *St Jerome,* all of whom had a very high opinion
of her and of Pinian. She kept the Christmas of 439 at Bethlehem, and died a week later. Her biography was written by her
chaplain, Gerontius.

St Melania the Elder (d. 410; f.d. 8 June) was the paternal
grandmother of Melania the Younger. Left a widow at twenty-
two, she was away from Rome from 372 to 379, mostly in Palestine where she was associated with St Jerome. She left Italy
finally at the Visigothic invasion, and died in Jerusalem. She had
a somewhat domineering personality, and her relations with her
granddaughter were not always easy.

MELCHIADES ◊ *Miltiades*

MELLITUS, bishop. D. at Canterbury, 624; f.d. 24 April. He was
one of the second band of monks sent by Pope ◊ *St Gregory I*
to England, and in 604 was consecrated the first bishop of the
East Saxons, with his see in London. He converted their king,
Sabert, but not his sons, who when their father died drove Mellitus out; for they had asked him to give them the 'white bread'
(the eucharist), and he had refused because they were not baptized. Mellitus withdrew to Gaul for a year with St Justus of
Rochester (◊ *Justus of Canterbury*), and soon after his return was
made archbishop of Canterbury, in 619. Bede says of him that
he suffered from gout but that in spirit he was healthy and active,
ever reaching out to the things of God: 'Noble by birth, he was
yet nobler in mind.' It was St Mellitus who built St Mary's
church at Canterbury, of which a fragment remains outside the

east end of the foundations of the abbey church of SS. Peter and Paul (St Augustine's).

MENAS, martyr. D. *c.* 303 (?); f.d. 11 November. Menas was in all probability born and martyred in Egypt, where his body certainly rested. All the earliest representations of him agree in showing him accompanied by two camels, of which no certain explanation is forthcoming; but it is not impossible that he was in fact a camel-driver. However, according to his legend he was an Egyptian soldier in the Roman army, serving in Phrygia, who was martyred at Cotyaeum under Diocletian; from there his body was brought back to Egypt for burial. This story was expanded and embellished with preposterous marvels, and the fame of the hero as one of the so-called soldier-saints grew in proportion: the little terracotta bottles (*ampullae*) for water from his shrine, brought away by pilgrims, have been found in all countries bordering the Mediterranean. That shrine was at Karm Abu Mina, south-west of Alexandria and Lake Mareotis, on the edge of the Libyan desert, where the ruins of the church and ancillary buildings have been laid bare, and many tokens of the cultus of St Menas found. He has been popularly looked on as one of the great saints of Egypt down to the present day.

MERCURY, martyr. Date unknown; f.d. 25 November. This is another of the Eastern 'soldier-saints', and as usual his legend is very highly coloured. It states that Mercury was a soldier of Scythian origin, who fought so well against invading barbarians that he gained the favour of Emperor Decius. Subsequently, being a Christian, he refused to join in a sacrifice to Artemis; after torture and angelic visitations, he was taken to his home in Cappadocia and executed at Caesarea. Another legend, peculiarly absurd, says that ◊ St Basil the Great learned from a dream that Mercury was sent from Heaven to kill Emperor Julian the Apostate in Persia in 363. All that seems sure is that a St Mercury, otherwise unknown, was venerated as a martyr at the Cappadocian Caesarea in the sixth century.

MERIADOC, or MERIASEK, bishop. Sixth century (?); f.d. 7 June. There is a church in Cornwall, at Camborne, dedicated in honour of this saint, who is venerated in Brittany as a bishop at Vannes. Nothing is known of his history (he may have come from Wales), but he is of interest as being the hero of a medieval play in the vernacular about a saint, the only example of such a thing surviving in Great Britain. It is called *Bewnans Meryasek*, 'Life of Meriasek', and was composed, or transcribed, in the Cornish language by a local priest in 1504. Unfortunately the play, with its local allusions, has no value as sober history, but the early church dedication suggests an actual connexion between Camborne and the St Meriadoc of Brittany.

MESROP, bishop. B. *c.* 345; d. at Valarshapat, 439; f.d. 19 February. St Mesrop the Teacher was the principal colleague of ◊ *St Isaac the Great* in developing the Armenian church. After serving in a civil capacity for a time he became a missionary among his people, and learned the necessity of an alphabet for writing the Armenian language. This he provided, and then turned his attention to organizing schools and the translation of the Bible. He himself made an Armenian version of the New Testament and book of Proverbs based on the Syriac, revising them by the Greek. Mesrop's missionary activities took him into Georgia, where also he had a literary influence, and he is said to have sent students as far as Rome in search of manuscripts. It was Mesrop and Isaac who began the formation of a distinctively Armenian liturgy of worship, based on that of the mother church of Caesarea in Cappadocia. The Armenian translation of the Bible has a special value for scholars, and it aroused an enthusiastic but passing interest in so unexpected a student as Lord Byron.

METHODIUS ◊ *Cyril and Methodius*

METHODIUS OF CONSTANTINOPLE, bishop. B. at Syracuse; d. at Constantinople, 847; f.d. 14 June. He is greatly venerated in the East as an outstanding supporter of sacred images during the second iconoclastic persecution. Under Emperor Michael II he was flogged for his activities and kept in close confinement for seven years. When Theodora became regent in 842 she appointed Methodius patriarch of Constantinople, and he at once summoned a council at which the lawfulness of venerating religious images was finally reaffirmed. At the same time, to emphasize this event, an annual festival 'of Orthodoxy' was instituted, which is still observed on the first Sunday in Lent in all Byzantine churches. Methodius was a prolific writer, especially of hymns, but practically nothing of his work remains.

St Methodius was first brought to Constantinople from his monastery on Khios by the patriarch *St Nicephorus* (d. 828; f.d. 2 June), who, because of his opposition to Iconoclasm, was deposed from his see in 815, and passed the rest of his life in exile in a monastery; he left a number of writings, including a world history.

METHODIUS OF OLYMPUS, bishop and martyr. D. *c.* 310 (?); f.d. 18 September. This Methodius is called 'of Olympus', in Lycia, but it is not known for certain of what see, presumably in Asia Minor, he was bishop, and even his martyrdom is not beyond question: he is remembered entirely for those of his writings that have survived. The best known of them is the *Symposium*, or *Banquet of the Ten Virgins*, a sort of dialogue in the manner of Plato; its theme is the excellence of virginity, and it ends with a hymn to Christ as the church's bridegroom. This *Symposium* was published in English in 1958. Others of his writings are on the resurrection of the body and on free-will.

MEWAN ◊ *Méen*

MICHAEL THE ARCHANGEL. F.d. 29 September. The festival of Michael the Archangel on this date originated in the annual commemoration of the dedication, before the seventh century, of a church in his honour near Rome. From the beginning of Christian history there is evidence for the honour in which Michael was held, and he was also venerated by the Jews. The well-known passage in the Apocalypse (Rev. xii, 7–9) about the 'war in heaven' contributed to his being honoured in the West as the 'captain of the heavenly host' and protector of Christians in general and of soldiers in particular. In the East he was looked on as special guardian of the sick: outside Constantinople there was a church bearing his name from the time of Constantine. Veneration for Michael was intensified by the vision of him said to have been seen on Monte Gargano in southern Italy between 492 and 496. This almost certainly gave rise to the legend of Mont-Saint Michel in France (◊ *St Aubert*); later there were vague local legends of a vision at St Michael's Mount in England, at the Stranberg near Stuttgart, and elsewhere. A great impression was made too by the story that, during a plague in Rome, Pope ◊ *St Gregory I* saw the archangel sheathing his sword above Hadrian's mausoleum (now called the Castle of St Angelo). All over Christendom chapels of St Michael were built on top of hills and mountains: one on the Skirrid Fawr near Abergavenny was resorted to even after the Reformation. A contemporary popular song, of American Negro folk origin (?), 'Michael, row the boat ashore! Alleluia!' seems to incorporate a reminiscence of the very old tradition of Michael as the receiver of the souls of the dead.

No other individual archangel had a feast in the Western calendar until the present century. The angel of the annunciation to Mary, *Gabriel* (Luke i, 26; ◊ i, 11 and Dan. viii, 16 and ix, 21) and *Raphael* are now commemorated with Michael on 29 September. From the meaning of his name, 'God heals', Raphael is assumed to be the angel who troubled the water (John v, 2–4), and he figures in the book of Tobit (Tobias iii, 25; v, 5ff. etc.). Both these archangels have long been venerated liturgically in the East.

MICHAEL GARICOÏTS ◊ under *Elizabeth Bichier*

MILDBURGA ♢ under *Mildred*

MILDRED, abbess. D. at Minster *c.* 700; f.d. 13 July. St Mildred (Mildthryth) was a daughter of Merewald, an Anglian ruler on the Welsh border, by his second wife, Ermenburga, a princess from Kent. For her education Mildred was sent to the nunnery of Chelles in France, where she refused an offer of marriage; on returning home she entered the convent at Minster in Thanet, which her mother had founded. She became abbess and died there, leaving a holy memory of gentleness and kindness, 'a comforter to all in affliction'.

Mildred's elder sister, St *Mildburga* (Mildburh; d. *c.* 700; f.d. 23 February) was foundress and abbess of Wenlock abbey in Shropshire, and her name too figures in many old English calendars. A third sister, Mildgytha, also a nun, their mother Ermenburga and an aunt, Ermengytha, were also popularly regarded as saints.

MILTIADES, pope. B. in Africa (?); d. in Rome, 11 January 314; f.d. 10 December. Very little is known about St Miltiades (sometimes called Melchiades); but he is well remembered because it was during his few years as bishop of Rome that Emperor Constantine decreed toleration for Christianity (and other religions). The classical era of persecution came to an end: the Christian church now had to meet more subtle trials and temptations. ♢ *St Augustine* praised St Miltiades as a man of moderation and peaceableness. He is commemorated as a martyr because he is said in earlier years to have suffered much in the persecution by Maximian. It was to Miltiades, or to his successor ♢ *St Silvester*, that Constantine gave the mansion called the Lateran: it continued to be the residence of the bishops of Rome for a thousand years, and the church of St John Lateran is still the pope's cathedral.

MODWENNA ♢ under *Edith of Wilton*

MONICA, laywoman. B. at Thagaste (?), *c.* 331; d. at Ostia, 387; f.d. 4 May. St Monica was the mother of ♢ *St Augustine* of Hippo, and it is from his writings that she is known. Her husband, Patricius, was a man of modest rank at Thagaste in North Africa; they had three children, of whom Augustine was the eldest, and when he was eighteen his mother was left a widow. Monica had tried to bring him up as a Christian, but she was over-ambitious for his worldly success, and he regarded her religion with scorn. His earlier vacillations and his liaison with a woman of unknown name caused Monica the deepest distress: it was at this time that a bishop whom she had consulted gave her the famous reassurance, 'It is not possible that the son of so many tears should be lost.'

When in 383 Augustine slipped away to Italy, Monica followed him, first to Rome and then to Milan, where she became an obedient disciple of ◊ *St Ambrose*. Three years later her devoted pertinacity was rewarded, when Augustine decided to receive baptism: she 'rejoiced triumphantly', and retired with him and his friends to Cassiciacum, a happy woman. After the baptism they set out to return to Africa. St Augustine records that at the port of Ostia on the Tiber he and his mother were joined in a most moving conversation on the everlasting life of the blessed; five days later she fell ill, and died there. St Monica had at times been a trying mother, and Augustine had not always been a considerate son; but he had come to recognize her as his true mother in the spirit as well as in the flesh: his own experience taught him to speak of parenthood as a sort of bishopric.

MONINNE ◊ under *Edith of Wilton*

MONTANUS and LUCIUS, martyrs. D. at Carthage, 259; f.d. 24 February. Montanus, Lucius and their fellows were a group of African martyrs, several of whom were clergy of ◊ *St Cyprian*, who had been executed in the previous year. The first part of their acts was written down by one of themselves. Eight of them were arrested on a false charge of complicity in a revolt against the procurator at Carthage. After interrogation they were remanded in custody; they were kept on short rations, and suffered greatly from hunger and thirst. One of them, the priest Victor, was singled out for immediate death. When dissension threatened among the prisoners, Montanus had a dream which he interpreted as a rebuke for insufficient charity on his part (other dreams or visions are recorded). Their imprisonment lasted several months, and then those in holy orders were condemned to death. Lucius went to the place of execution in advance, being so enfeebled that he feared he could not keep up with the others; but Montanus was full of vigour and exhorted the heathen among the bystanders to repentance and the brethren to faithfulness. One of the prisoners, Flavian, had been reprieved because of his popularity with the people; but he insisted that the plea made for him, that he was not a deacon, was untrue, and so he was beheaded three days later.

MOSES THE BLACK, desert monk. B. *c.* 330; d. in Sketis, *c.* 405; f.d. 28 August. Moses was an Ethiopian, a man of great physical strength and ruffianly character. He was a servant in an Egyptian household from which he was dismissed for his depredations, and he put himself at the head of a gang of robbers. It is not known how the conversion of this rascal came about, but converted he was, so thoroughly that he joined some monks in the desert of Sketis. The old Adam was far from dead in him, but he persevered valiantly, and with such good effect that he was chosen for the priesthood. As he stood clothed in white after ordination the bishop remarked to him, 'Now the black man is made white.' 'Only outside,' replied Moses; 'God knows I am still dark within.' He met his death when the monastery was raided by Berbers, against whom he refused to defend himself. Monks still live at the monastery where St Moses was buried, Dair al-Baramus in the Wadi Natrun.

MUNGO ◊ *Kentigern*
MUNNU ◊ under *Fintan*

N

NABOR and FELIX ◊ under *Gervase and Protase*
NARSES THE FIRST, bishop. B. in Armenia, *c.* 326; d. 373; f.d. 19 November. Narses or Nerses, called 'the Great', descended from ◊ *St Gregory the Enlightener*, was the father of ◊ *St Isaac the Great*. After his wife's death he was ordained priest, and became chief bishop of the Armenian church, which he directed in accordance with principles he had learned earlier at Caesarea. It is said that *c.* 359 he was superseded for denouncing the crimes of King Arshak III and for other reasons. He was recalled by King Pap, only to find it his duty to rebuke the life of that monarch too, who in any case shared his predecessor's objection to the ecclesiastical influence of Caesarea. We are told that Pap brought about the death of St Narses, by poison; but the truth of this is not certain.

There were two other sainted Armenian bishops of this name. The primate *Narses IV the Gracious* (d. 1173; f.d. 13 August), who has been called 'the Fénelon of Armenia', was the foremost Armenian writer and poet of the twelfth century; he made earnest efforts to draw his church out of its isolation. *St Narses of Lampron* (d. 1198; f.d. 17 July), archbishop of Tarsus, pursued the same object. He had some success, and shortly before he died the bishops of Lesser Armenia, west of the Euphrates, came into communion with the Roman church. 'To me,' Narses declared to critics of his endeavours, 'Armenians, Latins, Greeks, Egyptians, Syrians are all one. My conscience is clear.' He made translations into Armenian of the monastic Rule of St Benedict and St Gregory's *Dialogues*.

NATALIA ◊ *Adrian and Natalia*
NAZARIUS and CELSUS ◊ under *Gervase and Protase*
NECTARIUS KEPHALAS, bishop. B. 1846; d. on Aegina, 1920; cd by the Orth.ch., 1961; f.d. 9 November. The most recently canonized Greek saint. While rector of the Rhizarion ecclesiasti-

cal college, in 1904 he began the restoration of a nunnery on the island of Aegina, and from 1908 devoted himself wholly to organizing and directing this work. Bishop Nectarius was greatly revered during his lifetime, and his tomb at the convent has been a place of pilgrimage since 1953. A number of his letters have been published.

NEOT, monk. Date unknown; f.d. 31 July. The name Neot is familiar from the places called Saint Neot in Cornwall and Saint Neots in Huntingdonshire, but who he was has baffled all researches. Medieval legends say he was a monk of Glastonbury who became a hermit in Cornwall, and that after his death his body was removed to a monastery at Eynesbury on the Great Ouse. These legends associate him with King Alfred the Great; the nursery story of Alfred and the cakes is derived from a Life of St Neot which is no longer extant.

NEREUS and ACHILLEUS. Date unknown; f.d. 12 May. These martyrs, who according to Pope ◊ St Damasus were Roman soldiers who became Christians and refused to serve any longer, were buried in the cemetery of Domitilla on the Via Ardeatina. Their legendary 'acts', however, state that they were servants in the household of Flavia Domitilla and with her were exiled and put to death for their religion. By Flavia Domitilla the 'acts' perhaps intend the Christian woman of that name, a member of the imperial family and wife of Titus Flavius Clemens, who was banished to the island of Pandateria c. 96.

NERSES ◊ Narses

NICEPHORUS OF ANTIOCH, martyr. No date; f.d. 9 February. This Nicephorus is the imaginary hero of a wholly fictitious moral tale. It relates that two Antiochenes, Nicephorus a layman and Sapricius a priest, had a quarrel. On four separate occasions Nicephorus apologized and sought a reconciliation, but each time Sapricius refused his overtures. Then the priest was arrested and condemned to death as a Christian. While on his way to execution he was stopped by Nicephorus, who made a last attempt to gain his forgiveness; but Sapricius only turned his back. When he was about to be beheaded he suddenly offered to sacrifice to the heathen gods so that his life might be spared. Nicephorus in vain implored him not to apostatize, but he persisted and was released. Thereupon Nicephorus declared that he also was a Christian, ready to die in place of Sapricius: he was executed accordingly. This is said to have happened during the persecution under Valerian. The tale was doubtless inspired by Matthew xviii, 21–22 (with perhaps a side-glance at Luke x, 30–31), but it came to be accepted as a relation of fact, for which there is no evidence whatever.

NICEPHORUS OF CONSTANTINOPLE ✧ under *Methodius of Constantinople*

NICETAS THE GOTH ✧ under *Sabas the Goth*

NICETAS OF REMESIANA, missionary and writer. D. *c.* 414; f.d. 22 June. He became bishop of Remesiana (Bela Palanka in Serbia) *c.* 370, but little is known of his life except that he was an active and successful missionary among the Bessi, Goths, and Dacians to the south of the Danube. He left a number of writings, of which one is an important exposition of the Apostles' Creed and another a short treatise on the value of psalm-singing. He makes some excellent remarks about the people's singing in church: 'Sing wisely, that is, understandingly, thinking of what you are singing. ... Tunes should be in keeping with the sacredness of religion ..., not savouring of the theatre. ... Sing together, and do not show off'; and he adds, 'Neither must we give thought to what people like, for everything in our worship must be done as in God's sight, not to please men.' ✧ *St Paulinus of Nola*, whom Nicetas twice visited in Italy, writes highly of him as a poet and evangelist among the rude inhabitants of a frozen land; and some scholars in our own time have suggested that he was author of the *Te Deum*, that most majestic of Latin hymns.

NICETIUS OF TRIER, bishop. B. in Auvergne; d. at Trier, *c.* 566; f.d. 1 October. He was taken from the government of a monastery to be bishop of Trier *c.* 527. On his way to take up his appointment he reproved his escort of Frankish noblemen for turning their horses loose in a poor man's field of corn, and himself drove them out. This was a foretaste of his whole episcopate. The Franks were hardly more than barbarians, in part nominally Christian: Nicetius sought to teach them by the virtue of his own life and gained their respect by his fearlessness. But direct methods were necessary to discipline the leaders, and he made free use of excommunication, notably in the case of the cruel and incestuous King Chlotar I. This earned banishment for Nicetius in 560, but he was brought back by Sigebert I. Nicetius was outstanding among the Gallo-Roman bishops of Trier; he took part in and presided at half-a-dozen local councils and corresponded with distant persons, including Emperor Justinian at Constantinople. Two of the writings of ✧ *St Nicetas of Remesiana* were formerly attributed to St Nicetius of Trier, one being the treatise on psalm-singing.

NICHOLAS, bishop. Fourth century; f.d. 6 December. There was a church of St Nicholas at Constantinople in the sixth century, and from the ninth century in the East and the eleventh in the West he has been one of the most popular saints of Christendom: a patron of countries, provinces, dioceses, and cities, titular of churches innumerable, the saint of sailors, children, merchants, pawnbrokers, and others, celebrated in pious custom and folklore, and represented countless times in paintings and carvings. Yet what can be confidently stated of his personal history is no more than that he was a bishop of Myra in Lycia (south-western Asia Minor) during the fourth century.

On the other hand legend about him has been extensive and sometimes childish since his first 'biography' appeared early in the ninth century. The most influential part of the legend is the story of three girls whom Nicholas saved from prostitution by throwing three bags of gold as dowry into their window at night. The pictorial representation of this is said to have given rise (by confusion of the round bags with children's heads) to the tale of his bringing to life three murdered children hidden in a brine-tub. He is also said miraculously to have saved from death three unjustly condemned men, as well as sailors in distress off the Lycian coast. There is no historical support for the less sensational statements that Nicholas suffered for his faith before Constantine's accession and that he was present at the first general council at Nicaea in 325.

St Nicholas as patron of children is the origin of 'Father Christmas'. Presents were – in some countries still are – given on his feast day, and 'Santa Claus' is derived, via America, from the Dutch dialect form of his name, *Sinte Klaas*. In 1087 Italian merchants stole the reputed relics of St Nicholas from Myra and enshrined them at Bari in Apulia, where they still are: that is why he is sometimes called Nicholas of Bari. His emblem is three balls.

NICHOLAS THE FIRST, pope. B. in Rome; d. there, 867; f.d. 13 November. He was elected bishop of Rome in 858, while still a deacon, and occupied the see with distinction for nine troubled years. Among the matters with which he had to deal was the long dispute about the patriarchal see of Constantinople (◊ *Photius*), the turbulence of Archbishop John of Ravenna and the ambition of Hincmar of Rheims, and the matrimonial troubles of several important persons; among these last the bigamous marriage of Lothair II of Lorraine precipitated a struggle during which Nicholas deposed two German archbishops and Lothair's army threatened Rome. Faced by disorder or scandal, Nicholas could not rest till he had dealt with it; but he sometimes invoked the aid of persons considerably less moderate and reasonable than himself. A letter he sent to the newly baptized Khan Boris of the Bulgars has been characterized as 'a masterpiece of pastoral wisdom and one of the finest documents of the history of the papacy'; his generosity made him beloved by the people and his defence of justice and virtue earned the respect of his contemporaries generally. St Nicholas is one of the three popes to whom the epithet 'the Great' is given (the others are ◊ *St Leo I* and *St Gregory I*).

NICHOLAS OF TOLENTINO, Austin friar. B. near Fermo in Italy, *c.* 1245; d. at Tolentino, 1305; cd 1446; f.d. 10 September. This Nicholas joined the order of friars of St Augustine, and from 1275 till his death was stationed at Tolentino, not far from his birthplace in the March of Ancona. His life was passed principally in tireless pastoral work, and he was a very effective preacher; but his fame – formerly more widespread than today – was largely due to the numerous miracles attributed to him. The stories of some of these seem clearly to have been influenced by the legends about his namesake of Myra (◊ above), whose shrine was at Bari, further down the Adriatic coast. As he lay dying, St Nicholas quoted to his brethren the words of St Paul, 'I have nothing on my conscience: but that does not mean that I stand acquitted' (I Cor. iv, 4).

NICHOLAS VON FLUE, layman. B. at Flueli near Sachseln, 1417; d. at Ranft, 1487; cd 1947; f.d. 21 March. This Swiss patriot was born on the family farm not far from the Lake of Lucerne, and followed his father's calling. He took an active part in local public affairs, fought in two wars, and earned good promotion. During the campaign in the Thurgau the Swiss troops at Katharinental were faced by a situation which anticipated in miniature that at Monte Cassino in 1944; Nicholas prevented the destruction of the nunnery. By 1447 he was married to a farmer's daughter, and ten children were born to them; he was a successful farmer and a most respected figure in his neighbourhood, well known as a man more than ordinarily religious: from childhood he had been under the influence of a devout movement called the *Gottesfreunde*, 'God's Friends'. Then, in 1465, he suddenly retired from public life in protest against an unjust and oppressive decision of a local court. Two years later, in response to an inward call, he announced his wish to leave home and devote himself to divine contemplation as a hermit. His wife Dorothy recognized the call and gave her consent; but his relatives and neighbours were full of indignation, which he disregarded.

For twenty years Nicholas, 'Brother Klaus', lived in a cottage at Ranft, close to his old home; in time people flocked to him to get his advice on matters religious and temporal, attracted not only by his reputation for goodness and wisdom but also by what they heard of his extraordinary fasting from food. His visitors included men of political and ecclesiastical importance from abroad, but it was not till towards the end of his life that the events occurred that gave Nicholas von Flue a significant place in the history of Switzerland as a whole. The country was threatened with civil war between the urban and the rural cantons. On the suggestion of a priest, the cantonal deputies consulted the hermit of Ranft about the matters at issue. St Nicholas had already been approached by the authorities of Lucerne, and he now suggested terms for a general settlement; they were so statesmanlike that they were accepted at once (the Compromise of Stans, 1481), and Swiss peace and unity were saved. It is of interest that Nicholas could not read or write. He died five years later; his wife and children were by his bedside, and the Flue family still survives in Switzerland.

NICODEMUS OF THE HOLY MOUNTAIN, monk. B. on Naxos, c. 1748; d. on Mount Athos, 1809; cd by the Orth. ch., 1955; f.d. 14 July. This Nicodemus became a monk at Dionysiou on Mount Athos (the Holy Mountain) in 1775. He was one of the two best-known Greek religious writers of his age, as a canonist, hagiographer, liturgist, ascetic, and mystic. Among his works was a Greek version of Lorenzo Scupoli's *Spiritual Combat* and a volume of meditations modelled on the *Spiritual Exercises* of St Ignatius of Loyola. But his most famous book, compiled in collaboration with St Macarius of Corinth (who had been driven from his diocese by the Turks), was the *Philokalia*, first published in 1782 at Venice. This is a collection of passages from the spiritual writings of the Greek fathers and ascetics, which has had a deep and lasting influence among Eastern Othodox Christians; an Athonite abbot has written that 'Almost all the monks of the Holy Mountain regard St Nicodemus as their chief elder and spiritual guide'. Two volumes of extracts from the Russian version of the *Philokalia* were published in English in 1951 and 1954.

NICOMEDES, martyr. Date unknown; f.d. 15 September (B.C.P., 1 June). He was an early Roman martyr, buried in a cemetery on the Via Nomentana. Nothing else is known about him; he is referred to as a priest in the legendary 'acts' of ◊ SS. *Nereus and Achilleus*, where it is said he was put to death for giving honourable burial to the body of another martyr, Felicula.

NILUS OF ANCYRA, writer. B. at Ancyra; d. there, c. 430; f.d. 12 November. This Nilus became a disciple of ◊ St John Chrysostom when a student at Constantinople. On returning to his native Ancyra (now Ankara) he founded a monastery near by, where he wrote the works for which he is remembered. They were intended for his monks, and are mostly moral and ascetical treatises; a series of his short passages on prayer is printed in English in *Early Fathers from the Philokalia* (1954) (◊ under *Nicodemus of the Holy Mountain*), but it is a work of which the authorship is

253

questioned. Nilus also conducted a large correspondence and many of his letters are extant. For a very long time he was mistakenly identified with another Nilus, a contemporary, who with his son became a monk at Mount Sinai; the son was carried off in a murderous nomad raid, and the father, following in pursuit, recovered him near Beersheba.

NILUS OF ROSSANO, abbot. B. at Rossano, 910; d. at Tusculum, 1004; f.d. 26 September. He was a Calabrian Greek, and as a young man worked in the taxes department of his native town, living with a young woman who was probably not his wife. When she and their child died in 940 he joined a Byzantine monastery at Palma in Campania; he lived in this and other communities for forty years, becoming well known for his goodness and wisdom, and eventually being made abbot of St Adrian's at San Demetrio Corone. With his fellows he underwent alarming experiences during the intensifying Saracen attacks on southern Italy, and things became so bad that c. 981 Nilus withdrew his monks and found a refuge for them at Monte Cassino. They were then given a house of their own, first at Vallelucio and then at Serperi, near Gaeta. It was at this time that St Nilus made vigorous intercession with Pope Gregory V and Emperor Otto III for humane treatment of the fallen antipope John Philagathus, but not wholly successfully. The tradition is that just before he died St Nilus selected Grottaferrata in the Alban hills as the permanent home of his monks, and he is regarded as the founder of the Greek monastery which has been there from that day to this. But it was his third successor, *St Bartholomew of Grottaferrata* (d. 1055; f.d. 11 November), who established this house on a firm and lasting basis, directing it for some forty years. He was a personal disciple of St Nilus, and like his master was a hymn-writer and skilled calligrapher; he 'could not bear to see anyone in affliction without giving him comfort', says his biographer.

NILUS OF SORA abbot. B. c. 1433; d. 1508; cd by the Russ.Orth. ch., 1903; f.d. 7 April. Nilus (Nil), surnamed Maikov but commonly called Sorsky, of peasant origin, was a monk of Belozersk near Lake Beloe in Russia. From thence he went to Greece and lived for a long time on Mount Athos, where he made a deep study of monastic discipline and mysticism. Returning to Belozersk, in 1480 he established a small colony of semi-hermits near by, on the river Sora; they devoted themselves particularly to the study, translation, and diffusion of Greek ascetical writings. Nilus was essentially a man of freedom and moderation, who opposed religious formalism, exaggeration, and intolerance; but on the subject of monastic property his ideas were severe and uncompromising. Five years before his death he took the lead against

◊ *St Joseph of Volokolamsk* and the 'possessors': monks ought not to own landed estates, said Nilus, but should work for what they need; even their churches should be plain and bare, lest worshippers be distracted from the beauty of God. He had many supporters, but these 'non-possessors' were destined finally to lose the day after he was dead. During the nineteenth century there was a renewal of interest in St Nilus and his writings. A short instruction to his monks and a 'monastic rule', which is really a treatise on religious life, have been translated into English.

NINIAN, missionary. D. *c.* 432 (?); f.d. 16 September. The tradition about St Ninian (Nynia, Ninnidh) current in Bede's time was to the effect that he was a British bishop who had been instructed in the Christian faith at Rome and then preached the gospel among the southern Picts; his centre was at Candida Casa, 'White House' (said to be Whithorn in Galloway), so called from the stone church that he built there. Further particulars are given in the untrustworthy Life of Ninian written by ◊ *St Aelred*. There is much discussion and disagreement about Ninian and the extent of his missionary labours; the foundation at Whithorn appears subsequently to have exercised considerable influence among the Celtic-speaking Christians of the British Isles.

W. D. Simpson, *St Ninian and the Origins of the Christian Church in Scotland* (1940); M. Anderson, *St Ninian* (1963).

NINO, slave-girl. D. *c.* 340 (?); f.d. 15 December. Writing *c.* 403 Rufinus relates the story of how Christianity was first brought to Georgia (Iberia), as it was told him by a Georgian prince, Bakur. A Christian girl was captured and brought to Georgia as a slave (her name, Nino, was added later). People were impressed by her goodness and religious devoutness, and by her ability to cure disease in the name of Christ her God, a power which she exercised in favour of the Georgian queen. The king, too, when lost while hunting found his way again after calling on Christ for help. Thereupon he asked Nino to teach him this new religion, which she did. Directed by her, a church was built, and completed in such miraculous circumstances that the people clamoured to be Christians too. Whereupon the king sent a legate to Emperor Constantine, asking him to send clergy to Georgia. This story was amplified and made more circumstantial, and gave rise to a whole series of Nino legends, some of which 'tie in' her story with that of ◊ *SS. Rhipsime and Gaiana* in the adjoining land of Armenia. There seems no doubt that Christianity was preached in Armenia in the time of Constantine, but how far Prince Bakur's narrative represents historical happenings is very problematical.

D. M. Lang, *Lives and Legends of the Georgian Saints* (1956).

NOEL CHABANEL, martyr. B. in France, 1613; d. in Canada, December 1649; cd 1930; f.d. 26 September. He began his Jesuit noviceship at Toulouse in 1630 and in 1643 was sent to the Canadian mission, where he worked among the Hurons with ◊ *St Charles Garnier*. He felt a strong repugnance for the Indians and their ways, he found their language very difficult to learn and he suffered from unbroken spiritual depression: to fortify himself he made a solemn vow never to leave his post. At the time of Father Garnier's death Father Chabanel was away on pastoral duty, and he was never seen again. His fate was learned only through the guilty admission of an apostate Huron: he had set upon and killed the priest out of hatred for the Christian religion, and had thrown his body into the river.

NORBERT, bishop and founder. B. at Xanten, *c*. 1080; d. at Magdeburg, 1134; cd 1582; f.d. 6 June. St Norbert came of a noble Rhineland family, and till he was about thirty-five led a courtier's life at princely courts, although he was a clerk in lesser orders holding several benefices. He then underwent a sudden conversion, occasioned by a narrow escape from death. He was ordained priest, but the enthusiasm of his new reforming spirit exasperated some of the clergy at Xanten, who in 1118 denounced him as an unauthorized preacher and a hypocrite. Thereupon Norbert disposed of his goods for the benefit of the poor and made his way to Pope Gelasius II, who was then in Languedoc. The pope gave him leave to preach wherever he liked, which he proceeded to do with much effect in northern France. At Valenciennes he fell in with the young priest Hugh of Fosses, and in 1120 they started a community of canons regular in the valley of Prémontré near Laon. From very modest beginnings it developed rapidly into an order, the Premonstratensian Canons, with other abbeys and priories. St Norbert meanwhile continued his itinerant preaching as occasion served in France and Germany, and in 1126 was chosen archbishop of Magdeburg.

The diocese was in a bad state and Norbert took it in hand with his accustomed vigour. He met with much opposition, especially from the laity when he undertook the recovery of wrongfully alienated church property: more than one attempt was made on his life. In 1130 he put all his influence behind the cause of Pope Innocent II in his struggle with the antipope Pierleone, and shortly before his death he was appointed chancellor for Italy by Emperor Lothair II. In the barely twenty years that he lived after his conversion St Norbert made a mark on his era, especially by his inauguration of the Premonstratensian canons regular, whose way of life was a middle term between that of monks and that of the friars of the following century. In 1627 St Norbert's relics were transferred from Magdeburg to the church of the abbey of his order at Strahov near Prague. His emblem is a monstrance.

NORTH AMERICA, THE MARTYRS OF. All b. in France; d. 1642–9; cd 1930; f.d. 26 September (in the Society of Jesus, 16 March). ◊ *Antony Daniel, Charles Garnier, Gabriel Lalemant, Issac Jogues, John de Brébeuf, John Lalande, Noel Chabanel, René Goupil.*

F. Parkman, *The Jesuits in North America* (1922); J. Wynne, *The Jesuit Martyrs of North America* (1925).

NOTBURGA, domestic servant. B. at Rattenberg in Tirol, *c.* 1265; d. there, *c.* 1313; f.d. 13 September. She was a peasant's daughter, employed as kitchen-maid at the castle of the local magnate, Count Henry. She was caught giving away to the poor broken food she had been told to put in the pigsties, and her mistress dismissed her. She then worked for a farmer at Eben, and continued her benefactions, stinting herself of food for the benefit of others. Later on she was recalled to the castle, where she worked for the rest of her life. By the time her biography was written in 1646 the story of St Notburga was considerably embellished, notably by the charming legend of the sickle that suspended itself out of reach in the air in confirmation of her refusal to reap corn on a Sunday. Notburga is the patron saint of hired hands in Tirol and Bavaria; her body lies in a chapel at Eben. In art, her emblem is a sickle.

NYNIA ◊ *Ninian*

O

ODILIA, abbess. D. *c.* 720; f.d. 13 December. St Odilia (Ottilia and other forms) is the patroness of Alsace, and widely venerated in adjoining lands, but authentic particulars about her are almost wholly lacking. It appears that she was the daughter of a Frankish nobleman, Adalric, and that she founded a nunnery, of which she was abbess, at Hohenburg (Odilienberg) in the Vosges mountains. Popular tradition avers that she was born blind and was hated by her father on that account, but when she recovered her sight he was at length reconciled with her: the legendary details of this story put a more than ordinary strain on the reader's credulity. St Odilia's shrine on the Odilienberg became a celebrated place of pilgrimage, especially for those afflicted with blindness or eye diseases; it is still resorted to, and a bogus prophecy attributed to the saint was circulating in France as lately as during the war of 1939–45.

ODILO, abbot. B. in Auvergne, c. 962; d. at Souvigny, 1048; f.d.
1 January. St Odilo succeeded ◊ *St Mayeul* as fifth abbot of
Cluny in 994, and during his fifty-four years in office he brought
the other Cluniac houses into more and more close dependence
on the mother house. Among his general activities was the support he gave to the institution called the Truce of God, whereby
military hostilities were regularly suspended at certain times, a
measure that had economic as well as religious and social signifi-
cance. Odilo's concern for the people was also shown by the
lavish help he gave during several famines. In 998 he ordered
that in all Cluniac houses November 2, the day after All Saints',
should be observed in memory of and prayer for all the dead;
this observance, All Souls' day, afterwards spread to the whole
Western church. St Odilo's physical appearance was unimpressive,
belying the strength of his character; his duties involved him in
much travelling about, and it was on a journey of inspection that
he died, at the priory of Souvigny; he was about eighty-six.

ODO OF CLUNY, abbot. B. at Tours, 879; d. there, 942; f.d. 18
November. This Odo had been a monk at Baume-les-Messieurs
for eighteen years when in 927 he was appointed second abbot of
Cluny, in the household of whose founder, Duke William of
Aquitaine, he had been brought up. Under his rule the number
of monks there increased rapidly, and several visits to Rome enabled him to introduce the principles of Cluniac observance into
important Italian monasteries. He reformed, not without difficulty, a number of French houses along the same lines, and at
his death Cluny was well on the way to the height of influence it
attained under his successors, ◊ *SS. Mayeul, Odilo*, and *Hugh*.
Many anecdotes are told of St Odo, showing how he combined
the strictest discipline with a sympathetic heart and a lively sense
of fun. He died at his birthplace while on the way back from
Rome. He left a few writings, which include a biography of the
contemporary ◊ *St Gerald of Aurillac* and a long poem on
Christ's redemption of mankind.

Among the French monasteries reformed by Odo was the
famous abbey of Fleury. In the year that Odo died a bishop
came there from England to be professed a monk before being
promoted to the see of Canterbury (whose archbishops at that
time were monks). This was *St Odo* (or Oda) *the Good* (d. 959),
whose festival used to be kept at Canterbury on 2 June.

For a Life, ◊ under *St Gerald of Aurillac*.

OLAF, king of Norway. B. 995; d. at Stiklestad, 1030; f.d. 29 July.
He was the son of a Norwegian jarl, Harald Grenske; and at a
precociously early age was allowed to join a band of vikings. In
the course of his rovings he fought for Richard of Normandy,

and for Ethelred II in England against the Danes. In 1016 he made himself ruler of Norway. Olaf had recently been baptized, and he brought Christian clergy, perhaps some from England, into the country; like Olaf Tryggvesson before him, he used force and bribery to destroy heathenism and impose the new religion on his people. His rule caused widespread discontent and it was not long before he was driven out by the Anglo-Danish King Cnut. Olaf tried to regain his kingdom, but was killed in battle at Stiklestad on the Trondheim fjord.

In circumstances somewhat resembling those of ◊ St Eric of Sweden and others, Olaf Haraldsson became the national hero-saint of Norway: he had been zealous for Christianity (however crudely), he had died what was called a martyr's death, and his name was made to stand for Norwegian independence. His body was soon enshrined in what became the cathedral of Nidaros (Trondheim) and was a place of pilgrimage. In England churches were dedicated in his honour (St Olave's) in London, York, Exeter, and elsewhere.

OLGA ◊ under *Vladimir*

OLYMPIAS, widow and deaconess. B. *c.* 366; d. at Nicomedia (?), 25 July *c.* 408; f.d. 17 December. St Olympias was the principal and most beloved of the women who were faithful to ◊ St John Chrysostom after he was finally banished from Constantinople. At the age of eighteen she married the prefect of the city, Nebridius (on which occasion ◊ St Gregory of Nazianzus wrote her a letter of advice in verse), but less than two years later she was a widow. Her determination not to marry again involved her in serious difficulties, for she was extremely wealthy as well as personally charming; but she dealt with them perspicaciously and by 391 was free to make over huge sums to charitable purposes and to be consecrated a deaconess of the church. People began to impose on her, and Chrysostom warned her to be more discriminating in her benefactions. She led an austere life with other deaconesses, and after Chrysostom had been deported to Cucusus in 404 they had to suffer severe persecution for supporting his cause. When charged with conspiring to burn down the cathedral at Constantinople Olympias answered the prefect boldly and with a sharp irony, and later repeated her refusal to recognize Chrysostom's intruded successor. She was fined heavily, and from then on seems to have been harried from place to place until her death. Seventeen of Chrysostom's extant letters from exile are addressed to St Olympias. He gives her news of himself, thanks her for her services and entrusts her with further responsible commissions, sympathizes time and again with her trials and recurrent bad health, and encourages and praises her with eloquent enthusiasm. Her patience and dignity in adversity, her prudence and wisdom, her charity towards her oppressors, these, he tells her, 'have won a glory and reward which later on will make your sufferings seem light and passing, when you are confronted with unending happiness'.

OMER, missionary bishop. B. near Coutances; d. 1 November *c.* 670; f.d. 9 September. For twenty years St Omer (Audomarus) was a monk of the monastery founded by ◊ *St Columban* at Luxeuil. Then, *c.* 637 he was made bishop and went to minister among the Morini, who had lapsed into heathenism. His centre was at Thérouanne in the Pas-de-Calais, and he was assisted by ◊ *St Bertin* and other monks. With them he established the abbey of Sithiu on the river Aa, where the town of Saint-Omer now stands. Little is known of the life of St Omer; he was totally blind from at least the year 663.

OSBURGA ◊ under *Edburga*

OSMUND, bishop. B. in Normandy; d. at Old Sarum, 1099; cd 1457; f.d. 4 December. St Osmund came into England with the Normans, was appointed William the Conqueror's chancellor, and was officially connected with the Domesday survey. In 1078 he was appointed bishop of Salisbury. Here he finished building the cathedral, within the Norman fortress at Old Sarum, and its chapter of canons and their constitutions became the pattern for other English cathedrals. St Osmund is sometimes given the credit for compiling and arranging the 'Sarum use', i.e. that version of the Latin liturgy of worship which eventually was followed in most dioceses of England and Ireland until the Reformation; but this appears to have been the work of a later bishop, Richard Poore (d. 1237). St Osmund was devoted to his duties, his diocese, and his books, a strict disciplinarian but a man of moderation – in the troubles between King William II and ◊ *St Anselm* he tried to steer a middle course. The process of the canonization of Osmund of Salisbury was begun in 1228 and met with such extraordinary delays that it was not finished till 1457; there was not another English canonization until 1935 (John Fisher (◊ *John of Rochester*) and ◊ *Thomas More*).

OSWALD OF NORTHUMBRIA, king and martyr. B. *c.* 605; d. at Maserfelth, 642; f.d. 9 August. In 633 Oswald defeated and slew the Welsh king Cadwallon of Gwynedd in battle near Hexham, and so recovered the Northumbrian kingdom of his father Ethelfrith. While in exile Oswald had become a Christian at Iona, and he at once obtained missionaries from there to carry on the evangelization of his people. They were led by ◊ *St Aidan*, whose personal friendship with Oswald resulted in a very fruitful collaboration: Aidan was not fluent in English, and, writes Bede, 'it was a pleasing sight to see the king himself interpreting God's word to his thanes and chief men, for he had learned the Irish tongue during his long exile'. Oswald married Cyneburga, daughter of Cynegils, the first Christian king of Wessex, and had a certain overlordship in respect of the other English kingdoms; but the reign that began so promisingly lasted only eight years. The heathen Penda of Mercia took up arms against him, and Oswald was killed at the battle of Maserfelth (Oswestry?): tradition says that as he fell he was heard to pray for the souls of those who fell with him. St Oswald was a popular hero who seems to have well deserved his title of saint, which began to be given him soon after his death; that veneration spread even so far as central Europe, especially southern Germany and northern Italy.

After St Oswald's death southern Northumbria was ruled by his cousin *St Oswin* (f.d. 20 August). Of him Bede says that he was handsome in appearance and courteous in manner, 'and among his other qualities of virtue and moderation the greatest was humbleness', of which quality Bede gives an impressive example. In 651 Oswin was killed at Gilling in Yorkshire at the instigation of another cousin, King Oswy, and was popularly revered as a martyr.

OSWALD OF WORCESTER, bishop. B. *c.* 925; d. at Worcester, 992; f.d. 28 February. He came of a Danish family settled in England and was educated under his uncle St Odo of Canterbury, who sent him to the abbey of Fleury in France to learn monastic discipline. In 962 he was appointed bishop of Worcester, and he was closely associated with ◊ *St Dunstan* and *St Ethelwold* in the restoration of monasticism in England. His first foundation was at Westbury-on-Trym, near Bristol, but his greatest establishment was at Ramsey in Huntingdonshire, from which were founded Pershore, Evesham, and other houses. St Oswald was energetic in improving the standard of the parochial clergy, fostering education, and enforcing clerical celibacy, and in 972 he was made archbishop of York, where as a young man he had worked under his uncle, Archbishop Oskytel. But he retained Worcester as well, presiding over both dioceses; it is with Worcester that he was always principally concerned and there he died, just after fulfilling his daily Lenten observance of washing the feet of twelve poor men and serving them at table. A Life of St Oswald was written very soon after his death: it speaks of his gentleness and kindness, the love that the people had for him, and his gaiety when he came to die.

For a Life, ◊ under *St Dunstan.*

OSWIN ◊ under *Oswald of Northumbria*

OSYTH, queen. Seventh century; f.d. 7 October. The village of Saint Osyth in Essex, originally called Chich, has its name from this woman. All that is known about her is that she was the wife of Sighere, king of the East Saxons, and that she founded a nunnery at Chich, where she ended her days. In the twelfth century currency was given to various legends, as that she was martyred by Danish pirates. King Sighere's uncle, King *Sebbi*, of whose dignified death Bede gives an account, is named as a saint in the Roman Martyrology, on 29 August; he was buried in Old St Paul's.

OTTILIA ◊ *Odilia*

OTTO OF BAMBERG, bishop. B. in Swabia, 1062; d. at Bamberg, 30 June 1139; cd 1189; f.d. 30 September. Having been ordained priest, Otto was taken into the service of Emperor Henry IV, who in 1101 made him his chancellor and soon after named him bishop of Bamberg. For twenty years he was concerned in the conflict over the investiture of prelates by secular rulers and other high affairs of church and state; in these he was distinguished by his freedom from partisan spirit, and he never failed in care for the welfare of his diocese. In 1124, at the invitation of Duke Boleslav III of Poland, Otto undertook a missionary journey in Pomerania. His personality commended itself to the people, and he is said in a very short time to have converted 20,000 persons and established a dozen churches. But a good deal of the seed must have fallen on stony ground, for the number of backsliders necessitated another visit to Pomerania in 1128 to retrieve the situation. This time Otto built more solidly and he continued the supervision of his converts from Bamberg; but for some years his efforts were handicapped by the obstructionism of the neighbouring metropolitans. St Otto was a wise and very able prelate and a great encourager of monasticism; because of his initial work there he is regarded as the evangelizer of Pomerania.

OUDOCEUS ◊ under *Teilo*

OUEN, bishop. B. near Soissons, *c.* 600; d. at Clichy, 684; f.d. 24 August. Until he was about forty St Ouen (Audoenus) was an important official at the courts of the Frankish kings Chlotar II and Dagobert I, at the same time as his friend ◊ *St Eligius*, whose biography he wrote. Having founded the abbey of Rebais, he received holy orders and in 641 was appointed to the see of Rouen. He was tireless in his zeal as bishop, especially for the conversion of the remaining heathen in his diocese. But he could not avoid the entanglements of politics, first as adviser to the queen ◊ *St Bathild* and then in the violent era of the unscrupulous West Frankish mayor of the palace, Ebroin, to whom Ouen was said to have given a measure of support. Some relics of St Ouen were enshrined in Canterbury cathedral about the year 950.

P

PACHOMIUS, abbot. B. near Esneh in Egypt, c. 290; d. at Tabennisi, c. 346; f.d. 14 May. St Pachomius was the first monk, not simply to bring hermits together in groups, but to organize them with a properly communal life and a written rule, to be monks as the word is now understood. Particulars of his life are uncertain, but he is said to have been a soldier in the imperial army who on being released from service became a Christian. He put himself under the direction of an anchorite named Palemon, and c. 320 went to live at Tabennisi, on the Nile in central Egypt, with a few other monks. As the community grew Pachomius gradually organized it on the principles of living in common. A second monastery was established at Pabau and nine more followed, two of them for women, the first nunneries in Egypt. St Pachomius seems deliberately to have chosen the communal form of life as more desirable in itself and having a wider appeal than that of the solitaries. Both ◊ St Basil the Great and St Benedict were influenced by his written Life and the regulations which he drew up, but the original text of his Rule no longer exists.

PALLADIUS ◊ under Celestine I

PAMMACHIUS, layman. B. in Rome, c. 340; d. there, 410; f.d. 30 August. He was a Roman senator, married to a daughter of ◊ St Paula, and a man of learning and ability who spent much of his time in study and religious affairs. He was a friend of ◊ St Jerome and twice wrote to remonstrate with him for the violence of his language: first during a controversy in which Jerome had written depreciatingly of marriage, and again during Jerome's disagreement with Rufinus about the teaching of Origen. His wife died in childbirth in 397, and he received from ◊ St Paulinus of Nola a long letter of condolence, praising her goodness and his faith and fortitude. Henceforth Pammachius devoted himself and his wealth to good works, being associated with ◊ St Fabiola in the foundation and running of a hospice and hospital for travellers at Porto. He had a church in his house at Rome, remains of which have been found under the church of SS. John and Paul on the Caelian Hill.

PAMPHILUS, martyr. B. at Beirut, c. 240; d. at Caesarea Maritima, 16 February 309; f.d. 1 June. He studied at the Christian school at Alexandria, and spent the rest of his life at Caesarea in Palestine, where he was ordained priest. He taught in the school there, gathered a celebrated library (afterwards dispersed by the Arabs), and did important work on the text of the Bible. While in prison because of his religion he wrote a treatise, 'apology', in defence of Origen's teaching. Pamphilus was eventually put to death for his faith at the same time as ◊ *St Elias* and his companions; six other martyrs suffered with them. These martyrdoms were narrated by Eusebius, who admired St Pamphilus so much that he called himself Eusebius Pamphili, 'Pamphilus's Eusebius'.

PANCRAS, martyr. D. 304 (?); f.d. 12 May. He was a Roman martyr who was buried on the Aurelian Way. Nothing else is known about him; the story that he was a boy from Phrygia, martyred in Rome at the age of fourteen, is legendary. As in the church of St Felix at Nola, oaths taken in St Pancras's church at Rome, built over his tomb by Pope St Symmachus *c.* 500, were esteemed to have a special sacredness; a church at Canterbury was dedicated in his honour by ◊ *St Augustine of Canterbury*. The parish church of St Pancras in London gave that name to the borough and the railway-terminus.

St Pancras of Taormina (f.d. 3 April) is the subject of a bizarre Greek legend; it makes him a disciple of ◊ *St Peter* who was martyred in Sicily.

PANTALEON, martyr. D. *c.* 304 (?); f.d. 27 July. The cultus of this martyr was connected principally with Bithynia, where Emperor Justinian rebuilt his church at Nicomedia, but no authentic particulars of him have survived. He was soon made the subject of legends. According to these he was court physician to Emperor Galerius and was drawn from a life of self-indulgence by a Christian friend; when arrested during Diocletian's persecution, vain attempts were made to put him to death in six different ways before he was successfully beheaded amidst a halo of other marvels. Because of his alleged profession St Pantaleon became a very popular patron of medical men. A reputed relic of the martyr's blood kept at Ravello in southern Italy displays the phenomenon of liquefaction (cf. ◊ *St Januarius*).

PAPHNUTIUS, bishop. D. in Egypt, *c.* 350 (?); f.d. 11 September. He was a disciple of ◊ *St Antony* who was called from his solitary life to be a bishop in Upper Thebaid. During the persecution under Maximinus he was barbarously treated, being blinded in one eye and having a leg mutilated; on account of these sufferings he was treated with special deference at the first general council at Nicaea in 325. Some of the fathers of the council wanted to impose on married bishops, priests, and deacons the obligation of separating from their wives; St Paphnutius, himself a monk, distinguished himself by his opposition to this proposal; and the existing discipline, which was simply that clergy should not contract marriage after ordination, was upheld. Paphnutius was a faithful supporter of ◊ *St Athanasius*; it is said that at the council of Tyre in 335 he made a dramatic appeal to Maximus of Jerusalem, imploring him not to support the enemies of the faith for which he, Maximus, had suffered the same injuries as had been inflicted on himself, Paphnutius. He was one of the saints to whom the conversion of the legendary ◊ *St Thais* was attributed.

PAPYLUS ◊ *Carpus and Papylus*

PASCHAL BAYLON ◊ under *Diego*

PATRICK, missionary bishop. B. at Bannavem Taberniae, 385 (?); d. at Saul in Down, 461 (?); f.d. 17 March. The evangelizer of the Irish was a Romano-Briton, born at an unidentified place near the west coast somewhere between the Clyde and the Severn estuary; his father, Calpurnius, was a civil official and deacon, and his grandfather was a priest. When he was sixteen Patrick was carried off by raiders and enslaved in Ireland, where he was used as a herdsman, traditionally at Slemish in Antrim. During this time he learned to take religion seriously and became a man of intense prayer. After six years he made his escape, being carried by ship to the continent, and when he had got back home he was called in a dream to return to Ireland to preach Christ there. It is generally held that Patrick was trained for the priesthood in Gaul, being a disciple of ◊ *St Germanus* at Auxerre, after leading a monastic life for a time on an island off the south coast; but it is not impossible that his formative period was passed in Britain. In any case in 432 (the traditional date, but disputed) he went back to Ireland as a missionary bishop.

There were certainly Christians in Ireland before the coming of St Patrick (they had a bishop, Palladius), but no great impression had been made. It was Patrick who caused Christ's gospel to be welcomed far and wide in the north, the central parts, and the west, and brought an organized church into existence. At Tara in Meath, we are told, he confronted the high-king, Laoghaire, on Easter eve, kindled the light of the paschal fire on the hill of Slane, silenced the druids and gained a hearing for himself as a man of power. From his *Confession* may be learned something of the success of his preaching and priestly ministrations, the opposition and dangers he encountered from the heathen, and the criticisms of some who should have been his friends – they accused him of being an ambitious ignoramus. In 444 St Patrick established his episcopal see at Armagh; by then he had other bishops to help him and a considerable body of lesser clergy, and he was an encourager of monasticism; but as yet the Irish church did not have that monastic character it afterwards acquired. Towards the end of his life he made that 'retreat' of forty days on Cruachan Aigli in Mayo from which the age-long Croagh Patrick pilgrimage derives.

The only contemporary evidence bearing on St Patrick's life is found in his own writings: the *Confession*, in which he reviews his life and work, and the *Letter to Coroticus*, denouncing an attack on one of his congregations by that British chieftain's men. The hymn called the Breastplate (*Lorica*) is also attributed to him. These writings have been translated into English several times, most recently by Dr L. Bieler (1953). What stands out in them is St Patrick's sense of being called by God to the work he had undertaken, and his determination and modesty in carrying it out: 'I, Patrick, a sinner, am the most ignorant and of least account among the faithful, despised by many.... I owe it to God's grace that so many people should through me be born again to him.' Later sources are copious and of very uneven value, causing much disagreement among the learned, not least in the matter of chronology. The saint's emblems are snakes and shamrock.

J. B. Bury, *Life of St Patrick* (1905); L. Bieler, *Life and Legend of St Patrick* (1949); E. MacNeill, *St Patrick, Apostle of Ireland* (1964).

PAUL, apostle of the Gentiles. B. at Tarsus in Cilicia; d. at Rome, *c.* 67; f.d. 29 June, with ◊ *St Peter* (B.C.P. 25 January). Until his conversion to Christ, Paul was known as Saul. He inherited Roman citizenship from his Jewish father (Acts xxii, 28), who brought him up a strict Pharisee (ibid. xxvi, 5); he studied his religion under the celebrated Rabbi Gamaliel at Jerusalem (ibid. ᵛxii 3), and learned the trade of a tent-maker (ibid. xviii, 1–3). As a young man he was present and consenting when ◊ *St Stephen* was stoned to death; afterwards he 'made havoc of the church' (ibid. viii, 3), searching out Christians and handing them over to prison and even death. Then, while on the way to Damascus to persecute there, he had a sudden vision, in which Jesus Christ rebuked him and told him he was destined to take the Christian faith to the Gentiles, i.e. to non-Jews. Paul was duly baptized, and retired for a time to Arabia; then he came back to Damascus, but after three years his Jewish enemies became so threatening that he had to make his escape by night, being lowered over the city wall in a basket. From thence he went to Jerusalem, 'to see Peter', whom later he 'withstood to the face' because of his uncertain attitude in the disagreement about Gentile converts and Jewish observances. This happened at Antioch, the metropolis of the East, to which Paul had been called to help ◊ *St Barnabas* in his work of evangelization: it was the beginning of the great mission to the gentiles. Their converts raised a fund for the relief of the famine-stricken Christian community at Jerusalem, and Paul and Barnabas were commissioned to take it there (ibid. ix, 1–30; xi, 26–30).

From about the year 45 St Paul was on his three principal missionary journeys, beginning with Cyprus and going hither and thither in Asia Minor, Syria, Macedonia, and Greece (Acts xiii-xx). In each town he first preached in the Jewish synagogue before addressing himself to the heathen. At the end of a dozen years he went to Jerusalem, and his presence there caused such disorder that he was taken into custody by the Roman governor. After two years he appealed for trial in the emperor's court, and was sent to Rome, being shipwrecked at Malta on the way (ibid. xxi–xxviii). He remained under house-arrest in Rome for two years, and thereafter his movements are uncertain. He may have been condemned at his trial, and then executed; or he may have been acquitted, for there is some indication that he revisited Ephesus and other places, and perhaps even went to Spain. He would then have been again arrested, brought to Rome once more, and there put to death. In either case the tradition is that he was beheaded at the place now called Tre Fontane, and his body buried where the church of St Paul outside the Walls stands. (The belief that Peter and Paul were martyred on the same day is probably due to the fact that they have a joint feast day, on 29 June.)

Up to his first arrival in Rome, St Paul's life is related in considerable detail in the Acts of the Apostles, and there are further gleanings to be had from those numerous letters of his that form so precious a part of the New Testament (the authorship of certain of them, notably the one to the Hebrews, is questioned). In a famous passage he has himself emphasized the external conditions of his life as a Christian missionary: 'In journeyings often, in perils of waters, in perils of robbers, in perils by mine own countrymen, in perils by the heathen, in perils in the city, in perils in the wilderness, in perils in the sea, in perils among false brethren; in weariness and painfulness, in watchings often, in hunger and thirst, in fastings often, in cold and nakedness' (II Cor. xi, 26–27). These things and more were brought upon him by his faithfulness to his daily preoccupation, 'the care of all the churches'. A second-century document depicts Paul as a man of unimpressive physical presence ('small, bald, bow-legged,' etc; cf. II Cor. x, 10); the Acts and the Epistles testify to the loftiness of his spiritual stature and the transcendent qualities of his mind. For he was a great deal more than a tireless and powerful missionary: as religious thinker he has been through his letters a profound and enduring formative influence in the development of Christianity, and his greatness of mind and spirit becomes only more apparent as the centuries pass. The symbols of St Paul in art are a sword and a book.

H. V. Morton, *In the Steps of St Paul* (1949); A. Penna, *St Paul the Apostle* (1953); C. Tresmontant. *St Paul and the Mystery of Christ* (1957).

PAUL OF THE CROSS, founder. B. at Ovada in Piedmont, 1694; d. at Rome, 18 October 1775; cd 1867; f.d. 28 April. Paul Francis Danei was well brought up by devout middle-class parents. When he was twenty he volunteered for the Venetian army, but he soon found he was not meant to be a soldier and for some years led a life of retirement and prayer. During 1720 he underwent a process of spiritual enlightenment, in which it was borne in on him that he was called to found a congregation of missioners whose life and work should be specially centred on the Saviour's cross and passion (hence their name, Passionists). Paul was to experience such mystical communications all his life, and came to distrust them; however, he acted promptly on these first ones, and in 1727 he and his brother were ordained in Rome and started the first Passionist house, on the Monte Argentario peninsula in Tuscany. The first ten years were difficult, for both internal and external reasons; but the austere life of the missioners and the fervent preaching of their founder made their mark, and before he died the congregation was firmly established and a convent of enclosed Passionist nuns begun. St Paul of the Cross was always interested in the religious state of England; the leader of the first Passionists to work there, Father Dominic Barberi (d. 1849), who received J. H. Newman into the Roman Catholic church, was beatified in 1963.

PAUL THE HERMIT. D. *c.* 347 (?); f.d. 15 January. This Paul, sometimes called 'of Thebes', is traditionally regarded as the first Christian hermit. We are told that he went into the Theban desert as a young man, seeking a temporary refuge from the persecution under Decius; but he stopped there, living in a cave, for the rest of his life, which lasted over a hundred years. When he was nearing death he was visited by ◊ *St Antony* out of respect for his holiness. Antony eventually buried him, wrapped in the cloak ◊ *St Athanasius* had given Antony; two lions, we are told, helped to excavate the grave. ◊ *St Jerome* wrote a Life of Paul, the degree of authenticity of which has much exercised the minds of scholars; it confronts the reader with centaurs and satyrs, and a raven reminiscent of Elijah's. But it does not follow that Paul himself was a fictional character.

A late contemporary of the above was *St Paul the Simple* (f.d. 16 March), so called because of his ingenuous character. He was an Egyptian peasant who, when he was sixty, left his wife because of her unfaithfulness and offered himself to St Antony as a dis-

ciple. According to one account Antony accepted him only after a long series of tests of his obedience and determination to persevere; whether true or not, the narrative is very characteristic of the early days of monasticism in the deserts of Egypt.
H. Waddell, *The Desert Fathers* (1936).

PAUL AURELIAN, or OF LÉON, bishop. Sixth century; f.d. 12 March. This is one of the few British Celtic saints of whom a Life exists written before the later middle ages: it was finished in 884, by a monk of Landévennec in Brittany, named Wrmonoc. It relates in considerable detail that Paul Aurelian was the son of a chieftain in Britain and was educated at the monastery of ◊ *St Illtyd*; he became a monk and priest and with twelve companions migrated to Brittany, where they founded a number of churches; he was bishop at the place now called after him, Saint-Pol-de-Léon, and died in very old age at his monastery on the island of Batz.

As narrated by Wrmonoc the story of St Paul Aurelian is full of legendary or doubtful matter, but there is no doubt that he was a powerful missioner in Finistère. The Life incorporates some traditions of Welsh and Cornish origin, and there are considerable traces of the saint in Wales, where, as in Brittany, he was sometimes called Paulinus. The ancient church at the village of Paul, near Penzance, is dedicated in honour of Pol de Léon.

PAULA, Roman matron. B. in Rome. 347; d. at Bethlchem, 404; f.d. 26 January. According to ◊ *St Jerome*, Paula was connected through her mother with the Scipios and the Gracchi, and both her wealth and her virtues matched the distinction of her birth. She married the senator Toxotius, whose death left her a widow with five children when she was about thirty-three. Under the influence of her friend ◊ *St Marcella* and of St Jerome she led a retired and studious life, till in 385 she determined to settle near Jerome in Bethlehem, taking one daughter, ◊ *St Eustochium*, with her. Paula took the lead among the women of Jerome's group, building a communal house for them and another for the men, as well as a hospice for pilgrims; and she had charge of Jerome's personal welfare, which she found no light undertaking. She had learned Greek from her father and now applied herself to Hebrew, so that she could sing the psalms in their original words and profit more from her biblical studies under Jerome's direction. In his letters he praises Paula's efficient practicality and tactfulness; but he was alarmed by her excessive self-imposed mortifications, and warned her that her lavish gifts to charity would land her in difficulties, which they did: her death left Eustochium with a large debt. St Jerome wrote a rather rhetorical but impressive account of St Paula's death and funeral in Letter

108, which is a sort of biography of her; she was buried close to the birthplace of Jesus, beneath the church of the Nativity.
Stanbrook nuns, *St Paula* (1934).

PAULINUS OF AQUILEIA, bishop. B. near Cividale, *c.* 726; d. at Aquileia, 802; f.d. 11 January. Having gained a reputation as a scholar, this Paulinus was called to the court of Charlemagne in 776, where Alcuin of York was among his friends. In 787 he was appointed to the see of Aquileia, near his birthplace in northern Italy, and he was a very active prelate, taking a leading part in a number of church councils. He was concerned in sending missionaries to the Avars and other heathen, in concert with Pepin of Italy and the Danubian bishops, and he condemned the baptism of uninstructed or unwilling converts. Paulinus wrote two tracts against the heresy called Adoptianism, and a number of poems, hymns, and other works.

St Paulinus of Trier (d. 358; f.d. 31 August) was an early bishop of that see; in 353 he was banished by Emperor Constantius II, with ◊ *St Eusebius of Vercelli* and others, for opposing Arianism. He died in exile in Phrygia.

PAULINUS OF NOLA, bishop and poet. B. at Bordeaux, 353; d. at Nola, 431; f.d. 22 June. Pontius Meropius Paulinus belonged to a wealthy family of senatorial rank; his master in poetry and rhetoric was the poet Ausonius, who took a great interest in his pupil both then and later. Paulinus held several public offices and travelled widely, making many friends and in 379 visiting Nola for the first time. He was not baptized till *c.* 390; shortly afterwards, having lost his only child and being involved in grave difficulties – he was threatened with a charge of having killed his brother – he retired to Spain with his Spanish wife, Therasia. They sold some of their property, devoting much of the proceeds to relieving distress, with the unlooked-for result that the people of Barcelona clamoured for him to be admitted to the priesthood, and he was ordained accordingly.

In 395 Paulinus and Therasia went to live at Nola in the Campanian province of Italy. They had now given up marital relations, and with a few associates they led a sort of monastic existence, living frugally, celebrating the offices in church, studying, caring for the needy, receiving visitors. Many pilgrims came to the tomb of ◊ *St Felix of Nola*, and Paulinus built a large new church adjoining that of the tomb, with subsidiary buildings; the walls of all were covered with pictures of biblical subjects, which Paulinus hoped would help to keep the crowds orderly. In 409 he was chosen to be bishop of Nola, but not a great deal is recorded of the following twenty years. There exists a moving account by an eyewitness of his last few days; he died soon after the hour of Evensong, when the lamps were lighted, quoting the Psalmist, 'I have prepared a lamp for mine Anointed'.

As a poet St Paulinus stands beside, if a little below, the contemporary Prudentius. Thirty-five of his poems survive, of which fourteen are for ◊ *St Felix of Nola*'s feast day; one of these is well-known in English as the hymn 'Another year completed'. Among the others is a wedding-song for the marriage of the Julian who was afterwards bishop of Eclanum, one of the earliest of Christian wedding poems. One of the two poems addressed to Ausonius was translated by Henry Vaughan, 'the Silurist': 'I am not he, whom you knew then'. Of prose writings there are fifty letters, of interest for what they tell of the gentle and affectionate character of the writer and for the religious and personal topics they discuss. His correspondents include many of the outstanding Christians of his time, among them ◊ *St Augustine, St Ambrose, St Victricius, St Martin of Tours*, and Sulpicius Severus. A characteristic of St Paulinus' personal religion was his intense devotion to the saints and respect for their relics, most noticeable as regards St Felix.

PAULINUS OF TRIER ◊ under *Paulinus of Aquileia*

PAULINUS OF YORK, missionary bishop. D. at Rochester, 644; f.d. 10 October. When in 625 the princess Ethelburga, sister of King Edbald of Kent, went north to marry Edwin of Northumbria, she was accompanied by Bishop Paulinus as her chaplain; he was one of the second band of missionaries sent from Rome to England, in 601, and was consecrated for his office by ◊ *St Justus* at Canterbury. At York in 627, in circumstances related at length by Bede, King Edwin, his nobles, and many others were baptized by Paulinus on Easter eve (a much less favoured source, the Welsh Nennius, ascribes this baptism to a Welsh priest). Paulinus, a tall, dark man, 'of venerable and awe-inspiring appearance', followed this up by a series of missionary journeys over a wide area, going so far south as Lincoln, converting and baptizing large numbers. Pope Honorius I recognized Paulinus as archbishop at York, but before the letter arrived the first evangelization of Northumbria had come to an end: in 632 Edwin was killed fighting the Welsh Cadwallon and his Mercian allies, and Paulinus brought the widowed Ethelburga and her children back to Kent by sea for safety. He had left his deacon James to carry on the northern work as best he could, and passed his remaining years as bishop of Rochester. During the last years of King Edwin's reign there was such peace and order in his dominions that a proverb said 'a woman could carry her new-born baby across the island from sea to sea and suffer no harm' (Bede); he too received a certain cultus as a saint and martyr.

271

PEDROG ◊ *Petroc*

PEGA ◊ under *Guthlac*

PELAGIA THE PENITENT. No date; f.d. 8 October. The story told about this Pelagia, nicknamed Margarito because of the fineness of her pearls, is that she was a notoriously licentious dancing-girl at Antioch who caught the attention of Bishop Nonnus of Edessa: 'This girl,' he said, 'is a lesson to us bishops. She takes more trouble over her beauty and her dancing than we do about our souls and our flocks.' Happening to hear a sermon from the same bishop, Pelagia was moved to repentance and baptism. She went to Jerusalem and, disguised as a man, lived as a solitary in a cave on the Mount of Olives, under the name of Pelagius. There she died some years later.

It seems likely that the self-styled James who wrote this edifying tale founded it on the life of a woman at Antioch about whom ◊ *St John Chrysostom* tells a somewhat similar story in one of his homilies; but Chrysostom does not mention her name and there is no evidence that she was ever venerated as a saint. Combined with the legend of ◊ *Pelagia of Tarsus*, 'James's' highly-coloured narrative is akin to the tales of ◊ *Marina, Margaret* (Reparata), *Euphrosyne*, and others (and cf ◊ *St Eugenia*), and was doubtless their starting-point.

H. Delehaye, *Legends of the Saints* (1962).

PELAGIA OF ANTIOCH, virgin martyr. D. *c.* 304 (?); f.d. 9 June, originally 8 October. She is the historical Pelagia who has sometimes been confused with the legendary ◊ *Pelagia the Penitent*. It is known, again from ◊ *St John Chrysostom* (◊ under *Pelagia the Penitent*), that she was a fifteen-year-old Christian girl at Antioch who, when soldiers came to her home to seize her, eluded them and threw herself to death from the house-top to avoid outrage. She was venerated as a martyr and is named among the maiden martyrs in the canon of the Mass as used in the rite of Milan.

PELAGIA OF TARSUS, virgin martyr. No date; f.d. 4 May, originally 8 October. Her legend is that she was a beautiful girl un-willingly affianced to a son of Emperor Diocletian; when she became a Christian the young man committed suicide. Instead of punishing Pelagia, the emperor wanted her for himself; but she repulsed him, clung to her faith, and was roasted to death in a red-hot brazen bull. The idea that the various fictitious Pelagias and Marinas (the same name in Greek and Latin) are a christian-ized version of Aphrodite or Venus has been examined and firmly rejected by Hippolyte Delehaye.

PEREGRINE LAZIOSI ◊ under *Philip Benizi*

PERPETUA and FELICITY, martyrs. D. at Carthage, 203; f.d. 6

March. The Passion of SS. Perpetua and Felicity with their four male companions is perhaps the most moving and impressive of authentic narratives of early martyrs. The document was written in part by Perpetua herself, in part by another of the martyrs, Saturus, and completed by an anonymous hand after the martyrdom. Vibia Perpetua was a young married woman of good family (a widow?) with a baby in arms; Felicity was a slave-girl, far advanced in pregnancy, and Revocatus also was a slave; the other three men were Secundulus, Saturninus, and Saturus. At the time of their arrest at Carthage under an edict of Septimus Severus all of them except Saturus were still catechumens; they were baptized while under 'house-arrest', and soon after were shut up in the common jail. It was then that Perpetua received the first of the visions or dreams, of the ladder to Heaven, that are a feature of the narrative; and she was visited by her puzzled old father, a pagan: 'I grieved at the unhappiness of his old age'. She was worried, too, about her baby, who was eventually taken away home. At their trial all were condemned to death by wild beasts. Returned to prison, Perpetua had two dreams about her brother, Dinocrates, who had died as a small boy, dreams which present problems of interpretation; later she had a very remarkable vision of herself overthrowing Satan, in the guise of an 'evil-looking Egyptian', in a physical fight. Saturus records his vision of arriving in Heaven, where the elders before God's throne told them to 'Go and play'; and Perpetua said, 'I was merry in the flesh: now I am merrier still.' After a difficult labour, and brutal jeers from a warder, Felicity gave birth to a girl, who was at once adopted by a fellow Christian.

On the day of triumph the martyrs entered the arena 'with gay and gallant looks'; 'You judge us: God will judge you!' they exclaimed to the presiding procurator, Hilarion. Perpetua came last, 'true bride of Christ and darling of God, her piercing gaze abashing all eyes'. A detailed account is given of how she and Felicity helped one another when they were attacked by a savage cow, and of the encounters of the others with leopard, bear, and boar; finally each was killed by a sword thrust in the throat, after they had kissed one another 'that their martyrdom might be perfected with the rite of peace'. A first clumsy blow failed to kill Perpetua; she shrieked with pain, but guided the sword for a second blow: 'Perhaps so great a woman, feared by the unclean spirit, could not have been slain unless she so willed it.'
W. H. Shewring, *The Passion of SS. Perpetua and Felicity* (1931).

PERRAN ◊ *Piran*

PETER, leader of the Apostles. D. at Rome, *c.* 64; f.d. 29 June, with ◊ *St Paul* (B.C.P., Peter alone). He was a fisherman on the Sea of

Galilee, married, and brother of ◊ *St Andrew*, with whom he was called to follow Christ and be a 'fisher of men'. Originally he was called Simon; but Jesus gave him the Aramaic title of *Kepha* (John i, 42), meaning 'rock', of which the Greek equivalent becomes 'Peter' in English, the name by which we know him. The title was explained when, in reply to Simon's declaration 'Thou art the Christ, the Son of the living God', the Lord said to him, 'Thou art Peter, and upon this rock I will build my church', and conferred on him 'the keys of the kingdom of Heaven', and the power of 'binding and loosing' afterwards extended to the other apostles (Matt. xvi, 16–19; xviii, 18). The New Testament gives ample evidence of Peter's unique position among the apostles, and also makes clear his earlier misunderstanding of Christ's messiahship and the warm impetuosity of his character. Within a few hours of his assuring his Master 'Though I should die with thee, yet will I not deny thee,' he in fact denied all knowledge of him three times to the Jewish high-priest's servants (ibid. xxvi, 35, 69–75). But after the resurrection Peter was the first of the apostles to whom Jesus appeared: and subsequently the risen Lord elicited a threefold assurance of his love; whereupon Jesus reiterated Peter's responsibilities: 'Feed my lambs. Feed my sheep' (John xxi, 15–19).

This St Peter did boldly and faithfully, as can be seen from the Acts of the Apostles. He was the leader of the Christian community. He directed that the place among the apostles left vacant by Judas Iscariot be filled; he addressed the crowd at Pentecost; he did miracles in Christ's name – his very shadow was health-giving (Acts v, 15); he passed sentence on Ananias and Sapphira; twice he refused to be silenced by the Jewish council; he admitted the first Gentile, Cornelius, to baptism; he was imprisoned by Herod Agrippa, and escaped through divine intervention; he made missionary and pastoral visits to Samaria, Antioch (traditionally he was the first bishop there), and other places. At Antioch he was reproved by St Paul for temporizing over eating with Gentiles (Gal. ii, 11–21); afterwards Peter spoke strongly against imposing the obligation of circumcision on Gentiles: to them also, he said, the Holy Spirit is given and their hearts are purified by faith (Acts xv 7–11).

The tradition, age-long, but not explicitly recorded in the New Testament, that St Peter eventually went to Rome and was put to death there has been called in question from time to time in later ages; but the researches of modern scholars have done much to confirm the tradition. That he was martyred under Nero is undisputed; it is said that he was crucified, head downwards at his own request, but this is very uncertain. Tradition again points to a spot below where the altar of the Vatican basilica stands as his burial-place. The results of recent excavations there are impressive and of profound interest, but not wholly conclusive on this point.

There seems no good reason to doubt St Peter's authorship of the first New Testament epistle bearing his name, but the second is more questionable; on the other hand it is generally agreed that Mark's gospel represents Peter's teaching. Other early works claiming St Peter as their author, or written about him, are apocryphal; one of them, the *Acts of Peter*, is the source of the story that the saint, fleeing from persecution in Rome, met Christ on the road and asked him 'Lord, where are you going?' Christ answered, 'I am coming to be crucified again', and thereupon Peter turned back to meet his martyrdom. St Peter is symbolized in art by two crossed keys.

O. Cullmann, *Peter: Disciple, Apostle, Martyr* (1954); O. Karrer, *Peter and the Church* (1963); Lord Elton, *Simon Peter* (1965).

PETER ✧ *Marcellinus and Peter*

PETER OF ALCÁNTARA, mystic. B. at Alcántara in Spain, 1499; d. at Arenas, 1562; cd 1669; f.d. 19 October. Peter Garavito, son of a lawyer, studied at the university of Salamanca and joined the Franciscan friars of the Observance. For some years after his ordination to the priesthood his life was uneventful, spent mostly in preaching missions all over Estremadura, but all the time he was longing for a yet more rigorous following of the Franciscan rule. After he was elected head of the Estremadura province of his order in 1538 he was able to take definite steps in this direction, but his efforts were not well received. At length, *c.* 1556, he succeeded in establishing a friary at Pedrosa, from which the Alcantarine Franciscan reform developed and spread; the friars lived in small groups, in great poverty and austerity, going barefoot, abstaining from meat and wine, spending much time in solitude and contemplation. The high example set by St Peter himself, almost unbelievable in some matters, is known from the autobiography of ✧ *St Teresa of Ávila*. She received much help and encouragement from him in the founding of the first convent of reformed Carmelite nuns in 1562; he was also her confessor for a time, and had a significant part in the development of her mystical life. Peter of Alcántara was one of the outstanding Spanish mystics before St Teresa herself; he wrote a *Treatise on Prayer and Meditation* that has been translated into many languages, including English (1926).

PETER OF ALEXANDRIA, bishop and martyr. D. 311; f.d. 26 November. This Peter was elected bishop of Alexandria in 300, and during the times of persecution that followed he eventually went into hiding. Another bishop, Melitius of Lycopolis, trespassed on his jurisdiction, accusing Peter of being too easygoing with lapsed Christians; this led to a schism in the Egyptian church that lasted for several generations. Peter returned to his see, and when persecution began again under Maximinus he was put to death. Eusebius calls him 'an inspired Christian teacher . . . a worthy example of a bishop, both for the goodness of his life and his knowledge of the Scriptures'; to the Egyptians he was 'the seal and fulfilment of persecution', as being the last victim of public authority in the Alexandrian church. Several legendary stories became attached to his name. Among St Peter's fragmentary writings are some regulations of great interest, drawn up in 306: they deal with the treatment of those Christians who in varying degrees had failed under persecution.

PETER OF TARENTAISE, bishop. B. at Saint-Maurice near Vienne, 1102; d. at Bellevaux, 1174; cd 1191; f.d. 8 May. He joined the Cistercian order, an example followed by several other members of his family, and in 1132 became abbot of Tamié in the Tarentaise region of Savoy. In 1142 he accepted, very unwillingly, the bishopric of Tarentaise; he proceeded to adapt Cistercian principles to the restoration of a very decayed diocese with considerable success. Among his general concerns was the welfare of travellers to and from Switzerland and Italy, for whom he had the hospice on the Little St Bernard pass rebuilt; he also endowed a charity for the free distribution of food to hill farms in the spring; this, under the name of *pain de mai*, May-bread, was continued until the French Revolution. But Peter was apparently never really happy outside a monastery, for we are told that in 1155 he disappeared for a year and was found hiding in a remote Swiss abbey. He often visited the Grande Chartreuse, where he was looked after by a young monk later to be known as ◊ *St Hugh of Lincoln*. Peter's activity on behalf of Pope Alexander III against the antipope Victor led to his being commissioned to treat between Louis VII of France and Henry II of England; it was at this time that he died. Another Peter of Tarentaise became Pope Innocent V, who is a *beatus*.

PETER BAPTIST ◊ under *Japan, Martyrs in*

PETER CANISIUS, theologian. B. at Nijmegen in Holland, 1521; d. at Fribourg in Switzerland, 21 December 1597; cd 1925; f.d. 27 April. Peter Kanis was the son of a burgomaster at Nijmegen. He was sent to the university of Cologne, with the idea of his becoming a lawyer; but he turned to theology and, coming under the influence of the celebrated Jesuit Peter Favre, he entered the Society of Jesus in 1543. Between 1546 and 1562 he became known as a preacher, assisted at the Council of Trent, spent six months with ◊ *St Ignatius of Loyola* in Rome, taught in the first Jesuit school, at Messina, and reformed the university at Ingolstadt in Bavaria; from there he was sent to do similar work at Vienna, where he became a religious power in the city. Father Canisius had already given much attention to strengthening the faith of Roman Catholics in face of Protestanism, and he now began writing with the same object. In 1556 he was made provincial superior of the Jesuits in southern Germany, Austria, and Bohemia; first at Prague and then at Augsburg he worked with his usual astounding energy, founding schools, colleges, and clerical seminaries, preaching, writing, and giving missions (it has been estimated that he travelled 20,000 miles on foot and horseback in thirty years). Later he was stationed at Dillingen in Bavaria, at Innsbruck and finally at Fribourg, where he died.

St Peter Canisius, whom a modern Lutheran theologian referred to as 'a noble Jesuit, of faultless character', was an outstanding figure in the Catholic revival that followed the Council of Trent and he did more than any other single man to keep the south German peoples in the Roman Catholic church; he was also one of the exceptions among the controversialists of those days in that he was courteous, moderate, and understanding. He early realized the influence of pen and press, and gave every encouragement to printers and publishers; his own numerous writings caused him to be named a doctor of the church when he was canonized at Rome in 1925. His best-known works by far are the three catechisms of Christian doctrine for pupils of different ages: they had an immense diffusion in many languages, English and Scots versions being made in the author's lifetime and a Welsh one soon after his death.

J. Brodrick, *St Peter Canisius* (1963).

PETER CELESTINE ◊ *Celestine V*

PETER CHANEL, martyr. B. at Cuet near Belley, 1803; d. on Futuna, 1841; cd 1954; f.d. 28 April. The missionary Society of Mary was formed at Lyons in 1822 and one of its earliest members was a peasant's son, a young priest named Peter Chanel. He had for three years worked with good effect in a run-down country parish when in 1831 he was accepted as a member by the Marists. In 1836 the society was allotted the New Hebrides in the Pacific as a field for evangelization, and Father Chanel was one of the group of missionaries sent there. He was stationed on Futuna, an island where cannibalism had only recently been forbidden by the local ruler, Niuliki; with him were a laybrother and an English layman, Thomas Boog. They were at first well received; but, when Father Chanel had learned something of the language and gained the people's confidence, jealousy and fear were aroused in Niuliki. This was aggravated by the conversion and baptism of his son and other young men. Three years after his arrival, when his companions were away, Father Chanel was set upon by Niuliki's men and clubbed to death. When called on to justify his conversion, one of Chanel's catechumens had said of him, 'He loves us. He does what he teaches. He forgives his enemies. His teaching is good.' St Peter Chanel was the first martyr in the South Seas.

PETER CHRYSOLOGUS, bishop. B. at Imola, c. 400; d. there, c. 450; f.d. 4 December. Although St Peter Chrysologus ('golden speech') is included among the doctors of the church, since 1729, very little indeed is known about his life and all his writings have perished except a large collection of short sermons. There is no account of him earlier than nearly 400 years after his death, and little reliance can be put on it. He was made bishop of Ravenna c. 435, and was one of those who received a letter from the monophysite leader Eutyches protesting at his condemnation by ◊ St Flavian of Constantinople; in his reply Peter urged Eutyches not to cause dissension in the church and referred him to the teaching authority of the bishop of Rome. The sermons of Chrysologus are nearly all on gospel subjects, simple, practical, and clear, but without that eloquence that his surname suggests.

PETER CLAVER, missionary to Negro slaves. B. at Verdú in Catalonia, 1580; d. at Cartagena, 'in the Indies', 1654; cd 1888; f.d. 9 September. It was the old hall-porter at the Monitesión college in Majorca, ◊ St Alphonsus Rodriguez, who dispelled the young Jesuit Peter Claver's nervousness of being a priest and directed his attention to the religious needs of the New World. In 1610 Claver landed at Cartagena in what is now Colombia; he came under the influence of Father Alonso de Sandoval, another Jesuit who devoted his life to the local slaves; and after his ordination in 1616 Claver began the work that was to last for thirty-three years, summed up in his own words as being 'the slave of the Negroes for ever'. The slave-trade inflicted atrocious sufferings on its innocent African victims, whose religious squalor and neglect matched their physical state. Father Claver was at their beck and call from the moment a slave-ship docked at Cartagena; his mission was to relieve them and to redeem them (the number he baptized was enormous), and he worked in conditions that were often almost as terrible for him as for them. He did all he could to follow up the slaves at the mines and plantations to which they were allotted, and the opposition he encountered came from others as well as heartless slave-owners; but at least one Spanish lady, Isabel de Urbina, never ceased to help and encourage him. Father Claver also spent much time at the city jails, whose inmates included prisoners of the Inquisition. It is said that Claver had 'a great esteem' for the Inquisition, but he also had a deep compassion for the unhappy people – many of them Portuguese – who incurred its suspicion. He interested himself too in numbers of Englishmen and other foreigners, captured off marauding ships. His work in the hospitals aroused great admiration among his contemporaries; his care for the sick and diseased, whether white or black, showed extraordinary control over natural repulsions, but was often manifested in ways that now seem gratuitous and offensive.

A fellow Catalan said of St Peter Claver that 'unfortunately for himself he is a Catalan, pigheaded and difficult' (he also had the Catalan characteristic of fondness for music). But his defence of the destitute and oppressed against the rich and powerful needed strength of will and self-mastery as well as personal humility. His spirit was unbroken even by the shocking last four years of his life when, half paralysed and in constant pain, he was left in a small room, alone and ignored. A servant who had been told to look after him neglected the old man and treated him unkindly; ironically enough, the servant was a Negro. Claver did not complain: 'My sins deserve more punishment than this.' From the day of his death St Peter Claver was never again forgotten.

A. Valtierra, *Peter Claver* (1960).

PETER DAMIAN, theologian and reformer. B. at Ravenna, 1007; d. at Faenza, 1072; f.d. 23 February. Left an orphan when young, he was first in the charge of an unsympathetic elder brother and then of another brother, who had him well educated in the schools of Lombardy. In 1035 Peter joined the community of hermits founded by ◊ *St Romuald* at Fonte Avellana, of which he became the head. He was essentially a reformer in an age of reform, both as a monk and in his wider activities as cardinal-bishop of Ostia; but he was critical of some of the tendencies of the reforming popes of the time, and he exercised a strong influence in high ecclesiastical affairs. In his ideas about monasticism St Peter Damian always looked back to the example of the early desert monks, and in some respects he was not unlike ◊ *St Jerome* in character, critical, impatient, very outspoken, with the moral fervour of the prophet. His onslaught on clerical misconduct is called 'The Gomorrah Book' with reason; on the other hand he rebuked one bishop merely for playing chess. He wrote on a variety of important theological and canonical subjects and was enrolled among the doctors of the church by Pope Leo XII in 1828 without previous formal canonization. St Peter Damian's intransigence and severity have perhaps been overemphasized;

another side of him can be seen in his hymns, such as those on Heaven and on ◊ *St Gregory the Great*, whom he hails as 'apostle of the English people'.

O. J. Blum, *St Peter Damian* (1947).

PETER EYMARD ◊ under *John-Baptist Vianney*

PETER FOURIER, founder. B. at Mirecourt in Lorraine, 1565; d. at Gray, 1640; cd 1897; f.d. 9 December. He was an Augustinian canon regular at the abbey of Chaumozey, who at the age of thirty-two was appointed parish priest of the village of Mattaincourt in the Vosges; he laboured there for thirty years and his memory is still held in reverence locally as 'the good priest of Mattaincourt'. The parish was in a bad state religiously and otherwise, and the spread of Calvinism was one of the problems. Father Fourier concerned himself with every aspect of his people's needs, slowly effecting many reforms and improvements. He saw that there must be free schooling for children, and he had ideas about education that put him in the same category as ◊ *St Joseph Calasanz* and *St John-Baptist de La Salle*. With boys he failed; but for girls he found a partner in Alix Le Clercq (the process of whose canonization is well advanced), and together in 1598 they began to form the congregation of Augustinian canonesses of our Lady. The difficulties were immense, for the idea of teaching by nuns was still a novelty; the reputation of these canonesses today shows how well Fourier and Mother Alix laid the foundations. From 1622 to 1629 Father Fourier was inspecting the houses of his order in Lorraine and organizing them into a unified congregation, of which he was made superior general; but in 1636 political events caused him to go into voluntary exile, and he died soon after at Gray in Franche-Comté. His body was taken to Mattaincourt for burial.

PETER NOLASCO, founder. D. at Barcelona, 1256; f.d. 28 January. This Peter, said to have been a native of Languedoc, devoted his life to the rescue of captives from among the Moors, who were then in occupation of much of Spain; with this object he founded the Order of our Lady of Ransom ('Mercedarians') between 1218 and 1234. There is a deficiency of reliable documents about the life of St Peter and the beginnings of his order, and very little certain information is to be had; according to some writers ◊ *St Raymund of Peñafort* was co-founder of the Mercedarians with Nolasco. Equally obscure is the true history of *St Raymund Nonnatus* (d. 1240; f.d. 31 August), a Catalan said to have been received as a Mercedarian by St Peter Nolasco, to have voluntarily sold himself into slavery in Algiers to save others, and to have been made a cardinal at Rome in 1239. The explanation given for his curious nickname, Nonnatus, 'not born', is that he was taken from his mother's womb after her death in labour; accordingly he was looked on as a patron saint of midwives.

PETER ORSEOLO, doge of Venice. B. near Udine, 928; d. at Cuxa in Roussillon, 987; f.d. 10 January. In 976 the doge of Venice, Peter IV Candiano, was killed in a riot provoked by his attempt to set up a monarchy. In his place there was elected a member of the powerful Orseoli family, also named Peter (according to ◊ St Peter Damian, Orseolo had led a conspiracy against Candiano, but the statement is not verified). He had distinguished himself as a soldier, and he now showed high quality as a statesman in restoring order to Venice, and generosity in his treatment of the widow of Peter IV. Then in the autumn of 978 Peter Orseolo, without the knowledge even of his wife and son, left Venice and made his way to the monastery of Cuxa in the foothills of the Pyrenees. He was always of religious disposition and there is evidence which suggests he may have been meditating thus retiring from the world for a long time. After a few years in the monastery he became a hermit near by, doubtless encouraged thereto by ◊ St Romuald when he was at Cuxa. Forty years after his death St Peter Orseolo was officially recognized as a saint by the local bishop.

PETROC, abbot. Sixth century; f.d. 4 June. The large number of relevant ancient church-dedications and place-names in Devon and Cornwall and traces in Wales suggest that St Petroc (Pedrog) was of outstanding importance among the British Celtic saints. The medieval written Lives and other documents contain much fanciful matter and folklore, Cornish and other; but the available evidence in general gives support to the tradition that he emigrated from South Wales and landed in the Camel estuary, where Padstow became the chief centre of his monastic and missionary activities. In later life he is said to have withdrawn to a hermitage on Bodmin Moor. By the eleventh century Bodmin had become the centre of his cultus. The Augustinian canons regular there claimed to have his relics; in 1177 a disgruntled canon stole these relics and presented them to the abbey of Saint-Méen, near Rennes in Brittany: it took the intervention of King Henry II to get them back. However, the name of St Petroc was known among the Bretons before this disconcerting visit of his bodily remains to their land.

PHERBUTHA ◊ under Simeon Barsabba'e

PHILEAS, martyr. D. at Alexandria, c. 305; f.d. 4 February. He was bishop of Thmuis in Lower Egypt and a man of distinction and learning. While in prison for his faith at Alexandria he wrote a letter to his flock, describing the sufferings of the Alexandrian

Christians. He was put to death shortly after, together with an official, St Philoromus, who had protested to the prefect against the efforts made to make St Phileas apostatize. They both rejected the magistrate's appeal that they should save their lives by compliance for the sake of their wives and children. The extant account of their examination in court was most probably written up from the notes of an eye-witness.

PHILIBERT, abbot. B. in Gascony; d. at Noirmoutier, 684; f.d. 20 August. Under the influence of ◊ *St Ouen*, Philibert entered the monastery of Rebais of which he became abbot; but the monks were troublesome and he was inexperienced, so he left there to stay at other monasteries in order to remedy this. In 654, on land near Rouen given him by Clovis II and ◊ *St Bathild*, he established his own monastery of Jumièges. Having denounced the West Frankish mayor of the palace, Ebroin, for his misdeeds, Philibert was in 674 imprisoned and then banished; he founded another monastery, Noirmoutier, on an island near the mouth of the Loire, where he lived till Ebroin's death in 681. Philibert founded other houses for monks or nuns, and his example led to a great extension of monasticism in Neustria. Owing to the depredations of the Northmen the body of St Philibert lay in five different places in the thirty-nine years between 836 and 875, before finally coming to rest at Tournus on the Saône.

PHILIP, apostle. First century; f.d. 1 May, with ◊ *St James the Less* (in R.C.ch., 11 May). He was from Bethsaida, and after he had been called to be an apostle he brought Nathanael (◊ *St Bartholomew*) to Christ (John i, 43–49). When certain Greeks wanted to see Jesus it was to Philip they applied (ibid. xii, 20–22); and it was his request at the Last Supper, 'Lord, shew us the Father', that elicited Christ's declaration, 'He that hath seen me hath seen the Father ... I am in the Father, and the Father in me' (ibid. xiv, 8–9). It is possible that Philip preached the gospel in Phrygia and died, whether martyred or not, at Hierapolis, which claimed to have the grave of him and his daughters. Philip the Apostle is sometimes said to have been identical with Philip the Deacon, who occurs several times in the Acts of the Apostles; but this view appears to be mistaken.

PHILIP ◊ under *Felicity*

PHILIP OF HERACLEA, bishop and martyr. D. at Adrianople, 304; f.d. 22 October. At the time of Diocletian's persecution this Philip was the aged and revered bishop of Heraclea in Thrace. When his church was closed by the police he simply told them that God dwells in men's hearts, not within walls, and summoned the brethren for worship in the open air. He was ordered by the governor, Bassus, to hand over the church's sacred vessels and books: to the first Philip agreed, but, for the Scriptures, 'It is not fitting', he said, 'that you should ask for them or that I should give them up.' The bishop and his deacon, Hermes, were then scourged and the wanted goods seized. Afterwards Philip and Hermes refused in turn to make an act of worship of the emperors or of the goddess Fortune or of Heraclea's name-deity, Hercules. Later there was a fruitless interrogation by Bassus' successor, Justin, after which Philip was dragged back to jail by his feet. Together with Hermes and a priest called Severus he was confined rigorously for seven months, before all three were taken to Adrianople.

Justin interviewed them twice again, and he had Philip unmercifully beaten for his contumacy; they were then sentenced to death by fire. St Philip had been used so badly that he had to be carried to the stake. St Hermes, who was not much better, joked cheerfully and sent a last message to his son: 'Tell him to pay back whatever I owe, and to work hard for his living as I have done, and to behave well to everybody.' When the fire was lit the martyrs praised and gave thanks to God until the smoke suffocated them. St Severus followed them the next day.

PHILIP OF MOSCOW, bishop and martyr. B. at Moscow 1507; d. 1569; cd by the Russ. Orth. ch., 1636; f.d. 9 January. Theodore Kolyshov was a wealthy nobleman, who in his youth probably saw active service as a soldier. In his thirtieth year he entered the monastery of Solovetsk in the White Sea, and was given the name of Philip. He was made abbot in 1547, and distinguished himself not only as a religious superior but also as an agricultural engineer, devising a new system of drainage and irrigation for the monastic lands. In 1565 Abbot Philip was elected metropolitan of Moscow and primate of the Russian church, an office which he foresaw might lead to martyrdom, for the reigning tsar was Ivan IV, called 'the Terrible' or 'the Feared'. Two years had hardly passed when Ivan perpetrated a massacre of political suspects and innocent persons. Philip remonstrated with him privately, but only increased his rage. A few months later, when the tsar came to the cathedral at Moscow for the eucharistic liturgy, Philip openly rebuked him: 'At this altar we are offering a pure and bloodless sacrifice for men's salvation. Outside this holy temple the blood of innocent Christians is being shed. God rejects him who does not love his neighbour. I have to tell you this though I die for it.' The massacre went on, and Philip kept up his protest. Eventually Ivan obtained his deposition from office on absurd charges of sorcery and corrupt living. St Philip was dragged in chains from one place of confinement to another, lastly to the Otrosh monastery near Tver. Here, two days before

Christmas in 1569, he was choked to death with a cushion by an emissary of the tsar.

PHILIP BENIZI, Servite friar. B. at Florence, 1233; d. at Todi, 1285; cd 1671; f.d. 23 August. This St Philip studied medicine in the school of Padua, but soon gave up that profession and became a laybrother with the Servites. He was later admitted to the priesthood, and in 1267 was elected to the headship of his order. The story goes that, when Pope Clement IV died in 1268 and Philip was proposed as a candidate for the papal chair, he fled to the hills and remained in hiding for a time. He assisted at the general council at Lyons in 1274. Under St Philip's leadership the Servite friars made considerable progress; he was a talented and effective preacher, and was especially successful in pacifying the warring cities of northern Italy, where the factional strife of Guelfs and Ghibellines was at its height. While on such a mission at Forlì he was struck in the face by a Ghibelline, *Peregrine Laziosi*. This young man was so startled by St Philip's patient acceptance of the blow that he changed his ways, joined the Servites, and led a life of humility and care for others. Peregrine lived till 1345, and was cd in 1726 (f.d. 1 May).

D. B. Wyndham Lewis, *A Florentine Portrait* (1959).

PHILIP NERI, reformer and founder. B. in Florence, 1515; d. in Rome, 1595; cd 1622; f.d. 26 May. The man who was to be called 'the apostle of the city of Rome' was a son of a Florentine notary of good family. Philip was given a good education and then apprenticed in a relative's business; but he had come under the influence of the Dominicans at San Marco, where Savonarola had been a friar within living memory, and of the Benedictines of Monte Cassino, and at the age of eighteen he left the business and went to Rome. There he lived as a layman for seventeen years, at first earning his living as a tutor, writing poetry and studying philosophy and theology. Rome was at that time in a very demoralized state, and from 1538 Philip Neri began to devote himself to work among the young men of the city; he founded a brotherhood of laymen who met together for worship and to give help to pilgrims and the convalescent sick, which gradually developed into the great Trinity hospital. He spent much time in prayer, especially at night and in the catacomb of St Sebastian, where in 1544 he experienced an ecstasy of divine love which is believed to have left a permanent physical effect on his heart.

In 1551 Philip Neri was ordained priest, and went to live at the clergy house of San Girolamo, where he soon made a name as a confessor, being credited with the gift of reading hearts. But his principal work was still with young men. An oratory was built over the church, where religious addresses and discussions took place and enterprises for relief of the sick and needy organized. Here too were first held services consisting of a musical composition on a biblical or other religious theme, sung by solo voices and a chorus (hence the name *oratorio*). Other young clergy assisted St Philip, and by 1575 he had formed these into the Congregation of the Oratory; for this society, whose members do not take the vows which bind religious orders and congregations, he built a new church, the Chiesa Nuova, at St Mary's 'in Vallicella'. He became known throughout the length and breadth of Rome, and his influence over the Romans of his day, from the lowest to the highest, was incalculable.

But St Philip did not escape criticism and opposition: some were shocked by the unconventionality of his speech and actions and of his missionary methods. He sought to restore healthy and vigorous life among the Roman Christians quietly, working from within; he was not clerically-minded – the path of perfection was for lay people as much as for clergy and monks and nuns; he preached more about love and spiritual integrity than about physical austerity; the virtues that shone in him were impressed on others: love of God and man, humbleness and sense of proportion, gentleness and gaiety – 'laughter' is a word of frequent occurrence where St Philip Neri is concerned. Like ◊ *St Thomas More*, he is notably marked by that cheerfulness which is supposed to distinguish every saint, but which is more apparent in some than in others.

L. Poncelle and L. Bordet, *St Philip Neri and the Roman Society of his Times* (1932); Meriol Trevor, *Apostle of Rome* (1966).

PHILOMENA. In 1802 there were found in a burial-niche in the catacomb of Priscilla at Rome the bones of an adolescent girl. Archaeological indications were interpreted as proving that they were the remains of an early martyr, Philomena (Filumena) by name. In 1805 these relics were given to the parish priest of Mugnano, near Naples, who enshrined them in his church. At once there began an enthusiastic local veneration of the unknown martyr, and miracles and other answers to prayer were attributed to her intercession; among others, ◊ *St John Vianney* in France had an important part in popularizing the cult, which became widely diffused. In due course a purely fictitious account of Philomena's martyrdom was produced, to make up for the absence of any historical information or reference. Pilgrimages to Mugnano multiplied, churches were dedicated under the name of St Philomena, virgin martyr, and in certain places Mass was allowed to be celebrated in her honour on her feast day, 11 August; but her name was not added to the Roman Martyrology.

Meanwhile the science of archaeology was not at a standstill, and by the early years of the twentieth century scholars in the pertinent disciplines were practically unanimous that the bones found were not those of the Philomena named in the inscription, and that there was no good evidence that they were those of a martyr. For those who knew the facts the continuance of the cultus was therefore something of a scandal: for it was not a matter of some obscure or half-forgotten saint but of one for whom veneration was lively and widespread. At length in 1961 the pertinent authority in Rome ordered that the feast of Philomena was to be discontinued, the shrine at Mugnano dismantled, and her name expunged from any calendar in which it appeared.

On 5 July the Roman Martyrology names a different *St Philomena*, the story of whose cultus at San Severino in Italy is equally unsatisfactory and has remarkable points of resemblance to the above.

PHILOTHEUS ◊ *Hipparchus and Philotheus*

PHOCAS, martyr. Date unknown; f.d. 22 September. There was an early martyr named Phocas, who suffered at Sinope in Pontus, on the southern shore of the Black Sea; his sanctuary was there and he was widely venerated. That is all that can be safely stated. A panegyric of him preached by Bishop Asterius at Amaseia in Pontus early in the fifth century gives an account of him, but little reliance can be put on it. It tells that Phocas was a market-gardener at Sinope. One day soldiers called at his cottage; they had orders, they said, to kill a Christian named Phocas: where did he live? Phocas invited them to stay the night, and he would direct them in the morning. They did so, and during the night Phocas dug a grave in his garden. On the morrow he disclosed to his guests that he was Phocas; they carried out their orders, very regretfully. Already before the time of Asterius sailors in the Black Sea, the Aegean, and the Adriatic sang chanties in honour of their patron St Phocas; the incongruity of a gardener as a marine patron saint is not unexampled, as in the case of the younger St Simeon, who lived on top of a pillar.

St Phocas, bishop of Sinope (f.d. 14 July), and *St Phocas of Antioch* (f.d. 5 March), both called martyr, appear to be legendary figures derived in devious ways from the gardener.

PHOTIUS, bishop. B. at Constantinople, *c.* 810; d. there, *c.* 891; cd by the Orth. ch.; f.d. 6 February. Photius, a member of a Byzantine patrician family, was a man of very great ability and learning who until middle life followed a career of scholarship and public service at the imperial court, where he was secretary of state and filled other offices. Then, in 858, Emperor Michael III banished the patriarch Ignatius, and Photius, who up 'till then was a layman, was made patriarch in his place. From then on the life of Photius is the story of the difficulties between him and Pope ◊ *St Nicholas I* and his successor Adrian II, complicated by the fluctuations of Byzantine politics – a long, complex, and often obscure struggle which is a matter of general ecclesiastical history. It did not came to an end till 879 when, Ignatius being dead, Pope John VIII recognized Photius as legitimate patriarch of Constantinople and peace was restored between the churches. For Eastern Orthodox Christians St Photius was the standard-bearer of their church in its disagreements with the pope of Rome; to Roman Catholics he was a proud and ambitious schismatic: the relevant work of scholars over the past generation has done not a little to modify partisan judgements. All agree on the virtue of his personal life and his remarkable talents, even genius, and the wide range of his intellectual aptitudes: Pope Nicholas himself referred to his 'great virtues and universal knowledge'. Of his extensive writings the one of most general interest is the *Bibliotheca* or *Myriobiblion* (Eng. trans.), descriptions and summaries of 279 books of all kinds, including extracts from works whose text is no longer in existence. His *Mystagogy of the Holy Spirit* is important as the classical statement of Greek objections to the doctrine of the Holy Spirit's proceeding from the Father and the Son (Filioque).

The patriarch *Ignatius* whom Photius replaced figures as a saint in both Eastern and Western calendars (d. 877; f.d. 23 October). He was an upholder of the rigorist party in the Byzantine church, opposing the influence of the imperial court and its clergy in ecclesiastical affairs. In 857 he refused communion to Michael III's uncle, Bardas, who was accused of living in incest; this action helped to provide Ignatius's opponents with a pretext for getting rid of him. At the time of his death St Ignatius was under a cloud at Rome because of his failure to withdraw Greek missionaries from Bulgaria, where Pope John VIII claimed jurisdiction.

PIONIUS, martyr. D. at Smyrna, 250; f.d. 11 March. Pionius was a priest, a well-read and eloquent man, travelled and high-spirited, not disposed to suffer knaves or fools gladly. He was arrested, with a freedwoman named Sabina and another man, Asclepiades, after celebrating the anniversary of Smyrna's ◊ *St Polycarp*. They were called on to sacrifice to the gods, whereat Pionius explained to the crowd why they refused, and some lively heckling followed. At their two examinations, and when confronted by an apostate bishop at the altar of a pagan temple, Pionius spoke with quick wit and learned allusions; but he was excitable, and was told not to be so noisy. 'Don't you be so rough,' he retorted.

'Light a fire, and we will walk into it.' When he detected a breach of legal procedure he threw himself to the ground in protest, and struggled so violently that it took half-a-dozen men to overpower him. Finally the proconsul lost patience: 'You', he said, 'are like one of those men who would rather face wild beasts than pay a small debt. You are determined to die, so you shall be burnt.' What happened to his two companions is not recorded, but St Pionius suffered in the stadium, after a last refusal to save his life by an act of idolatry. There was martyred with him a priest of the Marcionite sect. St Pionius is one of the men to whom is due the preservation of the text of the letter that describes St Polycarp's martyrdom; he made a copy of it.

PIRAN, or PERRAN, abbot Sixth century (?); f.d. 5 March. It is now generally acknowledged that what is known as the Life of St Piran is nothing but an adaptation of the Life of ◊ *St Ciaran* of Saighir, made during the later middle ages when traditions about the Cornish saint had been lost, and that the identification of Piran with Ciaran is baseless. All that can be said of him is that his centre was probably at Perranzabuloe (Piran-in-the-Sand), south-west of Newquay, where there remains a tiny church, built perhaps only a little after his time. What were claimed to be his relics were kept in the neighbouring parish church, whence they were from time to time carried in procession to other churches during the middle ages. The miners of Breage and Germoe observed Piran's feast day as that of their patron saint until at least 1764. There was a considerable cultus of St Piran in Brittany.

PIUS THE FIFTH, pope. B. at Bosco in Liguria, 1504; d. in Rome, 1572; cd 1712; f.d. 5 May. Michael Ghislieri was of humble origin; at an early age he entered the Dominican order and made rapid progress as teacher and preacher. In 1556 he was appointed bishop of Nepi and Sutri, in 1557 cardinal and inquisitor general, and in 1559 bishop of Mondovì. He vigorously opposed the nepotism of Pope Pius IV, and at the conclave of 1566 was himself elected pope as Pius V, with the strong support of ◊ *St Charles Borromeo*. In his personal life he continued to be a devout mendicant friar; as pope he set himself to enforce the reforming decrees of the Council of Trent with energy and effect. His was a rigorous character; he made full use of the Inquisition and his methods of combating Protestantism were ruthless. He was drastic in his measures against such enormities as prostitution and bull-fighting. Pius V had a high estimate of papal power in secular matters, though sometimes showing little talent for dealing with them. In 1570 he declared Elizabeth I of England to be excommunicate and professed to release her subjects from their allegiance to her (it was on St Pius V's feast day, 5 May, 391 years later, that Queen Elizabeth II visited Pope John XXIII in the Vatican). That he also came into conflict with Philip II of Spain shows with what consistency he applied his principles. Although he was criticized for 'wanting to turn Rome into a monastery', St Pius had the respect of the Roman people, who knew his personal goodness and concern for everybody's welfare.

PIUS THE TENTH, pope. B. at Riese in Venetia, 1835; d. in Rome 20 August 1914; cd 1954; f.d. 3 September. Giuseppe Sarto was the second of the ten children of a family in very poor circumstances. His formal education began at the village school; and he was eventually ordained priest in 1858, when he was a year short of the usual minimum age. After seventeen years as curate and rector he was made a canon of Treviso, and in 1884 bishop of Mantua; in 1893 he was promoted to the see of Venice and nominated cardinal; and at the conclave of 1903 Cardinal Sarto was elected pope, taking the name of Pius X. Two outstanding events of his pontificate were the separation of church and state in France and the pope's sweeping decrees against the philosophical and religious movement which was given the unhappily-chosen name of 'Modernism'. In the first, Pius sacrificed ecclesiastical property for the sake of the church's freedom from civil control; in the second, the methods and excesses of lesser men reacted very unfavourably on public estimates of the pope. He was criticized too when it was sought to put a brake on what some regarded as extreme manifestations of social and political action, as when the French 'liberal' movement, called the Sillon, was condemned in 1910; the Action française, of opposite tendency, also was condemned, in 1914, but the decree was not made public until 1926. On the other hand, such important measures of his as the codification of canon law, the reorganization of the Roman ecclesiastical departments (the *curia*), the founding of an institute for scriptural studies, and the revision of the Latin translation of the Bible (the Vulgate) lay outside public controversy.

St Pius X had spent forty-five years in parish and diocesan work; he aspired 'to renew all things in Christ', and at the practical pastoral level his measures were highly beneficent: for instance, the first steps in the reform of public worship (especially its music), the encouragement of frequent, even daily, reception of holy communion, and of its reception by young children. He was essentially the loving, understanding parish priest, and every Sunday when pope he gave a simple address on the day's gospel passage to all comers, in one of the Vatican courtyards. Single-minded goodness and simplicity were his great characteristics, and they are seen in the gift of miracles with which he was credited even while he lived: accounts of healing, bodily or spiritual, that command assent by their very naturalness and simplicity. St Pius wrote in his will 'I was born poor, I have lived poor, and I wish to die poor'; he was embarrassed by Vatican ceremoniousness and certain papal conventions. Immediately on his death, sixteen days after the outbreak of the first world war, there was an insistent popular outcry for his canonization.

R. Merry del Val, *Memories of Pope Pius X* (1939); H. Dal-Gal, *St Pius the Tenth* (1954).

PLACID, monk. Sixth century; f.d. 5 October. When he was a boy, Placid's parents entrusted him to ◊ *St Benedict* to be brought up at Subiaco; there he had a narrow escape from drowning, being rescued by ◊ *St Maurus* in the seemingly miraculous circumstances narrated in ◊ *St Gregory I's Dialogues*. After his death Placid came to be venerated as a holy monk; and then in the twelfth century a legend grew up that he had gone to Sicily and there been martyred at Messina with several companions. The document in which the circumstances are set out is now recognized on all hands as a forgery.

PLAGUE AT ALEXANDRIA, MARTYRS OF THE. D. 262; f.d. 28 February. Reference has been made under ◊ *St Dionysius of Alexandria* to a fearful epidemic there in his time. He wrote afterwards: 'Most of our brethren were prodigal in their love and brotherly kindness. They supported one another, visited the sick fearlessly, and looked after them without stint, serving them in Christ. They were happy to die with them, bearing their neighbours' burdens and taking their disease and pain on themselves, even to the death which they caught from them. They put reality into what we look on as a courteous formula, accepting death as "humble servants" of one another. The best among the brethren died in this way ... Thus to bring oneself to the grave evinced such religious dutifulness and strength of faith that it seemed, indeed, not to fall short of martyrdom itself.' These selfless Christians are entered in the Roman Martyrology on 28 February, with the remark 'The faithful are wont religiously to honour them as martyrs.'

POLYCARP, bishop and martyr. D. at Smyrna, 23 February, c. 155; f.d. 26 January. During his long lifetime St Polycarp must have been an important Christian figure in western Asia Minor; ◊ *St Irenaeus of Lyons* tells us that he had 'known John and others who had seen the Lord', ◊ *St Ignatius of Antioch* on his way to martyrdom wrote a special letter to encourage him when he was a young bishop, and in old age he went to Italy to confer with the bishop of Rome, St Anicetus. After Polycarp's martyrdom his church at Smyrna wrote a long account of his death to the church of Philomelium in Pisidia, and the text of this letter has survived – the first authentic narrative of a Christian martyrdom after that of St Stephen.

Polycarp was betrayed by a servant and arrested one evening at a farm outside Smyrna. He was taken into the city and led before the proconsul in the stadium, where a crowd was assembled for the games. The proconsul urged him to forswear his religion: 'Take an oath by the emperor's guardian spirit; curse Christ.' 'I have served him for eighty-six years and he has done me no wrong,' answered Polycarp; 'How can I blaspheme my king and saviour?' The proconsul's cajoleries and threats had no effect, and the people yelled for the blood of the man 'who destroys our gods'. So, as he had already foretold, Polycarp was ordered to be burnt alive. He uttered a prayer of praise and glory to God, and when he had offered up himself and said Amen the fire was kindled: 'and the flames made a sort of arch, like a ship's sail filled with the wind, and they were like a wall round the martyr's body; and he looked, not like burning flesh, but like bread in the oven or gold and silver being refined in a furnace'. Then the executioner was ordered to stab Polycarp to hasten his end.

The annual festival of St Polycarp, still observed, is the first regular commemoration of a martyr of which there is record.

Narrative of the martyrdom trans. in Ancient Christian Writers series, no. 6 (1957).

PORPHYRY OF GAZA, bishop. B. at Salonika, c. 352; d. at Gaza, c. 420; f.d. 26 February. After years as a monk in the Egyptian desert and the Jordan valley Porphyry went to Jerusalem, where he earned his living as a shoemaker, having sold property he had inherited for the benefit of the poor. At the age of forty his religious reputation led to his being ordained priest, and in 396 he was made bishop of Gaza, where the people were still heathen. They openly resented the initial success of Porphyry's efforts to evangelize them, and he applied to the emperor, Arcadius, for permission forcibly to destroy idols and their temples. Leave was given, and the work was swiftly and violently carried out by imperial troops sent for the purpose. The result was to worsen Porphyry's position. His house was pillaged, he nearly lost his life, and the people of Gaza were at length brought to Christianity only by his patient teaching. These particulars are found in a Life of St Porphyry ascribed to his deacon Mark; but another Life seems to deny the bishop's earlier appeal to force.

Mark's biography is a valuable document for its picture of the last days of paganism around the eastern Mediterranean; it is also a witness to the reverence given at Jerusalem at the end of the fourth century to what purported to be a large piece of the wood of Christ's cross. St Porphyry was for a time custodian of this relic, in connexion with which he was cured of severe illness and forewarned of the burdens that were to be laid on him.

POTAMIAENA, martyr. D. at Alexandria, *c.* 202; f.d. 28 June. In circumstances that are not clear, this maiden repelled attempts on her chastity and was sentenced to be burnt as a Christian. The officer, Basilides, conducting her to execution treated her with consideration and kindness; she thanked him for his courtesy, and told him that when she was dead she would supplicate the Lord in Heaven on his behalf. Her mother, Marcella, suffered at the same time. Shortly afterwards Basilides was arrested as a Christian; he was baptized in prison and martyred by beheading.

POTHINUS, bishop and martyr. D. at Lyons, 177; f.d. 2 June. St Pothinus, their bishop, was the leader of the martyrs of Lyons (◊ under *Lyons*). He was ninety years old, infirm and ill, when he was taken into court through a jeering mob. He stood firm, answering the accusations brought against him, and when the governor asked who the Christian God was he replied, 'If you are worthy, you shall know.' At that Pothinus was repeatedly struck and kicked, and was taken off to prison nearly insensible. He never recovered from this ordeal, dying two days later.

PRIMUS and FELICIAN, martyrs. Date unknown; f.d. 9 June. These two, said to be brothers of a patrician family, were martyred at Nomentum (Mentana), near Rome, and buried on the Via Nomentana. The account of the circumstances is legendary; but they are of interest because they are the first martyrs of whom it is recorded that their bodies were later reburied within the walls of Rome: Pope Theodore I (d. 649) had them taken to the church now called San Stefano Rotondo.

PRISCA or PRISCILLA ◊ under *Tatiana*

PROCOPIUS, martyr. D. 303; f.d. 8 July. This martyr provides a classic example in hagiography of how a simple record of fact can be overlaid with nonsensical legend and eventually lost sight of, altogether or in part. The church historian Eusebius was bishop of Caesarea in Palestine, where Procopius suffered, at the time of the martyrdom. He tells us that Procopius was born at Jerusalem but lived at Scythopolis (Bethshan), where he was a church reader, exorcist, and interpreter of Syriac. He was a man of virtuous and abstemious life, kind, humble, and respected. At the beginning of Diocletian's persecution he was sent with other Christians to Caesarea, where he was brought before the magistrate, Flavian, and ordered to sacrifice to the gods. Procopius refused. Flavian tried to persuade him at least to sacrifice to the emperors. He again refused, quoting Homer: 'It is not good to have several masters: let there be one chief, one king.' This was taken as disrespectful to the emperors, and Procopius was at once put to death by beheading. This happened on 7 July in the first year of the persecution in Palestine, of which Procopius was the first victim.

Eusebius's account of who Procopius was and the circumstances of his death is entirely trustworthy. The legends that subsequently grew up about him take three principal forms. According to the most popular of these, the original name of Procopius was Neanias, born at Jerusalem, and he was made duke of Alexandria by Diocletian, who sent him to proceed against the Christians there. On the way from Antioch Neanias experiences a vision similar to that of ◊ St Paul on the road to Damascus, as a consequence of which he declares himself a Christian. He is taken in chains to Caesarea, where the governor Oulcion has him tortured and imprisoned. He is then baptized in a vision by Christ himself, and given the name of Procopius. Oulcion dies suddenly, and is succeeded by Flavian, with whom Procopius has long arguments, interspersed with bouts of unbelievable torture. At last Flavian pronounces sentence, and Procopius is executed. The narrative is decorated with marvels throughout. With the help of a miraculous cross, Neanias scatters and slays six thousand marauders; his mother, Theodosia, and twelve other noble ladies are suddenly converted and martyred; Procopius is healed overnight of the wounds inflicted by torture, and so on.

It will be noticed that of Eusebius's historical particulars only the names of some persons and places survive; even the hero himself is no longer a humble cleric of Scythopolis but a young heathen officer. The legends are sheer invention, and such was the confusion engendered by them that some compilers of calendars produced three martyrs named Procopius – the cleric, the officer, and an unexplained St Procopius of Persia. That the martyr described by Eusebius was publicly venerated is proved by the existence of shrines in his honour at Caesarea and Scythopolis from at least the fifth and sixth centuries.

H. Delehaye, *The Legends of the Saints* (1962).

PROSPER OF AQUITAINE, theologian. B. in Aquitaine, *c.* 390; d. at Rome after 455; f.d. 7 July. He was a lay theologian of distinction, but very little is known of his life; when first heard of, *c.* 428, he was living among monks in Marseilles. From *c.* 440 he was in Rome, employed in the papal chancery under ◊ St Leo the Great. The chief preoccupation of St Prosper's writing, in both prose and verse, is the upholding of ◊ St Augustine's teaching on grace and the combating of Pelagian tendencies. Perhaps

293

his best-known work, however, is his chronicle, from the creation of the world to the year 455. The treatise on God's universal saving will, entitled *De vocatione omnium gentium*, 'The Call of All Nations', has been published in English (1950), as well as his writings in 'Defence of St Augustine' (1963). It appears likely that in earlier life Prosper was married, for there is a poem addressed to a wife which many scholars attribute to him, rather than to ◊ *St Paulinus of Nola*; it is translated among the works of Henry Vaughan, 'the Silurist' (who ascribes it to Paulinus), 'Come, my true Consort in my joys and cares. . . .' St Prosper of Aquitaine has sometimes been wrongly identified with his contemporary, *St Prosper of Reggio*, who was a bishop in Emilia (f.d. 25 June); the Roman Martyrology still perpetuates this mistake.

PROTASE ◊ *Gervase and Protase*

PROTUS and HYACINTH, martyrs. Date unknown; f.d. 11 September. St Hyacinth is unique among Roman martyrs in that his epitaph and grave in the cemetery of Basilla on the Old Salarian Way were found intact in modern times (1845); in it were the charred bones of the martyr, who had been put to death by fire. Part of the empty tomb of St Protus was also found. Nothing more is known of them; the legend associating them with ◊ *St Eugenia* is wholly fictitious.

PULCHERIA, empress. B. at Constantinople, 399; d. there, 453; f.d. 10 September. In 414 the princess Pulcheria became regent for her young brother, the Byzantine emperor Theodosius II, a position that she filled with energy and ability. After Theodosius's marriage in 421 she continued, with some intervals, to exert good influence over him. She succeeded to the throne at his death in 450, and ruled as joint sovereign with the capable general Marcian, whom she married (as a young woman she had made a vow of celibacy; the marriage was a nominal one). The events of St Pulcheria's life belong to general secular and ecclesiastical history. Religiously, she was deeply devout, an active opponent of Nestorianism and Monophysism, and a great benefactress of the church and charitable causes. As a gesture of amends for her parents' bad treatment of ◊ *St John Chrysostom*, she in 438 had his bodily remains brought from Comana and enshrined in the church of the Apostles at Constantinople. Edward Gibbon wrote of Pulcheria: 'She alone, among all the descendants of the great Theodosius [I], appears to have inherited any share of his manly spirit and abilities.'

R

RADEGUND, queen. B. at Erfurt, 518; d. at Poitiers, 587; f.d. 13 August. As a child Radegund was carried off from her home in Thuringia by invading Franks, and at about the age of twenty was forced into marriage with King Chlotar I, a man of shocking character. She endured him with exemplary patience for some ten years, till his murder of her brother *c.* 550, when she left him. At Noyon she induced a bishop to take the risk of making her a deaconess, and soon after she established a nunnery at Poitiers. It was known as Holy Cross, the rule was that given by ◊ *St Caesarius* to the nuns of Arles, and here St Radegund made her home for the rest of her life. A close friendship came about between her and the poet Venantius Fortunatus, who became the nuns' chaplain; the gift to the convent of a reputed relic of Christ's cross was the occasion of his great hymns *Vexilla regis* and *Pange, lingua, gloriosi lauream certaminis* ('The royal banners forward go' and 'Sing, my tongue, the glorious battle'). Fortunatus loved to praise people, and he wrote of St Radegund: 'human eloquence is struck almost dumb by the piety, self-denial, charity, sweetness, humility, uprightness, faith, and fervour in which she lived.'

F. Brittain, *St Radegund* (1925).

RAINELD ◊ under *Gudula*

RAPHAEL THE ARCHANGEL ◊ under *Michael the Archangel*

RAYMUND NONNATUS ◊ under *Peter Nolasco*

RAYMUND OF PEÑAFORT, canonist. B. at Peñafort, in Catalonia, *c.* 1175; d. at Barcelona, 1275; cd 1601; f.d. 23 January. He joined the Dominican friars in 1222, after an already distinguished academic and preaching career at Barcelona and Bologna. In 1230 he was called to Rome, where he made the collection of conciliar and papal decrees which continued to be a standard work in use among canon lawyers for nearly 700 years; this was followed by the publication of an authoritative work on penitential discipline, the *Summa casuum*. In 1236 St Raymund returned to Spain and, after two years as master general of his order, devoted himself to the conversion of Moslems and Jews. In this connexion he encouraged ◊ *St Thomas Aquinas* to write his *Summa contra gentiles* and established schools for the teaching of Arabic and Hebrew. It is claimed that St Raymond had an important part, with ◊ *St Peter Nolasco*, in the founding of the Mercedarian order, but the truth of the matter is difficult to get at for want of reliable documents. He died in about his hundredth year.

REMI, bishop. B. near Laon, *c.* 438; d. at Rheims, 13 January, *c.* 533; f.d. 1 October. Remi (Remigius), son of a count of Laon of Gaulish descent, was appointed bishop of Rheims at the extraordinary age of twenty-two. The greatest external event in his long life was his baptism of Clovis I, king of the Franks. Traditionally this was in consequence of the influence of the king's Christian wife, St Clotilda, and of his victory over the Alemanni at the battle of Tolbiac, the baptism taking place at Rheims on Christmas day in 496. The true year and place are much disputed; but it certainly happened about that time and it was an event of great importance in French history. Not much else is known of St Remi, except that he was a zealous evangelizer of the Franks: 'by his signs and miracles,' it was said, 'he brought low the heathen altars everywhere.' ◊ *St Sidonius Apollinaris*, who knew him, testifies to his virtue and his eloquence as a preacher.

RENÉ GOUPIL and JOHN LALANDE, martyrs. B. in France; d. in North America, 29 September 1642, 19 October 1646; cd 1930; f.d. 26 September. These are the two of the North American martyrs who were *donnés*, lay helpers, of the Jesuit missionaries, and both were companions of ◊ *St Isaac Jogues*. Goupil, who had studied surgery, had had to leave the Jesuit noviceship because of ill-health; so he went to Quebec at his own expense, and there volunteered for the mission field. He shared Jogues' period of captivity at Ossernenon (Auriesville, N.Y.), suffered the same tortures, and was tomahawked for making the sign of the cross on the head of an Indian child. He was the first of the whole group to be killed. John Lalande, a native of Dieppe, suffered death at the same place four years later, the day after Father Jogues.

RHIPSIME and GAIANA, martyrs. B. in Armenia, *c.* 312 (?); f.d. 29 September. These two maidens and their companions have long been venerated as the first martyrs of the Armenian church, but no trustworthy particulars of them have survived. Their legend, associated with that of ◊ *St Gregory the Enlightener*, is wholly without historical value. It relates that Gaiana was the leader of a group of dedicated women at Rome, who fled together because one of their number, Rhipsime, had attracted the attention of Emperor Diocletian. They arrived eventually in Armenia, only to encounter the same trouble with King Tiridates. When Rhipsime repulsed him too he had the whole community put to the sword. One form of the legend says there was a single survivor, who became the ◊ *St Nino* who is honoured in Georgia. It is possible that they were really local martyrs under Maximinus Daia.

RICHARD OF CHICHESTER, bishop. B. at Droitwich, 1197; d. at

Dover, 1253; cd 1262; f.d. 3 April. Richard Wych, or 'of Wich', studied at Oxford, and perhaps at Paris and Bologna; in 1235 he became chancellor of his university, but was soon called away to be chancellor to ◊ *St Edmund of Abingdon* at Canterbury. He went with Edmund into exile and after his death was ordained priest in France; soon after his return to England he was elected bishop of Chichester, in 1244. This meant the rejection of King Henry III's candidate for the see, and it was not till 1246 that Richard was allowed to take full possession of it. He was a reforming prelate, of the stamp of his friends St Edmund and Robert Grosseteste of Lincoln, merciless towards simony and nepotism, of simple personal habits, generous in his charities, strict with his clergy, and happy among the humbler people of his flock; even before his troubles with the king were resolved he had succeeded in holding synods to legislate against abuses. St Richard died in the Maison Dieu at Dover, the day after consecrating a new church there in honour of his master, St Edmund. His biography was written by one of his clergy, Ralph Bocking.

M. R. Capes, *Richard of Wyche* (1913).

RITA OF CASCIA, nun. B. near Spoleto, 1381; d. at Cascia, 1457; cd 1900; f.d. 22 May. It is related of this saint that she wished to be a nun but deferred to her parents' wishes and married. For nearly twenty years she lived with exemplary patience with a husband who was rough, ill-tempered, and profligate. He came to a violent end and, after much difficulty, Rita gained admittance to a convent of Augustinian nuns at Cascia in Umbria, where she lived to the end of her days. A number of supernatural happenings are reported in her life, and she has a considerable popular cultus. But the earliest extant biography of St Rita was not written till nearly 150 years after her death, and it must be recognized that the details of her story are not well attested.

ROBERT OF CHAISE-DIEU ◊ under *Gerald of Aurillac*

ROBERT OF MOLESME, abbot. B. near Troyes, *c.* 1027; d. at Molesme, 1111; f.d. 29 April. Robert had a long experience of monastic life in several houses, trying with varying degrees of success or failure to promote the observance of a stricter interpretation of the Benedictine rule. About 1075 he established a monastery at Molesme in Burgundy; but it did not develop quite as he had hoped, and in 1098, with ◊ *St Alberic, St Stephen Harding*, and others of his monks, he emigrated to the forest of Cîteaux, near Dijon, and started over again. After only eighteen months it was arranged that Robert should leave Alberic and Stephen to carry on at Cîteaux and himself return to Molesme, which he governed till his death at a great age. To St Robert belonged the honour of being a founder and the first of the abbots of Cîteaux; his companions prepared the way for the great Cistercian movement carried on by ◊ *St Bernard*.

ROBERT OF NEWMINSTER, abbot. B. at Gargrave in Yorkshire; d. at Newminster, 1159; f.d. 7 June. After being parish priest of his native place, this Robert joined the Benedictines of Whitby, and later was one of those monks who at Fountains were accepted by ◊ *St Bernard* of Clairvaux into the Cistercian order. In 1139 Robert was chosen abbot of a new Cistercian foundation at Newminster, near Morpeth in Northumberland, from whence in due course he established other new houses at Pipewell in Northamptonshire and Roche and Sawley in the West Riding. He was a close friend of the hermit ◊ *St Godric* at Finchale, and a model monk and abbot.

ROBERT BELLARMINE, theologian. B. at Montepulciano, 1542; d. at Rome, 17 September 1621; cd 1930; f.d. 13 May. Roberto Bellarmino was one of the ablest and most effective of the theologians of the Roman Catholic church in its conflict with Protestantism; the impact of his polemical work was the greater because of his temperate spirit and the saintliness of his character. He entered the Jesuit order in 1560, and first came into living contact with Protestant teaching ten years later, when he was a professor and preacher at Louvain. Among his activities at the university there were the promotion of the study of Hebrew and preparatory work for revision of the Vulgate text of the Bible. Bellarmine's career as a controversialist began with the period from 1576, when he was teaching and writing at the Roman College, of which he was made rector in 1592; in 1599 he was appointed cardinal, and from 1602 to 1605 he was archbishop of Capua. At the two conclaves in this last year there was some possibility of his being elected pope. Among his very varied activities he entered into debate with King James I of England, Bishop Lancelot Andrewes, and the Scottish jurist William Barclay on the subject of kingly authority; and he was a moderating influence in the affair of Galileo, with whom he was on friendly terms.

In his later years St Robert Bellarmine wrote commentaries on the psalms and on Christ's seven 'words' from the cross, and other devotional works; that on the Psalms in particular he declared to be not a burdensome task but a labour of delight. His principal controversial writing was the three volumes of *Disputations* (1586–93), but his two Catechisms had an even wider circulation; his views on papal power in secular affairs, later embodied in a treatise, were too moderate for many and incurred the disapproval of Pope Sixtus V. Already between 1602 and 1638 several of Bellarmine's catechetical and ascetical writings were published in English (and one in Welsh), some editions being printed secretly in England. The old idea of St Robert Bellarmine as of cold and distant character was finally dispelled by the publication in 1899 of his 'domestic exhortations' to his Jesuit brethren, begun when he was a young man. Since his long-delayed canonization in 1930 he has ranked among the doctors in the Roman Catholic church.

J. Brodrick, *Robert Bellarmine, Saint and Scholar* (1961).

ROCH ◊ *Rock*

ROCK, healer. Fourteenth century; f.d. 16 August. St Rock seems to have been a native of Montpellier in Languedoc who nursed the sick during an epidemic in northern Italy. Legendary accounts of him say he was on pilgrimage to Rome when the plague began, and that he went from place to place healing the victims by supernatural means; when he was himself stricken at Piacenza he was first succoured by a dog. He recovered, and got home safely. But his relatives did not recognize him; he was put in prison as an impostor, and died there. Another account says this happened in Lombardy, where he was taken for a spy. St Rock is still invoked against physical disease in France and, as San Rocco, in Italy. The name is often spelt Roch. In art, he is often represented accompanied by a dog.

ROMANUS and DAVID ◊ *Boris and Gleb*

ROMANUS THE MELODIST, hymn-writer. Sixth century; f.d. 1 October. Romanus was the greatest and most original of the Byzantine hymn-writers. He was a Syrian from Homs, of Jewish origin, who served as deacon at Bairut and then moved to Constantinople. No more is known of his life, and of the thousand hymns with which he is credited only about eighty have survived. They are vivid and dramatic, and great liturgical poetry, but apt to be too long, discursive, and over-elaborate for modern taste. Romanus gave its classical form to the type of hymn called a *kontakion*, of which his first was traditionally the one for Christmas: 'On this day the Maiden gave birth to the Transcendent One. . . .' His subjects range over the Old and New Testaments and the church's festivals.

There are several other saints named Romanus, including a Palestinian deacon martyred at Antioch *c*. 304 (f.d. 18 November).

ROMARIC ◊ under *Arnulf of Metz*

ROMUALD, abbot. B. at Ravenna, *c*. 950; d. at Val di Castro in Piceno, 19 June 1027; cd 1595; f.d. 7 February. St Romuald is said to have 'fled the world' in horror when his father killed a relative in a quarrel about property. He became an important figure among those eleventh-century monks who sought to reform contemporary monasticism in the direction of greater solitude. He eventually left the Cluniac monastery of San Miniato, and for many years went from place to place, preaching the values of the solitary life, and establishing a hermitage here, a community there. The two most important of these foundations were the hermits of Fonte Avellana in the Apennines and the semi-eremitical monastery at Camaldoli, near Arezzo. St Romuald had considerable influence in his time, and after his death Camaldoli became the head of an organized group of houses; these hermit monks still exist as a small independent order of Benedictines. ◊ *St Peter Damian* was a disciple of St Romuald and wrote a biography of him.

ROSE OF LIMA, recluse. B. at Lima, 1586; d. there, 1617; cd 1671; f.d. 30 August. Isabel de Flores y del Oliva, known as Rose, was the first person in the Americas to be canonized as a saint; she was the daughter of Spanish parents in Peru. They were in straitened circumstances, and Rose worked hard to help support them, by growing flowers and doing embroidery and other needlework. She firmly declined to consider marriage; from the age of twenty she was a Dominican tertiary, and lived in a summerhouse in the garden of her home. Here she passed long hours in prayer; her retiringness and the cruelty of the penances she inflicted on herself provoked the criticism of her family and friends, and her mystical experiences and the temptations she suffered became the subject of an ecclesiastical inquiry. St Rose bore her adversities with uncomplaining patience, and her sympathy with the sufferings of others found an outlet in care for the sick poor, Indians, and slaves; she is looked on today as the originator of social service in Peru.

In the generation following there lived at Quito another South American Spanish girl, *St Mariana Paredes y Flores* (d. 1645; cd 1950; f.d. 26 May), whose story very closely resembles that of Rose of Lima. Mariana also ministered to the needy, and taught Indian children in her home: her penitential practices, however, were even more startling than Rose's, so extravagant in fact as to savour of morbid fanaticism. During an epidemic in Quito, Mariana publicly offered her life in expiation of the sins of others, and in fact died soon after. She and St Rose and others like them were simply seeking to follow Christ in his spirit and his sufferings: but the means were not always prudently chosen, and such saints pose delicate questions of religion and psychology.
F. P. Keyes, *The Rose and the Lily* (1962).

RUPERT OF SALZBURG, missionary bishop. D. at Salzburg, *c*. 710; f.d. 27 March. St Rupert appears to have been a Frank by nationality, and was bishop of Worms until the closing years of the seventh century, when he went as a missionary to Regensburg in Bavaria. There and at Altötting he had conspicuous success, and he extended his activities over a wide area along the Danube. His centre was Salzburg, where he founded the church and, getting more helpers from Franconia, built a monastery and a nunnery at the spots now called the Mönchberg and the Nonnberg. St Rupert was a characteristic example of the devoted monastic bishops who evangelized the Germans. An old tradition attributes to him the beginning of salt-mining at Salzburg, which when he took it over was the desolate ruin of the Roman town of Juvavum.

S

SABAS, abbot. B. near Caesarea in Cappadocia, 439; d. at Mar Saba, 532; f.d. 5 December. St Sabas was an outstanding figure among the early monks and his example and teaching had an important influence on the development of Eastern monasticism. As a young man he was a disciple of ◊ *St Euthymius the Great*. After living for years as a solitary and in various ascetical settlements in Palestine, about 478 he founded a *laura* or semi-eremitical community in a wild gorge between Jerusalem and the Dead Sea; it grew and prospered, and in 493 Sabas was given the oversight of all Palestinian monks living a similar life (as distinct from the cenobites). He took an active part in the public ecclesiastical history of his time, and was twice sent on missions to Constantinople by the patriarch of Jerusalem. His biography was written by Cyril of Scythopolis, a careful writer, who when a lad had met Sabas and been very impressed by him. St Sabas's monastery, now called Mar Saba, still exists, one of the oldest occupied monasteries in the world; it is peopled by monks of the Eastern Orthodox church.

SABAS ◊ *Sava*

SABAS THE GOTH, martyr. D. 372; f.d. 12 April. In the year 372 a Gothic ruler north of the Danube was persecuting his Christian subjects and among the victims was this Sabas; an account of him was written in a letter very soon after his death. He was a church reader, apparently at Targoviste in modern Rumania, and after his first arrest was released as an insignificant fellow, 'who can do us neither good nor harm'. Taken a second time, he was knocked about and tied up for the night, but refused a chance to escape. Sabas treated his military captors with defiance and spoke disrespectfully of their commander, who then ordered him to be drowned. He was tied to a pole and held down in the river Buzau till he was dead; 'this death by wood and water,' says the writer of the letter, 'was an exact symbol of man's salvation.'

Another famous Gothic martyr at this time was *St Nicetas*, who was burnt to death (f.d. 15 September). The bodies of both these martyrs were taken into Asia, Sabas to Caesarea in Cappadocia at the request of St Basil, and Nicetas to Mopsuestia in Cilicia; it thus came about that their memory was held in honour in the East.

SADOTH ◊ under *Simeon Barsabba'e*

SAHAK ◊ *Isaac the Great*

SALVATOR OF HORTA ◊ under *Diego*

SAMSON, abbot-bishop. B. in South Wales, *c.* 490; d. at Dol, *c.* 565; f.d. 28 July. It is more than possible that the existing Life of St Samson was written within half a century of his death, which would make it by far the earliest biography of a British Celtic saint. According to it Samson was educated and ordained at ◊ *St Illtyd's* school in Glamorgan; he then went to another monastery (on Caldey Island?) of which he became abbot and, after a visit to Ireland and a period as a hermit at an unidentified place on the banks of the Severn, he was consecrated bishop by ◊ *St Dubricius*. In consequence of a vision, he and other monks together crossed the sea to central Cornwall. After some time there they went to Brittany, where Samson established his monastery at Dol, which afterwards became an important episcopal see. He seems to have interested himself in Jersey and Guernsey (his name is also found in the Isles of Scilly), and he had a part in public affairs, going to intercede with the Frankish king, Childebert I, on behalf of the dispossessed Breton ruler Judual. Many miraculous deeds were attributed to St Samson, and to these the anonymous biographer gives ample space. There are ancient churches dedicated in Samson's honour in Cornwall, Brittany, and elsewhere; recent research tends to show that he was the leading churchman of the colonists from Britain who founded Brittany, and a chief figure in the history of the evangelization of Cornwall and the Channel Islands.

T. Taylor, *The Life of St Samson of Dol* (1925).

SARAPION ◊ *Serapion*

SAVA, bishop. B. *c.* 1175; d. at Trnovo, 1235; f.d. 14 January. Sava (Sabas) is the patron saint of the Serbian people. He was the third son of King Stephen I Nemanya, and in 1191 secretly became a monk on Mount Athos; four years later he was joined there by his father, who had resigned his throne. Together they founded a house for Serbian monks, Khilandari, which still exists as one of the seventeen 'ruling monasteries' on Athos. In 1208 Sava returned to Serbia, where the rivalry of his brothers had led to anarchy. He established himself at Studenitsa, and proceeded to organize the Serbian church properly, using monks who had come with him for pastoral and missionary work among the neglected people. He obtained emancipation from the jurisdiction of the Greek archbishop of Okhrida, and in 1219 was himself consecrated first archbishop of the Serbs by the Byzantine patriarch, then in exile at Nicaea. He took a prominent part also in secular affairs, materially contributing to the integration of the Serbian kingdom under his brother, Stephen II, 'the First Crowned'.

St Sava was always a monk at heart. He had left Mount Athos simply for the sake of his countrymen: 'If you listen to me, and if God enables me to do good among you, if you become holy and one in God, there will be twofold gain and salvation will be ours.' From time to time he would retire to an inaccessible hermitage near Studenitsa to gain strength for perseverance in the tasks he had set himself. He was active to the last, dying at Trnovo in Bulgaria on his way back from a journey in the East, during which he had founded a hospice for Serbian pilgrims to Jerusalem and arranged for the reception of Serbian monks at Mount Sinai and other distant monasteries. St Sava's memory is revered by both Orthodox and Roman Catholics in Yugoslavia.

SCHOLASTICA, dedicated maiden. B. at Norcia, c. 480 (?); d. near Monte Cassino, 543; f.d. 10 February. Practically all the little that is known about ◊ St Benedict's sister (traditionally his twin) is gleaned from ◊ St Gregory the Great's Dialogues. She was dedicated to God at an early age, but probably continued to live in her parents' home. Later on, however, she was living not far from Monte Cassino, whether alone or in a community does not appear; brother and sister used to meet once a year at a house near the monastery. On the last of these occasions, St Gregory tells us, Scholastica implored her brother to stay the night, 'so that we may go on talking till morning about the joys of Heaven'. Benedict would not. Whereupon Scholastica fell to prayer, and so fierce a storm suddenly arose that departure was impossible and she had her way. Three days later St Scholastica died. St Benedict was buried in the same grave with his sister, 'so death did not separate the bodies of these two, whose minds had ever been united in the Lord'.

SCILLITAN MARTYRS, THE. D. at Carthage, 180; f.d. 17 July. This name designates a group of seven men and five women from Scillium in North Africa; their authentic 'acts' is the earliest of such documents in Latin. After their arrest they were taken to Carthage and interrogated by the proconsul Saturninus, St Speratus being their chief spokesman. He was carrying a satchel, and when asked what was in it he answered, 'The sacred books, and the letters of a righteous man named Paul.' All agreed in refusing to give up their beliefs, and the offer of a month's remand in which to change their minds was ignored. They were therefore sentenced to immediate death by the sword, to which Speratus replied for them all, 'Thanks be to God.'

SEBASTIAN, martyr. Date unknown; f.d. 20 January. The name of St Sebastian is one of the best known among those of the early martyrs, in part because of his popularity as a subject among Renaissance painters. But almost nothing is known about him, beyond that he was a martyr, buried on the Appian Way at Rome and commemorated on 20 January. ◊ *St Ambrose* says he was born in Milan, where he was already venerated in the later fourth century.

The traditional story of St Sebastian is simply a romance, and the classic example of a legend which associates with the hero a number of known saints, and others whose existence is at least problematical, without regard to history or chronology. The nucleus of the narrative is that St Sebastian, born in Gaul, was an officer of the imperial guard in Rome under Diocletian; when it was discovered that he was a Christian, he was sentenced to be shot with arrows. The archers left him for dead, but his wounds were healed by the widow of another martyr (St Castulus). On learning this, Diocletian ordered that he be battered to death with cudgels, which was done. St Sebastian's emblem is an arrow.

SEBBI ◊ under *Osyth*

SENAN OF SCATTERY, abbot-bishop. Sixth century; f.d. 8 March. He was the principal of the numerous Irish saints of this name, and is credited with making a remarkable succession of monastic foundations on islands at the mouths of rivers and elsewhere, from the Slaney in Wexford to the coast of Clare. He finally settled on Scattery Island (Inis Cathaig) in the Shannon estuary, where there is still a fine round tower and other early remains. The stories that have survived about St Senan suggest a man of considerable complexity of character. He is said to have visited ◊ *St David* in Wales, but appears to have had no connexion with the Land's End parish of Sennen.

SERAFINO ◊ under *Ignatius of Laconi*

SERAPHIM OF SAROV, mystic. B. at Kursk, 1759; d. at Sarov, 1833; cd by the Russ. Orth. ch., 1903; f.d. 2 January. Prokhor Moshnin was the son of a builder, and in his twentieth year entered the monastery of Sarov; he took the name of Seraphim, and in 1793 was ordained priest. Thereafter his life reads like the story of a desert monk of Egypt in the fourth century. For sixteen years he lived alone in a shack in the neighbouring forest, growing vegetables for food, felling trees, studying the Bible and the writings of the Fathers, and praying continuously. In 1804 he was 'beaten up' by robbers and suffered badly from shock; he was cared for in the monastery for five months and then returned to his solitude. There for some years he in a measure emulated ◊ *St Simeon the Stylite*, spending much of his time in prayer on a high outcrop of rock. By 1810 Father Seraphim's strength was failing, he could no longer get to the monastery on Sundays and feast days. So he was given a small room in the house, where he could live as a recluse within the community. Here he continued to live so far as possible as before, giving help and comfort to all who came to him and directing the nuns of a neighbouring convent. On the second day of 1833 he was found dead on the floor of his cell.

It is said that several times during his life St Seraphim experienced visions of the Virgin Mary and other saints, the last time, in 1832, in the presence of a nun of Diveyevo; and there were attributed to him a number of cures of spiritual and physical ills. Among these, that of Nicholas Motovilov, who for three years had suffered from rheumatism and other complaints, is notable because it led to the beneficiary's writing down a conversation he had with Seraphim on the Holy Spirit in Christian life. This has more than once been published in English. Whatever elements of legend may have gathered round St Seraphim there is no doubt that he was a man of remarkable spiritual and prophetical gifts, who summed up in himself the Russian ideal of the holy monk and elder (*starets*); and the more-than-natural facial transfiguration recorded in the conversation with Motovilov – a spiritual irradiation manifesting itself outwardly in a 'blinding light' – is a phenomenon recorded of other outstandingly holy men and women in both East and West.

V. Zander, *St Seraphian of Sarov* (1973).

SERAPION OF THMUIS, bishop. D. in Egypt, *c.* 365; f.d. 21 March. Of a number of martyrs and other saints called Serapion, or Sarapion, the one whose name occurs most frequently was a bishop of Thmuis, in the Nile delta, in the middle of the fourth century. This is because of a sacramentary, a collection of liturgical texts, ascribed to him, discovered at the end of the nineteenth century. They are prayers intended primarily for the use of a bishop, and are valuable for the knowledge of early public worship in Egypt. In early life St Serapion was a follower of ◊ *St Antony* in the desert, and he was a friend and supporter of ◊ *St Athanasius.* His sacramentary has been published in English.

SERGIUS and BACCHUS, martyrs. D. *c.* 303 (?); f.d. 8 October. Traditionally these two were officers in the Roman army who, for absenting themselves when Emperor Maximian was sacrificing to Jupiter, were martyred at Resapha in Syria, south of the Euphrates. Certainly Sergius was buried at that place, which was renamed Sergiopolis, and it came to be one of the greatest pilgrimage centres of the East. Many churches bore the name of Sergius (sometimes with Bacchus), and his cultus was extraordinarily widespread and popular; the nomads of the desert looked on him as their special patron saint.

SERGIUS OF RADONEZH, abbot. B. at Rostov, *c.* 1314; d. at the Trinity monastery, 1392; cd in Russia before 1449; f.d. 25 September. Sergius and his parents were driven from home by civil war, and had to make a living by farming at Radonezh, north-east of Moscow. When he was twenty he took up a hermit's life, with his brother Stephen, in the neighbouring forest; they were in time joined by others, and what we are told of these hermits is reminiscent of the earliest followers of ◊ St *Francis of Assisi*, especially in their attitude to wild nature – in spite of the climatic and other differences between Umbria and central Russia. A Russian writer has said of their leader that 'he smells of fresh fir wood'. By 1354 they had become monks living a properly communal life; this change provoked disagreement, which might have permanently disrupted the community but for the selfless conduct of St Sergius. This monastery of the Holy Trinity (*Troitsa Lavra*) became to northern Russian monasticism what ◊ St *Theodosius*'s monastery of the Caves was to the Kievan province in the south. Sergius founded other monasteries, directly or indirectly, and his reputation spread far. He refused the metropolitan see of Moscow in 1378, but used his influence to keep the peace among the quarelling princes. When, according to tradition, Dmitry Donskoy, prince of Moscow in 1380, consulted him about continuing his armed revolt against the Tartar overlords, Sergius encouraged him to go on: the great victory at Kulikovo followed.

St Sergius is the most loved of all Russian saints, not simply for his influence at a critical time in Russian history but for the sort of man he was. In character if not by origin he was a 'peasant saint': simple, humble, grave and gentle, 'neighbourly'. He taught his monks that service of others was part of their vocation, and the examples that he held up to them were the men of old who had fled the world but helped their fellow men. Special emphasis was put on personal and communal poverty and the eradication of self-will. St Sergius was one of the earliest Russian saints to whom mystical visions were attributed, of the Blessed Virgin and in connexion with the eucharistic liturgy, and, as with St *Seraphim* of Sarov, a certain physical transfiguration by light was sometimes apparent in him. The people saw in him a chosen man of God, on whom the grace of the Spirit visibly rested. Many of them still go as pilgrims to his shrine in the Trinity monastery of Zagorsk.

N. Zernov, *St Sergius, Builder of Russia* (1939).

SEVEN BROTHERS, THE ◊ under *St Felicity*

SEVEN FOUNDERS, THE, of the Servite Order. Thirteenth century; cd 1888; f.d. 12 February. In the year 1233 a group of seven men, all well-known in the civic life of Florence, established themselves as hermits on Monte Senario not far from that city. This community developed into an order of mendicant friars, the Servants of Mary (Servites), which is still at work in the world. Their first leader was St Buonfiglio Monaldo (d. 1261). Outstanding among them was St Alexis Falconieri, whose modesty made him refuse holy orders. He helped in the foundation of a Servite community at Siena, and served the nascent order in various capacities as a laybrother. He outlived the other original founders, and is said to have been 110 years old when he died in 1310.

SEVEN SLEEPERS, THE. No date; f.d. 27 July. This legend is to the effect that seven young men were walled up in a cave at Ephesus during the Decian persecution (c. 250) and awoke to life again under Theodosius II, two hundred years later (the story is told at length in the *Golden Legend*). The long sleep is a common theme of myth and folklore, and the christianized version of it was already current in the sixth century. The tale was written as a pious romance, perhaps in connexion with controversy about the resurrection of the body; gradually the heroes of it came to be honoured as saints, whose alleged tomb was a place of pilgrimage. Almost as strange as the legend is that these young men should still be entered in the Byzantine church calendar and the Roman Martyrology.

SEVERINUS OF NORICUM, missionary. D. at Favianae, 482; f.d. 8 January. His place of origin is not known, but for a time he was a monk somewhere in the East. After 453 he settled in Noricum (Austria), then in the hands of barbarian settlers. He ministered to the people and proclaimed the gospel along the Danube from Vienna to Passau, establishing the first local monasteries, at Passau and Favianae. St Severinus seems to have gained the respect even of the Hun chieftain Odoacer. After his death his body was taken into Italy, where it finally rested at Naples. – There were other saints of this name – e.g. bishops in the March of Ancona, at Cologne, at Bordeaux (Seurin) – between some of whom there has been confusion.

SEXBURGA ◊ under *Etheldreda*

SHAHDOST ◊ under *Simeon Barsabba'e*

SHUSHANIK ◊ under *Susan*

SIDONIUS APOLLINARIS, man of affairs. B. at Lyons, c. 432; d.

at Clermont, *c*. 482; f.d. 21 August. Sidonius was by turns country gentleman, politician, man of letters, and ecclesiastic. He came of a noble family of Lyons, and married Papianilla, whose father Avitus became Roman emperor for a few months. From *c*. 452 Sidonius was engaged in high politics and public affairs, and about 470 was made bishop of Arvernum (Clermont-Ferrand in Auvergne); he was doubtless a layman at the, time, and he accepted the office reluctantly. He proved a good bishop, and when the Visigoths besieged Clermont he organized its defence; but the city fell in 475, and its captors imprisoned Sidonius for a while. Perhaps the happiest years of his varied life were those spent with his wife and family on his country estates, administering them, hunting and fishing, writing.

Of St Sidonius's writings there have survived twenty-four poems and 147 letters. His verse is uninspired, and some of it too much at the service of politic eulogy; but the letters are of extraordinary interest. In a style often inflated and pedantic, they give a living picture of provincial life and society, characters and events, during the break-up of the Roman empire in the West. An English translation of them was published in 1915.

C. E. Stevens, *Sidonius Apollinaris and his Age* (1935).

SIGFRID, missionary bishop. D. at Växjo, *c*. 1045; f.d. 15 February. St Sigfrid was prominent among the evangelizers of Sweden, but particulars of his work are confused and uncertain. Traditionally he was a priest of York, who with other Englishmen was sent to preach the gospel in Scandinavia. Sigfrid made his centre at Växjo in southern Sweden, and laboured with success in the Småland and Västergötland districts. It is said that it was he who baptized King Olaf Skotkonung.

SILAS. First century; f.d. 13 July. St Silas (Silvanus) was one of the 'chief men among the brethren', a companion and fellow worker with ◊ *St Paul*. He is referred to in the Acts of the Apostles xv, 22–40, xvi, 19–40 and elsewhere; in the epistles to the Thessalonians he is called Silvanus, and he is probably the secretary of that name mentioned in I Peter v, 12. There is a tradition that he died in Macedonia.

SILVANUS ◊ under *Felicity*

SILVESTER THE FIRST, pope. D. in Rome, 335; f.d. 31 December. Silvester, a Roman, was elected bishop of Rome to succeed ◊ *St Miltiades* within a year of peace coming to the Christian church in 313; accordingly, though little is known about him, his name frequently occurs in ecclesiastical history and in later legend. Of legends, the most important is that Emperor Constantine conferred on Silvester and his successors in the see of Rome primacy over all other bishops and temporal dominion over

Italy; this 'donation' has long ago been proved to be a fabrication. The first general council of the church was held at Nicaea in 325; Silvester did not attend in person, but was represented by two legates. He was buried in the cemetery of Priscilla on the Salarian Way, and he was one of the first non-martyrs to be venerated as a saint in Rome.

SILVESTER GOZZOLINI, abbot. B. at Osimo, 1177; d. at Monte-Fano, 1267; f.d. 26 November. This Silvester gave up the study of law to become a priest, and was given a canonry in the cathedral of his native town. He ministered there till he was fifty, when, after rebuking his bishop for the irregularity of his life, he resigned the benefice. After living for four years as a solitary, Silvester in 1231 founded a monastery at Monte Fano, near Fabriano in the Marches. Here he taught a very strict interpretation of the Benedictine rule, and so effectively that at his death a dozen monasteries were acknowledging his leadership. The Silvestrines still exist as a small independent Benedictine congregation.

SIMEON THE STYLITE. B. in Cilicia, *c.* 390; d. at Telanissus, 24 July 459; f.d. 5 January. The elder Simeon was the first and most famous of the pillar ascetics. He was the son of a shepherd, and from early youth subjected himself to ever-increasing bodily austerities, especially in fasting from food. For some twenty years he lived in various hermitages and monasteries in northern Syria. Then in 423 he began to live on a pillar, at Telanissus (Dair Sem'an). At first the pillar was low, but over the years its height was increased to some sixty feet; at the top was a platform, with a balustrade, which is calculated to have been about twelve feet square. There he spent the remainder of his life, thirty-six years. After his death a monastery and sanctuary were built over the spot, and amidst the imposing ruins the base of Simeon's column can still be seen.

The reason given for Simeon's adopting this extraordinary mode of existence was his wish to avoid the press of people who flocked to him for his prayers and advice (it has been amusingly put that, 'despairing of escaping the world horizontally, he tried to escape it vertically'). The contrary of course happened: many more people came to him, whether pilgrims or sightseers, from emperors downwards. Every afternoon he was at their disposal, teaching, exhorting, answering questions. He was full of kindliness and sympathy, and his discourses and instructions were marked by practical common sense and freedom from fanaticism. He was the occasion of many conversions to Christianity, especially among the Beduin Arabs. But his fame spread far beyond Syria, and people who could not make the long journey consulted him by letter. In an age and land of licence and luxury Simeon bore witness to the claims of virtue and selflessness in so striking a fashion that no one could fail to see it.

St Simeon had many imitators in the Near East, some of whom are numbered among the saints, such as ◊ *St Daniel the Stylite* and *St Simeon Stylites the Younger* (d. 592; f.d. 24 May). He is said to have been a stylite near Antioch from a very early age, and was ordained priest on a pillar; the platform at the top was big enough for him to celebrate the Holy Mysteries there, and people went up by ladder to receive communion from his hands. He also had a considerable influence on his contemporaries, and was greatly respected for his knowledge and wisdom.

SIMEON THE NEW THEOLOGIAN, mystic. B. in Paphlagonia, 949; d. at Constantinople, 1022; f.d. 12 March. This Simeon, whose annual festival is observed by the Orthodox church of Constantinpole, was brought up in that city and became a monk in the monastery of Studius. Looking for a stricter life, he migrated to the monastery of St Mamas, and was abbot there for some twenty-five years. Later, having incurred animosity, he organized a new monastery, where he lived out his life in peace. In St Simeon Byzantine mysticism reached its peak; he was in the spiritual tradition of ◊ *St John Climacus* and *St Maximus the Confessor*, and in recent times there has been a marked appreciation of his religious writings among Western students of them; some examples are given in English in E. Kadloubovsky and G. E. H. Palmer's *Writings from the Philokalia* (1951). The title 'new theologian' indicates the place given to Simeon in the East, as a man of God whose writings on divine things put him first among the successors of ◊ *St John* the Evangelist and *St Gregory of Nazianzus*.

SIMEON BARSABBA'E, bishop and martyr. D. at Ctesiphon, 341; f.d. 21 April. The persecution of Christians in Persia under King Shapur II was one of extreme violence and cruelty. Their chief bishop, this Simeon, was accused of treasonable correspondence with the Christian Roman emperor, Constantius II, and of other offences; he was ordered to conform to the Persian religion (Zoroastrianism). He protested his loyalty, but refused to comply: 'The sun,' he said, 'went into mourning when its Creator and Master died on the cross.' So, on a Good Friday, St Simeon and a large number of others were put to death. Some time later his sister, *St Pherbutha* (*Tarbula*; f.d. 22 April), a dedicated virgin, was charged with witchcraft; she, with her sister and another woman, was sawn asunder. Simeon's successors in the see of Seleucia-Ctesiphon were both martyred: *St Shahdost* (*Sadoth*; f.d. 20 February) was tortured and beheaded with many others in 342, and *St Barba'shmin* (f.d. 14 January) followed in 346. After that the see was vacant for nearly forty years; thousands of Christians perished, and many fled abroad during the persecution.

SIMEON SALUS, eccentric. D. at Homs, c. 590; f.d. 1 July. After living for many years as monk and hermit in Palestine, Simeon went to his birthplace, Homs in Syria, and devoted himself to caring for the most wretched and neglected among the people, especially harlots. To share the contempt in which social outcasts were held, he behaved in such strange ways that he was nicknamed 'the crazy' (*salus*). So outrageous did his conduct become, if it was reported correctly, that it seems likely that he was at times really out of his mind. He was treated by some as a hypocritical rascal; but others saw him as a prophetical and holy figure, and in the end this opinion prevailed.

In succeeding ages certain other ascetics were known as 'fools for Christ's sake': men who, by their senseless behaviour and shammed stupidity, deliberately courted humiliation and the scorn of their fellows; for instance, they went about half or even wholly naked. They were especially common in Russia, where in the sixteenth century they had a certain social influence; they appear there again in the nineteenth century. Some of these *yurodivy* were canonized by the Russian church, such as *St Basil the Blessed* (d. 1552; cd c. 1580; f.d. 2 August). He was a shoemaker's apprentice in Moscow; like Simeon Salus, he used to take goods from shops and give them away to the destitute, and there are stories of his rebuking the tsar, Ivan IV the Terrible. Basil gave his name to one of the Kremlin churches, in which he was buried.

SIMON, apostle. First century; f.d. 28 October, with ◊ *St Jude*. This Simon, called 'the Cananaean' and 'the Zealot' (both meaning 'the zealous'), was one of Christ's twelve apostles. Nothing else is known about him for certain. According to later accounts he preached the gospel in Egypt and Persia, and was martyred in Persia, some say together with St Jude.

SIMON ◊ *Peter*; and under *William of Norwich*

SIMON STOCK, Carmelite friar. B. in England; d. at Bordeaux, 1265; f.d. 16 May. A late tradition says that Simon's birthplace was Aylesford in Kent, but nothing much is known of him until c. 1247, when he was elected prior general of the Carmelite order. This was a difficult time in the order's history, and it was the English leader who consolidated its position; among the new foundations made at the period were four in university cities, Cambridge, Oxford, Paris, and Bologna. According to another late tradition, in 1251 St Simon experienced a vision of the Virgin Mary, as a consequence of which there arose what is known as the 'Scapular devotion', widespread among Roman Catholics; the authenticity of the occurrence is seriously contested by scholars. Two well-known Latin hymns to Mary are usually attributed to his authorship. In 1951 what remained of St Simon's relics were removed from Bordeaux to the old friary, now renewed, at Aylesford. The surname Stock is not found attributed to Simon till a century after his death.

SIXTUS THE SECOND, pope and martyr. D. in Rome, 258; f.d. 6 August. This Sixtus (Xystus) was elected to the Roman see in 257 and was martyred twelve months later. He was seized while addressing the faithful in the cemetery of Praetextatus on the Appian Way: he was either killed on the spot, or taken away for examination and brought back there for execution. He was slain by the sword, not crucified as a legend has it. With him, or on the same day, there suffered SS. Felicissimus, Agapitus, and four other deacons; ◊ *St Lawrence* soon followed them. The body of St Sixtus was carried across the road for burial in the cemetery of Callistus; he was one of the most revered martyrs of the early Roman church.

SOCRATES and STEPHEN ◊ under *Aaron and Julius*

SOPHIA, martyr. No date; f.d. 30 September. The mother of the legendary ◊ *St Faith* and her sisters. – There is a number of other obscure saints named Sophia, mostly eastern. The colloquial name of the great church called 'St Sophia' at Constantinople does not refer to any of them; it was dedicated to the Holy Wisdom (*he hagia sophia*), that is, to Christ as the incarnate Word of God.

SOPHRONIUS, bishop. B. at Damascus, *c.* 560; d. at Jerusalem, 638; f.d. 11 March. He is generally identified with Sophronius the Sophist (i.e. the Learned), who travelled about the Near East with John Moschus when Moschus was collecting material for his famous ascetical work called *The Spiritual Meadow*. Sophronius lived as a monk in Egypt and Palestine, and in 634 was made patriarch of Jerusalem. He was a distinguished leader of the opposition to the monothelite heresy, but his activities were cut short when the Arabs invaded Syria and took Jerusalem in 637. He had to act as the Khalif Omar's guide to the sacred places of the holy city, and did not long survive; but he seems to have strongly influenced Omar in his comparatively benevolent attitude towards the conquered Christians. Among the writings of St Sophronius is a panegyric of the Egyptian martyrs Cyrus and John, and with John Moschus he wrote a biography of their friend ◊ *St John the Almsgiver*, but it has not survived.

SPERATUS ◊ *Scillitan Martyrs*

SPIRIDION, bishop. D. *c.* 348; f.d. 14 December. St Spiridion (Spyridon) was a native of Cyprus, where he was a sheep farmer, with a wife and family to support. Though unlearned and of rustic manners, his virtues caused him to be chosen as bishop of Tremithus; he continued to pasture sheep while caring for his human flock. Most of the particulars of him that have survived are anecdotes of a legendary or uncertain character, but they suggest a man of shrewd and straightforward nature. He took some part in the wider ecclesiastical affairs of his time, but the statement that he was present at the Council of Nicaea is not well attested.

STANISLAS OF CRACOW, bishop and martyr. B. at Szczepanow, 1030; d. at Cracow, 1079; cd 1253; f.d. 7 May. This Stanislas is greatly revered in Poland, but there is much uncertainty about the events which led to the violent death because of which he is venerated as a martyr. He was elected bishop of Cracow in 1072, and the story commonly told is that he came into collision with the vigorous King Boleslav II on account of the disorders of the king's private life; the bishop several times fearlessly rebuked his sovereign and finally excommunicated him, whereupon Boleslav himself attacked and murdered Stanislas while he was celebrating Mass. But the available evidence is variously interpreted by historians.

STANISLAS KOSTKA ◊ under *Aloysius Gonzaga*

STEPHEN, protomartyr. D. at Jerusalem, *c.* 35; f.d. 26 December. All that is known about the first martyr for Christ is recorded in chs. vi and vii of the Acts of the Apostles. Stephen was 'a man full of faith and power', doubtless a Greek-speaking Jew, as he is named first of the seven deacons chosen by the apostles to look after the needs of Greek-speaking widows among the Christians at Jerusalem. He was also a zealous preacher, who 'did great wonders and miracles', and he was denounced to the Jewish council as a blasphemer. Being brought before the council he addressed it at length, summarizing the history of Israel and ending by calling his hearers stiffnecked men who resisted the Holy Spirit as their fathers had done; those fathers had persecuted the prophets, and now they themselves had killed the Holy One whom the prophets foretold. Looking upwards, 'Behold,' he said, 'I see the heavens opened, and the Son of Man standing at the right hand of God.' Thereupon they rushed him out of the city and stoned him. 'Lord Jesus, receive my spirit,' he cried, and falling on his knees prayed, 'Lord, lay not this sin to their charge!' Thus he fell asleep in the Lord. Standing by, approving this execution, was a young man from Tarsus, Saul by name; he was to become ◊ *Paul*, the apostle of the Gentiles.

STEPHEN ◊ under *Aaron and Julius*

STEPHEN THE YOUNGER, martyr. B. at Constantinople, 715; d.

there, 765; f.d. 28 November. When the Iconoclast persecution was renewed by the Byzantine emperor Constantine V, this Stephen was the foremost defender at Constantinople of the veneration of religious images. He was a hermit-monk on Mount St Auxentius, and in 761 was banished for his activities to the island of Proconnesus in the sea of Marmara. After three years he was brought before the emperor and questioned. Stephen produced a coin and asked if it were not wrong to treat the imperial effigy on it disrespectfully: 'Very well' – he went on – 'How much more then does he deserve punishment who stamps on an image of Christ or his mother, and burns it' (which was what was being done). He threw the coin to the floor and trampled on it. Constantine ordered him to jail, where he spent eleven months with over 300 other monks, living a sort of monastic life together. St Stephen continued to be resolute in his principles, and was finally battered to death. It is said that the emperor was not willing to order his death but – like Henry II and Thomas Becket (◊ Thomas of Canterbury) – provoked it by the intemperance of his language.

STEPHEN OF HUNGARY, king. B. at Esztergom, c. 975; d. at Buda, 15 August 1038; f.d. 2 September. Stephen was baptized when a lad, with his father Duke Geza, by ◊ St Adalbert of Prague. He married Gisela, sister of the Emperor ◊ St Henry II, and in 997 succeeded to his father's dukedom. Having reduced the country to order and consolidated his position, he received a royal crown from Pope Silvester II and in 1001 was crowned first king of Hungary. Stephen worked energetically for the conversion of his people to Christianity, setting up episcopal sees and establishing monasteries; among his foundations were the primatial see of Esztergom and the abbey of Pannonhalma. But his methods with recalcitrant pagans were marked by the roughness of the age and place, and at times there was lively resistance, in alliance with his political rivals. St Stephen holds an honoured place in Hungarian history, and seems personally to have had a better title to sainthood than some other royal and national heroes. His last years were embittered by ill-health and the shameless quarrels among his relatives about the succession to the crown. Stephen's relics were solemnly enshrined in 1083, at the same time as those of his only son Emeric (Imre), who also is revered as a saint. His father had taken much trouble to train this young man fittingly to succeed him, but he died prematurely, killed in a hunting accident in 1031 (f.d. 4 November).

STEPHEN OF PERM, missionary bishop. B. at Ust Yug, 1345; d. at Moscow, 1396; f.d. 26 April. He entered a monastery at Rostov in 1365 and spent thirteen years preparing himself for a missionary life. He was then ordained priest and went to proclaim the gospel to the Zyrians or Komi, just west of the Urals, among whom he had been born, although he was himself a Russian. He invented an alphabet for their language in order that public worship might be celebrated in their own tongue, and made many biblical and other translations, set up schools, and trained young men for the priesthood. His success as a missionary owed something to his fearlessness and vigour in defending the people against oppression from Novgorod and Moscow. In 1383 he was made bishop, with his see at Perm (now Molotov).

STEPHEN HARDING, abbot. B. probably in Dorset; d. at Cîteaux, 28 March 1134; f.d. 17 April. He went to school at Sherborne abbey and as a young man travelled abroad, eventually becoming a monk at Molesme in Burgundy. He left there in 1098, going with ◊ St Robert of Molesme, St Alberic, and others to Cîteaux, and when Alberic died in 1108 he succeeded him as the third abbot there. Of the three original founders of the Cistercian reform St Stephen was the most important; but his first years as abbot were extremely difficult, and it is possible that Cîteaux would have come to an untimely end had it not been for the arrival there of the young ◊ St Bernard and his followers in 1112; as it was, a dozen more Cistercian houses were founded during the next eight years, and many more followed. By 1119 St Stephen had drawn up the Charter of Charity (Carta caritatis), defining the spirit and providing for the unity of the association of Cistercian abbeys, a document of the first importance in Western monastic history. The high ideals, the careful organization, the austerity and simplicity of the Cistercian life are an index to the character of Stephen Harding; he was abbot for twenty-five years, during which he led Cîteaux from being a struggling 'lodge in the wilderness' to the headship of a great religious order. His fellow-countryman William of Malmesbury wrote of him that he was 'approachable, good-looking, always cheerful in the Lord – everyone liked him'.

J. B. Dalgairns, *Life of St Stephen Harding* (1946).

STURM, abbot. D. at Fulda, 779; cd 1139; f.d. 17 December. St Sturm was the son of Christian Bavarian parents. *St Boniface of Crediton* had him trained at Fritzlar, and after ordination to the priesthood he was a missionary in Hesse for three years. Then, with two companions, he retired to the forest of Hersfeld; but when Boniface determined to establish a monastery elsewhere, Sturm at length found a suitable site at Fulda, and in 744 he was appointed the first abbot there. Some years later he travelled to Monte Cassino to study Benedictine monastic life at its source. After the death of St Boniface, Sturm was involved in a long dispute about jurisdiction with the new bishop of Mainz, ◊ *St Lull*, and for a time was removed from his abbacy by order of King Pepin. His mission among the Saxons was prejudiced by the methods pursued by Charlemagne, who sought to convert them 'partly by conquest, partly by persuasion, partly even by bribes', as Sturm's contemporary biographer puts it. In the king's absence the Saxons revolted, and Fulda itself was in danger. Amidst the tumult of Charlemagne's return in arms, St Sturm died, worn out with years and labours.

Contemporary Life, trans. in C. H. Talbot, *The Anglo-Saxon Missionaries in Germany* (1954).

SULPICE, bishop. D. *c.* 647; f.d. 17 January. The very celebrated ecclesiastical seminary of Saint-Sulpice in Paris has its name from this Sulpicius, who was bishop of Bourges in Aquitaine; he was beloved by his people for his generosity and solicitude and for his defence of them against the tyranny of Merovingian kings. An earlier *St Sulpicius* (d. 591; f.d. 29 January), bishop of the same see, was sometimes given the name Severus; this has led to confusion with the author of the Life of St Martin of Tours, Sulpicius Severus, who is not numbered among the saints.

SUSAN, martyr. Date unknown; f.d. 11 August. There was a Roman martyr named Susan (Susanna) buried near the Baths of Diocletian, but her story appears to be wholly legendary. It tells that she was the beautiful niece of the bishop of Rome, St Caius, and was beheaded for rejecting the hand of Diocletian's partner Maximian; her father and two other uncles were put to death for supporting her. St Susan's festival is kept with that of ◊ *St Tiburtius*, but it is not known that they had anything to do with one another.

Several other Saints Susan appear in the calendars, of whom one, *Shushanik*, was the Armenian wife of a Georgian prince; it is said that she was martyred by the Persians, *c.* 473 (f.d. 17 October). The oldest existing work of Georgian literature is an account of her long sufferings.

SWITHIN, or SWITHUN, bishop. D. at Winchester, 862; f.d. 15 July. This saint's name is familiar enough in England but very little is known about him, except that he was the trusted counsellor of the Wessex kings Egbert and Ethelwulf, and was made bishop of Winchester in 852. His veneration as a saint appears to date from the removal of his bones from the churchyard into the cathedral, a century after his death. The origin of the saying that the weather on St Swithin's feast-day holds good (or bad) for the next forty days has not been ascertained; a similar superstition is associated with other saints in other lands.

SYMPHORIAN, martyr. Second or third century; f.d. 22 August. St Symphorian was one of the most revered martyrs of Roman Gaul; towards the end of the fifth century a church was built in his honour at Autun, where he suffered. The tradition about him at that time was that he showed contempt for the image of the goddess Berecynthia (Cybele) on her festival, and was accused before the governor, who tried in vain to convert him by argument and flogging. Symphorian was sentenced to be beheaded, and it is said that as he was taken out for execution his mother shouted encouragement to him from the city wall.
G. H. Doble, *St Symphorian* (1931).

SYMPHOROSA ◊ under *Felicity*

T

TARBULA ◊ under *Simeon Barsabba'e*

TARSICIUS, martyr. Third or early fourth century; f.d. 15 August. While carrying the consecrated host through a street in Rome Tarsicius was stopped and searched by bystanders; he tried to protect the host from profanation and was killed by his assailants. This happening is related in a verse inscription written by ◊ *St Damasus* in the fourth century. Later it was said that Tarsicius was an acolyte and that he was taking holy communion to some imprisoned Christians, though Damasus mentions neither circumstance. There is no reason to suppose that St Tarsicius was only a boy, and it is not unlikely that in fact he was a deacon; he was buried in the cemetery of Callistus.

TATIANA, martyr. Date unknown; f.d. 12 January. St Tatiana, who is venerated in the East, is said to have been a deaconess, martyred in Rome *c.* 228. Her 'acts', which are fabulous, are closely resembled by those of the virgin martyrs *Martina* (f.d. 30 January) and *Prisca* (f.d. 18 January), and it has been suggested that the first two, or all three, were the same person. There is no evidence for an early cultus of a Tatiana or Martina in Rome, and Prisca (or Priscilla) is difficult to identify.

TEILO, bishop. Sixth century; f.d. 9 February. There is plenty of evidence, both documentary and from place names and dedications, that St Teilo was widely venerated in southern Wales and Brittany. He was undoubtedly an influential churchman, whose principal monastic foundation and centre of ministry was at Llandeilo Fawr in Carmarthenshire; but information about his life is late, confused, and contradictory. It is said that he was born near Penally, by Tenby; and we are told among other things that he was with ◊ *St David* on his mythical pilgrimage to Jerusalem; that during the 'yellow plague' he went to Brittany and stayed with ◊ *St Samson* at Dol; and that after seven years he went back to Wales, dying at or near Llandeilo. Much of the writing about St Teilo was composed in the interests of the medieval see of Llandaff, which claimed him as its second bishop. He is co-titular of the cathedral there, with SS. Peter, Dubricius, and Oudoceus (Euddogwy). The last-named was claimed as Teilo's nephew and successor at Llandaff, but it is possible that he was a fictitious character, made up from legends about other persons.

G. H. Doble, *St Teilo* (1942).

TELEMACHUS ◊ *Almachius*

TELESPHORUS, pope and martyr. D. at Rome, *c.* 136; f.d. 5 January. Of the fourteen bishops who succeeded ◊ *St Peter* at Rome, to the end of the second century, every one is listed as a martyr. In the case of some of them, martyrdom is historically improbable, and for none of them does good historical evidence for the correctness of the tradition still exist, with one exception, St Telesphorus. Even for him the circumstances are not known: ◊ *St Irenaeus* (d. *c.* 202) simply says that he suffered a glorious martyrdom. St Telesphorus is said to have been a Greek, and he is commemorated in both the Greek and Latin churches.

TERESA, foundress and mystic. B. at Ávila, 1515; d. at Alba de Tormes, 1582; cd 1622; f.d. 15 October. With St Katherine of Siena, one of the first two women ever to be officially declared doctors of the Church, in 1970, was Teresa de Cepeda y Ahumada. She was a girl of good parentage and upbringing, naturally gifted and of lively disposition, who entered the Carmelite convent of the Incarnation at her native place, Ávila in Castile, when she was about twenty. She became a nun with determination, but without enthusiasm: she could not bear the thought of leaving her family. It was a large and easy-going community, whose members enjoyed the use of their own property and had free contacts with the outside world. Teresa at first suffered from serious ill-health; but she persevered in spite of the unpropitious conditions, and began to make deep progress in contemplation. As the years passed she was, too, frequently rapt in ecstasy, and among her spiritual experiences was the remarkable mystical piercing of her heart by a spear of divine love; she wrote a good deal about such things, but she did not give undue importance to them and clearly discerned their dangers. A strong influence upon her was the Dominican priest Domingo Bañez, who first taught her that God can be loved in and through all things.

It was not till she was middle-aged that, with the encouragement of ◊ *St Peter of Alcántara* and others, she resolved to found a convent under the original and strict form of the Carmelite rule. After many set-backs St Joseph's at Ávila was opened in 1562, the first house of reformed or 'discalced' (barefooted) Carmelites (followers of the mitigated rule were distinguished as 'calced', i.e. shod). During the next twenty years Mother Teresa travelled up and down Spain founding convents, seventeen in all, often in conditions of the greatest hardship. These communities were to be small, poor, strictly enclosed, and highly disciplined, with daily mental prayer as part of their rule. Under her influence the reform spread to the men of the order, outstanding among their leaders being ◊ St John of the Cross; but, whether friars or nuns, the 'discalced' were violently opposed and hampered by some of the 'calced'. (Eventually the Carmelite order was reconstituted with two independent branches.)

St Teresa is the classical example of one who combined the life of religious contemplation with an intense activity and common-sense efficiency in 'practical' affairs, and she recorded the results of both in literary form. The most important of her writings are the *Life* of herself up to 1562, written at the request of her confessors; the *Way of Perfection*, meant for the instruction of her own nuns; the high-spirited account of the establishment of her convents, the *Book of Foundations*; and *The Interior Castle*, the work above all which makes her a doctor of the spiritual life. The most up-to-date translation of all her works is that made by E. A. Peers (3 vols., 1963), together with three volumes of her vivacious letters (1957). St Teresa was a woman of both commanding and highly attractive personality, frank, affectionate, gay, and witty; Richard Crashaw's reference to 'the eagle and the dove' in her has become proverbial.

The *Autobiography* (Penguin) and *Book of Foundations*, several translations; V. Sackville-West, *The Eagle and the Dove* (1943); E. A. Peers, *Mother of Carmel* (1945); Life by Fr Silverio (1947); and many other books.

TERESA OF LISIEUX, nun. B. at Alençon, 1873; d. at Lisieux, 1897; cd 1925; f.d. 3 October. The parents of Marie Françoise Thérèse were Louis Martin, a watchmaker, and his wife, Zélie Guérin, five of whose daughters became nuns. In 1888 Teresa entered the Carmelite convent of Lisieux in Normandy, where two of her sisters already were. The nine years of life that remained to her were uneventful and 'ordinary', such as could be paralleled in the lives of numberless other young nuns: the daily round of prayer and work, faults of pride and obstinacy to be overcome, a certain moodiness to be fought, inward and outward trials to be faced; Sister Teresa stuck bravely to her 'little way' of simple trust in and love for God. Then tuberculosis showed itself, and she died after much suffering at the age of twenty-four.

Early in 1895 Sister Teresa had been told to write her recollections of her childhood, which she did, and afterwards added an account of her later life. After her death this book, heavily edited, was published under the title of *Histoire d'une âme*, 'The Story of a Soul'. Its success was sensational: it had an instant appeal in every language into which it was translated; veneration for the unknown nun of Lisieux spread everywhere, and miracles and answers to prayer were attributed on all sides to her intercession in Heaven. She was canonized in 1925, and a large church was built at Lisieux to accommodate the crowds of pilgrims to her shrine. Teresa Martin had become the most popular saint of modern times: she had shown innumerable people that sainthood is attainable by anybody, however obscure, lowly, untalented, 'ordinary', by the doing of small things and the discharge of daily duties in a perfected spirit of love for God.

Teresa's autobiography – far more widely read than that of her great Carmelite namesake of Ávila – was published and circulated in a version that was practically re-written, though not substantially falsified, by her sister, Mother Agnes. It was not till 1952 that the work of producing a facsimile edition of the manuscripts, restored to their original form, was undertaken. This authentic version of *The Story of a Soul* was first published in English in 1958, translated by Ronald Knox, under the title *Autobiography of a Saint*.

The *Autobiography*, above; biographies and studies by H. Petitot (1927), V. Sackville-West (1943), H. Urs von Balthasar (1954), E. Robo (1955), Ida Görres (1959), and many more.

THADDAEUS ◊ *Jude*

THAIS, penitent. No date; f.d. 8 October. Her legend relates that Thais was a notorious harlot, very beautiful and very wealthy, who lived in Egypt during the fourth century. ◊ *St Paphnutius*, or some other desert monk, was fired with the idea of bringing her back to a virtuous life, an enterprise in which he was successful at their first meeting. She made a public bonfire of her wardrobe and jewellery, and was then taken to a house of nuns, where she entered on a penitential course, never leaving her cell. After three years she was readmitted to the church's communion, and died a fortnight later. It is the general opinion of scholars that this is nothing more than a moral tale, written for edification; its starting-point may have been the Egyptian mistress of Alexander the Great, whose name was Thais.

THEBAN LEGION, THE ◊ *Agaunum, Martyrs of*

THECLA OF ICONIUM, virgin martyr. First century (?); f.d. 23

September. The legend of St Thecla derives from an apocryphal document, the *Acts of Paul*, written at a very early date, *c.* 170. It says that she was a native of Iconium (Konya in Asia Minor) who was converted to Christ by ◊ *St Paul*. She broke off an engagement to marry and dedicated her maidenhood to God, whereupon she was subjected to much persecution. After the failure of attempts to kill her by fire and by wild beasts, she at length retired to a cave at Meriamlik near Seleucia, where she lived for many years. When she was ninety she was again persecuted, by the local medical men who were jealous of her healing powers; she was saved from their hands by the rock of her cave opening to receive her, and so her life of martyrdom ended. Other details of this romance are no less fantastic, including incidents reminiscent of heathen mythology. Veneration of St Thecla was widespread in the early centuries and her sanctuary at Seleucia was a favourite place of pilgrimage. It is of course possible that St Paul had a disciple named Thecla who was martyred, and some scholars are of the opinion that this was in fact the case.

Among other Saints Thecla there was an Englishwoman, a nun of Wimborne who worked under ◊ *St Boniface of Crediton* in Germany; she died abbess of Kitzingen, *c.* 790 (f.d. 15 October).

THEODORE, martyr. Date unknown; f.d. 9 November. The tradition of St Theodore, called 'the Recruit', makes him a Roman soldier who, at Amasea in Pontus, refused to join his comrades in pagan worship. Having set fire to a temple of the Mother Goddess while on remand, he was cruelly tortured; in prison he was fortified by heavenly visions, and finally was killed by being thrown into a furnace. The story is untrustworthy, and its later forms so contradictory and complicated by incredible embroideries that another *St Theodore*, 'the General' (f.d. 7 February), was invented to account for them. There is good evidence that there was a martyred Theodore in Pontus; he was venerated from the fourth century and his burial-place at Euchaita was an important religious centre. He became the third of the great 'soldier-saints' of the East, with ◊ *St George* and *St Demetrius*, and a contest with a dragon seems to have been attributed to Theodore before it was to George.

THEODORE THE STUDITE, abbot. B. at Constantinople 759; d. at Akritas, 826; f.d. 11 November. He was the son of an imperial treasury official and in 794 succeeded his uncle as head of the monastery of Sakkoudion in Bithynia. After being banished for a short time for his refusal to countenance Emperor Constantine VI's divorce, he transferred his community to Constantinople, where they occupied the monastery founded by the Roman consul

Studius in 463. Under Theodore's direction this house developed remarkably, and his ideals and regulations have been a most potent and far-reaching influence in Byzantine monasticism. These reforms and developments were brought about under great external difficulties. From 809 to 811 Theodore was in exile on Prince's Island on account of further troubles arising out of the late emperor's adultery; and then in 814 Leo V the Armenian revived Iconoclasm as an imperial policy. To this Theodore organized public resistance, and he was again exiled. For seven years he was confined at various places with extreme rigour, even to being flogged by his gaolers. But he continued by letter to encourage his followers to keep up the struggle, and he sent an appeal to Pope Paschal I, who sent legates to Constantinople; but they achieved nothing. After the violent death of Leo V in 820, Theodore was released; however, he was not allowed to return permanently to the Studite monastery, and he died a semi-exile.

St Theodore stands out as a champion of the church's religious independence of the civil power, a defender of the legitimacy of sacred images, and a monastic reformer of genius. He has been called an incomparable agitator: he was certainly strong-willed and intransigent, even domineering; but there was a less rigid side to him, which can be seen in some of the more personal of his very numerous extant letters. There have also survived, as well as polemical writings, catechetical works, sermons, hymns, and epigrams. St Theodore was also a skilled calligrapher, an art which he fostered among his monks.

A. Gardner, *Theodore of Studium* (1905).

THEODORE OF CANTERBURY, bishop. B. at Tarsus, *c.* 602; d. at Canterbury, 690; f.d. 19 September. When in 667 the archbishop elect of Canterbury, Wighard, died in Rome before consecration, Pope St Vitalian took the appointment into his own hands and nominated to the vacant see a Greek monk from Tarsus in Cilicia, Theodore, who was not yet a priest at the time and over sixty years old. This surprising appointment proved to be an event of the highest importance in the history of the church in England. Having made a visitation of his province, Theodore filled its vacant sees and in 672 presided at the first council of the whole English church, at Hertford. In Northumbria he dealt firmly but considerately with the difficulties between ◊ St Wilfrid and St Chad, but himself became involved in serious differences with Wilfrid over the division of the see of York: the creation of new sees was one of Theodore's principal undertakings. His achievements were chiefly in ecclesiastical organization, administration, and discipline; but at Canterbury the school under the African abbot ◊ *St Adrian*, who had come with Theodore from Rome, earned a lasting reputation. St Theodore found the church in England an unorganized missionary body; he left it a fully ordered province of the universal church: his framework survived the upheavals of the sixteenth century and is still the basis of the diocesan system of the Church of England. 'It is difficult, if not impossible,' wrote the historian Bishop Stubbs, 'to overstate the debt which England, Europe, and Christian civilization owe to the work of Theodore.' His personal character can only be inferred from what he did; it is known that his decisions in moral and canonical problems were greatly respected.

W. Reany, *St Theodore of Canterbury* (1944).

THEODORE OF SYKEON, bishop. D. 613; f.d. 22 April. This Theodore was the bastard child of a girl who with her mother and sister kept an inn at Sykeon, a village in Galatia, and prostituted themselves to their customers. Later on his mother married and left him with his grandmother and his aunt, whom as a young man he converted to better ways. Theodore himself became a monk when on a visit to Jerusalem; he exercised considerable influence, founding monasteries in his own country, and in spite of his strong objection was elected bishop of Anastasiopolis, not far from Ankara, c. 590. He gave up this office after ten years and, after visiting his patron the emperor Maurice at Constantinople, lived as a monk again till his death at Sykeon. A long Life of St Theodore was written by one of his disciples; it is mostly a record of healings of the sick and the possessed and other marvels attributed to the holy man, and of anecdotes illustrating the virtues of his character; but it provides a lively picture of life in Asia Minor just before the Arab occupation.

E. Dawes and N. H. Baynes, *Three Byzantine Saints* (1948).

THEODOSIUS THE CENOBIARCH, abbot. B. in Cappadocia, c. 423; d. near Bethlehem, 529; f.d. 11 January. When he was about thirty he left his home and settled in Palestine, forming a small community close to Bethlehem. It grew rapidly, its monks being of several peoples and languages, and it was celebrated for its work for the sick, the aged, and the mentally deranged. When his friend and fellow-countryman ◊ *St Sabas* was appointed head of all hermit-monks in Palestine, St Theodosius was set over those living in community: this explains his name of 'Cenobiarch', i.e. chief of those leading a life in common. Theodosius was a staunch opponent of Monophysism, which led to his being removed from office for a short time by the Emperor Anastasius. He was about 105 years old when he died.

THEODOSIUS OF THE CAVES, abbot. B. at Vasilkov; d. at Kiev, 1074; f.d. 3 May. As a young man Theodosius (Theodossy)

shocked his mother by his ascetic habits and work among the poor
and distressed, and he had to overcome strong opposition from
her before he could join the monastic community at the Caves of
Kiev, c. 1032. He became second abbot there after the early
resignation of the founder, ◊ St Antony of the Caves, and it was
Theodosius who gave the monastery a solid foundation and direction to its mode of life. Antony had followed the austere and
solitary ideals of the Egyptian hermits, but Theodosius favoured
the broader and more active tradition, adopting the regulations
given by ◊ St Theodore the Studite to his monks at Constantinople. He found the caves at Kiev confined and depressing, and
enlarged and completed a range of ordinary buildings; he provided food and shelter for the sick and poor and travellers; and
he mixed freely with the outside world when he thought that any
good might be achieved thereby. He impressed on his monks that
they had to set a visible example to others of love, unity, and
harmony, and be ready to advise and help lay people who consulted them. The grand-princes of Kiev favoured the new monastery; but St Theodosius firmly maintained its independence of
exalted patronage, risking banishment for his rebukes to the
usurper Svyatoslav. He was a monk for forty years, and set the
standard for monasticism in early Russian Christianity. St Antony
and St Theodosius Pechersky were, wrote a Russian chronicler,
'the first great candles lighted in the name of Russia before the
universal image of Christ'.

An early Life is trans. in G. P. Fedotov's *Treasury of Russian Spirituality*
(1950).

THOMAS, apostle. First century; f.d. 21 December. Called 'Didy-
mus' (twin). The references to this apostle in St John's gospel give
a sharp impression of the sort of man he was: ready to die with
his Master (John xi, 16); drawing from Jesus at the Last Supper
the declaration 'I am the way, the truth, and the life' (ibid. xiv,
5–7); sceptical about the resurrection: 'Unless I see . . ., and touch
. . ., I will not believe', but when the risen Christ was made plain
to him, whole-hearted in his belief: 'My Lord and my God!'
(ibid. xx, 24–28). There is endless discussion about St Thomas's
subsequent life. In particular, did he take the gospel to India,
where for many centuries the Christians of Kerala have called
themselves 'St Thomas Christians'? That he did so, and was
martyred there, is the theme of a long document of the third or
fourth century, called the *Acts of Thomas*. This is one of the most
readable and intrinsically interesting of early Christian apocryphal
writings; but it is no more than a popular romance, written in the
interest of false gnostic teachings (e.g. the virtual necessity of
celibacy for Christians). It is not impossible that St Thomas should

have reached southern India, but the historical reality of his mission there cannot be considered proved. It was also said that he evangelized Parthia, and in the fourth century his relics were claimed to be at Edessa in Mesopotamia.

L. W. Brown, *The Indian Christians of St Thomas* (1956).

THOMAS OF CANTERBURY, bishop and martyr. B. in London, 1118; d. at Canterbury, 1170; cd 1173; f.d. 29 December. Thomas Becket was born in Cheapside of well-to-do Norman parents, and was given a good all-round education. About 1142 he entered the service of Archbishop Theobald of Canterbury, who sent him abroad to study canon law and in 1154 gave him deacon's orders and the archdeaconry of Canterbury; in 1155 King Henry II chose him to be the royal chancellor. Becket was on terms of intimate friendship with the king, and served him faithfully and well for seven years as statesman, diplomat, and soldier, appearing outwardly as the court ecclesiastic of extravagant worldly tastes and brilliant abilities. But when in 1162 Thomas was appointed to the vacant see of Canterbury, he changed from being, as he himself put it, 'a patron of play-actors and a follower of hounds, to being a shepherd of souls'. He threw himself into the duties of his new office, was profuse in alms-giving, lived very austerely, and soon came into conflict with the king. Of many points at issue between them, a crucial one for the archbishop concerned the respective jurisdictions of church and state over clergymen convicted of crimes. The situation became embittered, the bishops were divided in their views, and in 1164, after a stormy royal council at Northampton, Becket fled secretly to France.

It was six years before king and archbishop were apparently reconciled; but immediately Thomas arrived back in England, on 1 December 1170, the quarrel broke out afresh, over certain bishops whom Becket had disciplined for infringing his see's prerogatives at the king's instigation. Henry, in Normandy, fell into a passion of rage and uttered reckless words which, probably not intentionally, were Thomas's death-warrant. Four knights hurried across the Channel and, in the early evening of 29 December, killed the archbishop in a side chapel of his cathedral. Christendom was aghast; all over western Europe Thomas was spontaneously acclaimed as a martyr, and in 1173 Pope Alexander III (who had not given him unqualified support) formally canonized him. For nearly 400 years St Thomas's shrine at Canterbury was one of the three or four greatest pilgrim resorts of Europe. There has been disagreement about the character of St Thomas Becket. Imperious and obstinate, ambitious and violent he was. But all the time there were indications of more exalted qualities, and the years of exile at Pontigny and Sens were a time of preparation for the final ordeal; his last words, as reported by one eye-witness, were a key to his ideals as archbishop: 'Willingly I die for the name of Jesus and in defence of the church.' The story of Thomas of Canterbury has attracted dramatists from Tennyson's *Becket* through T. S. Eliot's *Murder in the Cathedral* to Anouilh's play *Becket*, which was made into a film in 1964.

Biographies by W. H. Hutton (1926), R. Speaight (1940), A Duggan (1962); D. Knowles, *Thomas Becket* (1970).

THOMAS OF HEREFORD, bishop. B. at Hambleden in Buckinghamshire, c. 1218; d. in Italy, 25 August 1282; cd 1320; f.d. 3 October Thomas Cantilupe, of noble Norman descent, received his education at Oxford, Paris, and Orléans; with his father he attended the general council of Lyons in 1245, and there probably he was ordained priest by Pope Innocent IV. He became professor of canon law at Oxford and chancellor of the university in 1262, supported the barons against King Henry III, and was for a short time chancellor of the kingdom under Simon de Montfort. Thomas held – by papal dispensation – a number of benefices in plurality; he took a careful interest in them, sometimes visiting them without warning to ensure that his vicars were looking after their parishioners properly. When in 1275 he was elected bishop of Hereford he was very zealous for the rights of the see against the encroachments of powerful neighbours, lay and clerical. But if he tended to litigiousness with the mighty, he made himself loved by his care and generosity towards the humbler members of his flock; he would sit up half the night preparing his sermons, and the abstemiousness of his life was proverbial. During his last years he was involved in disputes with his metropolitan, Archbishop Peckham, who early in 1282 excommunicated him. St Thomas took his case to Pope Martin IV in person, but before it could be considered he died, at Montefiascone near Orvieto. The cause of his canonization was facilitated by the number of miracles – large even for those days – reported at his tomb in Hereford cathedral, and by the interest of King Edward I, whose adviser St Thomas had been.

THOMAS OF VILLANUEVA, bishop. B. near Villanueva in Castile, 1488; d. at Valencia, 1555; cd 1658; f.d. 22 September. This Thomas's birthplace was Fuenllana, in the region of Don Quixote's La Mancha, but he was brought up at the adjoining Villanueva de los Infantes, where his father and mother set him an example of virtuous living and generous alms-deeds. After graduating at the new university of Alcalá, Thomas joined the Augustinian friars at Salamanca; soon after his priestly ordination in 1518 he was made prior of the house, and for twenty-five years he discharged responsible offices in his order, becoming well-known in

Spain as a most effective preacher. Thomas led an intense inner life of prayer, and was often rapt in ecstasy; on the other hand he suffered from the natural disabilities of absentmindedness and bad memory. In 1544, constrained by an order from his superiors, he accepted the archbishopric of Valencia.

As a bishop Thomas of Villanueva was distinguished by the poverty of his life and the freedom with which he used the resources of his wealthy see for the relief of the needy, in all ranks of society and without invidious distinctions between the 'deserving' and the 'undeserving': 'Anticipate the needs of those who are ashamed to beg,' he said, 'for to make them ask for help is to make them buy it.' He was specially open-handed in providing marriage-portions for girls and care for orphans and abandoned children. The diocese of Valencia had been neglected for many years; in the heavy task of restoring order among clergy and laity St Thomas combined firmness with tact and discretion, for which he was criticized by the advocates of more direct and authoritarian methods. He found a particular problem in the Moriscos, Moorish people who had been forcibly 'converted' to Christianity not long before; their consequent state of mind was such that they remained an unsolved problem for the archbishop. Many stories are told of his power of healing and other spiritual gifts, and of the reasonableness and charity of spirit, the quietness and straightforwardness with which he carried out his pastoral duties. From 1549 St Thomas suffered from a serious hernia and his general health rapidly worsened; in 1554 he asked – not for the first time – to be released from his office, but the reply was evasive and in the following year he died.

E. I. Watkin, in *Neglected Saints* (1963).

THOMAS AQUINAS, theologian. B. at Roccasecca near Aquino, c. 1225; d. at Fossanuova near Terracina, 1274; cd 1323; f.d. 7 March. This great medieval doctor of the church – esteemed by many the greatest – was one of the many children of Landulf of Aquino, a nobleman of Lombardic descent. He was educated by the Benedictines at Monte Cassino and at the university of Naples, where c. 1244 he joined the Dominican order. That he should want to be a mendicant friar was shocking to his noble relatives, so his brothers kidnapped him and shut him up for a year. But he would not change his mind. On his release he went to study under ◊ *St Albert the Great* at Paris and Cologne, and in 1256 he took the degree of master in theology. The rest of Thomas's relatively short life was devoted to teaching, preaching, and, above all, writing. But his academic career was not confined to one place: in 1259 he left Paris for Italy where he taught in several cities; from 1269 to 1272 he was in Paris again; and finally he went to

Naples. It was said of Brother Thomas that 'his wonderful learning owes far less to his genius than to the effectiveness of his
prayer'; and at the end of 1273 he left his great *Summa theologica*
unfinished, declaring: 'All I have written seems to me like so
much straw compared with what I have seen and what has been
revealed to me.' He was an incarnation of the Dominican ideal
of handing on the fruits of contemplation to others – 'a far
greater thing,' he said, 'than simply contemplating.' Having been
summoned to attend the general council at Lyons, he set out a
few weeks later; but he was already ill, and he died on the journey
at the abbey of Fossanuova.

Of St Thomas's voluminous philosophical and theological works
the most famous and influential are the *Summa contra Gentiles*
(1259–64), a treatise on God and his creation, and the *Summa
theologica* (1266–73), the classical systematic exposition of theology, a work of such extent and solidity that it has earned its
author the title of *Doctor communis*, 'universal teacher'. Both
these have been translated into English, the first in three volumes,
the second in twenty-two; more manageable introductions are his
Selected Writings (Everyman) and F. C. Copleston's *Aquinas*
(Pelican). The influence of St Thomas on his contemporaries was
less than that of ◊ *St Bonaventure* and St Albert; it subsequently
became enormous. In 1567 he was declared a doctor of the church
by Pope ◊ *St Pius V*; and in modern times an encyclical letter of
Leo XIII in 1879 encouraged a great revival of Thomistic studies
and a renewed interest in St Thomas's teaching, an interest not
limited within confessional boundaries. The authorship of certain
well-known eucharistic hymns has long been ascribed to Thomas
Aquinas, e.g. *Adoro te* ('Thee we adore, O hidden Saviour') and
Verbum supernum ('The Word of God, proceeding forth'); but
some doubts have been voiced on this matter in recent years. The
emblem of Aquinas in art is a star.

A. Walz, *St Thomas Aquinas* (1951); J. A. Weisheipl, *Friar Thomas d'Aquino*
(1973); studies by G. Vann (1940), G. K. Chesterton (1947), and others.

THOMAS MORE, humanist and martyr. B. in London, 1478; d. on
Tower Hill, 1535; cd 1935; f.d. 9 July, with ◊ *St John (Fisher) of
Rochester*. The Roman Catholic church canonized Thomas More
as a martyr; it is arguable that he was a fitting candidate for
canonization by the integrity of his God-centred life no less than
by his death. His father was a judge, living in Milk Street in the
City, and after two years at Oxford Thomas was admitted a
student of Lincoln's Inn; he was called to the bar in 1501, and
in 1504 entered Parliament. In the following year he married
Jane Colt, and three daughters and a son were born to them; but
the beloved Jane died young, and More then married a widow,

Alice Middleton, who could be a mother to his young children. More was a humanist and a reformer; 'a gentleman of great learning, both in law, art, and divinity'; a wit as gay as he was serious. Among his close friends were numbered Bishop Fisher and Dean Colet, Grocyn, Linacre, and 'Erasmus my darling'; by 1516 he had written his famous book *Utopia*. Under King Henry VIII he filled a succession of high posts and missions; in 1529 he was appointed lord chancellor, and as a judge he was acclaimed for his fairness, incorruptibility, and dispatch. More, who was a good theologian, took an active but temperate part on behalf of traditional Catholicism in the controversies precipitated by Luther.

But, when his career and reputation were at their height, there came King Henry's demand for a declaration of the nullity of his marriage with Katherine of Aragon. More was a close friend of the king, but had no illusions about his character; he believed the marriage to be valid, and in 1532 he resigned the chancellorship and retired from public life. In 1534, with Bishop Fisher, he refused to take an oath which involved the repudiation of papal religious authority, and he was committed to the Tower. During fifteen months' imprisonment he wrote a *Dialogue of Comfort against Tribulation*, and conferred much with his deeply-loved and loving eldest daughter, Margaret Roper. Nine days after the execution of St John of Rochester, More was tried in Westminster Hall on a charge of treasonably denying the king's supreme headship on earth of the church in England; he was found guilty and sentenced to death. He then repeated to the court that he could not go against his conscience, and wished his judges that 'we may yet hereafter in Heaven merrily all meet together to everlasting salvation'. The execution, by beheading, took place on Tower Hill on 6 July; he died, he told the crowd of spectators, 'the king's good servant – but God's first': his biographer R. W. Chambers calls these 'the most weighty words ever spoken upon a scaffold'. He was playful and witty to the last, and carefully adjusted his beard: just so did Perpetua tidy her dishevelled hair in the arena at Carthage.

Of St Thomas More's written works, *Utopia* stands in a class by itself; his writings against Luther and Tyndale and other polemics are now of interest and value chiefly to scholars; but his later writings and letters from prison should command a wider public than they probably do. The spirited *Dialogue of Comfort* has been compared with the devotional works of ◊ *St Francis de Sales* and Jeremy Taylor, but it is equalled, perhaps surpassed, by the *Treatise on the Passion of Christ*. *Utopia*, the *Dialogue of Comfort*, *Selected Letters*, and others have been republished in

329

recent years. A play about More, *A Man for All Seasons* (1960), by Robert Bolt, has met with considerable success.

Early Lives by William Roper and Nicholas Harpsfield, in Everyman edn; modern biographies by R. W. Chambers (1951), E. E. Reynolds (1953) and others.

THORFINN, bishop, B. at Trondheim; d. near Bruges, 1285; f.d. 8 January. This Norwegian bishop had a certain cultus in north-western Europe, but few particulars of his life have been preserved. He was perhaps a Cistercian monk near Trondheim before becoming bishop of Hamar. When he and other bishops fell out with King Eric II, over the freedom of episcopal elections and other matters, Thorfinn had to leave the country, and took refuge at the Cistercian abbey of Ter Doest near Bruges, where he died. A monk there at that time, Walter of Muda, wrote a poem extolling the resolute goodness of St Thorfinn's character.

THORLAC, bishop. B. in Iceland, 1133; d. at Skalholt, 1193; f.d. 23 December. When a very young priest he went from Iceland to study, which he is said to have done in Paris and Lincoln. There he acquired ideas of ecclesiastical discipline which were as yet not effective in Iceland, and on his return surprised his friends by refusing (after some hesitation) to marry a rich widow; instead he started a house of canons regular at Thykkvibaer. In 1178 he was consecrated bishop of Skalholt, and in face of much opposition set about a thorough reformation: he had the weighty support of his metropolitan in Norway, ◊ *St Eystein*, with whom Thorlac collaborated in drawing up a code of law for both clergy and laity. St Thorlac was canonized locally in 1198, and he is the subject of an Icelandic saga.

TIBURTIUS, martyr. Date unknown; f.d. 11 August. He was a Roman martyr, buried 'at the two laurels' on the Via Labicana. ◊ *St Damasus* wrote an epitaph for him, which gives no biographical particulars, and the references to him in the 'acts' of St Sebastian have no historical value.

There was another martyred *St Tiburtius* (f.d. 14 April), buried in the cemetery of Praetextatus on the Via Appia, with St Valerian and St Maximus. Nothing else is known of them; but all three were given parts in the legend of ◊ *St Cecily*, Tiburtius as her brother-in-law and Valerian as her husband.

TIKHON OF ZADONSK, writer and bishop. B. near Novgorod, 1724; d. at Zadonsk, 1783; cd by the Russian Orth. ch., 1860; f.d. 13 August. Tikhon Sokolov (christened Timothy) was the son of a village sexton, and when he was fourteen was entered at an ecclesiastical school at Novgorod to avoid military conscription. He became a priest-monk when he was thirty-four, and in 1763 was made bishop of the difficult diocese of Voronezh.

The state of his flock, clergy and laity, was very bad, and his efforts at improvement met with a discouraging response; he persevered, but his health gave way and in 1767 he was allowed to resign the see. He retired to the monastery of Zadonsk, north of Voronezh, and lived the rest of his life there, giving much of his time and small pension to people in need of help, spiritual and temporal.

The popularity of Bishop Tikhon's writings is the measure of his quiet, unspectacular influence. His masters were the Bible and the Fathers, particularly ◊ *St John Chrysostom*, and his aim was expository and pastoral, to help people in every walk of life to live 'in Christ', here and hereafter. He was gentle, moderate, and wide-spirited, but quick-tempered, a keen observer of people and of things, a foe to authoritarianism and to differing standards for clergy and laity. To those who excused their shortcomings on the ground that they were not monks he replied, 'My dears, all those words calling for love and poverty and service were spoken before there were any such things as monasteries.' And he had the gift of pithy observation, as when he warned the temperate against complacency, 'for Satan too never drinks'. A dozen of St Tikhon's letters and his last testament are translated in G. P. Fedotov's *Treasury of Russian Spirituality* (1950). He probably took his name from *St Tikhon of Amathus* (f.d. 16 June), an early Cypriot bishop, of whom ◊ *St John the Almsgiver* wrote.
N. Gorodetzky, *St Tikhon Zadonsky* (1951).

TIMOTHY, bishop and martyr. D. 97 (?); f.d. 24 January. He was a native of Lystra in Asia Minor, son of a gentile father and a Jewish mother. He was converted from heathenism by ◊ *St Paul*, whose companion and helper he became (Acts xvi, 1–4). Two of the New Testament epistles were addressed to him; and we learn from the first of them that Paul entrusted him with the supervision of the Christians around Ephesus. St Timothy is regarded as the first bishop of that city. A fourth-century account states that he was beaten to death by a mob for opposing the observance of a heathen festival.

TITUS, bishop. First century; f.d. 6 February. He was a convert and helper of ◊ St Paul, who clearly was very fond of him. Having appointed Titus to organize the church in Crete, Paul wrote a letter instructing him on how to discharge his duties among the Cretans, of whom Paul had a low opinion. St Titus is venerated as the first bishop of the Cretan city of Gortyna.

TORIBIO OF LIMA, bishop. B. at Mayorga in Spain, 1538; d. at Santa in Peru, 23 March 1606; cd 1726; f.d. 27 April. Toribio Alfonso de Mogrobejo, professor of law in the university of Salamanca and a layman, was appointed president of the court of the

Inquisition at Granada by King Philip II. He was still a layman when, in 1580, he was nominated to the archbishopric of Lima in Peru – a most difficult charge, religiously and geographically. The first of Toribio's three visitations of the huge and pathless diocese took him seven years, and he found it in a scandalous state: very many of the Spanish colonists, and not least their clergy, had succumbed to the temptations of their position, and large numbers of baptized Indians knew little or nothing about Christianity. Toribio proved a tireless and forthright reformer, no respecter of persons or tolerator of prescriptive abuses. As a missionary he had considerable success, for he took much trouble to learn Indian languages, and in this work he was associated with ◊ *St Francis Solano*. The college he organized at Lima in 1591 was the first seminary for training clergy in the Americas, and during the quarter-century of his episcopate his work in Peru had a salutary influence in other South American countries. In his extensive charities St Toribio showed delicate consideration for the feelings of those who were ashamed to appear poverty-stricken, and he befriended ◊ *St Rose of Lima*, whom he confirmed; he died first, but was not canonized till fifty-five years after her.

U

UBALDO, bishop. B. at Gubbio in Umbria; d. there 1160; cd 1192; f.d. 16 May. While dean of the cathedral at his native place, Ubaldo Baldassini induced the canons of the chapter to live a common life together, under the rule given by Peter degli Onesti to his community at Ravenna. Ubaldo himself wanted to be a solitary, but was advised otherwise, and he had to accept the bishopric of Gubbio. He was an admirable bishop, noted for his patience and forbearance, and his shrine is still a place of pilgrimage.

UGANDA, MARTYRS OF. All b. in Africa; d. at Namugongo and elsewhere, 1885–6; cd 1964; f.d. 3 June. The first of the twenty-two canonized victims of King Mwanga's persecution of his Christian subjects was Joseph Mkasa Balikuddembe, who was beheaded after having rebuked his royal master for his debauchery and for the murder of the Anglican missionary bishop James Hannington in October 1885. Six months later there was a literal holocaust, burnt-offering, at Namugongo, when there were burnt alive in a body thirty-two Catholic and Protestant men and boys. Many of them were young pages in Mwanga's household, from their head-man, Charles Lwanga, to the thirteen-year-old Kizito,

who went to his death 'laughing and chattering'. The description
of the passion of these young Africans, related by the head of
the White Fathers' mission in Uganda, reads like some narrative
of a martyrdom in the first Christian centuries. These and many
other Baganda suffered for their Christian faith, and in some
cases for refusing to minister to Mwanga's perverted sexual
habits.

J. P. Thoonen, *Black Martyrs* (1941); J. F. Faupel, *African Holocaust* (1962).

ULRIC OF AUGSBURG, bishop. B. near Zurich, 890; d. at Augsburg, 973; cd 993; f.d. 4 July. During the fifty years he was
bishop of Augsburg Ulric took a conspicuous part in ecclesiastical
and secular affairs and laboured zealously for the good of his
flock. He is now chiefly remembered as the first saint of whom
it is recorded that his canonization was solemnly decreed by a
pope, John XV, to whom an account of Ulric's life and miracles
was submitted at a council in Rome in 993. A letter against
clerical celibacy ascribed to St Ulric has been shown to be a
later forgery.

St Ulric of Zell (d. 1093, f.d. 14 July), a monk of Cluny, established the abbey of Zell in the Black Forest of Germany. Another
St Ulric (better, *Wulfric*; d. 1154; f.d. 20 February) had a local
cultus at Haselbury Plucknett in Somerset. He was a 'hunting
parson' at Deverill in Wiltshire, who ended his days as a recluse
at Haselbury.

ULTAN ◊ under *Foillan*

UNCUMBER ◊ *Wilgefortis*

URSULA and her maidens, virgin martyrs. Date unknown; f.d. 21
October. An inscription on stone found at Cologne records, not
very clearly, the rebuilding by one Clematius of a memorial
church on the site of the martyrdom there of a number of
maidens, of whom no names or other particulars are given. This
inscription was cut in the late fourth or early fifth century and
it provides all that is known historically about those martyrs
who became known as SS. Ursula and the eleven thousand
virgins.

They are not heard of again for some 400 years, when in the
ninth century the ramifying legend appears as taking shape. The
kernel of its developed form, of which there were Cologne and
Gaulish versions, is that Ursula, to avoid an unwanted marriage,
departed with her company from the island of Britain, where her
father was a king; on their way back from a visit to Rome, they
were slaughtered by Huns at Cologne on account of their
Christian faith. During the twelfth century this pious romance
was preposterously elaborated through the mistakes of imaginative visionaries; a public burial-ground uncovered at Cologne was

taken to be the grave of the martyrs, false relics came into circulation and forged epitaphs of non-existent persons were produced. The earliest reference which gives St Ursula the first place speaks of her ten companions: how these eleven came to be multiplied by a thousand is a matter of speculation. Other earlier references to the martyrs call their leader Pinnosa, and mention four or seven companions, but 'thousands' were already spoken of in the ninth century. One variation of the legend made the maidens come from the east and associated them with the martyrs of Agaunum (◊ *Agaunum, Martyrs of*). It seems that some young women were martyred at Cologne at an early date, but nothing else remotely resembling historical fact can be said about them.

V

VACLAV ◊ *Wenceslas*

VALENTINE, martyr. Date unknown; f.d 14. February. There was a church of St Valentine built on the Flaminian Way at Rome in the middle of the fourth century. His supposed 'acts' seem to derive from those of *SS. Marius and Martha*, who with their sons *Audifax and Abachum* (f.d. 19 January) were martyred in Rome but were said to be Persians; their burial place was on the Via Cornelia. It is likely that *St Valentine*, a martyred bishop at Terni (Interamna) whose feast-day is also on 14 February, is only a doublet of the Valentine above. There is nothing in either Valentine legend to account for the custom of choosing a partner of the opposite sex and sending 'valentines' on 14 February; it apparently arose from the old idea that birds begin to pair on that date, but it may have a more remote pagan reference.

VALERIAN ◊ under *Cecily*

VALERIUS OF SARAGOSSA ◊ under *Vincent of Saragossa*

VERONICA. F.d. 12 July. The story told of St Veronica is that she was a woman of Jerusalem who, filled with compassion at the sight of Jesus suffering on his way to Calvary, wiped his sweating face with a cloth; and on the cloth there was left an image of his features. There is no reliable evidence for any such happening, but the story has made a wide appeal to Christians for many centuries. There are variations and amplifications of it, and Veronica has been identified with various persons, historical and other, notably with the woman who had an issue of blood (Matt. ix, 20). A cloth purporting to be the original 'Veronica's veil' has been preserved in St Peter's at Rome, perhaps since the early eighth century; but St Veronica is not mentioned in the Roman Martyrology, and the inclusion of her action in the service called the Stations of the Cross has been objected to from time to time. The name Veronica, commonly explained as meaning 'true image', was given to the figured veil ('vernicle' in English), and may have been transferred from it to the compassionate woman.

VERONICA GIULIANI, mystic. B. at Mercatello, 1660; d. at Città di Castello, 1727; cd 1839; f.d. 9 July. She was mistress of novices at a convent of Capuchin nuns at Città di Castello in Umbria for thirty-four years and abbess for eleven, in which offices she was distinguished for her level-headedness and efficiency. Her inner life and personal experiences were of a very extraordinary kind and extremely well attested, making her case an outstanding one in the records of the phenomena of mysticism.

✦ VIATOR ◊ under *Justus of Lyons*

VICELIN ◊ under *Canute*

VICTOR OF MARSEILLES, martyr. D. *c.* 290 (?); f.d. 21 July. There has been a number of martyrs and other saints named Victor, of whom the best known is probably the one whose tomb in a church at Marseilles was one of the most popular pilgrim shrines of Gaul. According to his 'acts' he was put to death, with three guards whom he had converted, by order of the emperor Maximian; but the document is untrustworthy and it is not clear what elements of truth it contains.

VICTRICIUS, bishop. B. *c.* 330; d. at Rouen, *c.* 407; f.d. 7 August. While serving in the Roman army in Gaul Victricius became a Christian and, like his friend ◊ *St Martin of Tours*, refused further military service as incompatible with the gospel; for this he was flogged and nearly lost his life. Nothing more is known of him till he had become bishop of Rouen, *c.* 385. He was a vigorous missionary over a wide area, and did much to build up the young church in northern Gaul. His reputation was such that *c.* 395 he was sent for by the bishops in Britain to resolve certain difficulties, the nature of which is not known. It is evident that St Victricius was a man of importance in his era, who 'did all that he could, even if he could not do all that needed doing'; but there is no early Life of him, and most of the relevant information comes from the letters of ◊ *St Paulinus of Nola*, who also was one of his friends. A writing by Victricius on the Praise of the Saints has survived, and also an important disciplinary document addressed to him by Pope St Innocent I.

VINCENT OF SARAGOSSA, martyr. D. at Valencia, 304; f.d. 22 January. The deacon Vincent, most celebrated of Spanish martyrs, was put to death at Valencia in the persecution under Diocletian, but further trustworthy particulars are lacking. His countryman Prudentius devoted a poem to his praise and embroidered acts of his martyrdom have been preserved; we are given a highly imaginative picture of the tortures he endured without a tremor before dying from their effects, including roasting on a grid in much the same way as is narrated of ◊ *St Lawrence*. The fame of St Vincent spread very rapidly and far, as St Augustine testifies; several churches in England were dedicated in his honour in the middle ages. *St Valerius*, bishop of Saragossa (f.d. 28 January), is said to have shared his deacon's cruel imprisonment, but was simply sent into exile, where he died in peace.

VINCENT OF SOIGNIES ◊ *Madelgaire*

VINCENT FERRER, missioner. B. at Valencia, *c.* 1350; d. at Vannes, 1419; cd 1455; f.d. 5 April. Vincent Ferrer, whose father was an Englishman married to a Spanish woman, joined the Dominican friars in 1367 and soon made his mark as a powerful preacher, not least among Jews and Moslems. In the papal controversy that convulsed the Western church from 1378 he gave active support to the Avignon claimant Peter de Luna ('Benedict XIII'), whose counsellor and confessor he became. In 1399 Vincent left Avignon and for ten years engaged in intensive mission work in France, Spain, and other lands. He saw his mission in apocalyptic terms and drew huge crowds which reacted in 'revivalistic' fashion to his impassioned appeals and warnings; a troop of penitents, male and female, followed him from place to place. It was only to be expected that miracles should be attributed to him, and his reputation as a wonderworker was subsequently enhanced by the credulity of his biographers. In 1416 he made an effective contribution towards ending the papal schism by withdrawing his support from 'Benedict XIII', as did King Ferdinand of Aragón. Three years later St Vincent Ferrer died while on a preaching tour in Brittany.
H. Ghéon, *St Vincent Ferrer* (1939).

VINCENT PALLOTTI, founder. B. in Rome, 1795; d. there, 1850; cd 1963; f.d. 22 January. This Roman priest passed all his life in his native city, where as a young clergyman he gained a variety of experience, pastoral and other. At one period he was attached to a church where he was subjected to unbelievable persecution by other clergy, which he bore for years without complaint. From his devoted work among the people there emerged in 1835 the Society of Catholic Apostleship ('Pallottine Fathers'), for religious and charitable work in close collaboration with lay people; a corresponding society of women was also established. In 1844 Don Pallotti sent one of his most trusted priests to minister to the Italians in London, and since then his society has spread to many other parts of the world. He had a special concern for England and had numerous English, Irish, and American friends. One of them, Walter Tempest, was with him when he was given shelter at the Irish College in Rome in 1849. To the people of the city, St Vincent Pallotti was a nineteenth-century ◊ *St Philip Neri*.

VINCENT DE PAUL, founder. B. in Gascony, *c.* 1580; d. in Paris, 1660; cd 1737; f.d. 19 July. He was the son of a peasant farmer at Pouay in the Landes, and was ordained to the priesthood at the early age of twenty. For ten years he aimed no higher than a clerical life of ease; but under the influence of Peter de Bérulle (afterwards cardinal) and of some years' ministry among neglected peasants and convicts in the hulks, a great change came over him. He dedicated his whole life to the service of the poor. Groups of lay people were organized for charitable work, and at Paris in 1625 he founded the Congregation of the Mission (Vincentians, or Lazarists), a society of priests for missionary work, especially in country districts, and for the training of clergy. In 1633, with ◊ *St Louise de Marillac*, he founded the Daughters (or Sisters) of Charity, and members of these congregations are now found all over the world.

St Vincent de Paul's foundations were made in response to needs that he saw; there was no human suffering that he did not seek to relieve, and for the help of the religiously indigent he used the same bold and wise methods as for the material wants of galley-slaves, decayed gentry, or abandoned children. He approached each undertaking with the same humbleness and simple trust in Providence and his single-minded goodness and generosity stirred a like generosity in others; he attracted many helpers and followers, for all that he was by nature sharp-tempered and lacking in external advantages. Sensitiveness for the feelings of others characterized all that he did; it comes out clearly in the instructions he gave his missioners about their dealings with Protestants, who were to be treated as brothers, with respect and love, without patronage or condescension or contentiousness. As well as from the Vincentian fathers and the Sisters of Charity, the name of St Vincent de Paul is now well known from the charitable society of laymen founded in Paris in 1833 by Frédéric Ozanam. In 1948 the saint's life was made the subject of a film, *Monsieur Vincent*, by Bernard Luc and Jean Anouilh.

Biographies by E. de Broglie (1913), E. K. Sanders (1913), T. Maynard (1940), J. Calvet (1952); M. Purcell, *The World of Monsieur Vincent* (1964).

VINCENT STRAMBI ◊ under *Caspar del Bufalo*

VINCENTIA GEROSA ◊ under *Bartholomea Capitanio*

VIRGIL OF SALZBURG, bishop. B. in Ireland; d. at Salzburg, 784; cd 1233; f.d. 27 November. Virgil (Fergal) was an Irish monk, possibly of Aghaboe, who went abroad *c.* 740 and became abbot of a monastery at Salzburg, with jurisdiction over the local Christians. He appears to have been a somewhat difficult character and he incurred the strong disapproval of ◊ *St Boniface of Crediton* at Mainz, who twice delated him to Rome. On the first occasion Pope ◊ *St Zachary* decided in Virgil's favour. The other case concerned Virgil's cosmological speculations and their implications, which, as reported to Zachary by Boniface, the pope found very shocking. The incident has been the subject of much discussion and has been used and exaggerated for polemical purposes, but in fact it is far from clear what Virgil's ideas really were. He was both a man of learning and a successful missionary, and he was eventually consecrated bishop of the see of Salzburg. A particular field of his activity was the province of Carinthia, of which he is venerated as the evangelizer.

VITALIS ◊ under *Felicity*

VITUS, martyr. Date unknown; f.d. 15 June. This martyr has been venerated from early times but his true story has perished; he probably suffered in the Lucanian province of southern Italy. His legend, a late and fanciful compilation, associates him with Sicily; it asserts that he was put to death, with his former nurse Crescentia and her husband Modestus, during the persecution under Diocletian and after the usual torments and wonders. He was invoked against a number of bodily ills, particularly epilepsy and the complaint called 'St Vitus's dance' (chorea). As well as in Italy, St Vitus was specially celebrated in Germany, his reputed relics having been translated to the abbey of Corvey in Westphalia in 836. His emblem is a cock or a dog.

VIVIANA, or BIBIANA, martyr. Date unknown; f.d. 2 December. There was a church dedicated in honour of this martyr on the Esquiline hill at Rome in the fifth century, where her relics were said to be, but all historical knowledge of her is lost. She was later given a part in a legendary cycle which groups a number of saints, real or imaginary, round the fictitious story of one called Pimenius or Pigmenius, which in turn is related to the legend of ◊ SS. *John and Paul.*

VLADIMIR, prince. B. *c.* 955; d. 1015; f.d. 15 July. Vladimir's grandmother *St Olga* (d. 969; f.d. 11 July) was an early convert to the Christian faith among the Scandinavian rulers of the province of Kiev; she was the widow of Prince Igor and advanced in age when she received baptism at Constantinople, *c.* 957. She made strong efforts to induce others to follow her example, but it is from the time of her grandson that the definitive conversion of Russia is dated. After a good deal of hesitation, Prince Vladimir was baptized *c.* 989 and married Ann, sister of the Byzantine emperor, Basil II, the two events being closely connected. Vladimir's life had been brutal, bloodthirsty, and dissolute; but he took his new religion seriously and indeed sought to impose it by force on his people, not all of whom were willing to accept it. But the change of life attributed to him, his mildness towards criminals, his generosity to the poor, and the support he gave to the Greek missionaries, resulted in a picture of him that caused later generations to look on St Vladimir and St Olga as the first-born of the new Christian people of Russia and her borderland. They were esteemed to be saints, and Vladimir became the subject of a cycle of folklore and heroic poems. A descendant of his, Vladimir Monomakh, married Gytha, daughter of King Harold of England.

W

WALBURGA, abbess. B. in Wessex; d. at Heidenheim, 779 (?); f.d. 25 February. St Walburga (Waldburg), a nun of Wimborne, was sister to ◊ *St Willibald* and St Winebald, and like them joined ◊ *St Boniface of Crediton*'s mission in Germany. On the death of Winebald in 761 she succeeded to the headship of the double monastery of Heidenheim, and lived there till her death. This Englishwoman had the curious destiny of attaining a place in German folklore. The night of 1 May (the date of the transfer of her bodily remains to Eichstätt) became known as Walpurgisnacht and she was associated with witchcraft and other superstitions (cf. Goethe's *Faust*, pt. i, Walpurgis night in the Hartz mountains). Her shrine was much resorted to on account of a 'miraculous oil' said to exude from it.

WAUDRU, or WALDETRUDIS, widow. D. at Châteaulieu, *c.* 688; f.d. 9 April. The patroness of Mons in Belgium was outstanding in a very remarkable seventh-century family: her parents, Walbert and Bertilia, her sister, Aldegund of Maubeuge, her husband ◊ *Madelgaire* and their four children, Landric, Dentelin, Aldetrude, and Madelberte, are all venerated as saints. After her husband had become a monk, St Waudru devoted herself to the care of the poor and sick, and later built a convent on the site of the present town of Mons.

WENCESLAS, prince. B. in Bohemia, *c.* 907; d. at Stara Boleslav, 929; f.d. 28 September. Ludmilla, widow of Borivoy, founder of the Bohemian dynasty of Premyslid, had followed her husband into the Christian church. Her religious and political influence over her grandson Wenceslas (Vaclav, Wenzel) angered a semi-pagan party among the nobility, and in 921, during the regency of Wenceslas's mother Drahomira, Ludmilla was murdered. A few years later Wenceslas took over power; he set himself to promote Christianity and good order among his subjects, and pursued a conciliatory policy towards his German neighbours. The opposition became more bitter, Wenceslas's brother Boleslav taking the lead in it. In 929, Wenceslas having accepted an invitation to stay on his brother's estate, Boleslav picked a quarrel with him, and in the ensuing scrimmage Wenceslas was killed by Boleslav's supporters. Though they died only in some remote degree on account of religion, the young prince and his grandmother were acclaimed as martyrs; St Wenceslas became the great Bohemian hero and is the patron saint of modern Czechoslovakia; *St Ludmilla*'s feast day is also observed, on 16 September. The theme of the Christmas song 'Good King Wenceslas', written by J. M. Neale (d. 1866), is imaginary.

WENZEL ◊ *Wenceslas*

WERBURGH, abbess. D. *c.* 700; f.d. 3 February. She was one of the early English royal abbesses, daughter of King Wulfhere of Mercia and St Ermenilda. Most of the material concerning her is legendary; but she was associated with several religious houses and appears to have died at a nunnery at Threckingham in Lincolnshire. To save it from the marauding Danes, her body was translated to Chester, where her shrine was a place of pilgrimage until it was destroyed under King Henry VIII. Among other royal abbesses not mentioned elsewhere herein were *St Cuthburga* (d. *c.* 725; f.d. 3 September), who was the wife of King Aldfrid of Northumbria; afterwards she took the veil and founded the nunnery of Wimborne; and *St Cyneburga* (d. *c.* 680; f.d. 6 March). She too was married to a Northumbrian prince and later ruled a convent, at Castor in Northamptonshire; with her sister St Cyneswide and another relative, St Tibba, she was particularly venerated at Peterborough abbey. There were two other holy Cyneburgas, honoured at Gloucester.

WILFRID, bishop. B. in Northumbria, 634; d. at Oundle, 24 April 709 or 710; f.d. 12 October. St Wilfrid was educated in the monastery of Lindisfarne and then spent some years at Lyons and in Rome. He came back an intransigent supporter of Roman church customs as against the Celtic ways of northern England, and at the conference of Whitby in 664 he was chiefly responsible for the victory of the Roman party. He had already been given the monastery of Ripon and was soon appointed bishop of York; but he was prevented from taking over the see until ◊ *St Theodore of Canterbury* put him in possession of it in 669, displacing ◊ *St Chad*. When in 678 Theodore divided the diocese of York without Wilfrid's agreement, Wilfrid appealed to Rome; the case was decided in his favour, but when he returned to Northumbria he was imprisoned by King Egfrid, and then sought refuge in Sussex. From Selsey he energetically evangelized the heathen South Saxons, until he was recalled to the north in 686. But his troubles began afresh in 691; he had to retire to the midlands, and he again went to Rome to appeal for help. Eventually he agreed to a compromise, and at the time of his death was presiding over the see of Hexham from the Ripon monastery, where he probably had already introduced the Rule of St Benedict.

St Wilfrid was an outstanding figure of his time, a very able and courageous man, holding pertinaciously to his convictions in spite of consequent embroilments with civil and ecclesiastical authorities. He was the first Englishman to carry a lawsuit to the Roman courts, and was successful in helping to bring the discipline of the English church more into line with that of Rome and the continent. His vicissitudes and misfortunes have somewhat obscured his abilities as a missionary, not only among the South Saxons but also for a brief period in Friesland in 678–9; his preaching there may be taken as the starting-point of the great English mission to the Germanic peoples on the European mainland.

The Life by his disciple Eddius, tr. by B. Colgrave (1927) and by J. F. Webb in *Lives of the Saints* (Penguin); E. S. Duckett, *Anglo-Saxon Saints and Scholars* (1947).

WILGEFORTIS. No date; f.d. 20 July. The legend of this fictitious person is that her father, the king of Portugal, wanted her to marry the king of Sicily; but she had made a vow of virginity, and her prayers for help in her predicament were answered when a beard grew upon her face. The king of Sicily withdrew his suit, and her indignant father had her crucified. She was accordingly represented as a bearded woman hanging on a cross. This preposterous tale has nothing to do with the hermaphroditic cults of antiquity in Cyprus and elsewhere; it started from a misunderstanding of one of those crucifixes showing Christ wearing a long tunic (the Volto Santo at Lucca is a well-known example). Wilgefortis was known by a variety of names, Liberata, Livrade, Kümmernis, and others. In England she was called Uncumber, and was invoked by women who had troublesome husbands. The Roman Martyrology still refers to St Wilgefortis, virgin martyr in Portugal, under 20 July.

WILLEHAD ◊ under *Willibrord*

WILLIAM OF AEBELHOLT, abbot. B. in France, c. 1127; d. in Denmark, 1203; cd 1224; f.d. 6 April. He was one of the most revered saints of Denmark, and his extant letters are a valuable source for the history of the Danish church. He was a canon regular in Paris when c. 1171 he was invited by the bishop of Roskilde to undertake the reform of the abbey of Aebelholt; he carried out this difficult task successfully and became a religious power in Denmark. About 1194 he went to Rome on behalf of Ingelburga, sister of the Danish king, who had been repudiated by her husband, King Philip Augustus of France. This William is sometimes confused with *St William of Roskilde* (d. c. 1070), a bishop there whose name figures in Danish calendars; he is said to have been an Englishman.

WILLIAM OF MONTE VERGINE, abbot. B. at Vercelli, 1085; d. at Goleto near Salerno, 1142; f.d. 25 April. After leading a wandering existence for a time he settled as a hermit on Monte Virgiliano, now Monte Vergine, in the province of Naples. Being joined by others, he formed them into a community c. 1124, which later became the mother house of a congregation of hermit monks. But William was by choice a solitary and left the monastery to pursue his wanderings in southern Italy, in the course of which he made other foundations. Of these none survive except the Benedictine abbey of Monte Vergine, which is a very popular place of pilgrimage.

WILLIAM OF NORWICH. D. at Norwich, 1144; f.d. 26 March. The mutilated body of this twelve-year-old boy was found in a wood outside Norwich; five years later it was alleged that he was a victim of ritual murder by Jews. The authorities seem not to have credited the story; but the common people did, and William was venerated locally as a martyr. This is the first recorded accusation of the kind against Jews; belief in their killing of Christian children for ritual purposes was rife in the later middle ages, fed by a fanatical antisemitism. No instance of the charge has been substantiated, and it has been rightly called 'one of the most notable and disastrous lies of history'. Another case was that of the nine-year-old *Little St Hugh*, whose body was found in a well at Lincoln in 1255; a score of Jews were tortured and hanged on a charge of complicity in crucifying him. Cf. Chaucer's 'Prioress's Tale', in which Hugh is invoked. A prominent continental case was *St Simon*, a child of two and a half, said to have been done to death by a Jewish physician at Trento in northern Italy in 1475. No doubt these and other children were murdered; why and by whom is not known. In 1965 the cultus of Simon was officially abolished.

M. D. Anderson, *A Saint at Stake* (1964); C. Roth, *The Ritual Murder Libel and the Jews* (1935).

WILLIAM OF ROCHESTER ◊ under *William of York*

WILLIAM OF ROSKILDE ◊ under *William of Aebelholt*

WILLIAM OF YORK, bishop. D. at York, 1154; cd 1226; f.d. 8 June. The story of William Fitz Herbert as it has come down to us is almost wholly concerned with the bitter dispute that followed his election to the archbishopric of York in 1140. The election was challenged, particularly by the Cistercian monks of the province, who accused William of simony and incontinence, and King Stephen (who was probably his uncle) of exerting undue influence on the appointment. In 1143 Pope Innocent II permitted William's consecration, but the dispute continued; ◊ *St Bernard* of Clairvaux violently supported his Cistercian brethren, and Pope Eugenius III suspended the archbishop from his duties. William seems to have been negligent of his own interests, some of his supporters behaved with inexcusable violence, and in 1147 he was deposed. For six years he led an exemplary life in retirement at Winchester; then his three chief opponents died, and he was reinstated at York by Pope Anastasius IV. William was mild and conciliatory towards his enemies, but within a few months he was dead, perhaps from poison. He was well liked by the people, and the rumoured murder doubtless contributed to a popular demand for his canonization.

Half a century later a local cultus arose from a murder at Rochester, when in 1201, a citizen of Perth, said to be on pilgrimage to Jerusalem, was killed by his young travelling-companion. He was venerated as *St William of Rochester* (f.d. 23 May), but was never canonized.

WILLIBALD, bishop. B. in Wessex, *c.* 700; d. at Eichstätt, 786; f.d. 7 July. SS. Willibald, Winebald, and ◊ *Walburga* were the children of an eastern Wessex magnate of unknown name: he is venerated as a saint at Lucca in Italy (where he died) under the disguise of 'Richard, king of the English'. As a young man Willibald travelled in the Near East and then, from 730 to 740, lived as a monk at the abbey of Monte Cassino. He was the first known English pilgrim to the Holy Land and an account of his travels, the *Hodoeporicon*, was taken down from his own lips by a nun at Heidenheim; the text still exists. By Pope St Gregory III he was sent to Germany to help his kinsman ◊ *St Boniface of Crediton*, who ordained him priest and in 742 made him first bishop of Eichstätt. Willibald was a devoted pastor and missionary in Bavaria for over forty years, 'tilling the wide fields for the divine seed, sowing and cultivating them for harvest time'. At Heidenheim he founded adjoining monasteries for men and for women; of this establishment his brother *St Winebald* (Wynbald; d. 761; f.d. 18 December), who had been a missionary in Thuringia, was the first abbot. It became an important centre for the education of clergy. St Willibald was outstanding among those who carried on St Boniface's work, a man who 'set a good example by word and deed, zealous for good monastic observance, shunning all wickedness, godly and forbearing'.

The *Hodoeporicon* is trans. in C. H. Talbot, *The Anglo-Saxon Missionaries in Germany* (1954).

WILLIBRORD, missionary. B. in Northumbria, 658; d. at Echternach, 739; f.d. 7 November. Having been educated at the monastery of Ripon under ◊ *St Wilfrid*, Willibrord went to Ireland in 678, where he was ordained priest in 688. Two years later, with a number of other Englishmen, he landed in Friesland, of which he was to be the principal evangelizer, under the protection of Pepin of Herstal. He was consecrated archbishop of the Frisians by Pope St Sergius I in 695, and set up his episcopal chair at Utrecht. Thus was inaugurated the English colony in continental Europe that was to be so potent a religious influence for a hundred years. About 700 Willibrord established a second important missionary centre, the monastery of Echternach in Luxemburg. From 715 to 719 there was a grave set-back during the Frisian rising against the Franks; but the position recovered, and Willibrord was able to explore into Denmark and perhaps Thuringia. He was in touch with *St Boniface of Crediton*, and together they were responsible for instituting *chorepiscopi*, 'country bishops', in western Europe to help them in their work. St Willibrord's missionary achievement was not spectacular – the rapidity and number of conversions was exaggerated by later writers – but it was a solid laying of foundations; 'his charity was manifest in his daily unremitting labour for Christ's name's sake' (Alcuin). Every year on Whit Tuesday there takes place through the streets of Echternach and round the saint's tomb in the church an hours' long processional dance of pilgrims, each group accompanied by its own brass band. This has been done since before 1553, an unspoiled survival of ancient sanctified merry-making.

Early in the eighth century a monk of Echternach wrote out a calendar of saints, many of whom were connected with the scenes of Willibrord's life. This *Calendar of St Willibrord* is now in the National Library at Paris, and it is of great interest to students of hagiography; under the date 21 November 728 are several autobiographical lines written by Willibrord himself.

In the next generation there lived at Echternach for a time *St Willehad*, another Northumbrian missionary, first among the Frisians and then among the Saxons between the lower Weser and the Elbe. He died bishop of Bremen in 789 (f.d. 8 November). A. Grieve, *Willibrord, Missionary in the Netherlands* (1923).

WILLIGIS, bishop. B. at Schöningen in Brunswick; d. at Mainz, 1011; f.d. 23 February. He was a man of humble origin, who by 975 was imperial chancellor to Otto II, and archbishop of Mainz. He served also under Otto III and ◊ *St Henry II*, and left his mark as a capable and conscientious ecclesiastical statesman. Through his efforts Christianity increased in Schleswig, Holstein, and southern Scandinavia; he consecrated a succession of excellent bishops, and provided for the building of several great churches and other public works. Unhappily Willigis had a long disagreement with ◊ *St Bernward* of Hildesheim about jurisdiction over the nunnery of Gandersheim, a quarrel apparently provoked by one of the nuns, a sister of Otto III; at long last Willigis admitted he was in the wrong and gracefully withdrew his claims. This seems to have been the only blot on a vigorous and beneficent episcopate.

WINEBALD ◊ under *Willibald*

WINIFRED, or GWENFREWI. Seventh century; f.d. 3 November
Written information about St Winifred, called Gwenfrewi in Welsh, is too late and fanciful to allow reliable data about her life or death to be established. The legend current in the later middle ages makes her a niece of St Beuno, and says that she was pestered by the unwanted attentions of a chieftain's son, Caradoc, from Penarlâg (Hawarden in Flintshire). When she repulsed him he struck off her head with his sword, whereat the earth opened and swallowed him. Beuno restored Winifred's head to her shoulders and, thus brought back to life, she lived the rest of her days as a nun at Gwytherin in Denbighshire.

In 1138 Winifred's reputed relics were enshrined in the Benedictine abbey church at Shrewsbury, and in due course her cultus spread in England too. We are told that where her head fell at Holywell (Treffynnon, Welltown) a spring of water suddenly appeared. It acquired a reputation for the cure of disease, and King Henry VII's mother, Lady Margaret Beaufort, and others had it enclosed within a stone building. Pilgrimages to St Winifred's Well persisted after the Reformation, and they continue to this day. Two poems of Gerard Manley Hopkins are devoted to this saint.

There is evidence that the abbot *St Beuno* (f.d. 21 April) was a man of importance, but his story too, as written in 1346, is legendary. His name is particularly associated with Clynnog in Caernarvonshire, where sick people were still brought to his supposed burying-place towards the end of the eighteenth century. He may well have had a small monastery there.

P. Metcalf, *Life of St Winifride* (1712; ed. H. Thurston, 1917).

WINNOC ◊ under *Bertin*

WINWALOE, abbot. Sixth century; f.d. 3 March. The name of this saint appears under many forms; in French it is generally Guénolé. He was the founder of the great monastery of Landévennec in Breton Cornouaille; Landewednack on the Lizard peninsula in British Cornwall is the same name, and Gunwalloe near by also commemorates him. There is a long and tedious Life of Winwaloe, written at Landévennec in the ninth century; few trustworthy biographical particulars can be gleaned from this collection of legend. The cultus of the saint is still alive in Brittany.

WOLFGANG, bishop. B. in Swabia, *c.* 925; d. at Puppingen near Linz, 994; f.d. 31 October. He was educated at the abbey of Reichenau in Lake Constance, and afterwards taught at the cathedral schools of Würzburg and Trier; in 964 he joined the Benedictine monks of Einsiedeln. After a short and discouraging mission in Pannonia (Hungary) he became bishop of Regensburg in 972. Wolfgang presided there till his death, restoring canonical life among his clergy, reforming monasteries, and earning the love of his people and the respect of the imperial court. He was for a time tutor to the future emperor ◊ *St Henry II.*

WOOLOS ◊ under *Cadoc*

WULFRIC ◊ under *Ulric*

WULFSTAN, bishop. B. at Long Itchington, *c.* 1009; d. at Worcester, 1095; cd 1203; f.d. 19 January. St Wulfstan, or Wulstan, was educated at the monasteries of Evesham and Peterborough, and became a monk at Worcester. As prior of the house he restored its fortunes, religious and temporal, and was noted for his pastoral activity, and in 1062 he was made bishop of Worcester. After the Norman conquest he supported King William I and was allowed to retain his diocese, pastoral care for which was his principal interest. He fought the slave-trade in Bristol, enforced the discipline of priestly celibacy (a thankless task in those days), built new parish churches and refounded the monastery at Westbury-on-Trym, while keeping so far as possible the monastic régime in his own daily life. He was not a learned man, but this did not prevent him from being an effective preacher and an encourager of learning among his clergy, and he endeared himself to his flock. Professor David Knowles writes of St Wulfstan, 'He is, indeed, a most attractive figure, too little known to his countrymen ...; the last, and certainly one of the greatest, of the [early] bishops of pure English blood and culture.'

J. W. Lamb, *St Wulstan, Prelate and Patriot* (1933); David Knowles in *The English Way* (ed. Maisie Ward, 1933).

X

XYSTUS ◊ *Sixtus*

Y

YVES, priest and lawyer. B. at Kermartin near Tréguier; d. at Lovannec, 1303; cd 1347; f.d. 19 May. Yves (Ivo) Hélory was the son of a Breton landowner and was sent to the universities of Paris and Orléans, where he became a very competent civil and canon lawyer. He was appointed a diocesan judge, first to the bishop of Rennes and then to the bishop of Tréguier; in this office he was distinguished for his equity, incorruptibility, and concern for the interests of the poor and ignorant. In 1284 Yves was ordained priest, and from 1287 gave himself wholly to parochiel work, at Trédrez and Lovannec. His legal knowledge was always at the disposal of his parishioners, as were his time and his goods; he gave an example of frugal and unassuming living, and found his forensic experience valuable in the pulpit. His countrymen have always had a great regard for St Yves, 'an attorney who was an honest man' (lawyers, like bishops, are apt to have a 'bad press'); Yves is a favourite christening name in Brittany.

Z

ZACHARY, pope. B. at San Severino; d. in Rome, 752; f.d. 22 March. St Zachary was a Calabrian Greek by birth, and was elected bishop of Rome in 741. In public affairs he joined a conciliatory spirit with far-sighted wisdom. He came to terms with the Lombard king Liutprand, sanctioned the assumption of the Frankish crown by Pepin the Short, denounced the iconoclasm of the Byzantine emperor Constantine V, and gave every encouragement to the work of ◊ St Boniface of Crediton in Germany; two extant letters of the pope to Boniface are of great interest. St Zachary was an inveterate enemy to the trade in Christian slaves. His translation into Greek of ◊ St Gregory the Great's Dialogues spread knowledge of holy men of the West in the East.

A feast of St Zachary, father of ◊ St John the Baptist, with his wife St Elizabeth, is kept in Palestine and elsewhere on 5 November and other dates.

ZENO OF VERONA, bishop. B. in Africa; d. at Verona, c. 372; f.d. 12 April. He was bishop of Verona from 361 till his death, but little else is known of him except that he was a trained orator and zealous preacher. His sermons are of great interest for the information they give about Christian teaching, worship, organization, and life in the fourth century. They form the earliest collection of homilies in Latin, ninety-three in number.

ZITA, domestic servant. B. near Lucca, c. 1218; died at Lucca, 1278; f.d. 27 April. At the age of twelve Zita entered domestic service in the household of a well-off weaver in Lucca, and remained there all her life. She was intensely devout and punctilious in her work, qualities which did not commend her to her fellow servants, and her lavish gifts of food to the poor embroiled her with her employer. But as years passed she won respect by her patience and goodness, and she became a confidential friend of the family. In later life stories were told about her in Lucca, of supernatural manifestations and her good deeds, and at her death she was popularly acclaimed a saint and a patroness of maidservants.

RECENT CANONIZATIONS

ELIZABETH SETON, laywoman and foundress. B. in New York, 1774; d. at Emmitsburg, 1821; cd 1975; f.d. 4 January. Elizabeth Ann Bayley, the first native-born American to be canonized, came of a prominent New York family, and at twenty she married a professor of anatomy, Richard Seton. Five children were born of this happy union, but in 1803 Mr Seton died. Two years later Mrs Seton joined the Roman Catholic church. After some very difficult years she was enabled to establish in Emmitsburg a small religious community to care for the children of the poor. The rest of Elizabeth's life was devoted to the leadership and fostering of this community which has developed over the years into the wide-spread congregation of the American Sisters of Charity. St Elizabeth was a charming and cultivated woman of determined character. In face of all the social pressures of her 'world' she persevered in the religion and eventual way of life to which she knew God had called her. Of all the attendant discouragements and difficulties the hardest to bear were interior to herself; for example, she detested having to exercise authority over others and she suffered much from bouts of spiritual aridity. But she conquered in the Sign she had chosen and conquered heroically.

R J. Cushing, *Bd Mother Seton* (1964); D. Attwater, *Saints Westward* (1953).

OLIVER PLUNKETT, martyr. B. in Meath, 1625; d. in London, 1681; cd 1975; f.d. 1 July. After being made priest in Rome in 1654, Oliver Plunkett remained for twelve years in the papal service. He was then sent back to his native land as archbishop of Armagh and primate of All Ireland. The policies of Cromwell had brought the country to a state of religious disarray, not to say disorder. The new archbishop's vigorous efforts to remedy this were carried on under most harassing conditions, amid which he persevered for ten years. Then, in 1678, Titus Oates 'discovered' a non-existent 'popish plot' involving Plunkett. He was arrested in Ireland but, through the chicanery of political lawyers, was put to trial in London, charged with conspiring to subvert the realm.

Chiefly on the evidence of a renegade priest, he was convicted and sentenced to death. St Oliver was hanged at Tyburn, dying before the barbarities of disembowelling and quartering were carried out. His mutilated remains are now enshrined in part at Drogheda and in part at Downside Abbey in England.

A. Curtayne, *The Trial of Oliver Plunkett* (1953).

SOME EMBLEMS

Anchor: Clement I
Arrow: King Edmund; Giles; Sebastian
three Balls: Nicholas of Myra
laden Basket: Dorothy
Bear: Columban
Beehive: Bernard
Bell (and Pig): Antony
Book (and Sword): Paul
Breasts on dish: Agatha
two crossed Candles (or Comb): Blaise
Cardinal's Hat: Bonaventure
Cardinal's Hat (and Lion): Jerome
Cock (or Dog): Vitus
Cockleshell: James the Greater
Comb (or two crossed Candles): Blaise
the Cross: Helen
Cross saltire: Andrew
red cross on white ground: George
broken Cup (and Raven): Benedict
Dog: Rock
Dog (or Cock): Vitus
Dog, with torch in mouth (and Star): Dominic
Dove: David
Dragon: Margaret
Eagle: John the Divine
two Eyes in dish: Lucy
Forceps gripping tooth: Apollonia
Greyhound: Ferdinand III of Castile
Gridiron: Lawrence
Hind (or Stag): Eustace; Giles; Hubert; and others
ointment Jar: Mary Magdalen
two crossed Keys: Peter
bunch of Keys: Zita
butcher's Knife: Bartholomew
Lamb: Agnes
Last (or Shoe): Crispin and Crispinian
Lily: Antony of Padua
Lion: Gerasimus and other desert-dwellers
Lion (and Cardinal's Hat): Jerome
winged Lion: Mark
Man with wings: Matthew

SOME EMBLEMS

Monstrance: Clare of Assisi; Norbert; Paschal Baylon
Organ: Cecily
winged Ox: Luke
Pig (and Bell): Antony
Raven (and broken Cup): Benedict
finger Ring: Edward the Confessor
Shamrock (and Snakes): Patrick
Ship: Anselm; Bertin; and others
Shoe (*or* Last): Crispin and Crispinian
Sickle: Isidore the Farm-servant, Notburga
Snakes (and Shamrock): Patrick
Spade: Fiacre
pastoral Staff, with mouse running up it: Gertrude of Nivelles
Stag (*or* Hind): Eustace; Giles; Hubert; and others
Star: Thomas Aquinas
Star (and Dog, with torch in mouth): Dominic
Stigmata: Francis of Assisi, Katherine of Siena
Swan: Hugh of Lincoln
Sword (and Book): Paul
Tongs: Dunstan
Tower: Barbara
Wheel: Katherine of Alexandria
Windlass: Erasmus (Elmo)

There is a number of emblems or devices used in association with whole classes of saints. The principal ones are a *church building* for founders of churches or monasteries; a *crown* or other royal badge for royal persons; the *mitre* or the *pastoral staff* for bishops (sometimes for abbots or abbesses); the *palm* or a *sword* for martyrs; a *pen and book* for learned men; the triple *tiara* for a pope.

FEAST DAYS

This list gives the feast days only of saints mentioned in this book.

JANUARY

1 January   Almachius; Odilo

2 January   Caspar del Bufalo; Macarius the Younger, Seraphim of Sarov

3 January   Fulgentius; Geneviève

5 January   Simeon the Stylite; Telesphorus

7 January   Canute Lavard; Charles of Sezze; Lucian of Antioch

8 January   Abo; Gudula; Pega; Lucian of Beauvais; Severinus of Noricum; Thorfinn

9 January   Adrian of Canterbury; Philip of Moscow

10 January   Peter Orseolo

11 January   Paulinus of Aquileia; Theodosius the Cenobiarch

12 January   Benedict (*or* Benet) Biscop; Tatiana

13 January   Hilary of Poitiers (B.C.P.; ►► 14 January)

14 January   Barba'shmin; Felix of Nola; Hilary of Poitiers (►► 13 January); Kentigern (*or* Mungo); Macrina the Elder; Sava

15 January   Ita; Macarius the Elder; Paul the Hermit

16 January   Berard and his companions; Fursey; Honoratus of Arles

17 January   Antony the Abbot; Sulpice

18 January   Margaret of Hungary; Prisca

353

19 January	Audifax and Abachum; Canute IV; Henry of Uppsala; Marius and Martha; Wulfstan
20 January	Euthymius the Great; Sebastian
21 January	Agnes; Fructuosus of Tarragona; Meinrad
22 January	Anastasius the Persian; Vincent of Saragossa; Vincent Pallotti
23 January	Ildefonsus; John the Almsgiver; Raymond of Peñafort
24 January	Timothy
25 January	Juventinus and Maximinus; Paul (B.C.P.; ▶▶ 29 June)
26 January	Alberic; Eystein; Paula; Polycarp
27 January	John Chrysostom
28 January	Peter Nolasco; Valerius of Saragossa
29 January	Francis de Sales; Gildas the Wise; Sulpicius
30 January	Bathild; Martina
31 January	Aidan (or Maedoc) of Ferns; Cyrus and John; John Bosco; Marcella

FEAST DAYS

FEBRUARY

1 February Brigid (*or* Bride); Ignatius of Antioch

2 February Joan de Lestonnac

3 February Anskar; Blaise; Ia; Lawrence of Canterbury; Werburgh

4 February Andrew Corsini; Gilbert of Sempringham; Joan of France; Joannicius; John de Britto; Phileas

5 February Agatha; Japan, Martyrs in

6 February Amand of Maastricht: Dorothy; Photius; Titus

7 February Romuald; Theodore the General

8 February Cuthman; John of Matha

9 February Apollonia; Cyril of Alexandria; Nicephorus of Antioch; Teilo

10 February Scholastica

11 February Benedict of Aniane

12 February Julian the Hospitaller; Marina; Seven Founders, The

13 February Katherine dei Ricci

14 February Maro; Valentine (1); Valentine (2)

15 February Sigfrid

16 February Elias and his companions

17 February Finan; Fintan of Cloneenagh

18 February Colman of Lindisfarne; Flavian of Constantinople

FEAST DAYS

19 February Mesrop

20 February Shahdost; Ulric of Haselbury

22 February Margaret of Cortona

23 February Mildburga; Peter Damian; Willigis

24 February Matthias; Montanus and Lucius

25 February Ethelbert of Kent; Walburga

26 February Porphyry of Gaza

27 February Gabriel Possenti; Leander

28 February Oswald of Worcester; Plague at Alexandria, Martyrs of the

FEAST DAYS

MARCH

1 March	David (*or* Dewi)
2 March	Chad
3 March	Aelred; Cunegund; Marinus of Caesarea; Winwaloe
4 March	Casimir
5 March	Ciaran of Saighir; Gerasimus; Phocas of Antioch; Piran
6 March	Chrodegang; Colette; Cyneburga; Perpetua and Felicity
7 March	Thomas Aquinas
8 March	Felix of Dunwich; John of God; Julian of Toledo; Senan of Scattery
9 March	Dominic Savio; Frances of Rome; Gregory of Nyssa; Katherine of Bologna
10 March	Forty Martyrs, The
11 March	Eulogius of Córdoba: Pionius; Sophronius
12 March	Gregory the Great; Maximilian; Paul Aurelian (*or* of Léon); Simeon the New Theologian
13 March	Euphrasia; Gerald
14 March	Matilda
15 March	Clement Hofbauer; Louise de Marillac

FEAST DAYS

16 March	Heribert of Cologne; Julian of Antioch; North America, The Martyrs of (S.J.; ►► 26 September); Paul the Simple
17 March	Gertrude of Nivelles; Joseph of Arimathaea; Patrick
18 March	Cyril of Jerusalem; Edward the Martyr; Frigidian; Salvator of Horta
19 March	Joseph (►► 1 May)
20 March	Cuthbert; Herbert; Martin of Braga
21 March	Benedict; Enda; Nicholas von Flue; Serapion of Thmuis
22 March	Zachary
23 March	Gwinear
24 March	Gabriel; Katherine of Vadstena
26 March	Braulio; Ludger, William of Norwich
27 March	John the Egyptian; John of Damascus; Rupert of Salzburg
28 March	John of Capestrano
29 March	Berthold; Jonah and Berikjesu; Mark of Arethusa
30 March	John Climacus; Osburga

FEAST DAYS

APRIL

1 April   Hugh of Grenoble

2 April   Francis of Paola; Mary the Egyptian

3 April   Burgundofara; Pancras of Taormina; Richard of Chichester

4 April   Agape, Chionia and Irene; Ambrose (B.C.P.; ▶▶ 7 December); Benedict the Black; Isidore of Seville

5 April   Vincent Ferrer

6 April   William of Aebelholt

7 April   Nilus of Sora

9 April   Waudru

11 April   Gemma Galgani; Guthlac; Leo the Great

12 April   Sabas the Goth; Zeno of Verona

13 April   Carpus and Papylus

14 April   Justin; Tiburtius (2)

16 April   Benedict Labre; Bernadette; Magnus of Orkney

17 April   Donnan; Robert of Chaise-Dieu; Stephen Harding

19 April   Alphege; Expeditus; Leo IX

20 April   Agnes of Montepulciano

21 April   Anselm; Beuno; Simeon Barsabba'e

22 April   Conrad of Parzham; Pherbutha; Theodore of Sykeon

23 April   Adalbert of Prague; George

24 April   Euphrasia Pelletier; Ivo; Mellitus

FEAST DAYS

25 April   Mark; William of Monte Vergine

26 April   Cletus (*or* Anacletus); Stephen of Perm

27 April   Maughold; Peter Canisius; Toribio of Lima; Zita

28 April   Louis Grignion; Paul of the Cross; Peter Chanel

29 April   Hugh of Cluny; Robert of Molesme

30 April   Erconwald (▶▶ 13 May); Joseph Cottolengo;
Katherine of Siena; Marian and James

FEAST DAYS

MAY

1 May   Brieuc; James the Less and Philip (►► *11 May);
       Joseph (*►► 19 March); Peregrine Laziosi; Ultan

2 May   Athanasius

3 May   Theodosius of the Caves

4 May   Gothard; Monica; Pelagia of Tarsus

5 May   Hilary of Arles; Jutta; Pius V

7 May   Stanislas of Cracow

8 May   Peter of Tarentaise; Victor

9 May   Gregory of Nazianzus

10 May   Antonino; Isidore the Farm-servant

11 May   Asaph; Comgall; Francis di Girolamo; James the Less
       and Philip (R.C. ch.; ►► 1 May); Mayeul

12 May   Epiphanius of Salamis; Germanus of Constantinople;
       Ignatius of Laconi; Nereus and Achilleus; Pancras

13 May   Andrew Fournet; Erconwald (►► 30 April);
       Euthymius the Enlightener; Robert Bellarmine

14 May   Carthage; Michael Garicoïts; Mary Mazzarello;
       Pachomius

15 May   Dympna; Hallvard; John-Baptist de la Salle

16 May   Andrew Bobola; Brendan the Voyager; Fructuosus of
       Braga; Honorius of Amiens; Simon Stock; Ubaldo;
       John of Nepomuk

17 May   Paschal Baylon

18 May   Eric; Felix of Cantalice

361

FEAST DAYS

19 May   Celestine V; Dunstan; Yves (*or* Ivo)

20 May   Bernardine of Siena; Ethelbert of the East Angles

21 May   Godric

22 May   Rita of Cascia

23 May   Desiderius; Euphrosyne of Polotsk; Ivo of Chartres;
William of Rochester

24 May   David of Scotland; Simeon Stylites the Younger

25 May   Aldhelm; Gregory VII; Madeleine Sophie:
Marys, The Three

26 May   Augustine (*or* Austin) of Canterbury;
Mariana of Quito; Philip Neri

27 May   Bede; Julius of Durostorum

28 May   Bernard of Montjoux; Germanus of Paris

29 May   Mary-Magdalen dei Pazzi

30 May   Ferdinand III of Castile; Joan of Arc

FEAST DAYS

JUNE

1 June   Angela of Brescia; Nicomedes (B.C.P.; ►►
15 September); Pamphilus

2 June   Blandina; Erasmus (*or* Elmo);
Lyons, The Martyrs of; Marcellinus and Peter;
Nicephorus of Constantinople

3 June   Clotilda; Kevin; Uganda, Martyrs of

4 June   Francis Caracciolo; Petroc

5 June   Boniface of Crediton

6 June   Jarlath of Tuam; Norbert

7 June   Colman of Dromore; Meriadoc;
Robert of Newminster

8 June   Melania the Elder; William of York

9 June   Columba (*or* Colmcille); Pelagia of Antioch;
Primus and Felician

11 June   Barnabas

12 June   Eskil; John of Sahagun; Leo III

13 June   Antony of Padua

14 June   Basil the Great; Methodius of Constantinople

15 June   Edburga of Winchester; Germaine of Pibrac; Vitus

16 June   Cyricus and Julitta; John Regis; Lutgard;
Tikhon of Amathus

17 June   Alban (B.C.P.; ►► 22 June);
Botolph (*or* Botulf); Harvey

FEAST DAYS

18 June Elizabeth of Schönau; Ephraem;
Mark and Marcellian

19 June Boniface (*or* Bruno) of Querfurt;
Gervase and Protase; Juliana Falconieri

20 June Adalbert of Magdeburg

21 June Aloysius; Méen

22 June Alban (▶▶ 17 June); Nicetas of Remesiana;
Paulinus of Nola

23 June Etheldreda (*or* Audrey) (▶▶ 17 October);
Joseph Cafasso

24 June John the Baptist (*birth*)

25 June Febronia; Prosper of Reggio

26 June Anthelm; John and Paul

27 June Ladislas

28 June Austol; Potamiaena; Vincentia Gerosa

29 June Peter and Paul (▶▶ 25 January); Peter (B.C.P.)

30 June Martial of Limoges

FEAST DAYS

1 July   Simeon Salus

3 July   Aaron and Julius; Bernardine Realino;
Irenaeus of Lyons; Leo II

4 July   Andrew of Crete (1); Martin of Tours (B.C.P.; again on
11 November); Odo the Good; Ulric of Augsburg

5 July   Antony Zaccaria; Athanasius the Athonite;
Modwenna; Philomena of San Severino

6 July   Godelive; Mary Goretti; Moninne; Sexburga

7 July   Cyril and Methodius; Ethelburga of
Faremoutiers-en-Brie; Hedda;
Prosper of Aquitaine; Willibald

8 July   Elizabeth of Portugal; Procopius

9 July   John (Fisher) of Rochester and Thomas More;
Veronica Giuliani

10 July   Alexander (and the six other sons of St Felicity);
Amalburga; Antony of the Caves

11 July   Olga

12 July   John the Iberian; John Gualberto;
Nabor and Felix; Veronica

13 July   Eugenius of Carthage; Francis Solano; Mildred; Silas

14 July   Bonaventure; Camillus; Madelgaire (or Vincent of
Soignies); Nicodemus of the Holy Mountain;
Phocas (2); Ulric of Zell

FEAST DAYS

15 July   Edith of Polesworth and Edith of Tamworth;
          Henry II; James of Nisibus; Swithin; Vladimir

16 July   Helier; Mary-Magdelen Postel; Raineld

17 July   Alexis; Kenelm; Leo IV; Narses of Lampron;
          Scillitan Martyrs, The

18 July   Symphorosa and her seven sons

19 July   Arsenius; Macrina the Younger; Vincent de Paul

20 July   Jerome Emiliani; Margaret (1); Wilgefortis

21 July   Lawrence of Brindisi; Victor of Marseilles

22 July   Mary Magdalen

23 July   John Cassian

24 July   Boris and Gleb; Christine

25 July   Christopher; James the Greater

26 July   Ann; Bartholomea Capitanio

27 July   Aurelius and Natalia; Celestine I; Clement Slovensky;
          Pantaleon; Seven Sleepers, The

28 July   Nazarius and Celsus; Samson

29 July   Lupus of Troyes; Martha; Olaf

31 July   Germanus of Auxerre; Ignatius of Loyola; Neot

FEAST DAYS

AUGUST

1 August   Ethelwold; Faith (2), Hope and Charity

2 August   Alphonsus Liguori; Basil the Blessed

3 August   Peter Eymard

4 August   Dominic

5 August   Afra

6 August   Sixtus II

7 August   Cajetan; Victricius

8 August   Cyriacus; Hormidz; John-Baptist Vianney

9 August   Oswald of Northumbria

10 August   Lawrence

11 August   Attracta; Blaan; Susan; Tiburtius (1)

12 August   Clare of Assisi

13 August   Cassian of Imola; Hippolytus of Rome; Narses the Gracious; Radegund; Tikhon of Zadonsk

15 August   The Blessed Virgin Mary; Tarsicius

16 August   Joachim; Rock

17 August   Hyacinth of Cracow; Mamas

18 August   Florus and Laurus; Helen

19 August   Arnulf of Metz; John Eudes

20 August   Amadour; Bernard of Clairvaux; Oswin; Philibert

21 August   Abraham of Smolensk; Jane Frances de Chantal; Sidonius Apollinaris

22 August   Symphorian

FEAST DAYS

23 August	Philip Benizi
24 August	Bartholomew; Emily de Vialar; Joan Thouret; Ouen
25 August	Genesius the Actor; Genesius of Arles; Gregory of Utrecht; Louis of France
26 August	Elizabeth Bichier des Âges
27 August	Caesarius of Arles; Joseph Calasanz
28 August	Augustine of Hippo; Hermes; Joaquina; Julian of Brioude; Moses the Black
29 August	John the Baptist (*death*); Sebbi
30 August	Felix and Adauctus; Pammachius; Rose of Lima
31 August	Aidan of Lindisfarne; Paulinus of Trier; Raymund Nonnatus

FEAST DAYS

SEPTEMBER

1 September   Fiacre; Giles

2 September   Brocard; Stephen of Hungary

3 September   Cuthburga; Pius X

4 September   Marinus of San Marino

5 September   Bertin; Lawrence Giustiniani

6 September   Cagnoald

7 September   Cloud; Evurtius

8 September   Adrian

9 September   Ciaran of Clonmacnois; Isaac the Great; Joseph
of Volokolamsk; Omer; Peter Claver

10 September   Aubert of Avranches; Finnian of Moville; Nicholas of Tolentino; Pulcheria

11 September   Deiniol; Paphnutius; Protus and Hyacinth

12 September   Guy of Anderlecht

13 September   Eulogius of Alexandria; Notburga

15 September   Katherine of Genoa; Nicetas the Goth; Nicomedes (►► 1 June)

16 September   Cyprian (►► 26 September); Edith of Wilton; Euphemia; Ludmilla; Ninian

17 September   Columba of Córdoba; Hildegard; Lambert of Maastricht; Socrates and Stephen

18 September   Joseph of Copertino; Methodius of Olympus

369

FEAST DAYS

19 September   Emily de Rodat; Januarius;
Theodore of Canterbury

20 September   Eustace

21 September   Matthew

22 September   Agaunum, Martyrs of; Phocas (1);
Thomas of Villanueva

23 September   Adamnan; Linus; Thecla of Iconium

24 September   Gerard of Csanad

25 September   Cadoc; Euphrosyne; Finbarr;
Francis of Camporosso;
Sergius of Radonezh; Vincent Strambi

26 September   Colman of Lann Elo; Cornelius; Cyprian
(B.C.P.; ►► 16 September);
Cyprian and Justina; Nilus of Rossano;
North America, the Martyrs of (►► 16 March)

27 September   Cosmas and Damian; Elzear

28 September   Eustochium; Lioba; Wenceslas

29 September   Cyriacus the Recluse; Michael the Archangel;
Rhipsime and Gaiana

30 September   Honorius of Canterbury; Jerome;
Otto of Bamberg; Sophia

FEAST DAYS

OCTOBER

1 October   Bavo; Gregory the Enlightener; Nicetius of Trier;
            Remi; Romanus the Melodist

2 October   Leger

3 October   Gerard of Brogne; Hewalds (*or* Ewalds), the Two;
            Josepha Rossello; Teresa of Lisieux;
            Thomas of Hereford

4 October   Francis of Assisi

5 October   Maurus; Placid

6 October   Bruno (1); Faith (1) (*or* Foi, Foy)

7 October   Justina; Osyth

8 October   Bridget; Demetrius; Keyne; Margaret (2);
            Pelagia the Penitent; Sergius and Bacchus; Thais

9 October   Dionysius (*or* Denis) of Paris; Louis Bertrand;
            John
            Leonardi

10 October Daniel and his companions; Francis Borgia;
            Gereon; Paulinus of York

11 October Alexandar Sauli; Bruno (2);
            Canice (*or* Cainnech, Kenneth)

12 October Ethelburga of Barking; Serafino; Wilfrid

13 October Edward the Confessor; Gerald of Aurillac

14 October Callistus I; Justus of Lyons

15 October Euthymius the Younger; Teresa of Âvila;
            Thecla of Kitzingen

FEAST DAYS

16 October   Gall; Gerard Majella; Hedwig; Lull

17 October   Ethelbert and Ethelred of Kent;
Etheldreda (*or* Audrey) (B.C.P.; ►► 23 June);
Margaret Mary; Shushanik

18 October   Justus of Beauvais; Luke

19 October   Frideswide; John of Rila; Peter of Alcántara

20 October   Andrew of Crete (2); Bertilla Boscardin;
John of Kanti

21 October   Fintan of Taghmon; Hilarion; John of
Bridlington;
Ursula and her maidens; Viator

22 October   Donatus of Fiesole; Philip of Heraclea

23 October   Antony Claret; Ignatius of Constantinople

24 October   Felix of Thibiuca; Raphael

25 October   Chrysanthus and Daria; Crispin and Crispinian;
Gaudentius of Brescia; Isidore the Farm-servant
(in
U.S.A.); John of Beverley

27 October   Frumentius

28 October   Demetrius of Rostov; Faro; Jude and Simon

29 October   Colman of Kilmacduagh

30 October   Alphonsus Rodriguez; Marcellus the Centurion

31 October   Bee; Foillan; Wolfgang

FEAST DAYS

NOVEMBER

1 November	Benignus
3 November	Hubert; Malachy; Martín de Porres; Winifred
4 November	Charles Borromeo; Emeric
5 November	Zachary and Elizabeth
6 November	Illtyd; Leonard; Winnoc
7 November	Engelbert; Willibrord
8 November	Cuby; Four Crowned Ones, The; Godfrey (*or* Geoffrey) of Amiens; Willehad
9 November	Nectarius Kephalas; Theodore the Recruit
10 November	Andrew Avellino; Justus of Canterbury
11 November	Bartholomew of Grottaferrata; Martin of Tours (B.C.P.; again on 4 July); Menas; Theodore the Studite
12 November	Lebuin; Martin I; Nilus of Ancyra
13 November	Brice; Diego (*or* Didacus); Frances Cabrini; Homobonus; Nicholas I; Stanislas Kostka
14 November	Dubricius; Gregory Palamas; Josaphat of Polotsk; Lawrence O'Toole
15 November	Albert the Great; Fintan of Rheinau; Leopold of Austria; Malo
16 November	Edmund of Abingdon; Eucherius of Lyons; Gertrude of Helfta; Margaret of Scotland
17 November	Dionysius of Alexandra; Gregory the Wonderworker; Gregory of Tours; Hilda; Hugh of Lincoln

373

FEAST DAYS

18 November	Mawes; Odo of Cluny; Romanus of Antioch
19 November	Barlaam of Antioch; Elizabeth of Hungary; Mechtilde of Hackeborn; Narses I
20 November	Bernward; Edmund; Felix of Valois
21 November	Gelasius I
22 November	Cecily
23 November	Alexander Nevsky; Clement I; Columban; Felicity
24 November	Chrysogonus; Colman of Cloyne; Flora and Mary; John of the Cross
25 November	Katherine of Alexandria; Mercury
26 November	John Berchmans; Leonard of Porto Maurizio; Peter of Alexandria; Silvester Gozzolini
27 November	Barlaam and Josaphat; Gregory of Sinai; Virgil of Salzburg
28 November	James of the March; Katherine Labouré; Stephen the Younger
30 November	Andrew

FEAST DAYS

DECEMBER

1 December	Eligius; Natalia
2 December	Viviana
3 December	Cassian of Tangier; Francis Xavier; Lucius, 'king'
4 December	Barbara; Osmund; Peter Chrysologus
5 December	Birinus; Crispina; Sabas
6 December	Abraham of Kratia; Nicholas
7 December	Ambrose (►► 4 April)
8 December	Budoc
9 December	Hipparchus and Philotheus; Peter Fourier
10 December	Eulalia; Miltiades
11 December	Damasus I; Daniel the Stylite
12 December	Edburga of Minster; Finnian of Clonard; Vicelin
13 December	Lucy; Odilia
14 December	Spiridion
15 December	Mary di Rosa; Nino
16 December	Adelaide; Eusebius of Vercelli
17 December	Begga; Olympias; Sturm
18 December	Winebald
21 December	Thomas Didymus
23 December	Thorlac
25 December	Anastasia; Eugenia

FEAST DAYS

26 December   Stephen

27 December   Fabiola; John the Divine

28 December   Innocents, The Holy

29 December   Marcellus the Righteous;
Thomas of Canterbury

30 December   Egwin

31 December   Columba of Sens; Melania the Younger;
Silvester I

About the Author

Donald Attwater, born in 1892, was educated at Aldenham and later read law. While a soldier in the Near East in the First World War, he came into contact with the ancient Christian churches there; and, having drifted into writing and journalism, he set himself to make these churches better known among English-speaking readers. His two volumes on the *Christian Churches of the East* were published in 1935-7, and have sold steadily ever since. He then collaborated with a Jesuit scholar, the late Herbert Thurston, in bringing up to date the standard collection of *Lives of the Saints,* written by Alban Butler in the eighteenth century. This proved to be his apprenticeship to further work on the same subject. In 1956 he produced a second revision of Butler's *Lives,* in four volumes, followed by books on *Martyrs* (1957), *St John Chrysostom* (1959), *Saints of the East* (1963), a new translation of Hippolyte Delehaye's classical work on the *Legends of the Saints* (1962), and a biography of the stone-carver and engraver Eric Gill: *A Cell of Good Living* (1969). During the Second World War Donald Attwater was a civilian lecturer on history and current affairs in H.M. forces, an absorbing occupation in which he said he learned more than he taught. Mr Attwater died in 1977.